SD329 Signals and perception: the science of the senses

Book 2
Somatosensation, Hearing and Balance

This publication forms part of the Open University module SD329 *Signals and perception: the science of the senses*. Details of this and other Open University modules can be obtained from the Student Registration and Enquiry Service, The Open University, PO Box 197, Milton Keynes MK7 6BJ, United Kingdom (tel. +44 (0)845 300 60 90; email general-enquiries@open.ac.uk).

Alternatively, you may visit the Open University website at www.open.ac.uk where you can learn more about the wide range of modules and packs offered at all levels by The Open University.

To purchase a selection of Open University materials, visit www.ouw.co.uk, or contact Open University Worldwide, Walton Hall, Milton Keynes MK7 6AA, United Kingdom for a catalogue (tel. +44 (0)1908 858785; fax +44 (0)1908 858787; email ouw-customer-services@open.ac.uk).

FSC www.fsc.org MIX Paper from responsible sources FSC® C013436

The Open University, Walton Hall, Milton Keynes MK7 6AA

First published 2013

Edited and designed by The Open University.

Typeset by The Open University.

Printed in the United Kingdom by Latimer Trend and Company Ltd, Plymouth.

ISBN 978 1 7800 7336 1

1.1

Contents

Block 3 Somatosensation

Block 4 Hearing and Balance

Block 3 Somatosensation

Claire Rostron with Elizabeth Parvin, Heather McLannahan,
Stanley Bolanowski, Peter Cahusac and Ian Lyon

Learning outcomes

You should be able to do the following by the time you have completed this block. Note that the information in brackets indicates which module learning outcome(s) each block outcome relates to.

- Define and use, or recognise definitions and applications of, each of the **bold** terms in the text. (KU1)
- Understand the limitations of current research into signal transduction mechanisms in somatosensation. (KU1, KU2, CS1 and CS4)
- Explain the receptor mechanisms involved in the detection and coding of innocuous and noxious sensory events occurring in the skin. (KU2 and KU6)
- Understand the extent to which the plasticity of the cerebral cortex can affect the perception of touch, proprioception and pain stimuli. (KU1, KU4 and KU6)
- Explain the suggested basis for endogenous analgesia. (KU2)
- Use knowledge of pathways to comment on drug interventions, and their side effects in pain control. (KU5)
- Understand and explain some of the problems encountered in the treatment of pain. (KU5 and CS4)

1 Introducing somatosensation

> It is in moments of illness that we are compelled to recognise that we live not alone but are chained to a creature of a different kingdom, whole worlds apart, who has no knowledge of us and by whom it is impossible to make ourselves understood: our body.
>
> *(Marcel Proust,* À la Recherché du Temps Perdu*)*

In the opening quotation, the French novelist Marcel Proust offers an interesting perspective on the relationship between body and mind which, although somewhat dramatic, raises the important question of corporeal awareness at any one time. The term 'corporeal' simply means relating to the body, or having physical substance. Thus 'corporeal awareness' refers to our awareness of our physical body. This notion may lead us on to further considerations such as the degree to which our ability to interact with the world through our bodies is entirely automatic in our everyday lives, as well as what happens when this relationship is disrupted by illness, as in Proust's reflection above.

■ Spend a moment now with your eyes closed, preferably in a quiet place, and bring your conscious focus specifically onto your body. Try to be aware of the position of your body and the stimuli that it can detect outside of any faint background noise or changes in the light around you. Then slowly move your arms until they make contact with another object, or another part of your body. What stimuli were you aware of?

□ Almost certainly you would have been aware of touching when your arms or hands contacted another object and you may have been aware of some qualities possessed by the object you touched. For example, was it hot or cold? Smooth or rough? Before you moved your arms, you would have been aware of the position of your body and the relation of the various parts, one to another. Were you sitting or standing? Arms bent or stretched? For example, you would have known that your toes were at the end of your feet rather than on top of your head and that your head was where it should be, at the end of your neck! This sense, as you may recall from Block 1, is known as proprioception.

By spending a few moments focused on your body, you probably realised that you are party to an incredible amount of information about the state of your body at any one moment. However, this information does not fill the contents of your conscious awareness until you direct your attention to it.

An extensive range of sensory information is therefore transmitted to the central nervous system (CNS) to inform us of the sensory state of our bodies. This information is passed to the brain via peripheral nerves with their associated cell bodies located in the dorsal root ganglia (DRG). This collection of varied information about your body represents the signals for the somatic sensory system, or 'somatosensation'.

Such signals include the kind of information you probably noted in the exercise above, that is: touch, skin temperature and body position (proprioception). Somatosensation also includes information about pain, which we hope you did not experience during the exercise (unless you bumped into a sharp object or were bitten by an insect, for example). For the sake of completeness, you should also be aware that somatosensation encompasses information about the internal state of your body such as blood pressure, but this aspect is not covered in this module.

Given the variety of information processed by the somatosensory system, it is often divided up into subsystems for analysis. There are a number of different ways to do this, but we have chosen to focus on:

- touch in Chapters 2 and 3
- proprioception in Chapter 4
- pain in Chapters 5 and 6.

We have opted not to consider the sense of skin temperature separately, but rather have integrated this topic into several chapters. For example, thermal detection is discussed alongside pain in Chapter 5 because, as you will see, the receptors and the afferent pathways that can lead to the perception of pain are the same as those involved in detecting skin temperature. Another reason temperature is often discussed alongside pain is that we are not usually automatically aware of the temperature of our surroundings, or of objects in it, unless they are uncomfortable. However, there is some discussion of non-painful thermal sensation in Chapter 3 in the context of detecting the heat of objects being touched.

Given the plethora of sensory information contributing to corporeal awareness, the significance of somatosensation as a topic of study cannot be underestimated. An accurate perception of your own body and the boundaries of it are important for maintaining your health and safety, and therefore basic research into somatosensation may have implications in clinical settings. Also, somatosensory information necessarily needs to be combined with information from the other senses in everyday life to ensure successful interaction with the world. For example, it is integrated with vestibular information to ensure balance is maintained (which is discussed in Block 4) and with visual information to help locate our limbs in space (Block 5).

As you might imagine, somatosensation is a fascinating and complex topic that requires input from several disciplines. You should get a feel for the multidisciplinary nature of this subject as you work through this block, covering each of the different aspects of the system in turn. For now, however, you start your exploration of somatosensation by considering the topic of touch.

Sensing touch

2

Touch encompasses a range of sensations produced by the lightest of touches to pressure that is just short of painful. Perhaps surprisingly, physical contact with the skin is not always required for this perception. The movement of air can stimulate some of our touch receptors; for example, if you blow on the back of your forearm you may feel hairs move. It is the receptors around the hair follicles (embedded in the skin) that are stimulated in this instance. This large range of sensations should therefore give some hint of the range of receptors involved.

We begin our discussion of this sense by focusing on the signals transmitting touch information. We then move on to the location and properties of the different receptor types that receive touch information, and finally the process of signal transduction.

2.1 Tactile signals

It is necessary, in order to understand the nature of tactile signals, to know something of the medium in which the receptors are present. This medium is the skin, and its anatomical construction and properties allow us to detect a variety of touch-related stimuli in our daily lives.

2.1.1 The anatomy of skin

Skin is a multilayered coating covering the entire body, both inside and outside. In fact, in terms of surface area, it is the largest organ of the human body. Skin is a highly complex living structure that incorporates not only touch receptors and the nerves that innervate them, but also blood vessels, sweat glands, and other specialised structures.

Skin can be classified into three specific types with each type having its own complement of touch receptors and internal structure:

- **glabrous skin** or hairless skin, typified by the palm of the hand and the soles of the feet
- **hairy skin**, so called because of the presence of body hair
- **mucocutaneous skin**, which lines the entrances to the inside of the body, such as the nostrils.

Mucocutaneous skin is different from glabrous and hairy skin because it marks the junction between mucous membranes and skin. In this module, the focus is on glabrous and hairy skin because the features of touch sensation are similar in both tissue types.

The types of skin mentioned above differ in terms of their location, their mechanical properties, and the types of touch receptors that they contain. All of these factors affect the sensory capabilities of a given area of skin. Furthermore, recall from Block 1 that the types and density of touch receptors within it vary with body site. For example, the lips and the fingertips are highly sensitive when compared with the thigh or the back. (You can test this assertion for yourself when you complete Activity 2.1 later in the chapter.) The mechanical properties and receptors also vary with the gender and age of the individual.

Glabrous and hairy skin are both composed of an outside layer called the **epidermis** and an inside layer called the **dermis**, as shown in Figure 2.1. The dermis separates the epidermis from the underlying muscle, ligaments and bone. The border between the epidermis and dermis is specialised in that somatic or 'epithelial' cells are generated in this region, and these cells migrate over time to the surface of the skin. As they migrate, they begin to die, and eventually they form a relatively hard surface called the **stratum corneum**. It is the dead cells of the stratum corneum that are brushed away during everyday activities such as washing and grooming. For the most part, very few touch receptors are located within the epidermis.

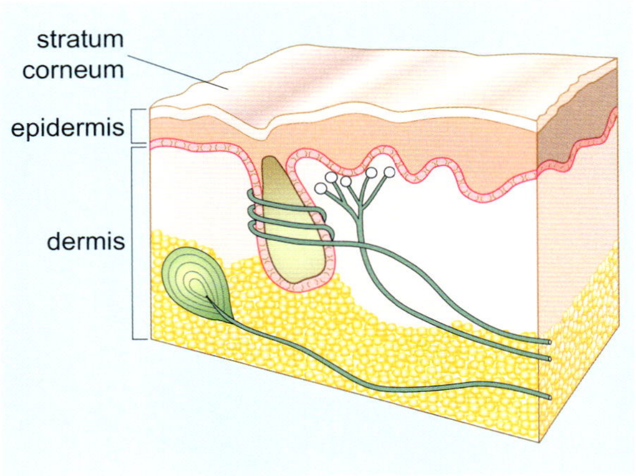

Figure 2.1 The layers of the skin.

2.1.2 The mechanical properties of the skin

From a physical standpoint, skin is a very complex material. Under some conditions it behaves like a viscous liquid (such as syrup) and in other circumstances it behaves like an elastic material. For this reason it is described as being 'viscoelastic'.

Mechanical inputs such as touch stimuli applied to the skin surface can produce viscous flow, but this is only usually the case for small displacements. Beyond that, they produce stresses and strains within the skin itself and these stimuli are detected by the touch receptors. Stresses are measures of the forces that are applied to objects within the skin, such as the touch receptors, while strains correspond to the deformation or stretching of such objects when a force is applied.

Box 2.1 describes two types of stress – tensile and shear – and shows how the moduli associated with these stresses can be calculated. Moduli are a quantification of how a substance reacts to stresses; for example, they indicate the extent to which a substance is deformed on application of a force.

Here, moduli are important because they aid understanding of how tactile sensory stimuli interact with the sensory receptors for touch.

Box 2.1 Calculating the moduli of tensile and shear stress

Tensile stress

Tensile stress describes situations where an object (for our purposes, skin) is stretched by a force. Figure 2.2 shows a typical situation. The tensile force F_T is applied over area A of the object and, as a result, the length of the object increases from l to $l + x$.

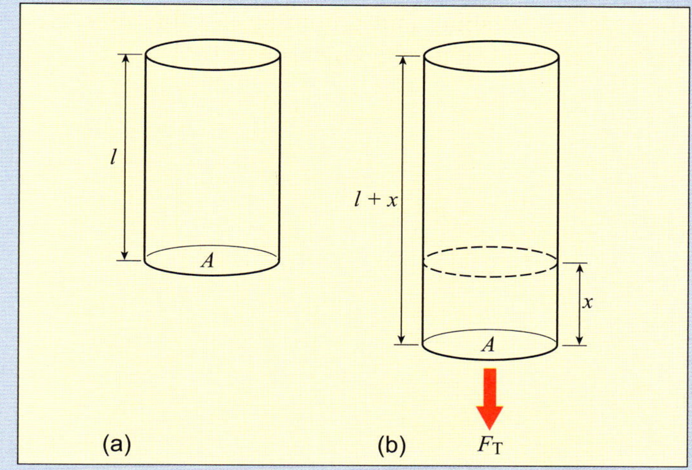

Figure 2.2 The stretching of an object by a tensile force: (a) before, and (b) after the force has been applied.

The tensile stress, s_T, experienced by the object is a measure of the force applied per unit area, and is calculated using the equation:

$$s_T = \frac{F_T}{A} \qquad \text{(Eqn 2.1)}$$

The tensile strain, ε_T, is a measure of the fractional increase in length of the object, and is calculated from the equation:

$$\varepsilon_T = \frac{(l + x)}{l} \qquad \text{(Eqn 2.2)}$$

where l = length and x = increase in length. (Note that this relationship is independent of the length of the object.)

An important quantity that is often quoted as a measure of a material's ability to withstand stretching when a force is applied is Young's modulus, Y. This quantity is defined by:

$$Y = \frac{s_T}{\varepsilon_T} \qquad \text{(Eqn 2.3)}$$

A large Young's modulus implies that a material is strong and can be subjected to a large tensile force with only a small extension in length resulting; a small Young's modulus implies that a material can be stretched easily. Some example substances are shown in Table 2.1 for comparison with the values of Young's modulus obtained for skin. The unit is the pascal (Pa), a measure of pressure. Note the large differences between different substances.

Table 2.1 Approximate values of Young's modulus for skin and other common substances.

Substance	Young's modulus/Pa
Rubber	$(0.7–2) \times 10^7$
Wood	$(3–7) \times 10^7$
Silk	4×10^9
Steel	2×10^{11}
Skin (young person)	$(1.3–1.4) \times 10^4$
Skin (older person)	$(6–8) \times 10^3$

(Source: Pailler-Mattei et al., 2008)

Shear stress

In a similar fashion, we can describe what happens when an object is subjected to a shearing force, as shown in Figure 2.3. The force, F_S, is applied over an area A_S and can be regarded as the equivalent of a torque, or couple. Its effect is to move the two parallel faces of the specimen in opposite directions without changing the perpendicular distance between them.

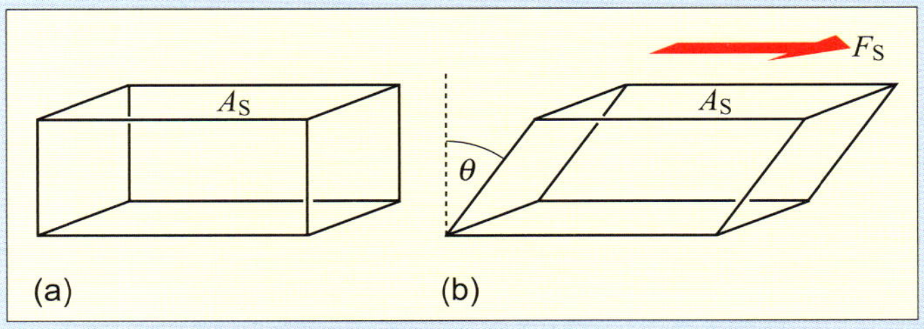

Figure 2.3 The deformation of an object resulting from the application of a shearing force: (a) before, and (b) after the force has been applied.

If the cross-sectional area of these faces is A_S then the shear stress experienced per unit area of the object, s_S, is given by the equation:

$$s_S = \frac{F_S}{A_S} \qquad \text{(Eqn 2.4)}$$

Note that this equation is very similar to Equation 2.1, but the force is now acting parallel to the area rather than perpendicular to it.

Just as tensile strain must be considered when determining Young's modulus, shear strain is an important factor when describing how objects react to sheering forces. In this case, the measure of the amount of shear is the angle θ by which the vertical sides of the object have moved as a result of the force applied (as shown in Figure 2.3b), and the shear strain, ε_S, is given by:

$$\varepsilon_S = \tan\theta \quad \text{(Eqn 2.5)}$$

Finally, the object's ability to withstand shearing can be described in terms of its shear modulus, G, which is defined by:

$$G = \frac{S_S}{\varepsilon_S} \quad \text{(Eqn 2.6)}$$

A large value of G implies a greater ability to withstand a shearing force, while a smaller one corresponds to a material that shears easily.

Study note

If you are not familiar with the mathematical function tan, please refer to the *Study Companion*.

2.1.3 Stimulating the touch system

As you can appreciate from the above discussion and Box 2.1, skin has rather complex mechanical properties. Moreover, these properties, along with those of the touch receptors within the skin, vary with position on the body and the characteristics of the individual (such as age). The mechanical properties of skin also vary for each of the skin layers, and with temperature (Zhou et al., 2010). As a result of this complexity, many different types of mechanical stimuli have been used to investigate how the touch system works.

For example, mechanical stimuli produced by pins or probes applied perpendicularly or tangentially to the skin have been used to determine the basic properties of mechanoelectrical transduction (the transduction of mechanical stimuli) and the transmission of the induced electrochemical signals to the CNS. These stimuli indent the skin and can be of a 'vibratory' nature, or of the 'ramp-and-hold' variety.

- The vibratory stimuli that are typically used range in frequency from 0.4 to 1000 Hz and to a maximum amplitude of 3 or 4 mm.
- Ramp-and-hold stimuli consist of a variable indentation of the skin by the probe, followed by a period when the probe is held at a constant static indentation until such time as the stimulus is withdrawn. The rate and depth of the initial ramp indentation and the duration of the hold state can be varied widely, as can the rate of withdrawal.

Other types of stimulus that have been used to understand touch include regularly repeating and non-repeating gratings moved across the skin surface, air puffs, embossed letters, and even everyday items such as sandpaper, cloth and steel wool.

2.2 Tactile mechanoreceptors

As established in Block 1, the detection of tactile information occurs via mechanoreceptors. These specialised neurons have their cell bodies located in the DRG next to the spinal cord, and can be classified on the basis of their various structural or morphological forms and physiological properties.

2.2.1 Types of mechanoreceptors

Different types of mechanoreceptors are found in the various layers of the skin, and they do not all respond to the same stimuli.

■ Why might there be variation in the types of mechanoreceptor found in the different layers? (Refer back to Section 2.1.1 if you are unsure.)

□ Different layers of the skin have varying mechanical properties, so the touch receptors present in these layers need to be able to detect slightly different mechanical signals.

The four main types of tactile mechanoreceptor are found in hairy and glabrous skin and are called:

- **Pacinian corpuscles**
- **Meissner's corpuscles**
- **Merkel's discs**
- **Ruffini's endings**.

These names were given in recognition of the nineteenth-century biologists who discovered each receptor type. Figure 2.4 shows the morphology and location of each mechanoreceptor type, as well as giving a brief indication of the sort of stimulus each one responds to. Note that although we are focusing on tactile mechanoreceptors in this chapter, some non-tactile (pain) receptors are included in Figure 2.4 because these are also embedded in the skin. Specifically, these are the free nerve endings, which are discussed shortly.

Some tactile mechanoreceptors have elements that are not standard components of a neuron directly attached to them, or located adjacent to them (Figure 2.5). These non-neural elements are referred to as accessory structures, and they are thought to impart particular response properties to the mechanoreceptor, and perhaps also to regulate their metabolic capabilities.

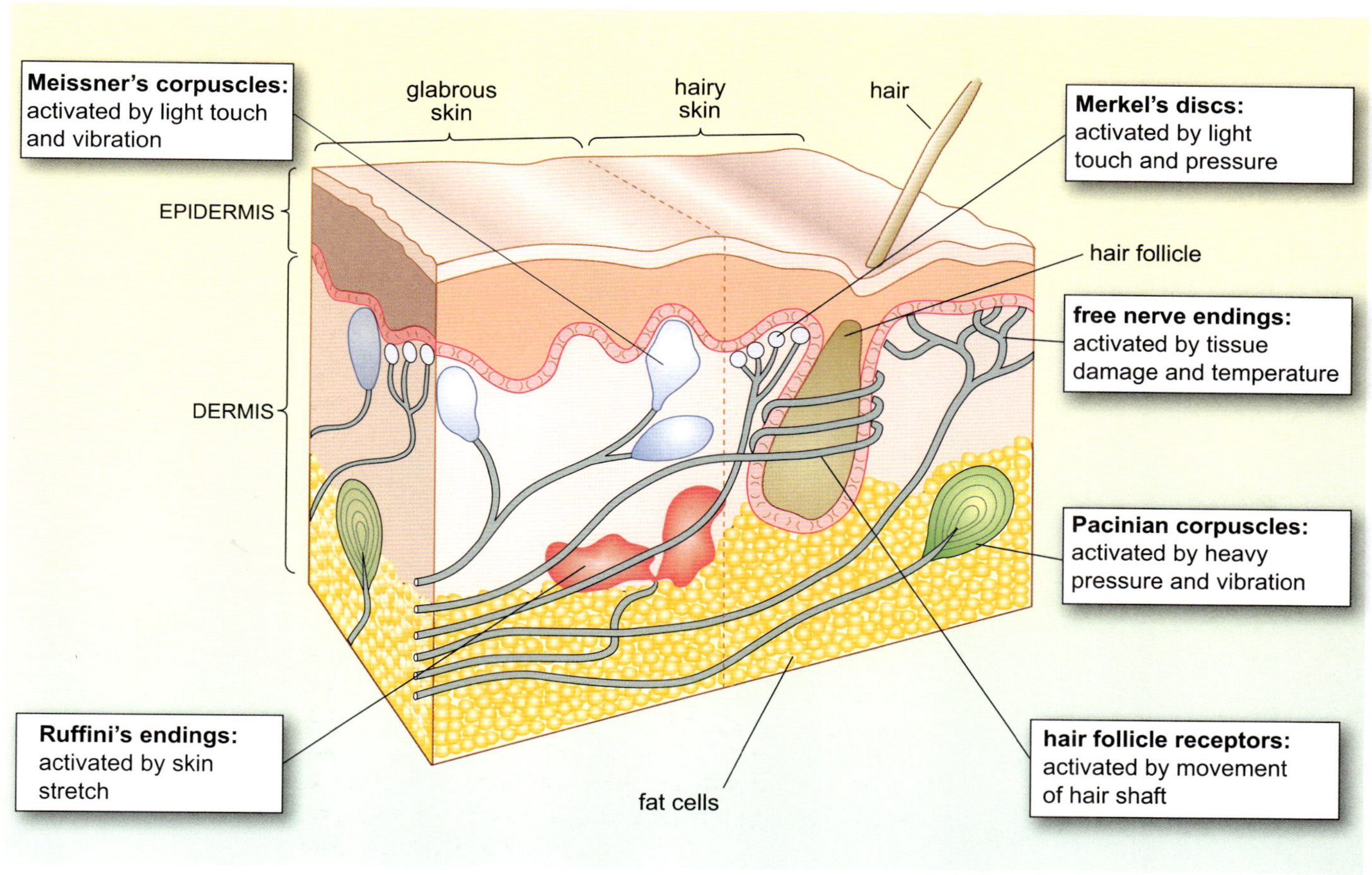

Figure 2.4 The morphology of skin receptors and the stimuli to which they respond.

Of the four main types mentioned above, two of these mechanoreceptors have accessory structures called capsules, in which the tip of the neuron is embedded. The capsules of these receptors are organised in specific ways that depend on the receptor type. The capsule surrounding the Pacinian corpuscle mechanoreceptor, for example, has an onion-like, layered arrangement. On the other hand, the Meissner's corpuscle has a capsule that looks like a woven basket. The Merkel's disc has an accessory structure to which it is closely attached but not encapsulated. Together with its accessory structure, the Merkel's disc receptor is referred to as the **Merkel cell neurite complex**.

The other types of mechanoreceptor that detect touch information are associated only with hairy skin. These are the **hair follicle receptors** and the **field receptors**. Hair follicle receptors come in three different types: down hair follicle receptors, guard hair follicle receptors and tylotrich hair follicle receptors. These types mainly differ in the sensitivity to movement of the hair located in the hair follicle. Field receptors are located over the joints in the fingers, wrists and elbows and they detect skin stretch when the joint is extended. These field receptors are therefore important for proprioceptive feedback, namely telling your brain where your various body parts are in relation to each other.

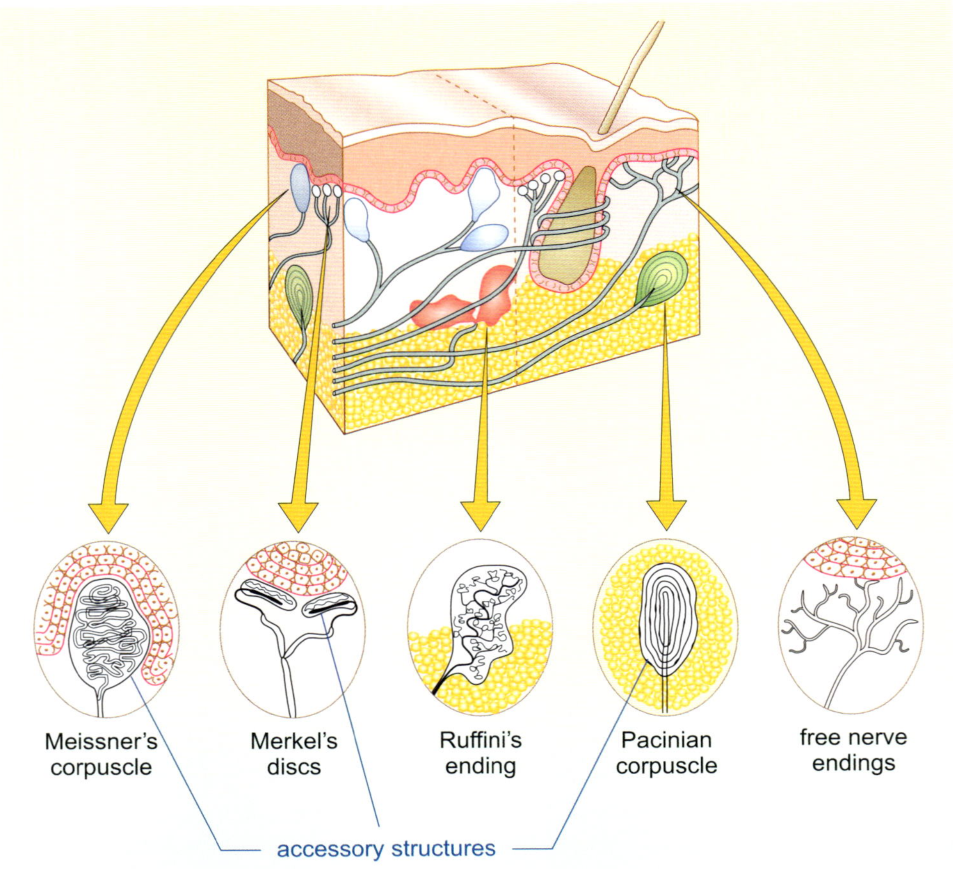

Figure 2.5 Some of the receptor types found in human skin.

There is another major class of mechanoreceptor in the skin and these are the **free nerve endings** which are shown in Figures 2.4 and 2.5. These are 'free' because they are not associated with, or attached to, any accessory structure or hair follicle. Free nerve ending mechanoreceptors are involved in the signalling of both proprioceptive stimuli and signals perceived as painful, and are discussed in more detail later. They are sometimes specifically referred to as **mechano-nociceptors** in order to distinguish them from those mechanoreceptors that relay non-painful or non-noxious information. (Recall from Block 1 that the term 'nociceptor' refers specifically to sensory receptors that detect painful stimuli.) However, like other types of mechanoreceptors, some free nerve endings are also responsive to light touch and pressure; for example, in the cornea of the eye, where they are the *only* mechanoreceptors to be found (see Box 2.2).

Box 2.2 The mechano-nociceptors of the cornea

Mechano-nociceptors are found throughout the body. In normal, undamaged tissue they are activated only by intense mechanical stimulation, such as pinching or heavy pressure. But the situation in the eye is somewhat different.

Almost certainly, you will have experienced that contact between the cornea (the outer layer of the eye) and the most minuscule of objects is instantly detected. And a good thing, too, because perceiving this signal normally results in you removing whatever it was that was in your eye long before there is any damage to the cornea.

This protective function of the mechano-nociceptors of the cornea also means that it takes practice to be able to insert a contact lens. Of course, once inserted, the wearer is generally not troubled by the feel of the lens in the eye, which is a good example of the principle of sensory adaptation (Block 1).

2.2.2 Structure of mechanoreceptors

Although there are clearly many different types of touch receptors, they all have one anatomical feature in common, besides their cell bodies being in the DRG. In all cases, shortly after the axon joint at the cell body, the neuron immediately divides into two processes known as bifurcating (branching into two) axonal processes. One axonal process enters the spinal cord via the dorsal root portion of the peripheral nerve and the other process goes to the skin (Figure 2.6).

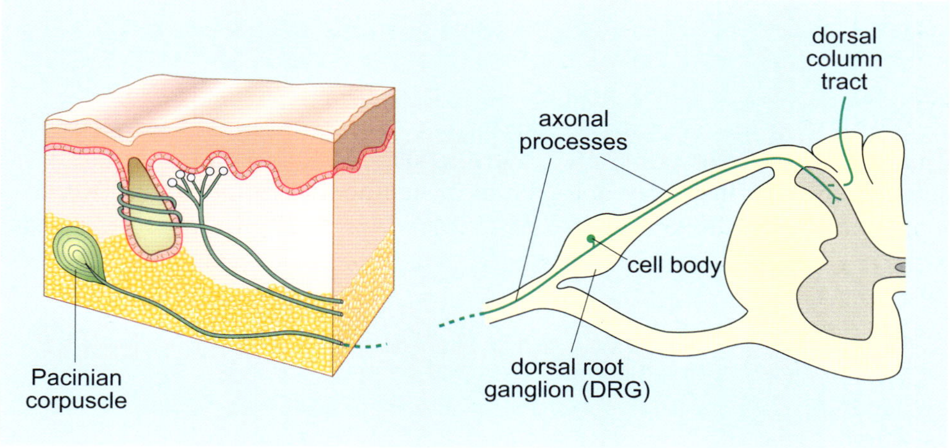

Figure 2.6 Location of the cell body of somatosensory mechanoreceptors and the bifurcating axonal processes, where one process goes to the spinal cord and the other to a receptor in the skin.

- ■ What typical structural feature is absent from these neurons?
- □ They do not have dendrites.

Some of the other structural features of mechanoreceptors have already been mentioned in this chapter. As you have read, many receptors in the skin have accessory structures closely associated with, or surrounding, the actual ending of the axonal branch in the skin. Other receptors have no associated connective tissue elements, and are thus free nerve endings. However, these structural differences are not the only distinctions that can be made between types of mechanoreceptors, and the remainder of this section examines functional variation.

2.2.3 Receptor activation

As well as being classified by structure, you saw in Figure 2.4 that the various types of mechanoreceptors respond best to different types of stimuli. The stimulus that a receptor best responds to is known as an adequate stimulus. Table 2.2 shows the adequate stimulus for each type of mechanoreceptor.

Table 2.2 Receptor types involved in touch and the stimuli that activate them.

Receptor type	Adequate stimulus
Meissner's corpuscles	stroking
Merkel's discs	pressure
Pacinian corpuscles	vibration
Ruffini's endings	skin stretch
Hair follicle receptors:	stroking
down hair follicle	stroking
guard hair follicle	light stroking
tylotrich hair follicle	stroking
Field receptors	skin stretch (in relation to joint movement)

The relationship between a stimulus, the mechanoreceptor(s) that is responding to it, and the sensation ultimately experienced can be difficult to ascertain.

- ■ Why might it be difficult to establish this relationship?
- □ Figures 2.4 and 2.5 show the mechanoreceptors embedded in fleshy, vascular tissue in the dermis, so it is quite difficult to observe which type(s) of receptor respond to any given stimulus. Also, it is hard (but not impossible) to isolate an individual receptor for study. When recording from a single axon within the peripheral nerve bundle it is, again, difficult to know what type of terminal receptor is at the other end!

Researchers, such as Gescheider et al. (1994), have devised ingenious ways to try to negate some of these issues. One example solution works on the basis that cooling the skin 'knocks out' some receptor types. Once these receptors have been knocked out, psychophysical techniques can be used to identify the range of stimuli that give rise to particular sensations (Table 2.3) and to postulate the receptor type that is responding (since those receptors that were not knocked out from cooling the skin must be the ones that are responding). Alternatively, modern techniques now enable receptors to be cultured so that their responses to some stimuli can be determined.

Table 2.3 Vibratory stimuli and the perceptions they elicit.

Receptor	Frequency of stimulation required/Hz	Perception described by subject
Merkel's discs	0.3–3	pressure
Meissner's corpuscles	3–40	fluttering
Ruffini's endings	15–400	buzzing
Pacinian corpuscles	10–500	vibration

Note that in Table 2.3 the stimuli applied were all vibratory. This may, at first glance, seem confusing, since Table 2.2 suggests vibratory stimuli are the adequate stimuli only for Pacinian corpuscles. However, in practice, receptors respond to a range of stimuli and the adequate stimulus is just the one to which they produce their greatest response. Note also that each of the mechanoreceptors listed in Table 2.3 produces a different perception when stimulated with specific frequencies of vibratory stimuli. This should not be taken to mean that these are the only vibratory stimuli these receptors respond to, but that these are the frequencies that the receptor types need to respond to in order to give rise to the different perceptions.

2.2.4 Touch and psychophysics

We introduced the concept of psychophysics in Block 1, referring to it as the study of the relationship between physical stimuli and the resulting perception. It is, in fact, the oldest field of the science of psychology and has historically centred around three approaches:

- Determining the smallest value of a stimulus that can be detected – a measure of sensitivity known as a 'threshold'.
- Gauging the subject's ability to distinguish between stimuli – a measure normally referred to as 'discrimination'.
- Directly asking about the stimulus; for example, questions specifically concerned with stimulus magnitude are called 'scaling procedures'.

These three methods have all been employed to investigate touch processing. For example, Figure 2.7 shows the results of a psychophysics investigation into the threshold for activation of Meissner's and Pacinian corpuscles. It also shows the overall threshold for human detection. The stimulus frequencies extend from a single stimulus to vibratory stimuli with frequencies over 1000 Hz. While you can see that the activation levels of different receptors can be associated with different stimulus frequencies, the graph also shows, in common with the other sensory systems discussed in this module, that the intensity at which we detect a stimulus varies according to its frequency. (You should note that the figure shows data gathered from one area of skin only.)

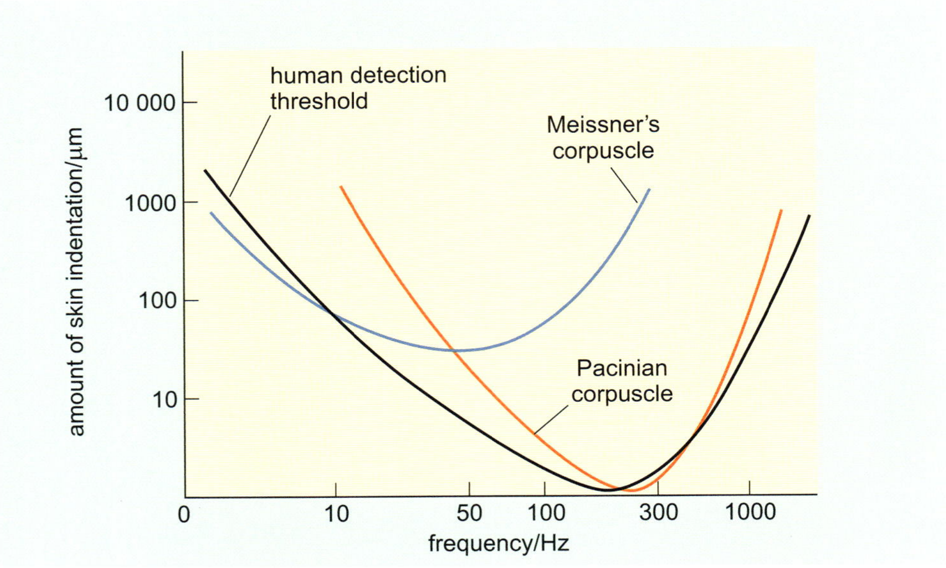

Figure 2.7 Graph of human detection threshold for skin indentation and activity of two different receptors at different frequencies of stimulation.

If you now study Figure 2.8a, you will see that the threshold for the detection of a single stimulus varies across the body surface. Note that the information in Figure 2.8a is logarithmic and these data were obtained using a fine nylon fibre (calibrated in mg) as a probe. The intensity of the pressure applied to the skin surface can be accurately calibrated and the lines represent the amount of pressure that can be applied before the probe is detected. In Figure 2.8b you can see differences in the ability to detect where a point stimulus is across those same regions of the body (also known as the stimulus localisation threshold).

Study note

If you are not familiar with this form of data representation, please read the section on logarithmic function in the *Study Companion*.

- ■ From Figure 2.8a, which parts of the body are the most sensitive and the least sensitive to pressure?
- □ The face is the most sensitive because the thresholds are lowest in the forehead, cheek, nose and upper lip. The hallux (big toe) is the least sensitive area shown; it takes almost twice as much pressure, in log units, to feel something on your toes than to feel it on your face.

While the hallux may not be very sensitive to pressure, Figure 2.8b shows that it is rather good at localising any stimulus that it does detect, as you probably know from experiencing a small stone in your shoe. Thus, the relative sensitivity of different parts of the body to pressure does not reflect their respective ability to accurately locate a stimulus.

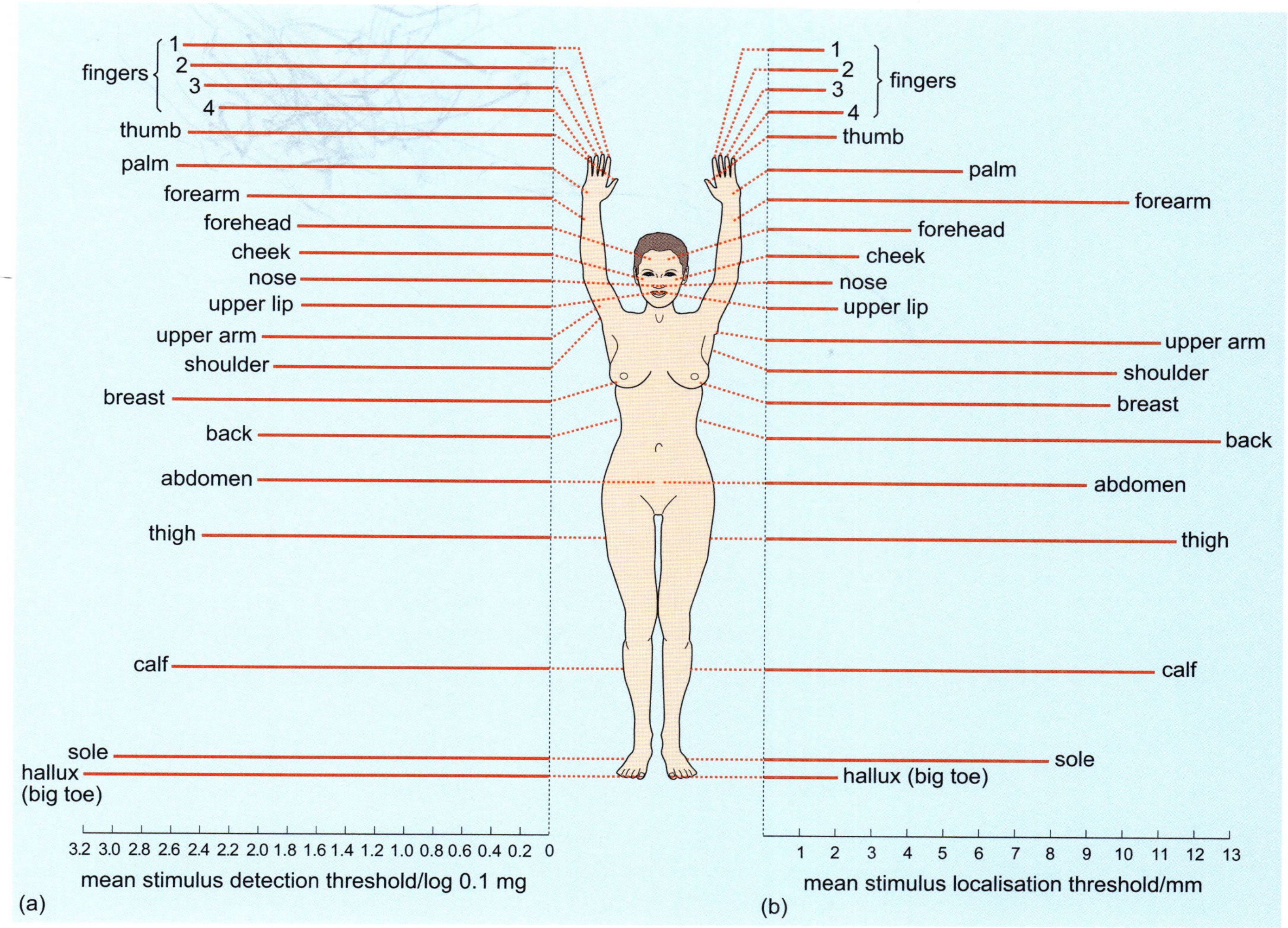

Figure 2.8 (a) Thresholds for detecting pressure obtained by applying a fine probe. (b) Stimulus localisation thresholds determined using a single-touch stimulus.

- Looking back through the data presented in this section, which results were obtained using the psychophysical approach of asking the individual about the stimulus?

- The results shown in Table 2.3 were obtained by applying stimuli to the skin and asking the subject for a description of the percept elicited.

An alternative approach to using psychophysics to explore touch involves both stimulating and recording from a single axon within the peripheral nerve bundle. In this way the response properties of the axon can be determined. This approach, along with stimulation-test results and **histological** examinations of the skin (i.e. a microscopic investigation of its structures), gives us a picture of the way in which the individual receptors detect particular aspects of a stimulus.

Nevertheless, you should not underestimate the difficulties of studying receptors that are scattered throughout the body. Most of the terminal receptive elements are tiny, and in some areas they are very densely packed. For example, the skin at the tip of your finger is innervated by around 300 sensory afferent axons per cm^2. Each axon terminal can branch as many as 25 times, with each branch being, functionally, a receptor. The areas of the body with high tactile acuity (such as the fingertips) must have numerous receptors. So do the same receptor types have differently sized receptive fields depending on where they are located, or do some receptor types have smaller receptive fields than others?

Valbo and Johansson (1978) discovered that there were two kinds of axons within the peripheral nerve bundles from the hands that had small receptive fields. The receptors involved are Meissner's corpuscles and Merkel's discs. Both of these receptor types are found close to the surface of the skin, just below the epidermis, although some Merkel's discs are in the epidermis. There are also deeply located receptors in the hands, such as Pacinian corpuscles, and these have large receptive fields. It seems, then, that each type of receptor has a characteristic receptive field size ('small' or 'large'), although the actual dimensions of a small field vary depending on the precise body location. But why should there be two types of receptor with small receptive fields?

■ What is the difference in adequate stimuli between Merkel's discs and Meissner's corpuscles?

□ These two receptor types best signal the presence of slightly different stimuli: pressure and stroking, respectively (see Table 2.2).

Finally, we can also detect our skin stretching or being stretched. Try pulling a few funny faces to experience the feel of skin stretch. Ruffini's endings and field receptors are believed to be the major responding sensory receptors in this situation.

As these receptors have different adequate stimuli they will fulfil slightly different functions that are necessary for stimulus discrimination just below the surface of the skin. They also differ in their rate of adaptation, which is discussed in the next section.

2.2.5 Receptor adaptation

Table 2.4 shows another way in which mechanoreceptors can be classified: on the basis of differences in how responses recorded from the axons of each receptor type change over time when the skin receives a constant pressure stimulus. This property is termed the rate of sensory adaptation, and was explained briefly in Block 1 in terms of the way your response to a stimulus (such as an odour in your immediate environment) can change over time, despite there being no change in the actual stimulus.

Table 2.4 Receptor types found in hairy and glabrous skin, classified by rate of sensory adaptation as well as location.

Hairy skin receptor type	Glabrous skin receptor type	Location in skin	Adaption to constant pressure stimulus
Pacinian corpuscle	Pacinian corpuscle	deep	rapid
Hair follicle receptor	Meissner's corpuscle	superficial	rapid
Merkel's disc	Merkel's disc	superficial	slow
Ruffini's ending	Ruffini's ending	deep	slow

You can see from the table that some mechanoreceptors adapt rapidly to constant pressure, while others adapt more slowly. In order to illustrate this idea, try the following exercise.

Blow gently on the back of your hand, but move your hand slowly around while trying to keep a steady current of air flowing through your lips. Now think also about the part of your body that is supporting you, your feet (if you are standing) or your bottom (if you are sitting).

■ Which part of your body was experiencing the greater pressure as a result of the stimulus applied?

□ Your feet (or bottom) would be experiencing more physical pressure than the back of your hand.

■ Which stimulus was the more noticeable?

□ Many people find blowing on the back of their hand produces the more noticeable stimulation.

■ Why might this be so?

□ The sensory system is particularly alert to *changes* in stimulation and, however hard you try, it is difficult to produce a completely steady air flow when you blow on your hand. Also, you were asked to move your hand while blowing on it, which ensured that the stimuli were constantly changing. In contrast, there are likely to have been very few (and minor) changes in pressure on your feet (or bottom) while you were completing the exercise.

Sensory adaptation occurs because it is not necessary or desirable for us to be continuously aware of unchanging stimulation (such as the pressure on our bottom when sitting). The fact that we are unaware of unchanging stimuli is due to rapidly adapting receptors. For example, Meissner's corpuscles, Pacinian corpuscles and hair follicle receptors only produce action potentials at the onset or termination of a stimulus (Figure 2.9). They are, therefore, suitable for signalling *dynamic* aspects of stimuli, such as when a stimulus is changing; additionally, they can provide information about the rate of change of the stimulus.

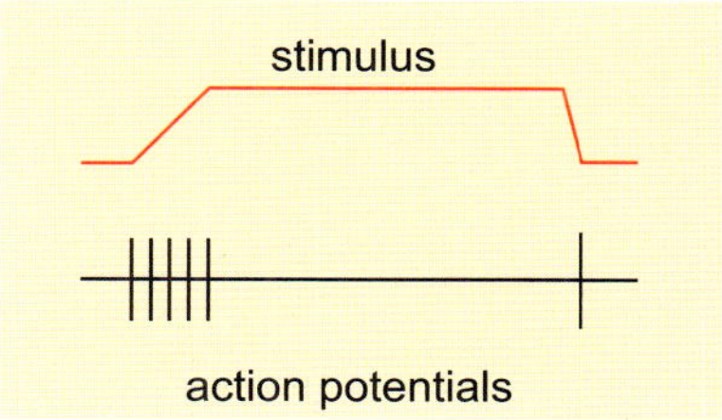

Figure 2.9 Firing of rapidly adapting receptors at the onset and the termination of a stimulus.

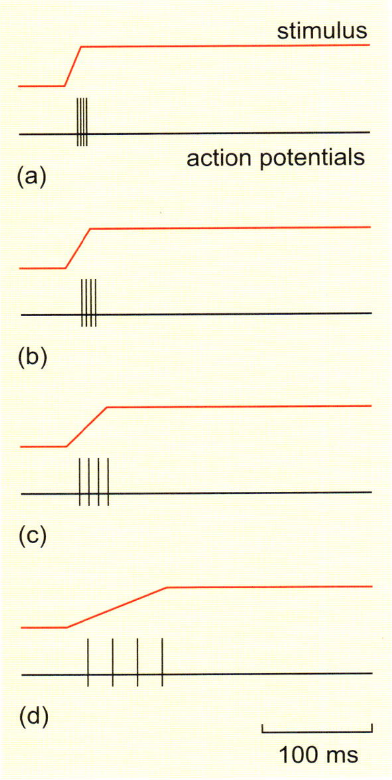

Figure 2.10 Responses from a rapidly adapting receptor to four different rates of application of a 'ramp-and-hold' stimulus.

Figure 2.10 shows how the firing rate of a rapidly adapting receptor (e.g. a Meissner's corpuscle) increases with the speed of application of a ramp-and-hold stimulus. The rate of application is shown by the slope of the 'ramp', which is fastest in trace (a) and slowest in trace (d). The number of action potentials generated is the same in each case, but the frequency of firing is highest with the most rapidly applied stimulus. Slowly adapting receptors (e.g. Ruffini's endings and Merkel's discs) can also serve this function, but additionally, since they generally maintain their firing during the stimulus, they can also convey information about the *static* aspects of stimulus intensity, and function as intensity detectors.

How does this behaviour relate to how we feel objects? Consider your fingertips: they have two types of receptor close to the surface of the skin – Meissner's corpuscles and Merkel's discs – each doing a slightly different job. First, Meissner's corpuscles alert you to a single skin contact and also, as just explained, to changes in pressure (i.e. to the dynamic aspects of the stimulus) such as might occur if a rough surface, sandpaper for example, were to be rubbed across your skin. In other words, they give information about the texture of the material. But suppose that you had a piece of sticky tape stuck to your finger. Once there, the pressure would not alter and Figure 2.10 shows that after an initial burst of activity the Meissner's corpuscle receptors would rapidly stop firing in this scenario.

However, Merkel's discs would continue to fire for longer (Figure 2.11), although even they would adapt and stop firing eventually. So while Merkel's discs remain active you would continue to be aware of the presence of the sticky tape, and the small receptive fields associated with this receptor type would give you the precise location. If you did not manage to remove the tape you would soon be able to ignore it, as the receptors adapt to the unaltered pressure imposed. This is because a small stimulus results in the lowest frequency of action potentials in both the initial burst of electrical activity and the following period of maintained response (Figure 2.11a). Applying larger stimuli (Figures 2.11b and 2.11c) represents more intense pressure on the skin surface, and the frequency of action potentials increases accordingly.

With these two receptor types capable of responding to a range of stimulus attributes, what purpose can be served by the skin having the more deeply located Pacinian corpuscles and Ruffini's endings, with their large receptive fields? For example, as a result of its large receptive field, a Pacinian corpuscle cannot 'tell' the brain exactly where the stimulus (such as the sticky tape) is. Also, a Pacinian corpuscle is a rapidly adapting receptor, tending to respond with only one or two action potentials when a stimulus is applied or removed, and is therefore not very sensitive to the rate of application or the magnitude of the stimulus. This situation is shown in the graphs in Figures 2.12a and 2.12c, where the responses to two different intensities of stimulation are the same: a single spike in action potential voltage.

However, Pacinian corpuscles are very sensitive to oscillating stimuli such as those shown in Figures 2.12b and 2.12d. Here, each cycle of the stimulus generates an action potential. These oscillating stimuli are perceived as vibration, and a Pacinian corpuscle might best be described as a vibration detector. Table 2.3 shows Ruffini's endings have very similar properties.

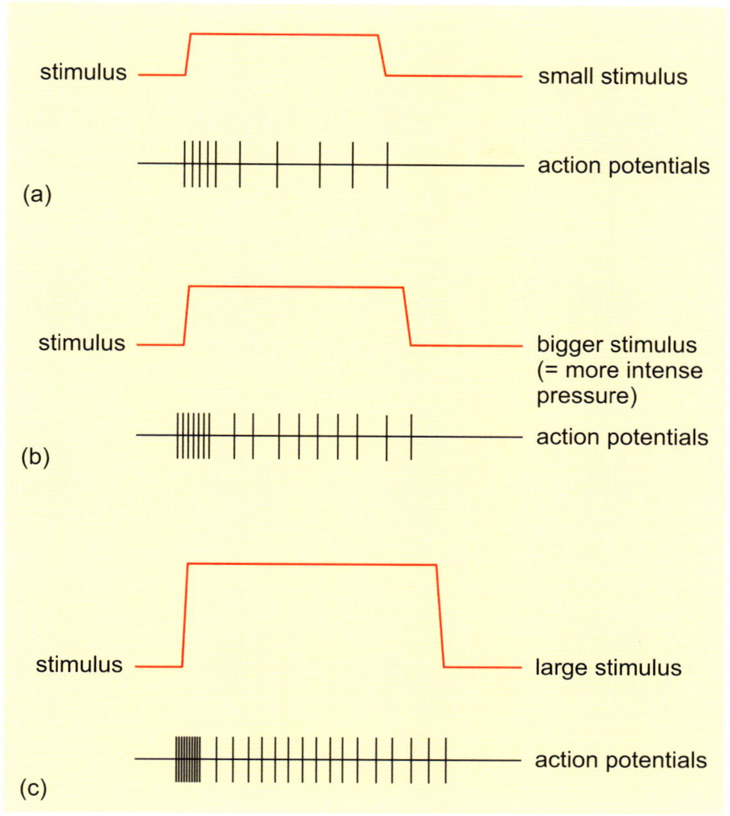

Figure 2.11 Firing of slowly adapting receptors in response to stimuli of different intensities.

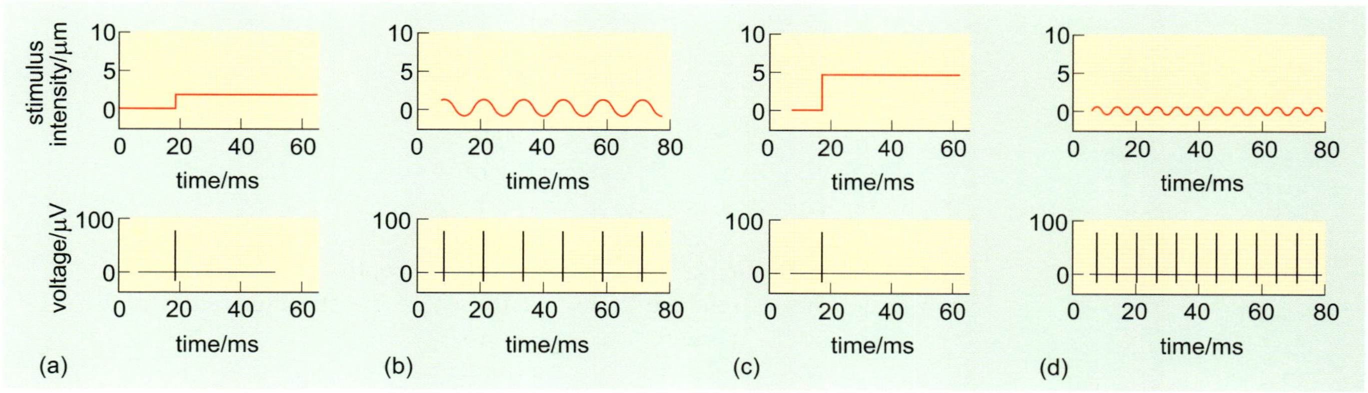

Figure 2.12 Response characteristics of Pacinian corpuscles to different stimuli. The upper graphs show the form of the stimulus applied; the lower graphs display the action potentials generated by these stimuli.

From Table 2.3 we can therefore surmise that neither Ruffini's endings nor Pacinian corpuscles are much use at detecting a single event. They are, however, very sensitive to repetitive stimulation (i.e. higher frequency vibrations). The usefulness of being sensitive to a high frequency is not immediately obvious, but it is what alerts you to the fact that something is slipping from your grasp (or, should you be climbing a ladder, it is the first indication that you are slipping!). This information is pretty useful to tool-using animals like humans.

2.2.6 Receptive-field organisation

A final characteristic that helps define the various response properties of the tactile mechanoreceptors is their receptive-field organisation. This can be seen in Figure 2.13, where fast adapting (FA) and slow adapting (SA) receptors have each been split into two subtypes: FAIs and SAIs have small, well-defined receptive fields while FAIIs and SAIIs have fairly large receptive fields. It is also noteworthy that while the FA-type and SA-type responses are found all along the somatosensory pathway, even within the somatosensory cortex, the receptive fields increase in size dramatically from the periphery to the cortex. This indicates that activity from many adjacent mechanoreceptors converges on cortical neurons, thus increasing the receptive field size.

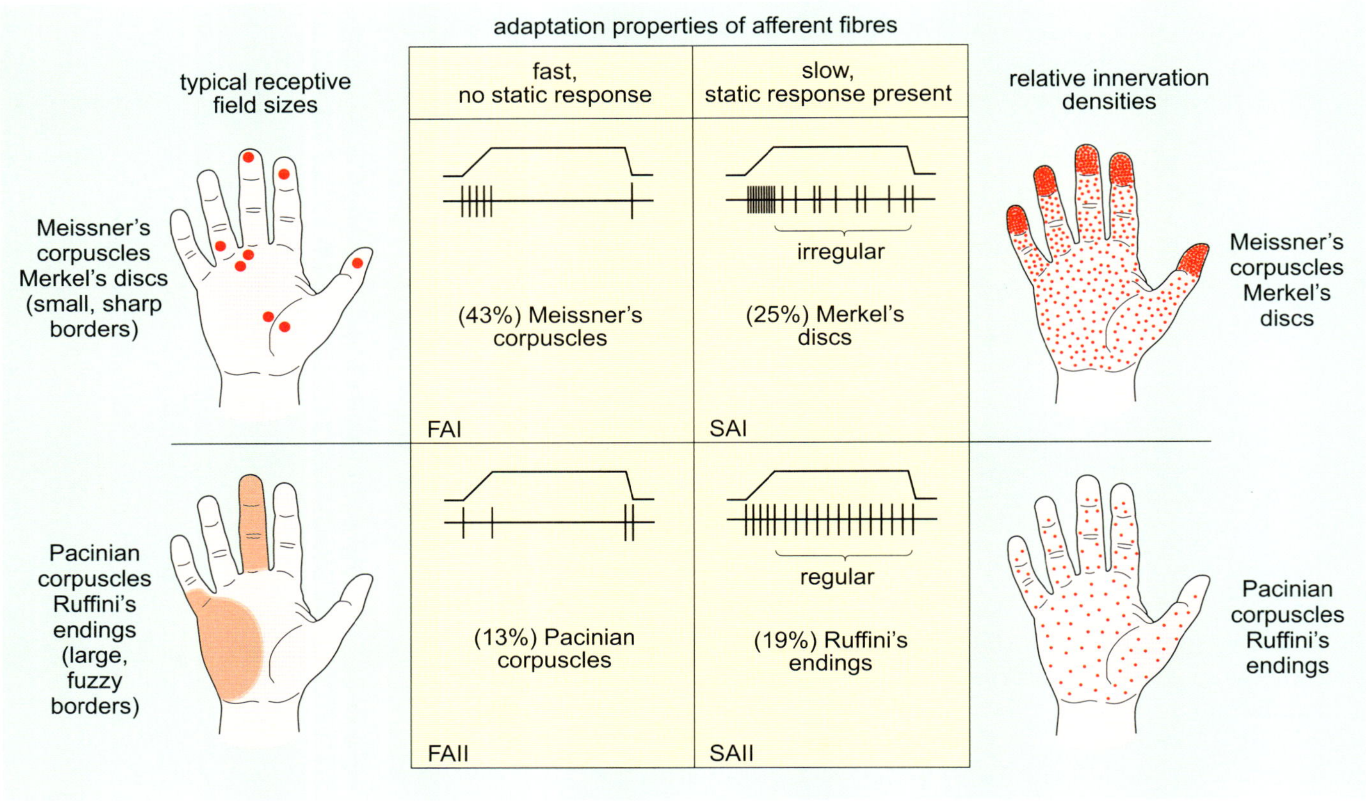

Figure 2.13 Physiological classification of the mechanoreceptive afferent fibres found in the skin of human hands.

Figure 2.13 also shows the different densities of the various receptor types on the hand (shown on the right of the figure). For example, the FAIs and SAIs have a fairly high density in the fingertips, with the density decreasing from the fingertips to the palm. In fact, this is one reason why the fingertip is more sensitive than the palm or the arm. The different patterning of action potential discharge in response to ramp-and-hold stimulation is shown in the four central pale yellow boxes in the figure. They also show the presumed receptor type. The hands to the left of the central panel show that Type I afferents have small discrete receptive fields, while Type II afferents have large receptive fields with fuzzy borders. The hands on the right show that Type I afferents innervate the fingertips more densely than they do the palm of the hand.

The combination of receptor density and receptive field size in mechanoreceptors affects the ability to discriminate stimuli in terms of the number of stimuli being applied to the skin. This is illustrated rather nicely by the two-point touch discrimination threshold experiment, which is described in Activity 2.1.

Activity 2.1 Two-point touch discrimination threshold experiment

Allow 1 hour

(*Relevant module learning outcomes: KU1, KU2, CS3 and PS2*)

This activity is an investigation of the ability of different areas of the body to distinguish a one-point stimulus from two-point stimuli placed on the skin. It is an example of an experiment aiming to examine stimuli using the psychophysical concept of discrimination and requires some basic apparatus and the help of another person, as explained below. Note that you can come back to this activity before the end of the chapter if it is not convenient for you to complete it now.

The experiment

When two points are applied lightly to the skin, usually two separate stimuli are felt. However, when the two points are close together, only one stimulus is felt. Different regions of the body vary in the amount of separation at which two points are felt, rather than one. A transition point for an aspect of sensation is referred to as its threshold and so, in the context of this experiment, this separation is called the 'two-point discrimination threshold'. The aim of this experiment is to investigate your capacity, or that of a participant, to use the sensation of touch to make such a distinction by comparing two-point discrimination thresholds for different areas of the body.

The following details describe how to measure the density of touch receptors using the two-point touch discrimination threshold test. You must read them all (and the experimental notes) before beginning your tests. The procedure requires the assistance of a helper, and you need to decide which of you will be the participant and which will make the measurements.

You will also need the following equipment:

- a large paper clip
- a notebook to record your data
- a scarf or other piece of cloth to serve as a blindfold
- a ruler or tape measure with a scale in millimetres.

First, carefully straighten the paper clip and then bend it into a 'U' shape. If you do not have a paper clip, any other stiff wire that can be bent into a 'U' shape with a fixed separation between the tips will be fine. This is the instrument that will be applied gently to the skin of different areas of the body during the experiment in order to generate responses.

Then follow the procedure below (which assumes your helper is the participant).

1 Select (and agree with your participant) which of the body areas listed in Table 2.5 you are going to investigate. (You may investigate all of them, if you wish.)

2 Explain to your participant that you are going to gently touch their skin with the paper clip and then ask them to tell you how many points they can feel. Tell them that you will sometimes touch one point and at other times two points on the skin, and demonstrate the procedure. Emphasise that you are going to apply the points gently to the skin and that this will not be at all painful.

3 Blindfold your participant and ensure that he or she is seated comfortably.

4 Carry out a trial run to familiarise your participant with the procedure – so touch them with one and then two points and ask them what they feel.

5 Next, choose the first area to investigate and then apply either two points or a single point in a random order, beginning with the points close together, slowly separating the points for each successive two-point attempt. At each attempt, ask your participant if they feel one or two points. Do not tell your participant if they are correct, but simply note down their response. You will need to keep widening your two points until your participant tells you they can detect two points, so make as many attempts as necessary before this occurs. Then repeat the process in the same body area, this time beginning with the points wide apart, and slowly bring them together for successive two-point measurements until they can feel only one point stimulus.

6 Repeat the sequence described in Step 5 for each of the other areas you wish to investigate.

7 For each body area tested, take the mean of the two smallest distances at which your participant reports two points (i.e. the mean threshold values), and note down this value.

Some typical results are given in Table 2.5. The blank column is for you to write in your measured values for comparison.

Finally, you might like to post your findings in a discussion forum on the module website to share with your tutor group and comment on what this tells you about the density and size of receptive fields.

Table 2.5 Two-point discrimination threshold for various areas of the body.

Area of body	Typical mean threshold/mm	Your calculated mean threshold/mm
Index finger	2	
Upper arm	47	
Palm of the hand	13	
Forehead	18	
Thigh	46	
Sole of the foot	22	

Notes on this experiment

- Be careful when applying the stimuli. The points of the paper clip may be sharp and should only be lightly touched on the skin.
- Be particularly careful if you examine sensitive areas like the face, and keep the points well away from your participant's eyes.
- For reliable results, great care is needed when applying the points to the skin. Try to apply the same pressure for each measurement and to touch the two points on the skin simultaneously.

The thresholds for detecting two different stimuli as opposed to one vary across areas of the skin because, in order for two different points to be felt, the stimulation must occur in two *non-overlapping* areas of neuron receptive fields. If the regions of the body have densely packed receptors with small receptive fields that do not overlap then this increases the sensory system's ability to detect two separate points, and the threshold of detection will be lower (as in the skin of the index finger; see Table 2.5). In contrast, the skin of the thigh contains a lower density of neurons with larger receptive fields that do overlap and so here discrimination of two points requires much greater point separation, typically 46 mm (Table 2.5).

2.3 Intermediate chapter summary

- Several types of mechanoreceptors are capable of detecting touch signals.
- These receptors can be classified and differentiated in a variety of ways. However, in all cases, transduction occurs at the axonal tips.
- Elucidating the properties of receptors is a piecemeal process, and we know more about some types than others. This is partly due to technical difficulties in isolating receptors, and also because most research efforts have focused on the fine discriminative abilities of our fingertips.
- There are also problems associated with interpreting results gained from the study of individual receptors' responses to simple stimuli, when these receptors work collaboratively in a living organism to provide the sensations we call touch.

2.4 Mechanoelectrical transduction

Our knowledge of mechanoelectrical transduction in the skin is unfortunately still somewhat limited. As explained in Section 2.2.3, one reason for this is that the receptors are embedded in highly vascularised skin, making it difficult to obtain receptor-potential activity via electrophysiological recording techniques (which involve inserting very fine electrodes into the tissue).

Some of what is known regarding the transduction mechanisms of these mechanoreceptors has been learned by experimenting on Pacinian corpuscles isolated from the membrane enclosing the intestines of a cat, as these corpuscles are anatomically and physiologically similar to those located within human skin. Figure 2.14a shows a light micrograph of a single Pacinian corpuscle, while Figure 2.14b is a schematic diagram defining the various components forming the receptor. It is generally accepted that the mechanisms of transduction found for Pacinian corpuscles are common to the other tactile receptors.

It is now known that both the tensile and the shear strains set up within the skin by mechanical stimulation are the adequate stimulus for transduction in tactile mechanoreceptors (Ingber, 2006). Although they are not believed to be directly party to the transduction mechanism, the non-neuronal elements of skin receptors do seem to mediate between the stimulus and the receptor's response. For example, an intact Pacinian corpuscle does not continue to respond to steady pressure, but it will do so if the corpuscle accessory structure has been dissected away from the axonal tip. In these artificial circumstances the receptor potential is maintained, although the afferent fibre's response still adapts (i.e. it does not continue to fire).

When a mechanical stimulus is applied either via the skin or directly to a receptor (for example, a Pacinian corpuscle), the accessory structure acts as a mechanical filter, transmitting the applied strain to the unmyelinated portion of the membrane where transduction occurs. The strain at the level of the mechanosensitive membrane induces strain-sensitive (stretch) channels to respond by increasing their conductance to certain ions. Sodium (Na^+) ions in particular are involved, although a contribution from potassium (K^+) ions may also occur.

The electrochemical forces for Na^+ are such that if Na^+ channels increase their conductance then these ions will rush into the neuron, causing depolarisation. The increase in conductance as a result of activating strain-sensitive channels underlies the receptor potential. It has been determined that the receptor potential is probably not mediated by neurotransmitters or other substances released by the surrounding accessory structure. If the receptor potential is of sufficient amplitude, an action potential will be generated and propagated along the axon to locations within the CNS.

The action potential set up on the more proximal portion of the tactile receptor (i.e. the axon) operates as typically described in neurons in Block 2. Voltage-sensitive Na^+ ion channels are opened once a threshold has been reached. They are subsequently closed and the axon membrane returns to its resting potential via activation of K^+ channels. It is believed that the site of

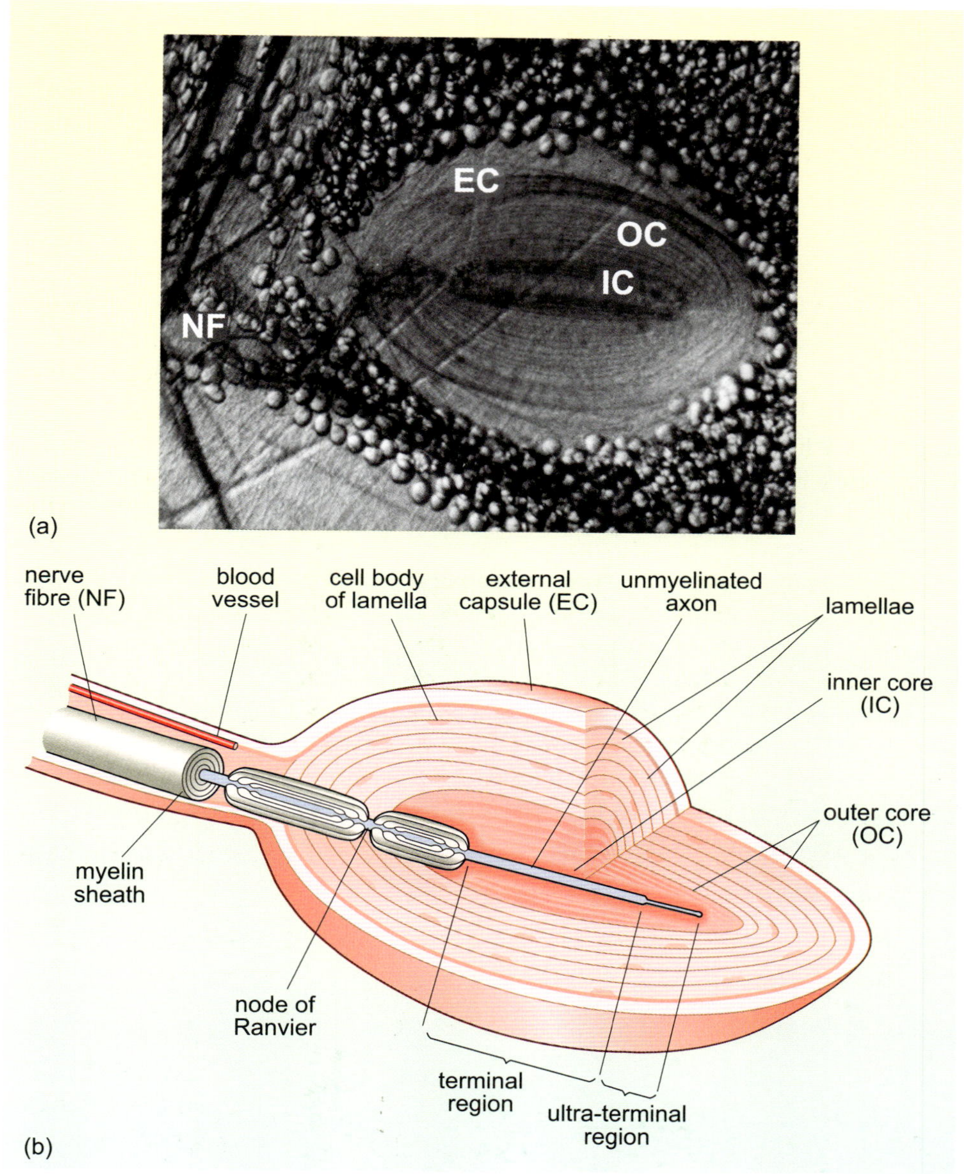

Figure 2.14 A Pacinian corpuscle: (a) light micrograph and (b) schematic diagram of a cross-section. In (a): EC = external capsule; OC = outer core; IC = inner core; NF = nerve fibre.

receptor potential generation and action potential initiation are different. Specifically, the receptor potential arises in the unmyelinated portion of the neurite and the action potential probably originates near the unmyelinated–myelinated juncture, perhaps at the most distal node of Ranvier.

- What happens to the movement of Na^+ ions once the voltage-sensitive Na^+ channels are opened?
- These ions move into the neuron down the electrochemical and concentration gradient.

- What is the mechanism by which the axon returns to its resting potential once K^+ channels are activated?
- The K^+ ions move out of the neuron by flowing down the electrochemical and concentration gradient, which makes the inside of the neuron slightly more negative than the resting potential (the refractory period), before the Na^+–K^+ pump returns the membrane potential to the resting potential.

The specific location of the mechanoreceptive channels responsible for the receptor potential is speculated to be in elements called 'filopodia' that project from the unmyelinated axon. However, other theories regarding the locus of transduction as it relates to the shape of the terminal neurite have also been proposed (Ingber, 2006).

Figure 2.15 shows that once a stimulus is sufficient for a receptor potential to be generated (at S_0), the relationship between the amplitude of the stimulus and the magnitude of the receptor potential is linear at low stimulus amplitudes (up to stimulus S_1), and becomes saturated at higher intensities. Beyond saturation point, the receptor response remains at a constant value of *P*. That is, receptor potentials are graded responses, unlike the action potential, which remains the same size whatever the amplitude of the stimulus. Thus, as the size of the receptor potential increases, the greater the number of action potentials produced. This means that as the stimulus amplitude increases, there is an increase in the firing rate as measured in action potentials per second.

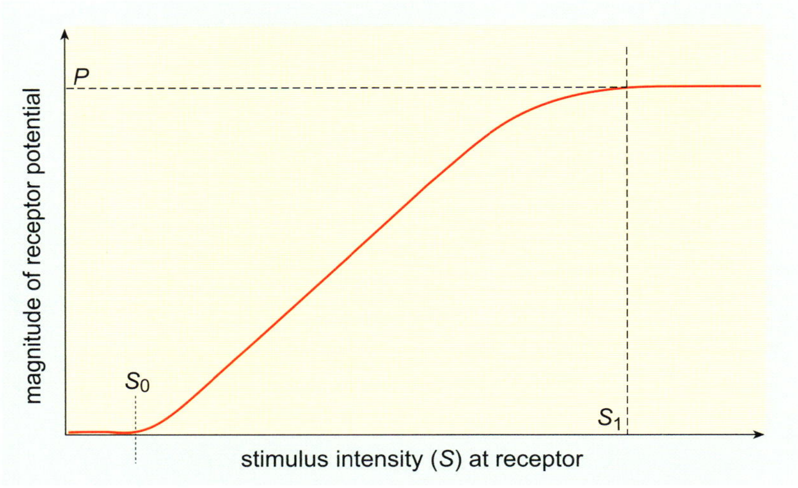

Figure 2.15 The relationship between stimulus intensity and response of the neuron.

It has been proposed that the mechanism that produces increased amplitude of the receptor potential for increases in stimulus amplitude is a result of a spatial summation of activity from discrete transduction sites that are added together to produce the activity of a larger amplitude. It has been speculated that these transduction sites are the filopodia and the suspected stretch-sensitive channels that are probably located on them.

2.4.1 Somatosensory fibre classifications

Before we move on to examine the routes touch information may take in the CNS, consider the properties of axons that respond to touch signals. The axons that comprise the peripheral nerves can be divided into myelinated ('A-type') and unmyelinated ('C-type') axons.

- ■ How is the speed of action potential affected by the presence of myelin?
- □ Myelin increases the speed of action potential conduction by allowing saltatory transmission.

The axons that transmit touch information are A-type, so they are myelinated. A-type axons can actually be further divided and labelled using Greek suffixes into Aα, Aβ, and so on. Each division has different diameters and therefore conduction velocities.

- ■ What is the relationship between axon diameter and conduction velocity?
- □ The greater the diameter, the greater the conduction velocity.

This distinction is particularly relevant when looking at somatosensation as a whole, because different types of somatosensory information travel in discrete types of axon. For example, the kind of touch information discussed in this chapter is transmitted in Aβ axons, which have a diameter of 6–10 μm and a conduction velocity of 36–60 $m\ s^{-1}$. These correspond to the Type I fibres mentioned in Section 2.2.6. By contrast, temperature information travels in Aδ axons, which have a smaller diameter of just 1–6 μm and a conduction velocity of 6–36 $m\ s^{-1}$. These, along with C fibres, correspond to Type II fibres.

You should note, however, that although specific types of somatosensory information can travel in certain types of axons, they may also travel in the same types of axons. For example, you will see later that some proprioceptive information may also be carried in Aβ axons, so these are referred to as general sensory afferents.

Activity 2.2 Consolidating somatosensory fibre classifications

Allow 30 minutes throughout the block

(*Relevant module learning outcome: KU2*)

As you have just read, there are several different types of axon fibres carrying somatosensory information. In order to keep track of these different types, you should draw up your own version of Table 2.6 (or download the blank version from the *Block 3 Activities* resource on the module website). You will need enough room to record information about each of the four fibre types listed below, which you will gain as you work through the *whole* block.

Table 2.6 Summary of axon types.

Axon type	**Specialised name**	**Diameter/µm**	**Function(s)**
Aβ			
Aδ			
Aα			
C			

You can begin completing your table now by recording the information for Aβ and Aδ fibres outlined above. Note that you will need to adapt your notes for one fibre type later in the block in the light of additional information, so remember to revisit your notes each time you come across new, relevant details. When you have completed the table, compare your notes to the activity feedback provided alongside the answers to this chapter's self-assessment questions.

We have now discussed some of the properties of mechanoreceptors as well as some of what is known about the process of mechanoelectrical transduction. You will read more about current knowledge of mechanoelectrical transduction, and be able to appreciate the limitations of available techniques of study, later in the block, once you have covered the basic principles of proprioception and nociception (the sensation that arises from activation of nociceptors). Mechanoreceptors also underlie these sensory processes.

Next, however, we explore the processing of tactile information beyond transduction.

2.5 Somatosensory afferent pathways

Recall that tactile mechanoreceptors have their cell bodies located in structures called dorsal root ganglia (DRG). These ganglia are collections of the cell bodies of pseudounipolar neurons, which use a range of different neurotransmitters.

■ What is unusual about the structure of a pseudounipolar neuron compared with a unipolar neuron?

□ The term pseudounipolar reflects the fact that these neurons have axons that branch into two portions.

These pseudounipolar neurons are arranged along both sides of the dorsal aspect of the spinal column. One branch innervates the skin and the other innervates the spinal cord. Each vertebra of the spinal column has two DRG associated with them (left and right), and they form the basis of the spinal nerves that innervate specific regions of the body surface called dermatomes. The dermatomes are organised topographically (Figure 2.16), meaning that they are arranged in a clear layout corresponding to the position of the inputs.

The taxonomy of these nerves refers to the location of the root ganglion in question and uses:

- 'C' to refer to cervical
- 'T' to thoracic
- 'L' to lumbar
- 'S' to sacral.

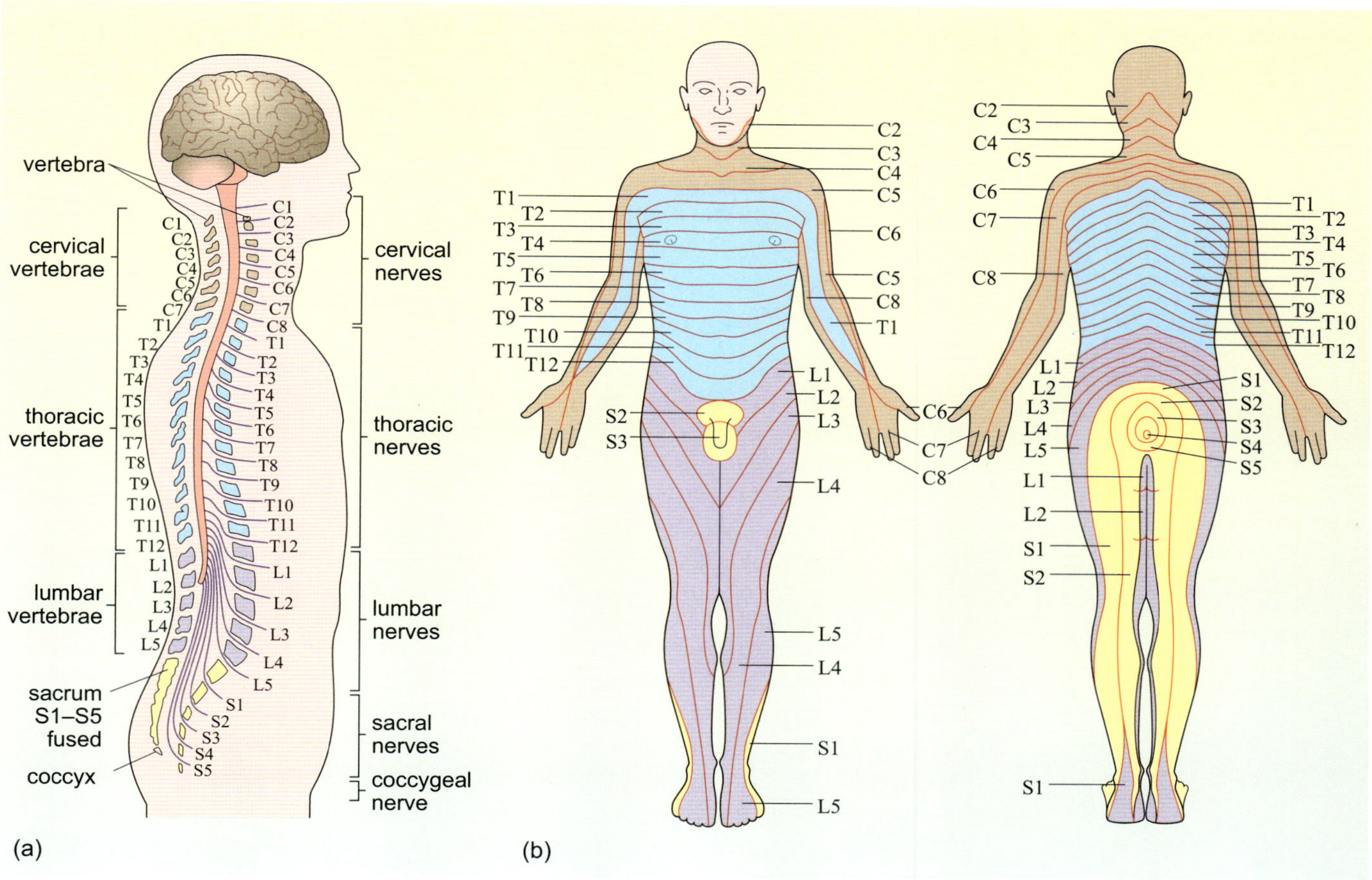

Figure 2.16 (a) Location of pseudounipolar neurons with respect to the vertebrae. (b) Dermatomes corresponding to the nerves in (a).

Note that there is a separate, but parallel system for sensing the mechanical and other somatosensory experiences on the face. This system is called the **trigeminal system** and it operates in a manner quite similar to that of the spinal nerves.

Routes from the spine to the brain

Neural activity arising in the spinal nerves as a result of mechanical stimulation of the mechanoreceptors is passed across the DRG and enters the dorsal horn of the spinal column, where it takes one of three routes.

The first route operates entirely at the spinal-cord level to control responses of motor neurons in the ventral horn of the spinal cord. This essentially forms the first component of sensorimotor integration, because these neurons are involved in controlling muscles that are responsible for the movements of the body in reflexes. For example, a stimulus such as someone tickling your foot excites mechanoreceptors that, via interneurons in the spinal cord, project to motor neurons in the lower limb, stimulating them to operate a withdrawal reflex that moves your foot away from the source of the tickling.

Unlike the first route, the remaining two routes for touch information access higher regions in the brain. The first of these is referred to as the **dorsal column/medial lemniscus tract**. This pathway is really divided into two portions; one is the dorsal column and the other is the medial lemniscus tract. In the first part of this pathway the incoming activity is directly passed upward in the spinal column via tracts called the dorsal columns (Figure 2.17). These bilateral dorsal columns are myelinated fibre tracts in the posterior region of the spinal cord. They form a direct pathway of activity to brainstem structures called the **dorsal column nuclei (DCN)**.

The DCN comprise two separate structures both located in the **medulla**. These are the gracile nucleus and the cuneate nucleus. Fibres from the lower limbs and trunk innervate the gracile nucleus while fibres from the upper limbs and trunk innervate the cuneate nucleus. Since these are direct pathways, no synapse is present between the site of mechanoelectric transduction and the dorsal column nuclei. Consequently, these neurons are long, some being more than a metre in length.

The first synapses of this pathway are located within the DCN and the projection neurons from these structures are considered to be the second-order neurons of the somatosensory system. The axons of these neurons cross the midline to form the second part of the pathway called the medial lemniscus tract, which projects directly to the somatosensory nuclei of the thalamus (Figure 2.17): the **ventral posterior lateral thalamic nucleus**. From the thalamus the information is transferred to the **primary somatosensory cortex (S1)**. This is located in the post-central gyrus of the cerebral cortex, a region known as the parietal lobe.

The second pathway to reach higher brain regions originates in the synaptic regions within the spinal cord, the central grey matter. Via a single synapse, the neural activity is relayed towards the brain in a pathway called the **spino-cervical-thalamic tract**. This term refers to the entire pathway shown in red in the diagram either side of the lateral cervical nucleus. As the name implies, the pathway originates in the spinal column, projects to the cervical nucleus at the level of the neck and, after synapsing there, the projection neurons merge with the dorsal column/medial lemniscus tract, subsequently synapsing in the ventral posterior lateral nucleus in the thalamus (Figure 2.17).

S1 consists of four different cortical areas referred to using the numbering system of Brodmann (1, 2, 3a and 3b). The secondary somatosensory cortex (S2) is located just lateral to this region (Figure 2.18) and it receives information from S1.

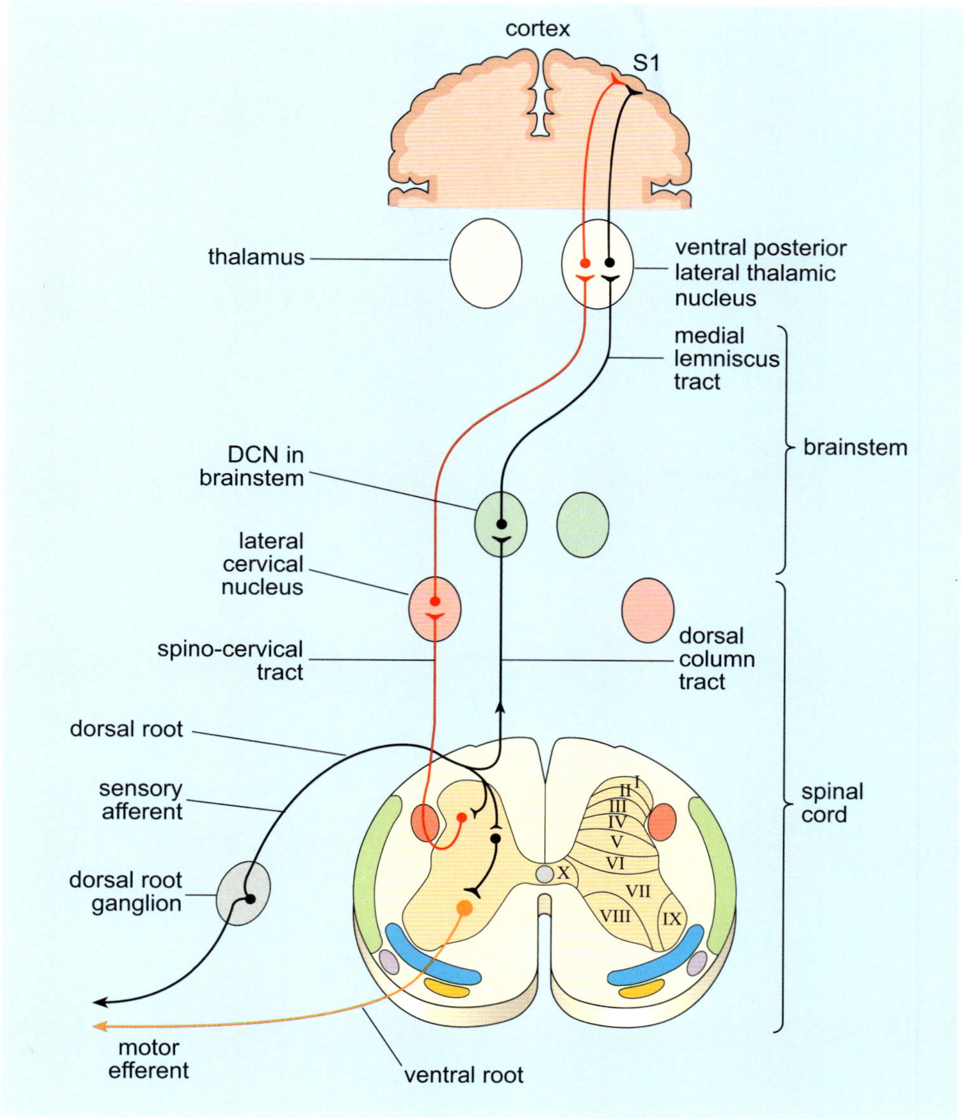

Figure 2.17 An overall view of the tactile pathways.

The neurons in the ventral posterior lateral nucleus of the thalamus have antagonistic receptive fields. The antagonistic subfields in this case are arranged by 'centre/surround', which refers to the fact that the receptive fields are organised into an inner circular field and an outer, surrounding circular field, with opposing effects. You can explore the effects of this receptive field organisation in Activity 2.3 at the end of the next section. You should also bear in mind that similar antagonistic receptive fields are found in other sensory systems such as vision.

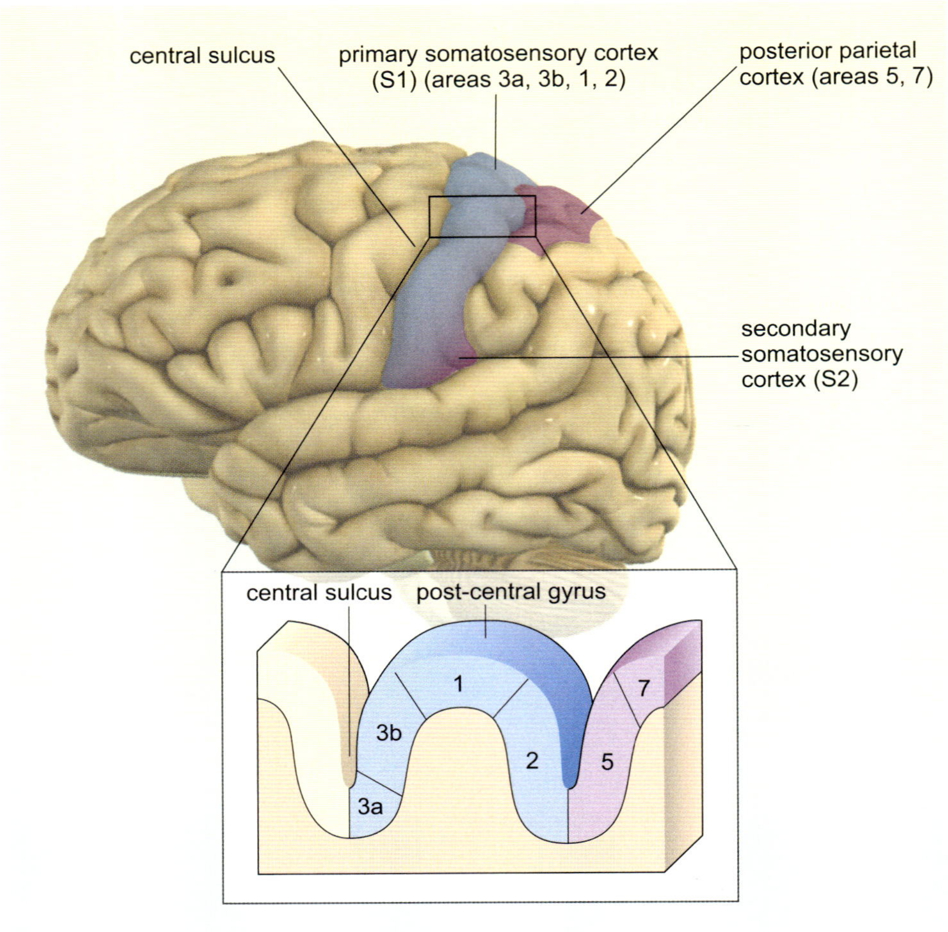

Figure 2.18 Somatosensory areas of the cortex. All of the illustrated areas lie in the parietal lobe (not shown), adjacent to the posterior parietal cortex.

2.5.1 Somatosensory representations in the cortex

Somatosensory representation in S1 was long thought to be topographically organised according to body parts in a manner known as the **somatosensory homunculus**: the model 'little man' that is produced by mapping the responsiveness of the neurons in the somatosensory cortex. The somatosensory homunculus was first proposed by Penfield and Bodrey (1937). It is shown in Figure 2.19 alongside the motor cortical representation of body parts, which are organised similarly to produce a **motor homunculus**.

The homunculi look somewhat distorted because the size of cortical representation is determined by the density of receptors, such that larger areas of primary somatosensory (or motor) cortex are devoted to areas of the body with the most dense receptor distribution. The idea was that this map is fixed and represents a simple physical map of stimulation sites around the body. However, the somatosensory homunculus has been challenged on both counts. The first is explored in Box 2.3 with a study showing that S1 represents the *perception* of touch rather than the physical tactile sensation.

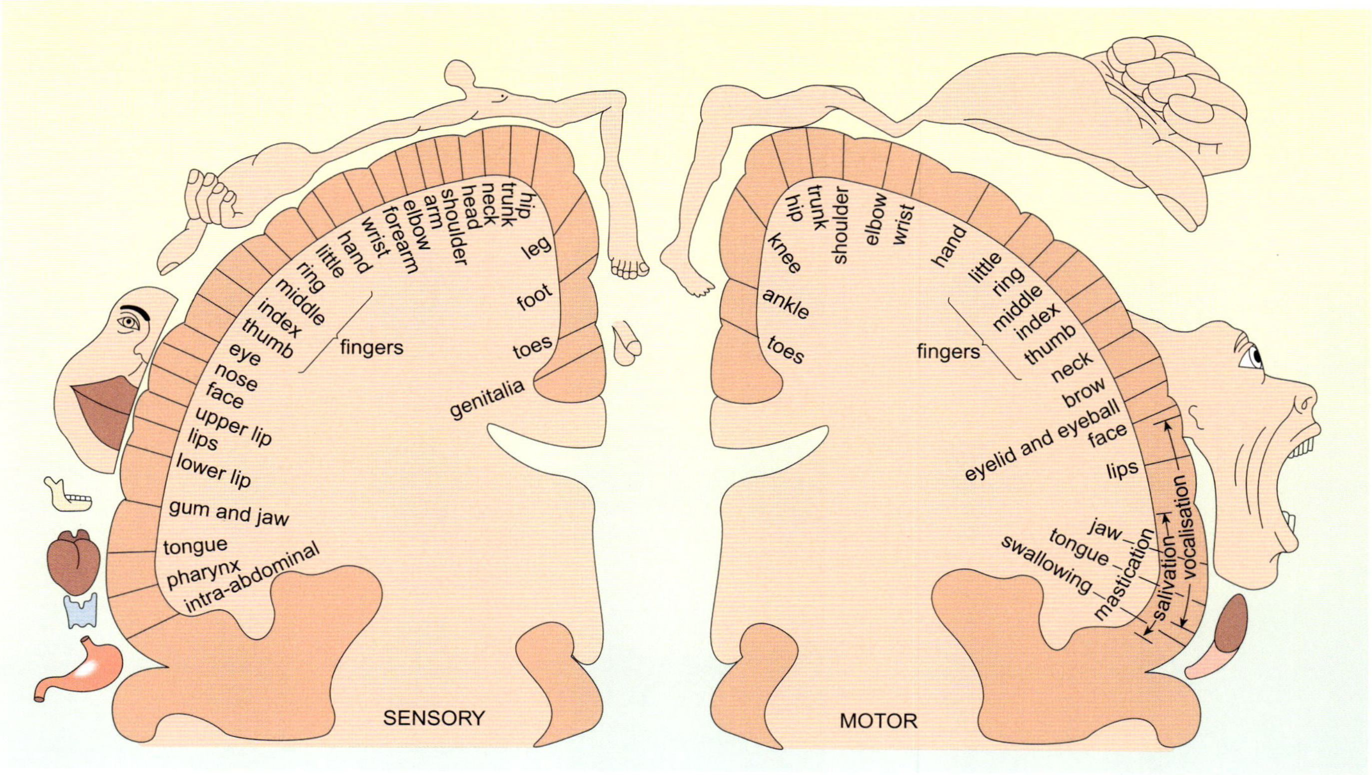

Figure 2.19 Somatosensory and motor homunculi.

Box 2.3 The perceptual nature of the primary somatosensory cortex homunculus

Blankenburg et al. (2006) conducted a study to determine whether S1 responded to a perceived rather than an actual mechanical stimulus. To do this, they used an illusion called the cutaneous rabbit illusion. In this illusion the skin at the wrist is repeatedly rapidly stimulated followed by the skin near the elbow. This actual pattern of stimulation at these two sites leads to the illusionary perception of touch at intervals along the skin between the two stimulation sites. However, these interval sites are not actually mechanically stimulated. The perception is said to be very much as if a rabbit is hopping along the forearm.

Crucially, functional magnetic resonance imagery (fMRI) scans of participants' brains that were taken during the illusion showed activation in the region of S1 representing the percept location on the forearm. This result provided convincing evidence that S1 and the somatosensory homunculus represent the *perception* of the body rather than the actual physical location of stimuli, illustrating rather nicely that perception may be something entirely different from the corresponding sensation.

The next chapter discusses the perception of touch in more detail, where the changeable plastic nature of S1 body image representation is explored through the concept of body schema. This is the second aspect on which the somatosensory homunculus put forward by Penfield and Boldrey (1937) has been challenged. For now, though, you should end this section by completing Activity 2.3.

Activity 2.3 Receptive fields in touch pathways

Allow 1 hour

(*Relevant module learning outcomes: KU1, KU2 and PS1*)

Now would be a good time to complete this activity, which is available from the *Block 3 Activities* resource on the module website. It offers the chance to review your learning from the two-point touch experiment which you carried out in Activity 2.1 and to explore two-point touch discrimination in Braille, as well as the function of lateral inhibition in the tactile pathways.

2.6 Chapter 2 summary and questions

- A variety of mechanoreceptor types detect touch information. Each type has specific structural features, adequate stimuli, adaptation rates, location and receptive fields.
- Psychophysical techniques have been used to establish the frequencies and intensities of stimuli to which the different receptor types respond.
- The Pacinian corpuscle is the largest of the receptors, making it the easiest to study. Much of the research on transduction has been carried out on this mechanoreceptor, although the findings are thought to generalise to other receptors.
- The transduction mechanisms are not fully understood, but it is thought that there are stretch-sensitive ion channels on the filopodia. These channels are believed to be responsible for allowing ion movement across the most distal portions of the neurite, resulting in a receptor potential and, if sufficient in amplitude, an action potential.
- All of the receptors are modified sensory neurons with their cell bodies in the dorsal root ganglion (DRG). Their axons enter the dorsal horn of the spinal cord. There are two ascending pathways, both of which project via the thalamus to the somatosensory cortex, as well as a local circuit that provides an input to the motor system at the spinal level.
- Somatosensory representations in the cortex were thought to follow a fixed somatosensory homunculus similar to the motor homunculus. Recent work has challenged this simplistic notion, showing that the somatosensory homunculus represents perceived touch rather than touch sensation.

Self-assessment questions

Question 2.1

What is a Merkel cell neurite complex and how does this differ in terms of its anatomical arrangement from a Pacinian corpuscle?

Question 2.2

How do Meissner's corpuscles and Pacinian corpuscles differ in their properties, innervations, densities and receptive field sizes?

Question 2.3

Draw the three routes for skin receptor afferents entering the spinal cord.

Question 2.4

It would appear that the somatosensory homunculus in the primary somatosensory cortex (S1) represents perception rather than stimulation. What evidence is there for this?

The perception of touch

3

The presence of such a variety of tactile mechanoreceptors, as discussed in Chapter 2, emphasises that touch is not a unitary sensation. Thus, perceptual experiences that arise from tactile stimulation are mediated by a medley of sensory inputs that somehow come to be interpreted as a unified experience by the brain.

Touch is generally regarded as the experience of physically encountering objects in our environment, but is actually far more sophisticated than this. In fact, when we touch objects we are able to perceive many features of them, such as their weight, stiffness, temperature and thermal conductivity. These qualities quickly allow us to formulate an idea of what the object is and what it is made from. This concept highlights rather nicely what is different about touch compared with other senses: when we use it we receive information about our body itself, as well as the information about what it is that we are touching. This chapter considers how some of these features are perceived.

3.1 Active and passive touch

Imagine yourself at the supermarket in the fruit and vegetable section. A bright red mango catches your eye and you pick it up to give it a gentle squeeze: this one's too soft – it's overripe. Another one you test is too hard, but the next one yields ever so slightly to gentle pressure from your thumb – it's perfect. This voluntary touch exploration process is known as **active touch**, or haptics. In this example the softness (or hardness) of the mango was tested, and this is a property that can best be determined by active touch. If, instead, the mango was pushed against your immobile hands, an example of **passive touch**, you would not get the same experience of hardness, and your judgement would be poorer as a result.

You can experience both active and passive touch if you examine one immobile arm using the hand of your other arm. Here, the active touch comes from the hand doing the explorative touch while the passive touch experience comes from the immobile arm. Your own tests (say with a mango) will confirm, as formal experiments have, that active rather than passive touch is the superior method of obtaining information about objects through our somatosensory system.

3.1.1 Different types of active touch

Psychologists Susan Lederman and Roberta Klatzky (1987) produced a descriptive taxonomy of touch exploration that shows the different ways in which we can actively engage with an object. They asked blindfolded participants to use their hands to try to identify objects, and observed a number of ways in which the hands work together to acquire information. These methods are depicted in Figure 3.1.

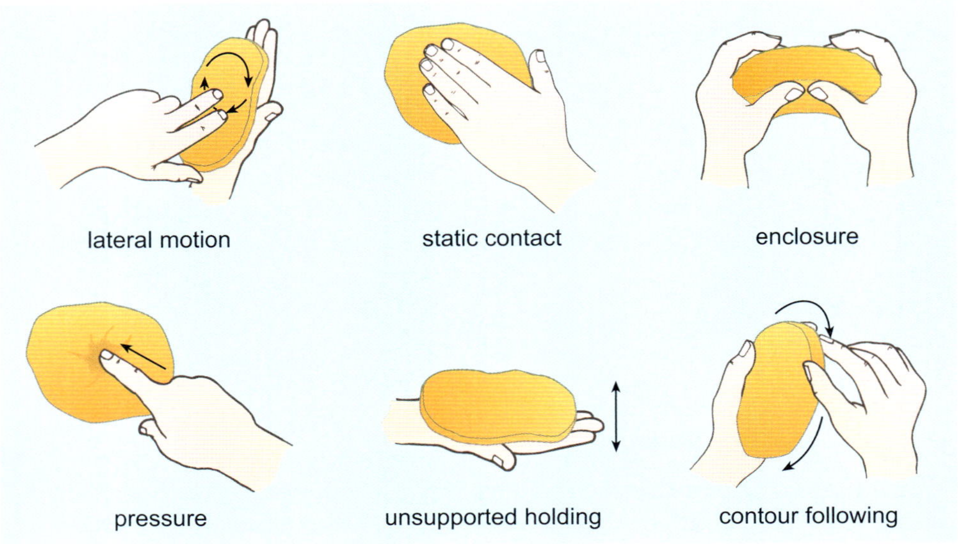

Figure 3.1 Examples of Lederman and Klatzky's taxonomy of touch.

Under this taxonomy:

- 'lateral motion' is used to obtain surface texture information (roughness)
- 'static contact' is used to determine the temperature of the object or its thermal conductivity (Box 3.1 has more information on 'thermodetection'), and so gives clues to the material used in the object's construction
- 'enclosure' requires the fingers to mould around the shape of the object to obtain shape and volume information
- 'pressure' is applied by one hand to the object held by the other hand (this operation can also be done with one hand) to determine hardness
- 'unsupported holding' consists of hefting the object up and down, and is used to determine the weight of the object
- 'contour following' is used to obtain exact shape information.

Lederman and Klatzky (1998) found that recognition of common objects by active touch was extremely accurate and fast. Blindfolded participants manipulating common objects such as a golf ball, scissors and a light bulb usually took less than 5 seconds for correct identification. Of course, as well as the tactile component of this task there is also a strong cognitive element, since the participant's perceptions must also be actively compared with their memory of similar perceptions produced by these objects in order to find a direct match. However, this factor makes successful blinded tactile object exploration an even more amazing feat, given that all of this information processing happens in less than 5 seconds!

Box 3.1 Thermoreceptors and the use of temperature in touch

Touching an object using static contact (see Figure 3.1) can give us quite a lot of information about the material(s) it is made of based just on its thermal conductivity. For example, metals are good conductors of heat so picking up a metal gardening implement on a cold day is an unpleasant experience as the warmth from your hand is conducted away by the metal. However, it is an experience that you can avoid by wearing woollen gloves because wool is a poor conductor of heat, especially if it has a loose weave that traps pockets of air, which is an even worse thermal conductor than wool.

Thermoreceptors are sensitive to small changes in skin temperature but operate collectively over a wide dynamic range, spanning painful (noxious) heat to noxious cold. They are of primary importance in the regulation of body temperature, but note that this module discusses only those receptors that are located on the skin. Mostly, thermodetection takes place without us being consciously aware of the physiological changes that are made. When we do become aware, we alter our behaviour, for example by putting on more clothes or turning up the heating if the ambient temperature is low, or wearing gloves if we need to grasp cold metal tools.

Thermodetection occurs via temperature-sensitive ion channels, of which the best understood are the transient receptor potential (TRP) family ion channels. There are at least six different types of thermo-TRPs known at the time of writing. These can be classified as shown in Table 3.1. They are found on DRG neurons that contain both Aδ and C fibres.

Table 3.1 Thermo-TRPs and the stimuli to which they respond.

Channel	Temperature sensitivity/°C	Alternative means of stimulating receptor	Thermosensing function
TRPV1	37–45	capsaicin, lidocaine	noxious heat sensor
TRPV2	>52	growth factors	extreme noxious heat sensor
TRPV3	32–39	camphor, oregano	innocuous warmth and noxious heat
TRPV4	27–34	anandamide, arachidonic acid	innocuous warmth
TRPM8	25–28	menthol, eucalyptol	innocuous cold
TRPA1	≤17	mustard oil, bradykinin	innocuous cold, noxious cold

Note that as well as responding to temperature, thermo-TRPs respond to non-thermal stimuli as indicated in the third column of Table 3.1. This, for example, explains why eating spicy food (containing capsaicin) leads to the experience of heat in the mouth and why menthol triggers a cooling or cold sensation.

The chemical name for capsaicin is *trans*-8-methyl-*N*-vanillyl-nonenamide, and it acts via the ionotropic vanilloid receptor called TRPVR1, which is associated with the TRPV1 ion channel shown in Table 3.1. These receptors are so named because they are *t*ransient *r*eceptor *p*otential *v*anilloid *r*eceptors, meaning that they bind vanilloid compounds. You will meet these receptors again in Section 5.1.2. Thus, you should note that the term TRP refers to the ion channel itself (in this case, TRPV1), while the alternative term TRPVR refers to the *receptor* associated with the thermal sensing ion channel (in this case, TRPVR1).

The perceived temperature of an actively manipulated object is important in assessing its material nature. Objects that feel cold at room temperature, such as those made from metal, have a high thermal conductivity. Skin surface temperature (the face is especially sensitive) is closely monitored to provide information about the ambient temperature as part of the body's thermoregulatory system. Rapid adaptation to skin temperature occurs so that what we actually experience perceptually is *relative* temperature as you will now see in Activity 3.1.

Activity 3.1 Rapid adaptation to skin temperature

Allow 15 minutes

(*Relevant module learning outcomes: KU1, KU2 and PS2*)

You will need three medium-sized bowls of water to complete this activity: one cold (but not near-freezing, and hence noxious), one at approximately room temperature, and one hot (but not so hot as to scald). The bowls should be around three-quarters full of water.

Once you have set up your bowls of water, place your left hand in the bowl containing the hottest water and your right hand in the bowl with the coldest water, and keep them there for 1 minute. Next, remove each hand from its bowl and place both hands simultaneously into the bowl of room-temperature water. What is your perceptual experience of temperature in each hand? Make a note of this and see if you can explain your observation. Feedback on this activity is provided alongside the answers to this chapter's self-assessment questions.

Our hands are most suitably adapted to perform active touch as they work together to grasp, prod, press, rub and heft the tested object. The pulp of our fingertips is equipped with a dense array of highly sensitive tactile receptors that map to a large somatosensory cortical representation in the brain (recall the somatosensory homunculus from Chapter 2). The tactile acuity of the fingertips is only surpassed by the tip of the tongue. The fact that the tip of the tongue has the highest acuity results in the common experience of the magnified perception of small objects in the mouth, for example, food stuck in the teeth. (This phenomenon is known as Weber's illusion, because Ernst Heinrich Weber (1795–1878), Professor of Physiology at Leipzig University, was the first person to study the acuity of different regions of the body.)

However, despite this high acuity, curiously the tongue is unable to feel a pulse at the wrist. (You might like to test this for yourself.)

■ Why is it that the tongue cannot feel a pulse on the wrist while a finger can, despite the tongue's far greater tactile acuity?

□ The receptors in the tongue are not sensitive to the stimulus being generated by the pulse at the wrist. So while the tongue may generally have a far greater tactile acuity, this means nothing if the receptors in question cannot detect a stimulus of a given nature.

Active touch is routinely used in many professions: the surgeon's palpation of an afflicted body region, and a wool grader's judgement of the wool quality as determined from the softness and fineness of the fleece, are just two examples.

3.1.2 Movement and proprioception in active touch

You have seen how active touch can be used to determine an object's features such as hardness or temperature, but it is also very commonly used to assess weight. Think about when you last made a cake and picked up the bag of flour to get a sense of how much was left in the bag from its weight. It is likely that you engaged in some unsupported holding, moving the bag of flour up and down to help you guess its weight. Therefore, when we use active touch to gauge weight, movement becomes essential for accurate performance. Weber was possibly the first person to emphasise the importance of movement in touch:

> Man is in some way helped by the knowledge of his own bodily movement when he examines objects by touch. When we move our arms in a particular direction intentionally and deliberately, we achieve the best perception of the direction of the object under examination. In this way we gain information about the shape of objects that we handle and touch all over. We also perceive weights more clearly when we feel by kinaesthesis the muscular or nervous force necessary to lift the objects.
>
> *(Weber, 1978)*

This assertion seems counterintuitive because you might think that weight would be better determined by controlled activation of the relevant cutaneous receptors produced by placing the object onto the palm of a stationary hand resting on a table top (as in accurately weighing out flour on a kitchen scale). In fact, if you watch someone judging the weight of an object you will find they heft the object up and down and even toss it from hand to hand. These movements take time, and what appears to be happening is that the particular information being sought (weight) is being isolated as an *invariant* from the changing flux of movements and their correlated tactile sensations. This is how American psychologist James J. Gibson (1983) described the process in his influential book *The Senses Considered as Perceptual Systems*, adding that it is a kind of filtering out of proprioceptive information, leaving the 'pure' information about the object.

What is striking about our experience of feeling an object with our hands is the unity of the percept despite the multiple tactile sensations stemming from up to ten moving fingertips. The tactile sense of object unity can be upset when the positions of fingers are forced out of their usual order, as with the so-called Aristotle's illusion (see Activity 3.2).

Activity 3.2 Aristotle's illusion

Allow 5 minutes

(*Relevant module learning outcomes: KU1 and PS2*)

Loosely cross your index finger and your middle finger and place a pencil in the 'V' formed by their intersection (Figure 3.2). Now close your eyes and gently slide the pencil between the two fingers, touching the two outer surfaces of both of them. You should experience a perception of being touched by two pencils.

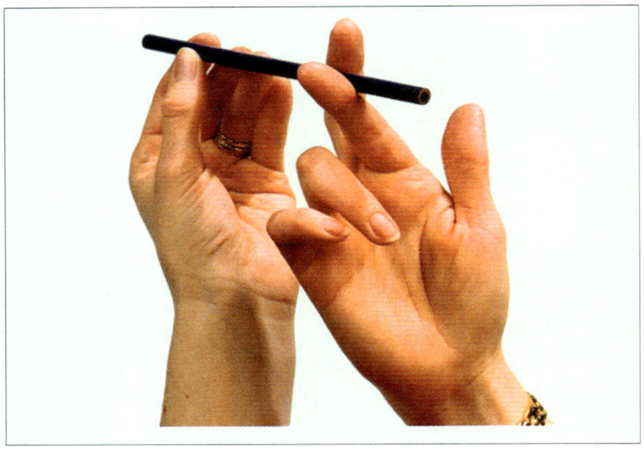

Figure 3.2 Testing Aristotle's illusion.

The perception that we hope you experienced is known as Aristotle's illusion. The explanation for the illusion is that the pencil is rubbing the two *outside* surfaces of the pair of fingers and it would normally only be possible to do this simultaneously by using two pencils. Once again, as in Block 1, we are noting the importance of expectation of the world around us and of assumption when building a percept based on sensation.

To recap, when we use active touch we must know where the various parts of our body doing the touching (usually our fingers) lie relative to one another, and this requires the sense of proprioception and a functioning **body schema**.

This term relates to the postural proprioceptive map of our body parts in relation to one another.

Our index finger lies next to our thumb, and if we pick up a pen between these two digits, the pen stimulates sensory receptors on the inner surfaces of both finger and thumb. If we did this with our eyes closed then the sensory afferent information would inform us that we had been successful in this manoeuvre. We expect these anatomical relationships between the various parts of our body to remain constant, and we use this knowledge when we interpret incoming signals from the skin.

During hand movements, tactile detection thresholds are increased for areas of skin that are not in contact with the target of exploration (object), while they are decreased for the involved skin areas. That is, those areas in contact with the object become more sensitive while those not in contact with it become less sensitive. This 'sensory gating' mechanism improves the signal-to-noise ratio, allowing manipulated objects to be the focus of attention.

Somewhat surprisingly, Weiskrantz and Zhang (1987) described a related effect that was apparent in a patient with hemianaesthesia (lack of touch sensation on one side of the body) following a right hemisphere stroke. The patient could, when blindfolded, accurately localise a touch on her left insensate hand only when she used her (sensate) right hand to do this, or when she touched her insensate hand using an object held in her sensate hand. Furthermore, another person's touch to the insensate hand was not perceived or localisable, and she could clearly discriminate between her active touching of her own fingers on the insensate hand and the fingers of the experimenter placed interdigitated with her own. Thus, active touch by the patient's sensate hand appeared to somehow reduce the tactile threshold in the insensate hand, although no definitive mechanisms by which this could have occurred are reported in the paper.

Active touch is also used to explore objects, and to determine their hazardous nature. This involves the transient activation of nociceptors in the skin (i.e. free nerve endings), which signal potential or actual tissue damage. Hence, we might warily check the sharpness of the edges of a flint stone before fully grasping it. Indeed, self-application affects pain and pleasure sensations: it is the very predictability of movements made during active touch that explain why it is difficult to tickle yourself, and why we are less sensitive to a noxious stimulus that is self-applied.

In studying this section, you should now be aware that active touch is used far more in our daily lives than we are normally aware of – reaching into a pocket to retrieve keys or coins; getting dressed; doing buttons up; peeling an orange; and so on. However, usually these operations are accompanied by other sensory input from vision and hearing. All of these manoeuvres require the remarkable exploratory, manipulatory and sensory capacities of our hands – capacities that we are likely to very much take for granted unless, for example, we are visually impaired.

3.2 Neural correlates of touch perception

The preceding section discussed active and (to a lesser degree) passive touch. Although active touch is very effective when using areas of the body with a high density of receptors, such as the fingertips, in animals, active touch often involves various appendages like nails, claws, or beaks. These extensions are used to probe and explore the environment. Using one of your fingernails, try probing into the wood grain of a table and consider where you are actually experiencing the scraping sensation. It is perhaps surprising to realise that the sensation is localised to the tips of the fingernails themselves, yet the mechanoreceptors responsible are located at the root of the nail.

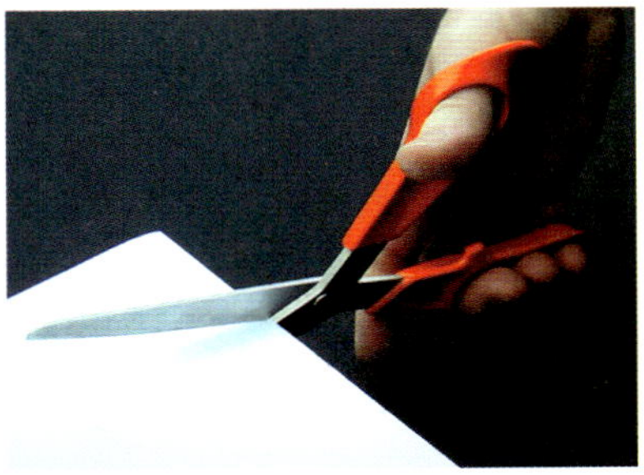

Figure 3.3 Cutting paper with a pair of scissors.

There seems no limit to how far we can extend our perception in this way. A blind or a sighted person exploring the ground with a cane experiences the gravel, tarmac or carpet at the end of that tool. Similarly, grasping a bolt with a pair of pliers results in feeling the contact at the jaws of the pliers, yet all of the receptors are in the hands, arm muscles and tendons. Cutting paper with scissors gives us a sensation at the very cutting edge of the scissors (Figure 3.3). We feel the cutting action at the blades of the scissors even though our sensory receptors are in the skin, joints and muscles associated with the hand. It is interesting that the control and sensation are attributed to the wrong blade because of their crossed construction (i.e. we experience the top blade as being controlled by our thumb, whereas in fact it is controlled by our fingers).

These examples bring us back to the concept of the somatosensory homunculus (see Box 2.3) and the second ground on which the model was challenged. The challenge relates to the notion that representations in the somatosensory cortex are fixed in nature. If they were, it would be impossible for somebody with visual impairment to perceive touch at the end of their cane. However, it has been shown that representations in the somatosensory cortex can be altered to encompass external objects following repeated experience of working with (using) these objects (Cardinali et al., 2012). Thus, a functioning body schema is essential for integrating sensory experience with proper motor action.

An everyday example is that of the learner driver who worries immensely about driving down a narrow lane lined with parked cars, while a seasoned driver seems to intuitively know ('sense') where the edges of the car are in relation to other obstacles. Unlike the learner, the seasoned driver does not feel an instinctual urge to 'breathe in' to make themselves smaller in this instance! In this case, of course, the entire car is the tool that has become incorporated into the body schema.

In Chapter 2 you learned that both pathways carrying touch information to the brain (namely the dorsal column/medial lemniscus tract and the spino-cervical-thalamic tract) reach the primary somatosensory cortex (S1), and that S1 actually processes information from the opposite side of the body. Electrical recordings of single neurons in this area of the cortex in monkeys have revealed that cortical responses occur following manipulation of complex tactile objects. Iwamura and Tanaka (1993) found that at the level of the S1, features such as the edges of objects were being coded for by the firing of neurons. The neurons had very large receptive fields on the contralateral hand, comprising a whole finger or more. There were also neurons that coded the joint positions of individual fingers. What is more, neurons in Brodmann's area 2 (part of S1, see Figure 2.17) were especially sensitive to the active manipulation of particular object shapes (either a sphere or a rectangular block shape). Indeed, many neurons *only* fired during active grasping of an object, since passive probing or movement of fingers gave no response.

Later, DiCarlo and Johnson (2002) found that in the monkey the responses of neurons in Brodmann's area 3b to dot patterns presented to the finger pads were independent of the application velocity of the pattern. We have here, therefore, the complex integration of kinaesthetic and tactile information to extract shape and roughness characteristics about objects: haptic form perception depends, as Gibson (1983) said, on 'the covariance of cutaneous and articular motion'. The responses of these neurons appear to represent a low-level analysis necessary for object recognition by active touch. The cortical area that fully integrates the necessary sensory and motor information may be an area within the parietal cortex, such as Brodmann's area 5.

3.3 The importance of touch

In evolutionary terms, touch is arguably one of the oldest and most fundamental senses of all. Primitive unicellular organisms can feel but not see or hear. Serious disorders, or congenital defects, of the sense of touch are extremely rare, more so than for other senses. These historic factors may explain the common notion of the salience of touch: when we are suspicious about the authenticity of coins or a flower, we subject them to various mechanical tactile tests. It has been said that touch educates the other senses.

There are also revealing figurative uses of the words derived from touch perception. So, for example, when we say that a person is 'in touch' we mean that the person is in direct communication. Other phrases tap common experience and emotions: finding something 'deeply touching' or 'a gripping experience'; being tactful, tactless or touchy; 'grasping' an idea, or getting a 'slap on the wrist', and so on. The everyday usage of 'feeling' to describe our basic emotions and our sense of how things are, in phrases such as 'you know how I feel about you' and 'I feel it is the right decision', contrasts with 'Yes, I see' when referring to understanding and knowledge. This usage reflects our belief that feeling is a more primitive sense than seeing.

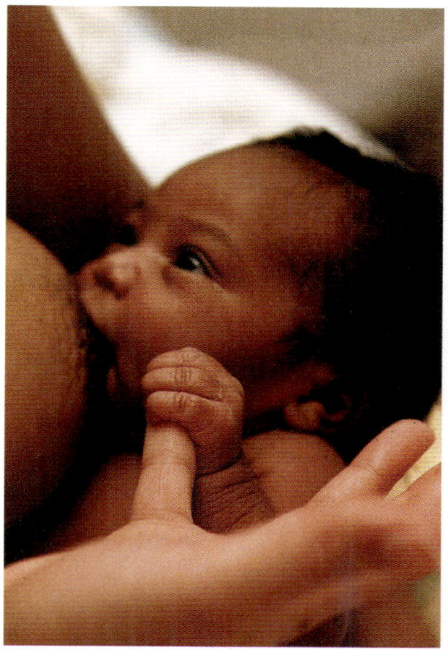

Figure 3.4 The importance of touch: the close bond between mother and breastfeeding baby.

It is certainly the more important sense for establishing and maintaining social bonds. Right from the first moments of life, when the most sensitive part of a baby's skin grasps the mother's nipple, to the moment of death when the living will tend to clasp the dying – even if in a sanitised, western hospital, it is only the hand that is held – it is touch that provides the all important contact between individuals (Figure 3.4). The handshake and shaking hands on a deal for more formal relationships, and the less formal but stylised kiss on each cheek, both involve the most sensitive parts of the skin but are not common to all cultures.

The importance of touching and being touched in intimate relationships is too well known to need describing here. An interesting insight into its importance in everyday life was gained from an experiment carried out at a library some decades ago (Fisher et al., 1976). After the librarians checked out the borrowers' books they made hand-to-hand contact in returning books to some of the people. On leaving the library, borrowers were asked for their opinions on a number of the library's facilities. Overall, those whose hands had been touched not only rated library facilities more highly, they were also more likely to judge that the librarian had smiled at them. However, the librarians had actually been instructed to smile at no one.

3.4 Touch illusions

Having stated how important touch is, it is clear that, like senses such as vision, the somatosensory system is subject to illusions and can be fooled (an example has already been described in Activity 3.2). In fact, some of these illusions are direct analogues of common ones found in vision – such as the Bourdon and the Müller–Lyer illusions (Figure 3.5). In the tactile Bourdon illusion, the top straight edge of an angular metallic object feels curved when it is handled, despite the fact that it is straight. The equivalent visual perception can be created when looking at the object from the side (Figure 3.5a). Similarly, in the Müller–Lyer illusion (Figure 3.5b), although both horizontal lines are the same length, the bottom one generally appears longer when perceived by the eye and is commonly *felt* to be longer when a person interacts with the lines using a tactile embossed drawing.

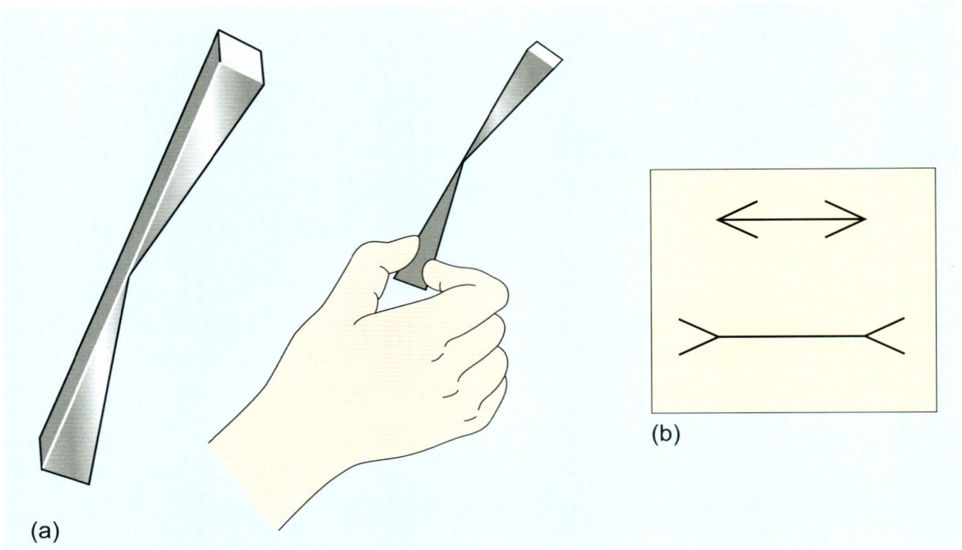

Figure 3.5 The Bourdon and the Müller–Lyer illusions, (a) and (b) respectively, which can be experienced in both their visual and tactile forms.

Another example of illusion that depends on a curious interaction between stimuli (here, mechanical and thermal) is the silver Thaler illusion. Weber described this illusion in 1846 using large (heavier than 50 g) coins (the silver

Thalers) at different temperatures, placed on a participant's forehead. He discovered that one very cold coin felt as heavy as two body-temperature coins stacked on top of each other. You can readily demonstrate this for yourself using three large modern coins at different temperatures. The biological basis of this illusion appears to depend on the fact that some slowly adapting mechanoreceptors in the skin also respond to cooling, thus producing an increased response when the colder coin is placed on the skin.

However, perhaps the most impressive and important of all somatosensory illusions is the size–weight illusion (Figure 3.6). Here, two objects of exactly the same mass but of different size (volume) are *perceived* to be of different weight, such that the larger object feels lighter than the smaller object. The illusion also occurs in blindfolded participants, as long as they are allowed to feel the size of the two objects before lifting them. To control for an effect that might be due to differences in pressure on the skin that the different-sized objects cause, the objects can be fitted with identical lifting rings, but the illusion remains unchanged and is extremely robust. Augustin Charpentier, who first described this illusion in 1891, used two spheres – one 40 mm in diameter and the other 100 mm in diameter – of identical mass (266 g). Participants perceived the larger sphere to be lighter than the smaller sphere, an effect that could be nullified by increasing the weight of the larger sphere by 66 g (nearly 25% of the total weight: this is a large effect).

Figure 3.6 In the size–weight illusion the smaller object is perceived as being heavier than the larger one when lifted, despite their identical physical weight.

What is more, the size–weight illusion is perceived from approximately 3 years of age, and even occurs under microgravity (i.e. in outer space). It is of interest that the illusion can also be produced by manipulating visual cues. For example, when the objects to be lifted are placed in the context of the railroad track illusion (placing the objects at different points on a pair of converging lines, which mimic railroad tracks receding into the distance from the point of the viewer), greater lift force is applied to what looks like the apparently larger object (because it is perceived to be 'further up the track').

The size–weight illusion is of some significance because it shows us how important expectations are. The percept formed by looking at the relative sizes of the two objects suggests that the body will need to use more force to lift the larger one, which influences how the weight of each is perceived when they are actually handled (this is why an unexpectedly empty suitcase feels so light). The illusion challenges the simple notion that the neural outputs of sensory receptors in the skin, muscles and tendons can directly code the perceived properties (in this case, heaviness) of an object.

3.5 Sensory deficits and touch perception

The importance of touch information is most clearly illustrated when deficits exist in other sensory systems, such as hearing or vision. Indeed, the profoundly deaf percussionist Evelyn Glennie reports that she 'hears' (feels) low-frequency sounds with her feet, and higher-frequency sounds with her face, neck and chest. This ability exists because the most sensitive form of somatosensation is that used to detect vibration. This fact is nicely exploited by mobile phone technology, which offers the option of discreet vibratory rather than intrusive auditory signals to alert people to calls and messages.

At the receptor level it is estimated that Pacinian corpuscles can detect 300 Hz tissue oscillations that cause displacements as small as half a micrometre. The corpuscles occur deep in both hairy and glabrous skin, the soles of feet, and in other more unusual places such as in the diaphragm and the peritoneal connective tissues. As well as allowing musicians like Evelyn Glennie to hear music, it is this sensitivity to vibration that allows people with impaired hearing to dance to music.

Touch can also provide critical information to people with visual impairments who use active touch as they move their fingertips over raised dot patterns representing letter symbols (Braille). The spacing of the dots within Braille patterns are just within the two-point discriminative power of the fingertips. Slowly adapting receptors, associated with Merkel's discs, in the superficial skin of the fingertips are responsible for the acuity demanded by Braille reading and other fine discriminative abilities of our hands. (However, the tongue, which has the greatest tactile acuity, lacks Merkel's discs.) Experienced Braille users can read up to 100 words per minute, a third of the rate for silent visual reading by sighted participants, and may use a 'reading' finger from each hand, for example the index fingers, side by side as they detect the dot patterns.

There is evidence that areas of the cortex used for visual processing in sighted people (occipital cortex) are recruited during Braille reading in people who have been blind or visually impaired from an early age. Experiments by Cohen et al. (1997) used brief periods of transcranial magnetic stimulation (TMS, see Box 3.2) to transiently disrupt the occipital cortex during tactile reading tasks. Braille reading was disrupted by this stimulation in people who had become visually impaired at an early age, who reported 'missing dots', 'phantom dots' or that the 'dots don't make sense'. It is worth noting that speech, and language in general, was not affected by the stimulation.

Box 3.2 Transcranial magnetic stimulation

Transcranial magnetic stimulation (TMS) is a technique that is used to investigate the functioning of brain areas. It involves electrically stimulating the brain from outside the skull by passing an electrical current through a copper wire coil encased in plastic and held over the head. This is referred to as the 'magnetic coil' because it generates a magnetic field, which is able to pass through the skull and disrupt processing in areas of the brain. It is typically used to target areas of the cortex close to the surface of the brain because targeting deeper structures requires very large coils and increased difficulty in achieving the desired effect.

TMS is a technique that can either stimulate or inhibit the brain regions it targets, depending on the nature of the magnetic field generated.

The same stimulation in sighted participants had little effect on the tactile reading of embossed Roman letters, and in these participants the stimulation only interfered with visual discriminations. It seems, then, that some of the special tactile discriminative abilities underlying Braille reading can be explained by the redeployment of the 'visual' cortex for tactile reading skills. Other studies using TMS in sighted people have shown that the visual cortex is important for tactile discrimination of orientation, indicating that the cross-modal processing of information in sensory cortical areas may be more widespread than was previously thought.

Touch is also used by people who have both visual and auditory impairment in the Tadoma method of 'listening' to speech. The listener places their hand lightly across one side of the speaker's face such that the thumb is placed over the lips and the fingers splayed out across the cheek and neck, and vibrations and movements of the jaw and lips are used to perceive speech.

One device intended to help a blind person to detect remote objects uses a video camera and a large array of tactile stimulators that is placed on the participant's back. The brightness output of the camera is then converted into a vibrating 'image' on the tactile array. What interested the first investigators to do this – Paul Bach-y-Rita et al. (1998), and also in his later work with Stephen Kercel (2003) – was that blind participants began to experience objects (such as a cup on a table) as being 'out there' rather than as a felt image on their backs. This 'seeing' experience depended on the person being able to manipulate the camera to scan the scene – again illustrating the importance of active self-initiated movement. To what extent people who are visually impaired and have tried this method are able to see, in the same way as sighted people do, is debatable. However, it was intriguing that when the camera's zoom was inadvertently operated, an experienced user raised his arms in front of his face to avoid collision with the 'looming' object.

Given the involvement of the redundant visual cortex in reading Braille, it is interesting to speculate whether the same area is also deployed for this substituted vision in people who are blind. Despite the initial successes of these laboratory studies over 30 years ago, it has proved technically difficult to implement such tactile–visual substitution systems for practical use by blind people. Bach-y-Rita went on to develop a miniaturised video system with a 49-point electro-tactile array on a dental retainer accessed by the tongue. Although he passed away in 2007, his research has inspired others to continue to work in the field of sensory substitution.

The phenomenon of 'facial vision', where blind people seem to be aware of objects and can navigate around them, was thought to be a 'tactile' experience involving the face (Supa et al., 1944). It was believed that blind people had increased sensitivity to touch sensation on the face, including sensing temperature, pressure and air changes. Later experiments, however, showed that the ability is in fact due to the auditory pick-up of changes in the nature of reflected sounds while moving the head around (Cotzin, 1950). It is thought that the 'tactile' perception results from **synaesthesia** between the auditory, vestibular and kinaesthetic senses, whereby sensations in the auditory modality, for example, produce tactile perceptions. Thus, the term 'synaesthesia' simply means that sensory stimulation in one sense generates perception in another.

3.6 Concluding remarks on touch

Chapters 1 and 2 discussed the nature of the touch signal, and how this stimulation is conveyed to touch receptors located in the skin. They focused on the sensory transduction process for innocuous touch in mechanoreceptors and illustrated the brain pathways that this transduced signal takes from the receptor neuron in the dorsal root ganglia to the spinal cord, brainstem, thalamus and cortex. After establishing the neurophysiology of touch sensation, this chapter continued to explore aspects of touch perception, focusing on the importance of touch in our everyday lives and the susceptibility of the touch system to illusion. In addition, it highlighted the remarkable importance of touch information in social communication and in the presence of deficits in other sensory systems. You should also now recognise that touch information is often integrated with proprioceptive information, which is the focus of the next chapter.

3.7 Chapter 3 summary and questions

- The somatosensory system is highly significant and, in some respects, has primacy over the other senses.
- Active touch is vital for normal interactions with the world.
- Somatosensory representations of touch in the cortex are not fixed, since body schema can alter following active tool use, such that touch is felt or anticipated at the end or outer edges of the tool in question.
- As for the other senses, somatosensory illusions can occur. The study of these illusions often reveals how the somatosensory system normally functions. The size–weight illusion, for example, shows us how important expectation is. That is, we lift an object using a force that we perceive (having learned from experience) as being appropriate for the size of the grasped object.

Self-assessment questions

Question 3.1

Explain why the concept of body schema is important for active touch.

Question 3.2

When cutting a piece of paper with a pair of scissors we ‘feel’ the cutting sensation on the scissor blades. Explain briefly the physiological mechanisms behind this.

Question 3.3

What evidence is there for cross-modal processing in cortical areas?

Proprioception

4

Around the beginning of the last century, the English neurophysiologist Sir Charles Sherrington coined the term proprioception, deriving it from the Latin *proprius*, meaning 'own'. Sherrington defined proprioceptors as receptors sensitive to stimuli that 'are traceable to the actions of the organism itself' (Sherrington, 1902).

You should recall from Block 1 that proprioception therefore refers to the sense we have of our own body position and movement, and you will see in this chapter that the importance of this sense cannot be underestimated. Without a properly functioning proprioceptive system, movement of our body and interaction with objects on a daily basis becomes severely limited.

As was done with touch in Chapter 2, we begin by outlining the receptors that are able to detect proprioceptive information before briefly considering the route such information takes to the brain. The majority of this chapter, however, is concerned with perception and the loss of proprioception.

4.1 Receptors for proprioception

According to Sherrington's definition of proprioception, any receptors detecting information relating to our own bodies can be considered proprioceptors. If you move your head, you stimulate the vestibular system and probably the visual system too which provides another example of how multiple systems combine to inform us of the world around us.

Proprioception may be divided into dynamic (or kinaesthetic) and static forms. Dynamic proprioception refers to an awareness of body parts moving through space relative to one another, while static proprioception refers to their stationary position. Generally, however, the term proprioception is used more narrowly than this. It is reserved for a series of receptors in our joints, muscles and tendons that can provide our central nervous system (CNS) with information about the position (or angle) and movement of our joints. One exception to this grouping of proprioceptors is the touch receptors in the skin. Although these clearly have an **exteroceptive** function (namely, they detect information that comes from outside the body), it appears that they can also contribute to our sense of joint position and therefore may also be considered to be proprioceptors.

■ Which type of touch receptor, discussed in Chapter 2 of this block, detects skin stretch over the joints of the fingers, hands and arms?

□ Field receptors (see Section 2.2.1).

There are four kinds of **joint receptor** (Figure 4.1) and, as with the receptors responsible for our sense of touch, each differs from the others in its morphology, location and responsiveness (Table 4.1).

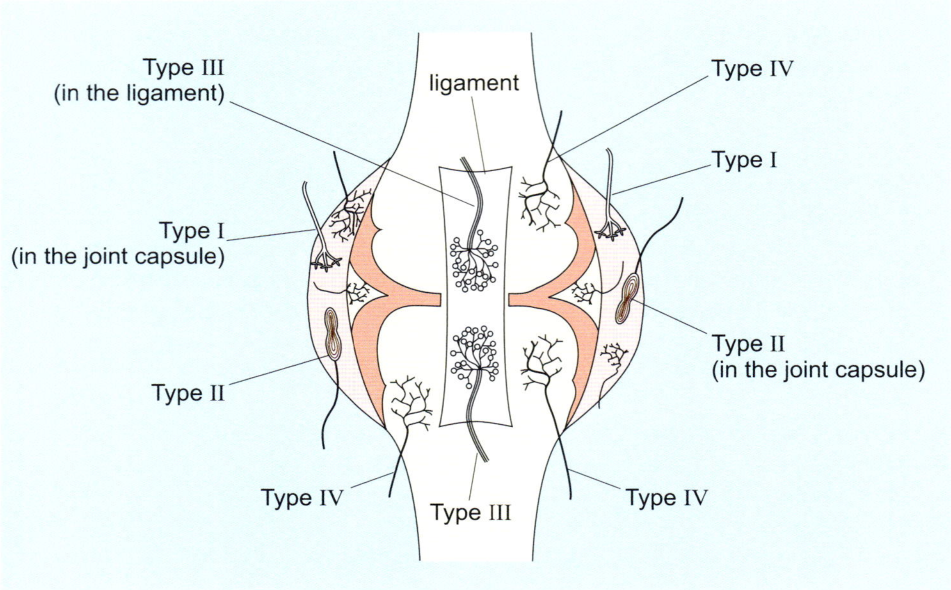

Figure 4.1 Schematic diagram of a joint showing the locations of the four joint receptor types.

Table 4.1 Types of joint receptor, their locations and response characteristics. Note that free nerve endings and Ruffini's endings are the same as those in skin signalling pain and touch, respectively.

Joint receptor (and type)	Location	Responsiveness
Ruffini's endings (I)	joint capsule	low activation threshold slowly adapting
Pacinian endings (II) (accelerator receptors)	fibrous region of capsule	low activation threshold fast adapting
Golgi-type endings (III)	ligaments intertwined with collagen strands	high activation threshold slowly adapting
Free nerve endings (IV)	joint capsule and connective tissue	extremely high activation threshold slowly adapting

You can see from Table 4.1 that the free nerve endings have a very high threshold for activation.

- ■ What kind of joint position do you think they would respond to?
- □ They may respond to any joint position that could be painful.

Indeed, the free nerve endings signal when the joint has reached the limit of its potential and this information is continuously integrated with that of the other joint receptors to provide information about speed of movement and deviation from the preferred orientation.

- ■ Following joint-replacement surgery, such as that for hips or knees, proprioception remains intact. What does this tell us about the receptors for this sense?
- □ The other proprioceptors found in muscles and tendons must be sufficient because the joint receptors can be lost (when the actual bones are replaced with artificial versions) and proprioception is maintained.

In line with this, sensation provided by the four types of joint receptor works in tandem with input from the Golgi tendon organs and the muscle spindles. **Golgi tendon organs** detect the force of muscle contraction because they lie encapsulated between the muscle and the tendon (Figure 4.2).

The term 'Golgi tendon organ' refers to the sensory receptors themselves, which essentially are the nerve endings of a Ib afferent neuron that branches extensively within the Golgi capsule. These branches, containing the Golgi tendon organ receptors, intertwine with collagen fibrils connecting muscle to tendon. As the force of a muscle contraction increases, more groups of muscle fibres are recruited and so the number of Golgi tendon organs that are active increases.

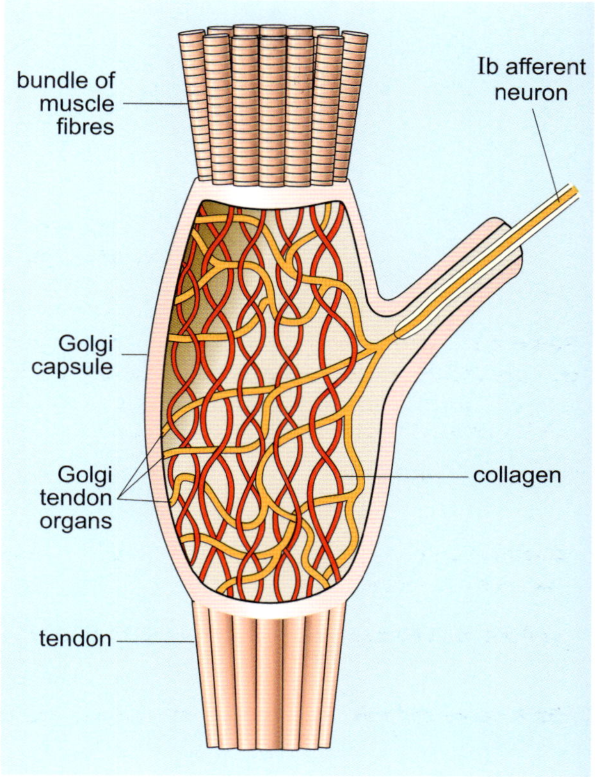

Figure 4.2 Golgi tendon organs lie within a capsule between a small group of muscle fibres and the tendon to which they attach.

By contrast, the **muscle spindles** (Figure 4.3) lie within the muscles and they can signal the stretching of a muscle. The muscle spindle contains a type of muscle called 'intrafusal', from the Latin *fusus* meaning spindle; so-called because these organs look like the spindles used by weavers. There are three types of intrafusal fibres, which differ in their signalling properties:

- dynamic nuclear bag fibres
- static nuclear bag fibres
- nuclear chain fibres.

The intrafusal muscle is innervated by the free nerve endings of two types of sensory afferent neurons. They can be distinguished because of a size difference. The large axons have diameters of 12–20 μm and are known as 'Ia' and 'Ib' fibres; the small afferents are termed group II fibres and have diameters of about 6–10 μm. Both types are myelinated.

Away from the proprioceptive apparatus found attached to connective tissue and inside muscles, the peripheral nerves close to the skin surface have a different nomenclature. Here, the large fibres (>10 μm in diameter) are called 'Aα' and those of diameter 6–10 μm are 'Aβ' fibres.

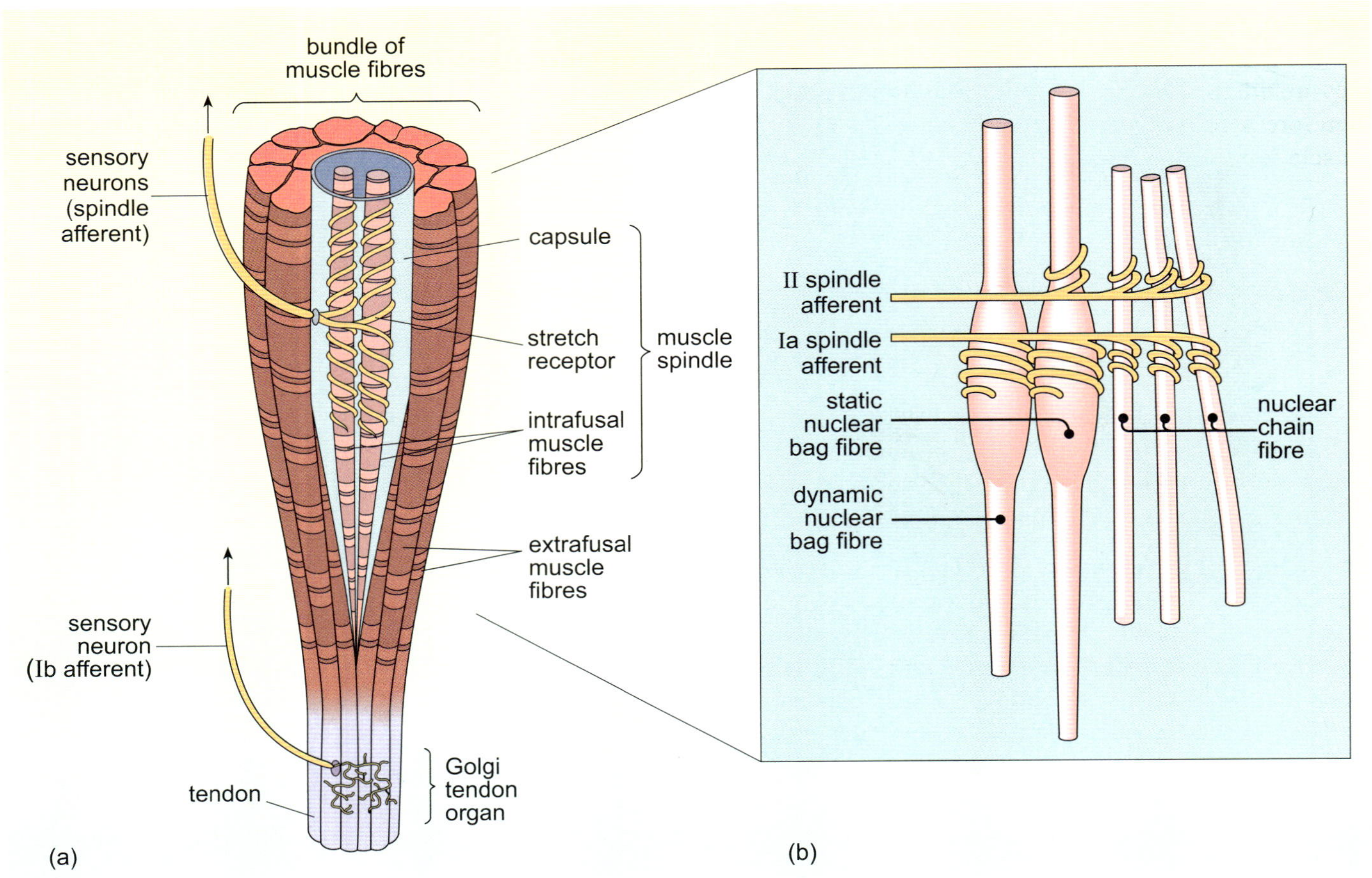

Figure 4.3 Schematic diagrams of (a) a muscle spindle encapsulated in skeletal muscle within a group of extrafusal muscle fibres, and (b) the group Ia and group II afferents.

- ■ How do you think the functioning of the different-sized fibre types mentioned above differs?
- □ They conduct action potentials at different velocities. The large fibres conduct more rapidly than the small fibres.

Study note

Remember to complete your table for Activity 2.2 using information in this section.

The fine endings of each receptor type in the muscle spindle entwine around different areas of muscle as shown in Figure 4.3b. As long ago as the early 1930s, recordings taken from individual axons within muscle spindles showed that when muscles are passively stretched the large primary Ia fibres detect the initial stretching of the surrounding muscles, increasing the rate at which they fire action potentials as the stretch develops, but fall back to a steady rate of firing once the muscle maintains a particular length (Figure 4.4). By contrast, the group II secondary fibres respond more slowly as the stretch develops and they maintain their firing rate throughout the stretch. Muscle spindles are therefore sensitive to being stretched, and provide the CNS with signals of muscle length, and rate of change of length.

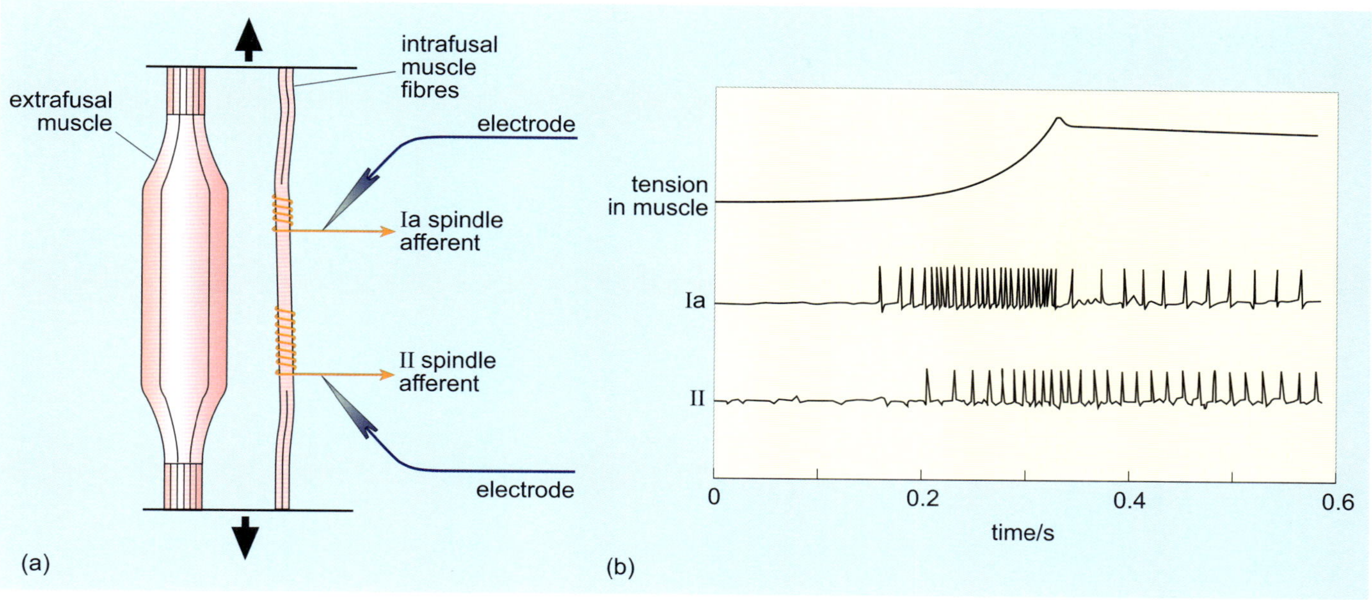

Figure 4.4 (a) The recording arrangement for measuring action potential within muscle spindles. (b) Traces obtained for muscle tension and firing patterns of the spindle afferent fibres.

Muscle spindles also have a motor nerve supply from a gamma (γ) motor neuron. We now have evidence that this motor supply is used to set the sensitivity of the spindles according to prevailing circumstances, and this idea of muscle spindle 'tuning' is discussed in the next section.

4.2 'Tuning' of muscle spindles

As discussed above, it is the γ motor neurons that project from the CNS to the intrafusal muscle spindles. Those neurons projecting to the ordinary contractile muscle fibres are α motor neurons. The motor system of the spindles is often referred to in its entirety as the **fusimotor system**.

Spindle afferents are wrapped around the central portion of the spindle and contain stretch receptors. The location of these afferents alongside those of the α and γ motor input can be seen in Figure 4.5a, which shows the muscle at rest. That is, when the spindle itself is stretched, ion channels are opened causing an influx of Na^+ ions, which may lead to an action potential (sensory signal). Thus, the process of transduction within the muscle spindles takes exactly the same form as discussed for tactile mechanoreceptors.

When a muscle contracts (due to the firing of its α motor neurons), the resultant shortening of the muscle would cause the spindles to become slack and unresponsive (Figure 4.5b) if it were not for the fact that the γ motor

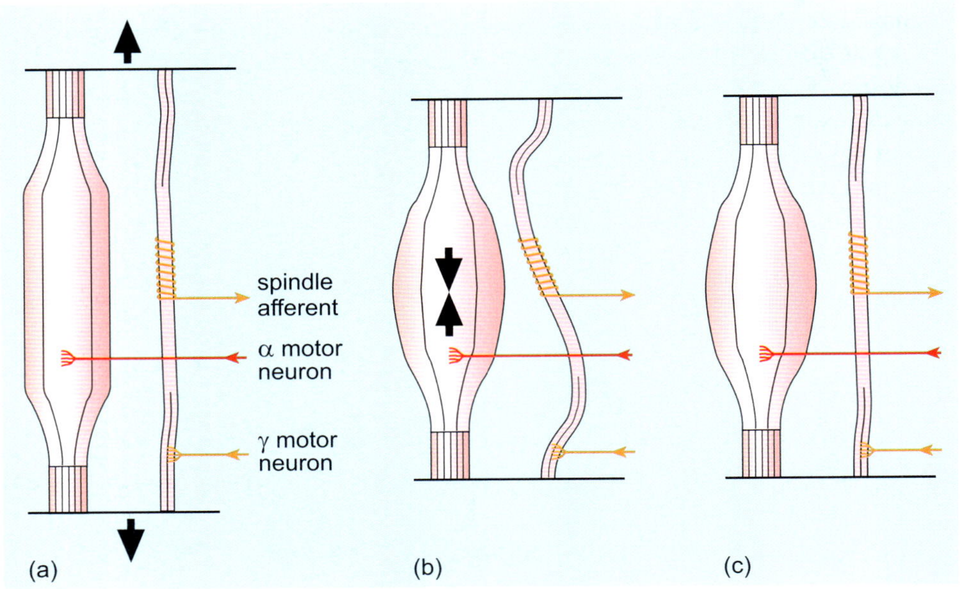

Figure 4.5 The basic action of the fusimotor system. See the text for explanation of parts (a)–(c).

neurons also fire. This activity, which mirrors that in the main muscle, contracts the end portions of the spindles and stretches the central sensory portion. This tension takes up the slack in the spindles and keeps them in the operating range where they can still fire an action potential (Figure 4.5c). This pattern of activity is described as **alpha–gamma co-activation** (α–γ co-activation).

The very presence of a separate motor system for the spindles, as opposed to a motor system for the muscles, suggests that it must in some way function independently. There must be more to it than just α–γ co-activation where both are activated together. In practice, however, evidence for such independent function has proved difficult to find, not least because the γ fibres are of such small diameter that it is very difficult to record from them.

The first demonstration of independent control of the γ fibres was made in 1985 by the physiologist Arthur Prochazka in a series of ingenious and technically demanding experiments. Prochazka et al. (1985) worked with cats that were free to move but wore various electrodes connected to a small transmitter. Because, under these conditions, it is not possible to measure activity in γ fibres directly, their activity had to be inferred from other measurements. The output of muscle spindles – that is, the activity in the spindle afferents – depends on three factors:

- the contractile activity in the muscle
- the degree of stretch of the muscle
- the activity in the fusimotor system.

If you measure the first two factors, together with spindle afferent activity, you can estimate the level of γ activity.

Prochazka et al. (1985) found that the background level of fusimotor activity was set at different levels according to the circumstances, or to what the cat was doing. The results are summarised in Figure 4.6. As you can see, two types of fusimotor fibre have been distinguished: static and dynamic (see Section 4.1). Firing in dynamic γ fibres increases the sensitivity of the spindles to the rate of muscle stretch, whereas firing in static fibres increases sensitivity to absolute muscle length. Recruitment of these two types of γ fibre can be predicted from the type of activity in which the animal is engaged. During activities in which muscle length changes slowly and in a predictable fashion, only the static γ neurons are active. However, under conditions in which muscle length may change rapidly and unpredictably, dynamic γ neurons are activated.

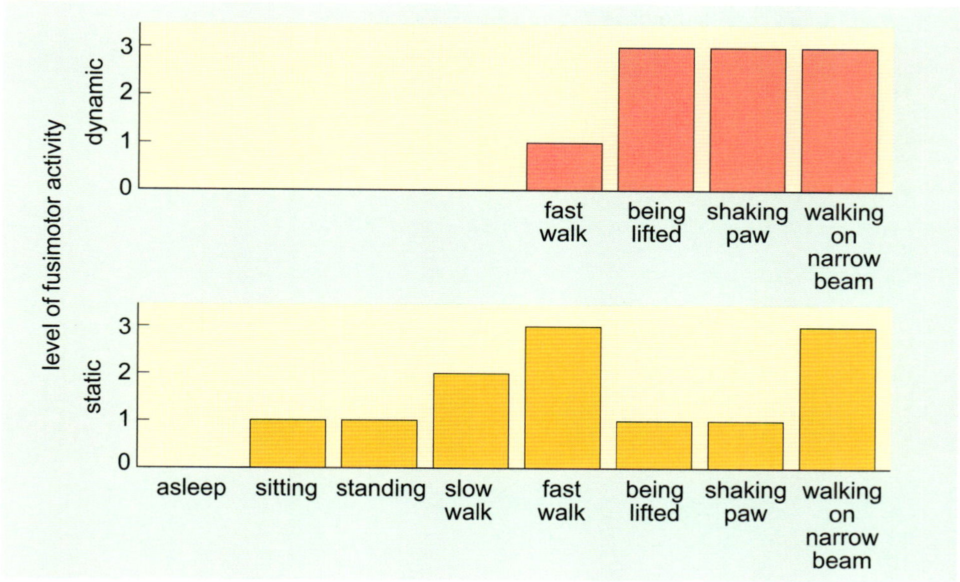

Figure 4.6 Activity in two types of cat fusimotor fibre measured for a range of activities. Recruitment of the two types of γ fibre can be predicted from the nature of the activity. (Based on Prochazka et al.,1985)

This observed behaviour, then, is an example of the CNS adjusting an incoming signal at source. It is effectively 'tuning in' the receptor based on the prevailing conditions. It also appears to be an example of fine tuning in the proprioceptive system, with independent control of dynamic and static fusimotor fibres. It is worth noting that this behaviour is often predictive in nature: namely, the animal is preparing itself for what is likely to happen. It should now be apparent why, despite the technical difficulties involved, it was necessary for the animals to be free to move during this study. Results such as these could only have been found in animals free to engage in a range of natural activities. Similar results have also now been found in humans (Ribot-Ciscar et al., 2008).

4.3 Muscle conditioning

The activity of muscle spindles is also affected by previous activity of the muscle (either contraction or length changes). This is because muscles display **thixotropy**, or a change of state briefly on the application of force.

In resting muscles, relatively long-lasting, stable cross-bridges have been shown to form between proteins (Proske and Morgan, 1999), and these lead to a degree of muscle stiffness that causes slackness if the muscle is subsequently shortened. You may have experienced this yourself if you have sat in a particular position for a long time and then got up and walked around. The formation of cross-bridges also happens in flexed and extended muscles if held in a fixed position for a period of time and these cross-bridges can then lead to errors in proprioception, as shown in Activity 4.1.

Activity 4.1 Proprioceptive errors following muscle conditioning

Allow 5 minutes

(*Relevant module learning outcomes: KU2 and PS2*)

In this activity you are going to condition your forearm muscles and then test them for resulting proprioceptive errors. To test for proprioceptive errors you need to remove the contribution of visual information to your sense of limb position by shutting your eyes. First, however, you need to condition your forearm muscles by holding your arms in opposing positions, which can be done with your eyes open.

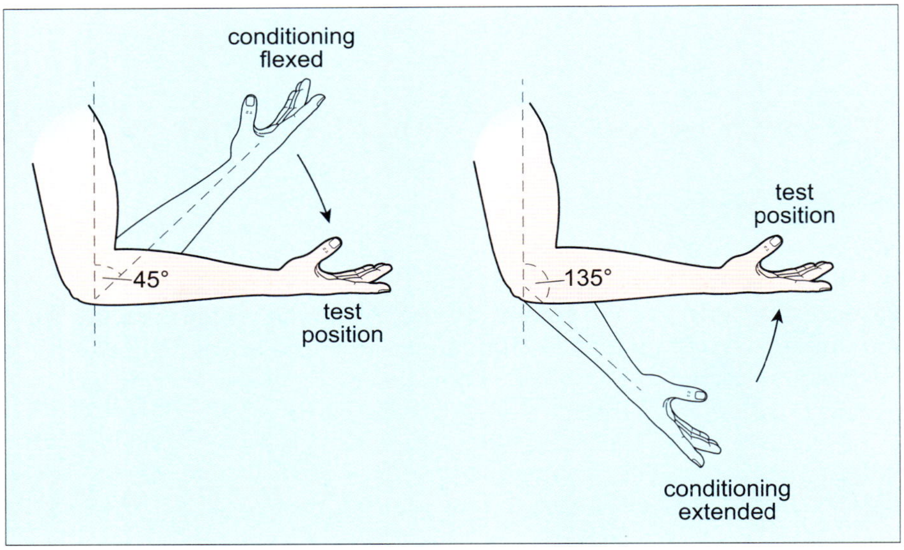

Figure 4.7 Arm positions for the muscle conditioning activity.

Hold both arms down by your side and then flex one arm up towards your face until there is a 45° bend (roughly) between your upper arm and forearm.

Next, raise your other forearm to form an approximate 135° bend. (The outlined arms in Figure 4.7 show these conditioning arm positions.)

Hold these positions for 60 seconds, counting the time to yourself. Then, with your arms still in the conditioning positions, close your eyes and try to bring both forearms into parallel alignment in front of you with a 90° elbow bend (see the 'test position' in Figure 4.7). Now open your eyes.

What did you find? Did you manage to get both your forearms exactly parallel to each other? Feedback on this activity is provided alongside the answers to this chapter's self-assessment questions.

The receptors described above are all modified DRG neurons and so, with the exception of Golgi tendon organ information, they feed into the same somatosensory pathways described in Chapter 2. Although some of these transduced proprioceptive signals are thought to reach the somatosensory cortex via the spino-cervical-thalamic tract, the majority are processed subcortically by the cerebellum because the information travels in the spinocerebellar tract (from spinal cord to cerebellum).

At the cortical level there is parallel processing of some proprioceptive information, with the muscle-spindle afferents ascending in the spino-cervical-thalamic tract projecting to Brodmann's area 3a of the primary somatosensory cortex (S1), while joint-receptor afferents ascending in the spino-cervical-thalamic tract project to area 2, which is still within S1.

4.4 Perception of proprioception

So far, we have explained what information is detected by proprioceptors and have indicated that these receptors provide us with a sense of body position and movement. Next, we consider the function of proprioception in a little more detail because it may not be immediately obvious what a sense of joint position and movement might be useful for.

Certainly, we are not ordinarily very aware of information derived from proprioceptors. We can perhaps see how it might be important for the maintenance of posture and the control of movement, and might imagine that disruption of such a system could contribute to an increased risk of falls. If the CNS needs to maintain a joint at a particular position for some reason – perhaps when applying consistent pressure to the acceleration pedal of a car – information that the joint is drifting away from this position is clearly useful. If the body needs to move an arm so that you can pick up a mug of tea, it needs to know where the arm is at the outset in order to work out what movement is required.

However, it turns out that this sense of the position and movement of our own body has a deeper significance than this, and is fundamental to the way we experience not only ourselves but also the outside world. This concept is far from being intuitively apparent, and one reason for this is that you cannot turn off your proprioceptors in the same way that you can close your eyes, block your ears or anaesthetise your skin. This sense is always with us, unless you are unfortunate enough to have an illness that affects it (Section 4.7). Indeed, as the following sections explain, proprioception is so central to our experience that it is very difficult to imagine life without it.

4.4.1 Proprioception and corporeal awareness

At the start of this block we mentioned the idea of corporeal awareness, which is awareness of our own physical body. Proprioception contributes to our experience of ourselves by creating what the physiologist Sir Henry Head described in 1911 as the 'body schema' (a term you met in Chapter 3). Head clearly explains the concept in the following passage.

> For this combined standard, against which all subsequent changes of posture are measured before they enter consciousness, we propose the word 'schema'. By means of perpetual alterations in position we are always building up a postural model of ourselves which constantly changes.
>
> *(Head and Holmes, 1911)*

The idea, then, is that all parts of our body (including the hierarchy of joints, e.g. from torso to fingertip) are continuously mapped and updated by information from receptors in our muscles, tendons, joints and skin. Note that the body schema is distinct from body image, which may be preserved in the cases of people with loss of proprioception. Body image depends on visual sensation and is a visual map of our body parts in relation to one another.

Body schema can be manipulated in an interesting illusion involving the artificial stimulation of muscle-stretch receptors by applying a vibratory stimulus to a large muscle, such as that in the forearm. Activation of the muscle spindles results in the perception that the arm has moved to a new position in space, despite remaining stationary. Similarly, if a participant touches the end of their nose with an index finger while their biceps muscle is vibrated, they feel their arm extending, and their finger and nose feel longer.

The concept of a body schema can be elaborated on in surprising ways. Henry Head noted in this respect that objects that become part of conscious body movements become incorporated into the schema, even 'a woman's power of localization may extend to the feather in her hat' (Head and Holmes, 1911). We gave the example of a person using a cane as an extension to touch perception in Chapter 3, and another example of this phenomenon is found in the use of sticks, cues, clubs, bats and racquets to hit balls in sport. These objects become part of the person's body schema because they are tools for action. Proficient racquet-sport players are able to switch quickly between sports, even though the so-called 'sweet spot' (the optimal part of the object with which to strike the ball) moves by as much as 30 cm from the player's grip when changing from a table tennis bat to a badminton racquet. Some gifted sports players are said to have 'touch', reflecting their uncanny ability to gently 'feel' or 'stroke' the ball (or shuttlecock), rather than just hit it.

More bizarrely, perhaps, is our ability to incorporate a motor vehicle into our body schema as we drive it along. The expanded body schema might partly explain how preoccupied we can get about others' driving behaviour, for example when we are impeded by another driver. When hit by another vehicle we can feel it as a direct assault on ourselves. Even a minor collision, not involving anyone else, can cause considerable shock.

Short-term alterations to cortical representations in S1 accommodate this expanded body schema, illustrating the remarkable plasticity of the somatosensory homunculus.

4.4.2 Proprioception and perception of the external world

We are able to reach out and touch things in the space around us without having to watch what we are doing, and we are reasonably proficient in this task. This is easy to demonstrate. Just look at an object in your immediate surroundings, close your eyes and reach out and touch it, then open your eyes and see how accurate you have been.

This apparently simple feat is cleverer than it first seems. When you look at something, your eye is rotated to bring the image of the thing onto the most sensitive part of the retina, the fovea. Then, in order to relate the position of the object being looked at to 'your' position (say, the position of the shoulder of the reaching arm), the CNS makes some computation based on the position of the eye in the head and the position of the head with respect to the torso.

A person who is lacking afferent pathways such that they have a loss of proprioception from the neck down cannot perform this task, partly because they cannot determine the position in space of a visual target relative to their shoulder. In order to reach for things, people with this impairment have to watch closely what they are doing. This is in stark contrast to the majority of people's everyday experience, where the most cursory glance at, say, a mug of tea is all that is needed for someone to reach out and pick it up successfully.

This evidence, then, is an illustration of the role of proprioception in the control of movement. But this same proprioceptive information (and possibly some similar type of computation) also shapes our perception of the space around us.

A group headed by the French neuroscientist Marc Jeannerod investigated this idea using the technique of muscle vibration (Biguer et al., 1988). In their experiment, participants sat in darkness looking at a small illuminated target in front of them. When vibration was applied to their neck muscles on one side, participants reported that they saw the target move to the other side (no head movement had occurred). When asked to point to the target they in fact pointed to the side of its real position, consistent with the illusion of target movement that they had experienced.

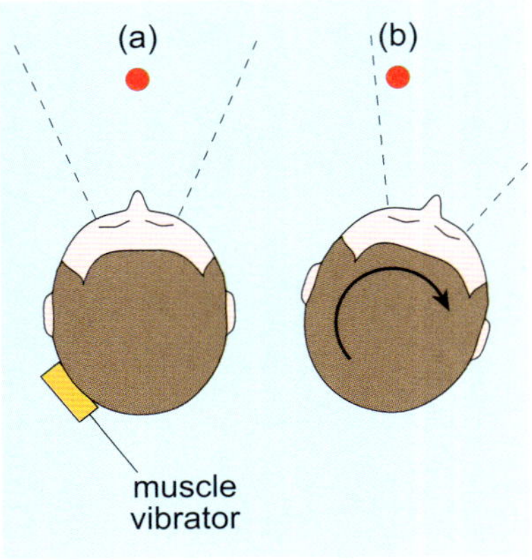

Figure 4.8 (a) Vibration of the left neck muscles produces (b) the illusion of rotation of the head to the right. If the head really moves to the right, a stationary target would appear to move left in the visual field.

The explanation for this illusion is that the CNS interprets the vibration, let us say of the left side of the neck, as a stretching of the muscles on this side: something that would normally occur when the head turns to the right. If the head were to turn to the right (and the eyes remained in the same position in the head), the target would appear to move to the left (Figure 4.8). Since, in this case, the target does not *actually* move to the left – this is an illusion – the CNS interprets this outcome as a movement of the target to its right.

This experiment demonstrates that our perception of the position (with respect to ourselves) of objects that we see is dependent on proprioception. It also suggests that what we think of as 'ourselves' in this context is the torso, rather than the head. This observation, in turn, infers that our spatial perception arises out of a movement (in this case, reaching) control system.

Proprioception in other animals

It seems that the harder you look, the deeper the influence of proprioception goes. It may, in fact, be the basis of our understanding of the 3D world in which we live. This can be more easily appreciated by comparing the abilities of jointed animals like ourselves with soft-bodied creatures, such as octopi.

It is because we bend in relatively few and well-defined places (i.e. our joints) that we are able to compute reasonably easily the position of our body parts. This is not so for an octopus, where the position of each part depends on the degree of contraction of muscles all over the rest of its body. As a result, jointless animals appear to lack the equivalent of our proprioceptive position sense. They cannot appear to tell where their limbs are unless they are looking at them (Wells, 1960).

Furthermore, we can pick up and examine an object, say a cube, with our hands and, without needing to see it, build up a mental picture of its shape by turning it in our hands and moving our fingers over it. We can do this because throughout this period of active touching we know where our fingers are relative to each other. We could easily distinguish between, say, a cube and a pyramid in this fashion. An octopus, however, appears unable to do this. It cannot (for a food reward) learn to distinguish by touch a cube from a sphere. In contrast, it is very much able to distinguish between different textures.

Similarly, creatures like octopi appear limited in their ability to understand the 3D space in which they move. They are, for example, unable to learn to negotiate all but the simplest mazes. Jointed creatures, on the other hand, can monitor the number of steps they have taken and the angle of any turns that they have made. They can readily learn to run even quite complex mazes without the need for exteroceptive cues. They can build structures, such as honeycombs and webs, which necessitate accurate measurement of lengths and angles.

It seems likely that our ability to understand the 3D space we live in, which appears as 2D representations on the retinae, is based on proprioception. In fact, philosophers have suggested that cognition in general might be based on our early experience of moving in our environment, since this is how we first learn to distinguish between ourselves and the rest of the world.

You have seen that proprioception enables us to create a sense of ourselves and our environment. At the start of Section 4.4, we suggested these functions were crucial elements of proprioception, and indeed they are. However, recall that balance and posture are also reliant on proprioception and are therefore discussed next.

4.4.3 Balance control and perception of whole body orientation

Proprioceptors play an important role in human balance control. Our balance when standing is a rather precarious state of affairs. Our centre of mass is high (about the level of the top of the hips) compared with the size of our base of support (the area of the feet). A relatively slight tilt in any direction is therefore enough to cause us to lose our balance. For this reason, life-size statues of human figures have to be made with large and heavy bases but we have a more sophisticated system for ensuring that we remain upright!

The CNS must maintain the orientation of our body with respect to gravity within very tight limits. We have what are effectively 'gravity receptors' in the vestibular system of the inner ear. But these alone can only tell the CNS about the orientation, with respect to gravity, of the head. In order for the CNS to know about the orientation of the torso, it also needs to know the relative position of the head. This information is best provided by proprioceptors in the neck, and it is interesting to note that the neck musculature is unusually richly endowed with muscle spindles.

There is considerable evidence that proprioceptors are involved not only in the control of our orientation but also in our perception of it. Part of this evidence has come from muscle vibration studies, as in the example in the previous section. Vibration of a muscle or its tendon stimulates the spindles within it, and the CNS appears to interpret this as stretch of the muscle. For example, if the flexor muscles of the wrist are vibrated, an illusion of extension of the wrist is produced although the wrist itself remains static. Conversely, vibration of the extensor muscles produces an illusion of wrist flexion (Figure 4.9a).

Figures 4.9b and 4.9c show another interesting further finding. If a participant leans against a wall with their hand and the flexor muscles or tendons of the wrist are vibrated, the illusion produced is now of whole-body movement. Furthermore, the direction of the whole-body movement is reversed simply by changing the orientation of the hand (and still vibrating the flexor muscles). With the fingers pointing forward, the illusion is always of the body swaying forward, and vice versa. In both cases, this is how the body would move were the wrist really extending.

Results such as these demonstrate that proprioceptive signals from the whole body are integrated by the CNS when arriving at an estimate of body orientation and movement. In this case, the signals from the wrist flexor muscles in the arm are interpreted according to the posture of the arm and wrist, and indeed of the whole of the rest of the body.

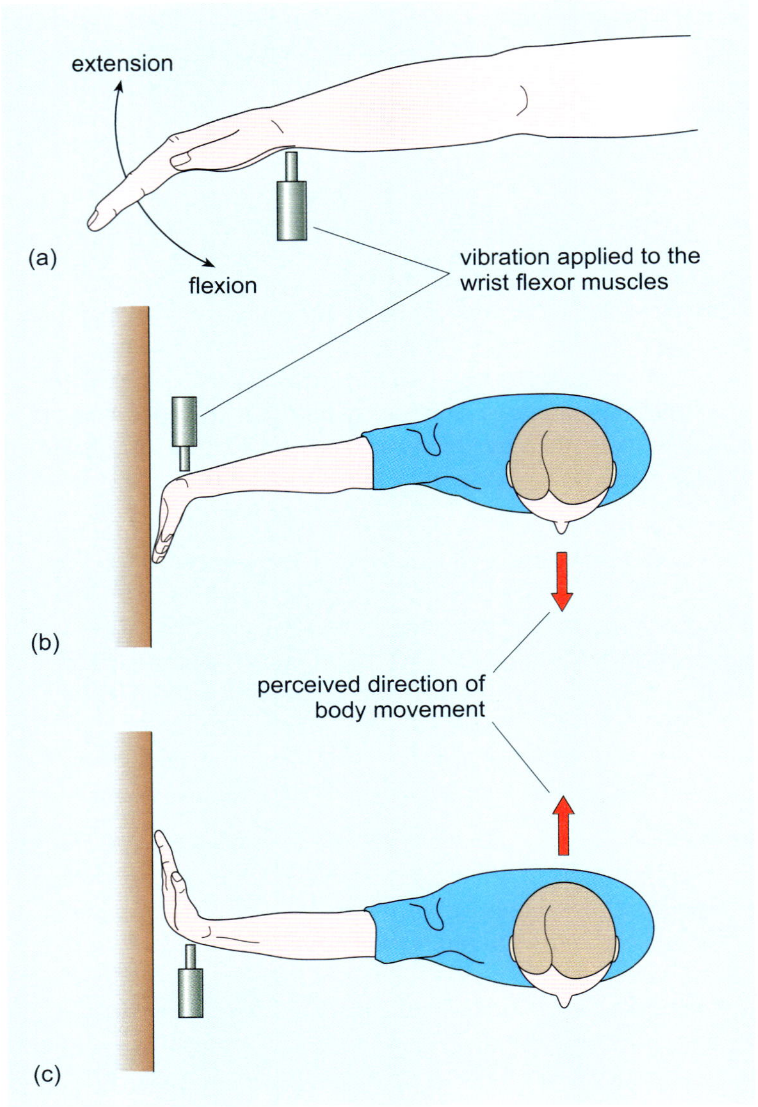

Figure 4.9 Vibration applied to specific muscles of the wrist produces an illusion of wrist extension or flexion when the hand is free (a), but an illusion of whole-body motion when the body is partly supported by the hand (b and c).

Activity 4.2 Balancing act

Allow 5 minutes

(*Relevant module learning outcome: PS2*)

It is easy to demonstrate the importance of the integration of vision with our perception of body position when performing a dynamic activity involving balance. To prove this, do the following activity. First, stand still, then close your eyes. You will probably find this task easy.

Now make the task a bit more difficult by standing on one leg and closing your eyes. You should try this now but be aware that some people lose their balance very rapidly, so make sure you have some stable props (table, chairs, the wall) nearby to assist you in regaining your balance and avoiding a fall and do not do this activity close to anything sharp or breakable.

Try to notice what goes wrong when you balance on one leg with your eyes shut and how you attempt to correct it. Feedback on this activity is provided alongside the answers to this chapter's self-assessment questions.

It is clearly necessary to be able to distinguish the difference between head movements caused by the movement of the neck when you tilt your head to one side, and the same movement caused by the leaning of the whole body when you might be about to lose your balance (as in the activity above).

■ Suggest how this distinction might be made. (Ignore the contribution of the visual system because in the activity your eyes were shut!)

□ There are several possibilities. Given Activity 4.2, your first suggestion might be that if you have not issued any motor commands to tilt your neck then a moving head means that your body is losing balance. Joint receptors in the neck and muscle spindles in neck muscles contribute information that tells us whether our neck and head are moving *relative* to the rest of the body or *together with* the whole body.

Also, when standing on one leg, the difference in the pressure on the soles of your two feet will be large compared with when you are standing on two feet, but there will also be detectable differences in pressure across the foot that remains on the ground. The detection and interpretation of these variations should help to guide the muscular movements that must be made to keep you upright.

One thing is almost certainly clear from the activity: without vision, it is far more difficult to keep your balance when standing on one foot. You probably felt yourself swaying when you had your eyes shut, and the foot and leg muscles working rather hard to keep you upright.

Why should lack of visual input make such a difference? The answer to this question is not really known, but balancing on one leg is a tricky operation and the senses work synergistically to achieve this. Removing one source of guidance cues (visual, in this case) impoverishes our ability to act effectively. However, despite the importance of visual cues, balancing on one leg with your eyes closed is achievable. As you will see in Activity 4.3, the reverse is also possible: vision can compensate for the loss of proprioception, but only after considerable learning and effort.

You might have experienced temporary loss of proprioceptive input yourself, perhaps in a limb that becomes numb ('goes to sleep'). This can happen, for example, when prolonged steady pressure cuts off the blood supply, thereby impairing the functioning of nervous tissue. On release of the pressure the limb quickly returns to normal, but if you try to stand on a numb leg it collapses, because without the somatosensory feedback the brain does not know where the leg it is and cannot control it. Episodes such as these give people with fully functioning somatosensory systems a tiny insight into the frightening world of life without proprioception.

4.5 Consequences of proprioception loss

If you are sitting comfortably, close your eyes and touch your nose with your index finger. If you achieved this goal then you have just passed one item from a battery of clinical tests for somatosensory function. Unless you have a rare disorder, this manoeuvre should be accomplished easily and fairly accurately (say, with an error of a centimetre). The tip of your finger is separated from your nose by nine joints, so this little trick demonstrates our remarkable ability to coordinate limb position and movement information (proprioception) with touch. A few individuals with **peripheral neuropathy**, a condition that can be caused by viral infection and that destroys proprioceptive neuronal fibres, are unable to do this task.

4.5.1 Cases of peripheral neuropathy

The American neurologist Oliver Sacks, in his well-known book *The Man Who Mistook His Wife for a Hat* (1985), includes a chapter entitled 'The Disembodied Lady'. It describes a woman who experienced a precipitous and permanent loss of her sense of proprioception, and was unable to feel the position or posture of her torso and head, or the disposition of her limbs.

Other cases of peripheral neuropathy have arisen among people who overindulge in vitamin B_6, although in these cases the symptoms are reversible when a normal diet is resumed. Two more cases of peripheral neuropathy were described in great detail by Cole and Paillard in 1995. In one of these cases the proprioceptive loss was from the neck down, and in the other, from the mouth down. Both individuals also lost their sense of touch but not temperature and pain. One of them was said to no longer experience tickle, but did feel itch. In Sacks' case study, the deficit was more purely proprioceptive as all the other senses of touch, temperature and pain were only marginally affected. All of the cases described by Sacks (1985) and Cole and Paillard (1995) had normal vestibular function (described in detail in Block 4), so that they could position, move and orientate their heads normally according to gravity.

- ■ Would you expect individuals with peripheral neuropathy to have altered body schema and/or body image?
- □ Body schema would be altered as this concept relies on proprioceptive information, but body image should remain intact because it relies on visual information.

Indeed, when one person ('GL') with peripheral neuropathy was tested for the ability to localise a thermal stimulus presented to a small patch of skin on one arm, she was only able to do so when she could see the stimulus. By contrast, when her body was covered with a sheet, she was still unable to point using her other arm to where the stimulus was presented but could describe where the stimulus was given, and mark on a schematic body diagram the precise position (Cole and Paillard, 1995).

In some of the cases mentioned above there was a loss of other types of somatosensory information as well as proprioception.

■ Why might the loss of somatosensory information not be consistent in all cases?

□ The specificity of the loss depends on which somatosensory fibres have been damaged.

A specific loss of proprioception arises when the peripheral neuropathy selectively affects large afferent fibres which convey impulses from proprioceptors and touch receptors in the skin – a condition called large fibre sensory neuropathy. The small fibres, which convey heat and pain, are unaffected. Large fibre sensory neuropathy that has arisen following a viral infection is extremely interesting because the loss experienced is very specific. The motor fibres of subjects are apparently entirely unaffected, such that motor function or muscle strength is normal. This is not the case when spinal injury leads to complete severance of the spinal cord. Here, the motor as well as the sensory signals are interrupted, resulting in a total inability to contract the muscles below the level of the injury.

Individuals with a large fibre sensory neuropathy find that, although their motor function is intact, they are initially unable to move purposefully. To begin with they are typically unable even to support themselves in a sitting position. In order to regain any purposeful motor function they have to painstakingly relearn how to hold and move themselves. However, they never regain anything like the motor function of someone without the condition. Their posture and movements are impoverished and critically dependent on vision. Furthermore, they need considerable attention. Sitting in a chair, for example, requires constant vigilance to avoid falling out of it, and closing their eyes is likely to lead to such a fall regardless of the concentration given to avoiding it. Observations such as these give us some indication of the importance of proprioception to the control of our everyday movements.

But of more direct interest here is the perceptual loss experienced by such people. Lacking proprioception, they are unaware of where the various parts of themselves are unless they can see them. If you ask them to close their eyes and you move their arm, they have almost no idea where you have moved it to and cannot reach out and touch it with the other hand without looking.

However, the unaffected small sensory fibres in people with large fibre sensory neuropathy means that such individuals do have some bodily sensitivity, for example to heat. In the case of the aforementioned individual GL, she could tell which part of her arm had been given a thermal stimulus and say, for example, 'It's over my left wrist', but, without being able to see her arm, she did not know where her left wrist was and could not point to the stimulus position (Cole and Paillard, 1995).

4.5.2 Loss of conscious proprioception

Peripheral nerve damage can be contrasted with another pathological condition that apparently results in a loss of proprioception, this time within the CNS. Cole and Paillard (1995) described the interesting case of an individual who experienced damage to the left parietal area of the cerebral cortex. Parts of the parietal cortex are thought to be involved in the representation of 3D space within the brain. Among other deficits, this individual lost the sense of touch in her right arm. She was completely unaware of pressure applied to her right arm, even when the pressure was very strong.

However, Paillard tried a very interesting experiment. He asked the individual to put on a blindfold and then with his finger applied pressure to a point on her insensate right hand. After one second's pressure, he removed his finger and said 'here'. This was a cue for the individual to reach across with her left hand and touch the spot where she believed the pressure had been applied. Her condition meant that she was not conscious of any pressure having been applied but, none the less, cued by the word 'here', she was able to touch the correct location, albeit with some degree of error.

The test was repeated for a total of 18 stimulus sites on the right hand. This task must have felt to this individual like pure guesswork, and Paillard reports that she made comments such as, 'But I don't understand that … I don't feel anything and yet I go there with my finger. How does that happen?' As an extra control, Paillard interspersed at random ten 'false' trials in which he said 'here' without having applied any pressure to the right hand. Although the individual was not conscious of these trials being any different from the legitimate ones, she did not respond (by reaching with her left arm) in any of them. Thus, her loss was apparently only of the *consciousness* of her proprioception.

Below the level of her consciousness the system was working relatively well, and this was reflected in the fact that her movement control was much better than that of individuals such as GL. On the other hand, because GL's small afferents were intact, she could detect some peripheral stimuli and tell which part of her was being stimulated, something that Paillard's individual could not do. Thus, GL must have had some sort of internal 'mapping' or 'image' of her body, but this image had become detached from any positional information: a state of affairs that it is impossible for us to imagine.

In discussing neurological syndromes, Paillard suggested a distinction between awareness of the 'what' and the 'where' of the stimulus, corresponding to the terms suggested by Larry Weiskrantz (1996): awareness *that* and awareness *of*, in talking about conscious experience. It seems that individuals lacking a body schema due to proprioceptive nerve damage can both locate *where* the tactile stimulus was applied on their own body (when allowed visual feedback) and know *what* the stimulus was: their perception of the stimulus is accurate in relation to their body image. However, access to somatosensory information about limb position and body posture is completely lost in these cases: their affected body schema denies them access to sensorimotor space.

A further interesting finding from these cases is that they show normal performance in what is called the 'waiter's tray effect'. That is, they are able to lift off an object (say a filled wine glass) with one hand from a tray held in the other hand, without the tray rising up due to the sudden decreased load. This result is achieved by affecting an appropriate postural reduction in the upward force applied to the tray in synchrony with the lifting of the glass. The timing of this adjustment is therefore crucial. The appropriate adjustment fails to occur when another person lifts the glass, and is the reason why you should not remove items from a tray carried by a waiter! The normal response in neuropathy patients suggests that the neural mechanisms for this form of postural adjustment are centrally programmed through the motor system, and are not dependent on proprioceptive feedback.

Most people report that, under normal circumstances, they are not particularly aware of the position and movement of their own bodies. Interestingly, the wording of the previous sentence hides an assumption or a preconception: namely, that our bodies are separate in some way from 'us'; my body is something that the real me 'owns', or, when some part of it hurts, just puts up with. This conception of ourselves is particularly marked in western culture.

In his book *A Leg To Stand On* (1984), Oliver Sacks describes his experience of a temporary loss of proprioception and sensation in a leg following an accident. Sacks was shocked and dismayed to discover that, rather than feeling like himself minus a leg, he now felt almost like someone else. A part of *him* had been taken away. The presence of his leg had been an integral part of his everyday experience of himself but, because it had always been there, he was not aware of this. Sacks found that similar perceptions were common in others who had experienced forms of 'de-afferentiation' (the interruption or loss of sensory fibres). These reports suggest that our conception that our bodies are somehow not the real us, but just a convenient bit of machinery 'bolted on', may be seriously misleading.

Activity 4.3 Consequences of proprioception loss

Allow 1 hour

(*Relevant module learning outcomes: KU5, KU6 and CS1*)

Access and watch the abridged version of the BBC television programme *Horizon* (1997) entitled 'The Man Who Lost His Body', which is available from the *Block 3 Activities* resource on the module website. It tells the story of Ian Waterman, one of the very rare individuals – there are fewer than a dozen known worldwide – who have lost their sense of proprioception through the loss of large fibre sensory afferents. However, Ian is the only person with this condition who is known to be able to stand and walk unaided. As you watch the video there will be questions to consider.

As well as loss of proprioception function as a consequence of nerve damage, our sense of proprioception can be altered in other ways, as you will discover in Activity 4.4.

Activity 4.4 Core reading

Allow 2 hours

(*Relevant module learning outcomes: KU1, KU5 and KU6*)

Access the core reading associated with this chapter, which is available from the *Block 3 Activities* resource. This reading is an integral part of the module, so you should treat it as you would treat the module text and devote an adequate amount of time to studying it. You will find questions and guidance on how to approach your reading of this text in the activity.

4.6 Concluding remarks on proprioception

In this chapter you read about an array of proprioceptors and their distribution around the body. The transmission pathways for proprioceptive information that lead from sensation at the level of the receptors to perception were discussed, as was how the proprioceptive system can be fooled by illusions, just like the other sensory systems. Finally, the integrated nature of proprioception into our everyday experience of the world was emphasised because we are usually largely unaware of proprioception and cannot therefore 'turn it off'. The importance of proprioception has been highlighted by considering the impact of damage to the proprioceptive system, particularly with the case of Ian Waterman who is rare in his ability to use visual information to compensate for the loss of proprioceptive information.

The final two chapters in this block move on to consider noxious forms of somatosensation by discussing the sensation of nociception and the perception of pain.

4.7 Chapter 4 summary and questions

- Experiments to find out which receptors provide the CNS with proprioceptive information have proved technically difficult, but there are known to be four types of joint receptor that contribute to our sense of proprioception, along with Golgi tendon organs and muscle spindles.
- It has also been demonstrated that the CNS does not merely passively receive proprioceptive information from these sources, but 'tunes in' the receptors according to context.
- We integrate and use the information from many receptors to orientate ourselves, position ourselves and to achieve a conscious awareness of the physical space around us and our place within it. This includes information derived from vestibular and visual sources as well as from proprioception.
- As with other senses, loss and illusion give an insight into the complex processing and interactions between senses that give rise to perceptual experiences.

Self-assessment questions

Question 4.1

Name the routes that non-painful proprioceptive somatosensory information can take from the spinal cord to the brain.

Question 4.2

Describe the process of alpha–gamma (α–γ) co-activation and why it is necessary.

Question 4.3

Distinguish the afferent sensory nerve input to the Golgi tendon organ and to the muscle spindle.

5 The neurophysiological basis of pain

> Unless suffering from one of those rare forms of hereditary indifference to pain, no human is without the experience of pain. Yet humans have always had difficulty in conveying a unified concept of pain since it can include subjective states ranging from mere unpleasantness to extreme physical agony, or the feeling of sadness and desolation accompanying an episode of major depression.
>
> *(Frederick Lenz, co-author of* The Human Pain System*)*

You read in Block 1 that pain can be set apart from the other sensations because it is unpleasant. The stimuli that give rise to pain are varied in nature and are explored in the first section of this chapter in the context of discussing the types of receptors that detect these sensations (nociceptors).

Pain is a complex perceptual experience that can have very prominent cognitive and emotional facets as well as sensory components, as the quotation above suggests. It is known, for example, that psychological pain such as that caused by the death of a loved one can trigger responses in the same brain areas that are activated in the perception of pain that ensues following tissue damage. Of course, tissue damage is something to be avoided, and so pain is very useful in alerting us to this damage so that we can take immediate action to ameliorate its effects. The unpleasant experience of sensing that pain may also help us learn to avoid similar episodes of tissue damage in the future.

Once we have recognised that tissue damage has been done, it is necessary to contain the damage and to start the healing processes as soon as possible. When the pain has done its job of communicating to us that there is a problem, it would be nice for it to stop; unfortunately, it often continues. In the short term this may be a good thing because it may force restitution. But when pain persists long after healing is apparently complete, it is recognised as a clinical syndrome, and a problem in its own right. Conversely, the complete inability to feel any pain, which arises very rarely as a result of a hereditary disorder rather than as a result of a disease such as leprosy or diabetes, is also a recognised clinical syndrome.

The focus of most research on pain is somewhat different from that undertaken for the other senses because it concerns how to control or relieve the perception of pain. One way to approach this challenge is to find out more about the neurophysiological basis of pain, which is considered in this chapter with specific reference to one of the key theories of pain circuitry: the gate-control theory. The perceptual aspects of pain, as well as its clinical management, are covered in detail in Chapter 6 of this block.

5.1 Nociception

Nociception is the sensation generated by stimuli that activate nociceptors. This process can be clearly dissociated from the perceptual experience of pain, which has the cognitive and emotional components mentioned in the introductory section of this chapter. Indeed, as you will learn in Chapter 6, pain is not always closely related to nociception. The following sections consider the process of nociception.

5.1.1 Nociceptor nerve fibres

There are two types of peripheral nerve fibre that are sensitive to stimuli that cause tissue damage. These fibres, and the associated receptors, are collectively known as nociceptors. As with the other types of somatosensory receptors, all nociceptors have cell bodies located in the DRG.

Table 5.1 shows the different types of nociceptors that are known to exist. The majority of these consist of polymodal nociceptor which have unmyelinated axons called C fibres. These fibres are always <1 μm in diameter and so they conduct action potentials relatively slowly. The other type of nociceptor fibre is small myelinated Aδ fibres. As C fibres form the majority of nociceptors, the rest of this section mainly focuses on these.

Table 5.1 Types of nociceptor.

Receptor type	Stimuli to which they respond	Fibre type
Polymodal nociceptor	chemical, thermal, mechanical	C
Thermo-nociceptor	temperatures <5 °C and >45 °C	Aδ
Mechano-nociceptor	intense pressure, e.g. pinching	Aδ

Study note

The information in Table 5.1 will help you to complete the table you created in Activity 2.2.

Both types of fibre terminate in the skin (for example, between the epithelial cells) and in other body tissues as extensively branching networks of very fine (0.5 μm) nerve terminals (Figure 5.1a). Because they have no specialised connective tissue capsule around them, these nociceptor terminals are called free nerve endings, like those discussed in Chapter 2 on the sensation of touch. You should also recall that proprioceptors are another example of free nerve endings.

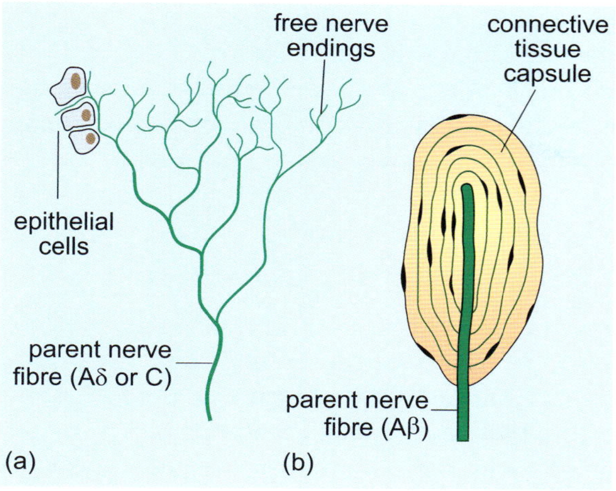

Figure 5.1 The structure of (a) free and (b) encapsulated nerve endings.

Free nerve endings are found in all parts of the body except ~~inside bones and~~ the brain. Unlike Aβ afferent fibres, which have mechanoreceptive nerve endings that are 'tuned' by their connective tissue capsule to a particular kind of movement stimulus (e.g. a Pacinian corpuscle, Figure 5.1b), free nerve endings can have a variety of membrane receptors on their surface. Nerve endings that are associated with C fibres can respond to, for example, mechanical or chemical stimulation. This means that a range of stimuli, such as physical distortion of the axon terminal membrane or changes in the concentration of various ions in the extracellular fluid (including changes in H^+ ions resulting in changes in pH), can trigger inward sodium currents. This flux generates receptor potentials and, when these are sufficiently large, a train of action potentials.

Unlike the mechanoreceptors at the ends of Aβ fibres, whose discharge adapts more or less rapidly to a sustained stimulus, C fibre activity can be very slow and can be non-adapting. In other words, after a single noxious stimulus, C fibres may continue firing action potentials for some time. Just as a wound does not disappear when the injuring stimulus is removed, so the activated C fibres do not stop firing and the perception of pain may continue.

Sometimes, C fibres also exhibit enhancement following continued stimulation, meaning that they sensitise. This phenomenon is called wind-up. The sensitisation process that can occur in C fibre receptors is an important part of pain sensation since it leads to **hyperalgesia**, or enhanced responsivity, following tissue damage (Gold and Gebhart, 2010). This increase in sensitivity occurs because the threshold of activation of the receptor is lowered as a result of the damage, and is in marked contrast to the other sensory systems, in which sensory adaptation takes the form of a decrease in responsiveness. This is not to say that nociceptors only show sensitisation, and an example of desensitisation (a decrease in responsiveness) is discussed shortly.

The rest of this section examines transduction in nociceptors. The process of transduction in response to mechanical stimuli in these receptors is very similar to that discussed for touch mechanoreception in Chapter 2. Therefore, the following two sections focus on the transduction process for nociception in the context of the response of polymodal nociceptors to chemical and thermal stimuli.

5.1.2 Chemical transduction in polymodal nociceptors

When tissue is damaged, cell walls are ruptured and intracellular materials spill out into the extracellular space. A number of the chemicals released into the extracellular space in injured tissue can activate the free nerve endings, or potentiate their response to other physical or chemical stimulation.

Potassium (K^+) ions are normally at a low concentration in the extracellular space, but leakage from damaged cells increases this. Some free nerve endings are activated directly by this rise in extracellular potassium concentration. Tissue damage often also leads to an increase in extracellular acidity (a decrease in pH/increase in H^+), which can activate free nerve endings.

As part of the body's response to damaged tissue, **mast cells** (a subtype of white blood cells, or 'leucocytes') release a number of chemicals including histamine, adenosine triphosphate (ATP), serotonin (5HT) and cytokines (small proteins that act as signalling molecules) such as nerve growth factor (NGF). Serotonin is also released by blood platelets following damage to blood vessels (Figure 5.2a). All of these compounds produce pain (or an itching sensation) if injected into the skin. Chemicals released as a result of tissue injury can activate enzyme cascades, which are discussed in Section 5.3 when detailing the inflammatory response.

Thus, broken or damaged cells release chemicals that affect neighbouring nociceptors in a number of ways. First, they may have direct effects on receptor firing rates and, second, they may sensitise the nociceptors so that they become more readily active when they encounter noxious stimuli, a phenomenon referred to as hyperalgesia. Alternatively, the nociceptor may become active in response to a previously innocuous stimuli, which is an effect referred to as allodynia. Examples of chemicals affecting nociceptors in this way are shown in Table 5.2.

Table 5.2 The effect on nociceptors of some chemicals released by (or in response to) damaged cells.

Chemicals that activate	Chemicals that sensitise
Potassium (K^+)	prostaglandins
Histamine	substance P
Bradykinin	acetylcholine (ACh)
Serotonin (5HT)	adenosine triphosphate (ATP)

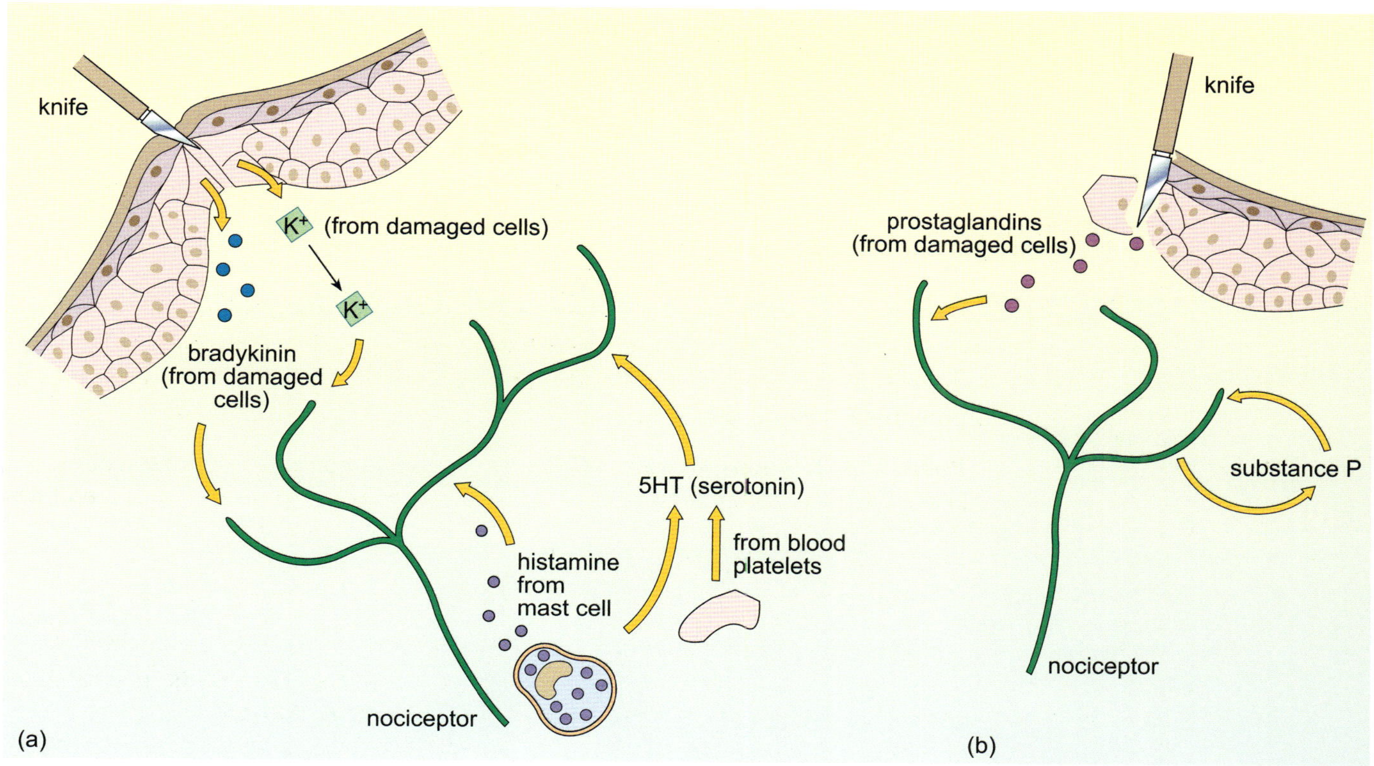

Figure 5.2 (a) Direct effects on nociceptors following cell rupture. Release of certain substances from the damaged cells, mast cells and platelets causes nociceptors to fire. (b) Indirect effects on nociceptors, e.g. sensitisation, arising from prostaglandins and the nociceptor's own transmitter substance P.

Causes of direct receptor activation

One example of direct receptor activation as a result of chemical stimulation is that caused by chilli peppers. These fruit contain the chemical *capsaicin*, which was mentioned in the context of thermoreceptors in Box 3.1. Capsaicin can cause skin irritation when chilli peppers are handled and it also excites the internal mucosa (skin) of the mouth and gut to a point that some people find unbearable. Other people enjoy the hot, spicy sensation that capsaicin adds to the experience of eating chilli peppers, which illustrates rather nicely how perception has a subjective element that is unique to each individual.

You may recall from Box 3.1 that the chemical name for capsaicin is *trans*-8-methyl-*N*-vanillyl-nonenamide and it acts via ionotropic vanilloid receptors called TRPVR1 (Figure 5.3). These receptors are so named because they are *t*ransient *r*eceptor *p*otential *v*anilloid *r*eceptors, meaning that they bind vanilloid compounds. These receptors are ligand-gated ion channels that allow the entry of the cations Ca^{2+} and Na^+.

■ What is the ligand in the example we are discussing?

□ The ligand is the substance that binds to cause the opening of the ion channels – in this case, it is capsaicin.

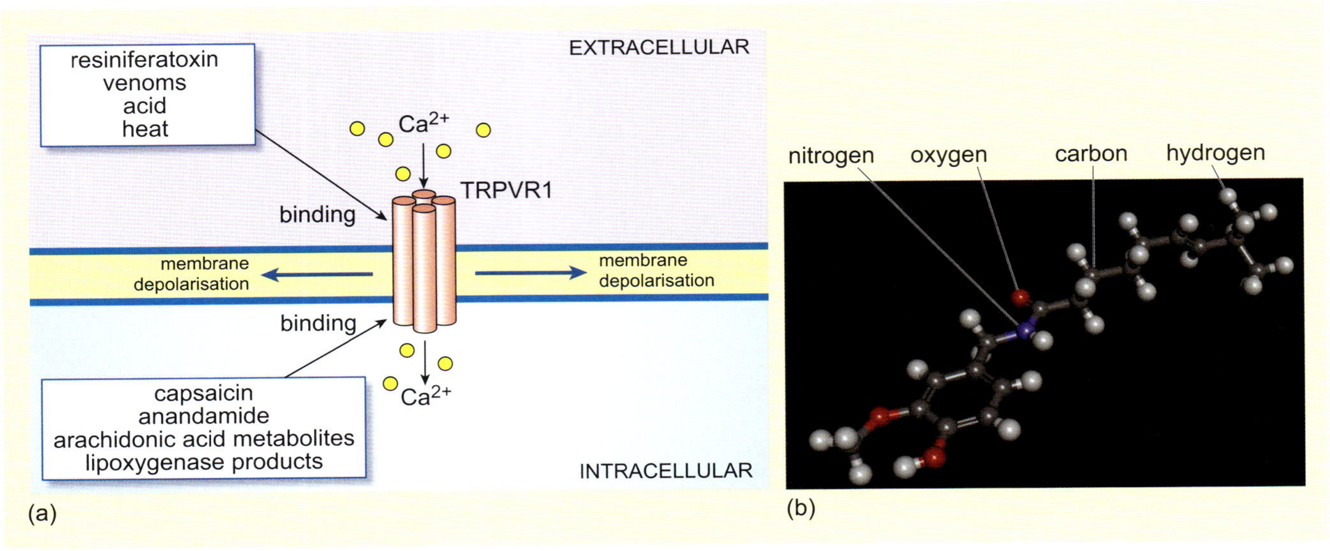

Figure 5.3 (a) Schematic diagram of the TRPVR1 receptor. (b) The *trans*-8-methyl-*N*-vanillyl-nonenamide (capsaicin) molecule that binds to it.

- ■ What effect does the opening of cation channels have on a neuron?
- □ Na^+ (and Ca^{2+}) ions will enter the neuron down electrochemical and concentration gradients and depolarise the nociceptor.

The TRPVR1 receptor site is on the inside of the neuron so capsaicin has to pass through the neuronal membrane in order to activate the receptor attached to the ion channel. The receptor is also activated by heat, acid, anandamide (an endogenous cannabinoid substance) and a number of other chemicals (Figure 5.3a), which illustrates the polymodal nature of this receptor type. The TRPVR1 receptor is extremely complex in that sometimes activation can occur from extracellular binding sites and sometimes from intracellular binding sites.

TRPVR1 is typically a heat-sensing receptor and the associated channel opens at temperatures of 37–45 °C. The application of capsaicin causes the TRPVR1 associated channel to open regardless of temperature, but the fact that TRPVR1 is primarily a heat-sensing channel explains why individuals who eat capsaicin report a burning sensation in the mouth, as discussed previously.

Somewhat counterintuitively, the repeated application of capsaicin can actually result in pain relief, and the substance is in fact used as a common treatment for arthritis. Researchers have found that initially applying capsaicin to the skin lowers the threshold of activation of the TRPVR1 receptor by thermal, chemical and mechanical stimulation. However, desensitisation of the receptor occurs with repeated application. This effect ultimately prevents chemicals such as substance P from being released peripherally. Additionally, substance P is involved in transmitting the nociceptive signal from the nociceptor to the CNS in the dorsal horn of the spinal cord and, as capsaicin depletes the amount of substance P available, the signal is no longer transmitted effectively.

Another example of direct receptor activation occurs with ATP, which also opens channels for Na^+ and Ca^{2+}. This receptor type is part of a family called the P2X receptor family. ATP is released by rapidly growing tumours and also by damaged cells, particularly in areas of the body affected by **ischaemia**: a condition where blood flow is substantially reduced. This situation happens, for example, when muscles around blood vessels go into spasms, and it can be the cause of certain kinds of headache (particularly migraine), as well as angina and muscular cramps. Muscle spasms have a directly constricting effect on blood flow and possibly also affect mechano-nociceptors directly by pulling them. Of course, once the nociceptors respond they may also release substance P from their terminals at the peripheral site of ischaemia and the complex chemical cascade of sensitisation and activation will be triggered.

5.1.3 Thermal transduction in nociceptors

We have already mentioned that TRPVR1-associated channels are heat sensing and that these channels open at temperatures in the range 37–45 °C. Figure 5.4 shows the response of a polymodal nociceptor to a range of heat stimuli from just below 40 °C to just below 60 °C. Thermo-nociceptors, which are not the same as the thermo-responsive polymodal nociceptors (see Table 5.1), also respond to temperatures in this range. Given the range of temperatures the polymodal nociceptor responds to, it is clear that there must be other heat-sensing channels involved besides TRPVR1.

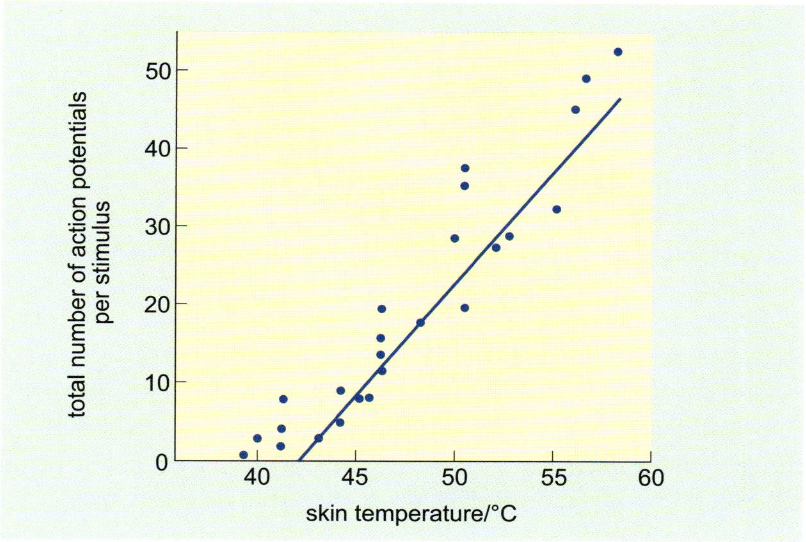

Figure 5.4 The response of a polymodal nociceptor to heat stimuli of various temperatures.

The perception attached to the firing of polymodal nociceptors in response to such a range of thermal stimuli of different temperatures differs. As the temperature rises, the increased rate of firing of a polymodal nociceptor is experienced as intense pain and most of us know to our cost that even if we remove ourselves very rapidly from a painful heat source, tissue damage will already have occurred, and we will have burnt skin.

Figure 5.5 shows how an initial exposure to a noxious radiant heat stimulus can affect the subsequent firing responses in a polymodal nociceptor generated by the same hot stimulus. In Figure 5.5a, the upper trace (blue) shows the action potentials generated by the first application of the stimulus. The lower trace (black) shows the response to a second application made 4 minutes after the original stimulus, when the nociceptors have been sensitised and both hyperalgesia and allodynia are exhibited.

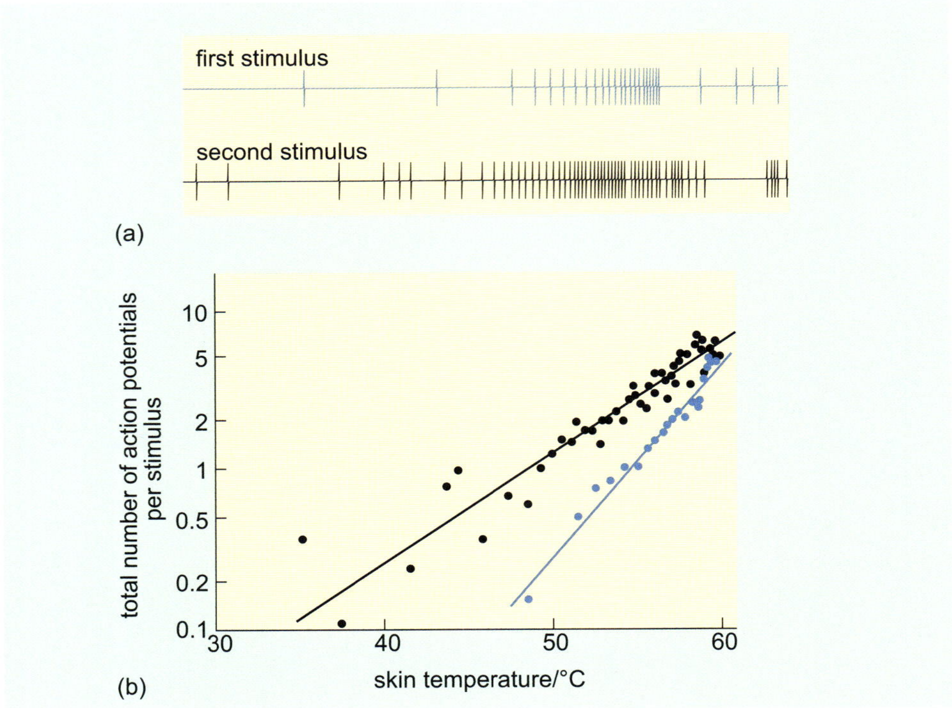

Figure 5.5 Sensitisation of polymodal nociceptors by repeated application of noxious heat stimulation.

As Figure 5.5b shows, at any given skin temperature during the episode of heating, the magnitude of the response to the second stimulus (black dots) is greater than the response to the first stimulus (blue dots). Thus, if we move close to the heat source, again we are likely to experience pain at a temperature that previously just felt pleasantly warm.

It should be clear by now that the range of stimuli that give rise to activity in nociceptors is rather wide, and we are really only beginning to understand the complex transduction mechanisms. Indeed, the properties and types of nociceptors that exist in humans is an area of intensive research, as the next activity demonstrates.

Activity 5.1 Core reading

Allow 2 hours

(*Relevant module learning outcomes: KU1, KU2, KU3 and KU6*)

Access the core reading associated with this chapter, which is available from the *Block 3 Activities* resource on the module website. This reading is an essential part of the module, so you should treat it as you would the module text and devote an adequate amount of time to studying it. You will find questions and guidance on how to approach your reading of this text in the activity.

5.2 Itch signalling

You may be wondering why we have included information on itch signalling here in a chapter on nociception. The reason is that itch signals are also detected by receptors located at the end of C fibres, and in some cases are mediated by the TRPV1 channels discussed in Box 3.1. Finally, as you will see in Chapter 6, chronic itching can be an unintended side effect of the administration of pain relief in the form of opioid analgesics such as morphine, and so an understanding of itch signalling is vital in relieving this unpleasant side effect of some of our most effective painkillers.

Itch, or more technically **puriception**, has been mostly studied in relation to histamine, which is the best known **puritogen** (substance that causes itching). Many people with allergies will know this to their cost! Histamine causes itching via activation of histamine receptors, one of which – the H1 receptor – is associated with TRPV1 channels. This form of itch can be relieved by administering antihistamines. However, not all forms of itch can be relieved in this way, which suggests there are non-histaminergic mechanisms of itch.

Furthermore, itch is a rather interesting phenomenon because it and pain appear to counteract each other. That is, a wide range of noxious stimuli are known to be able to inhibit itch (Ikoma et al., 2006). It is a common response, for example, to scratch an itch in order to relieve it. However, in most cases this cessation of sensation is only temporary, and the itching actually becomes worse! Precisely why this happens is unclear because scientists do not yet fully understand puriceptive mechanisms and the extent to which these can be separated from nociceptive mechanisms. The discovery in the dorsal horn of the spinal cord of mice of the presence of a gastrin-releasing peptide receptor (GRPR), which mediates only puriception, indicates that there may well be a labelled line code for itch (Sun and Chen, 2007), at least in the nervous system of mice!

■ Recall from Block 2 what a ‘labelled line code’ is.

□ The term refers to the neural coding of distinct sensory qualities. The idea is that distinct sensory qualities are encoded by distinct neurons (and therefore perhaps specific receptors).

The role of the dorsal horn of the spinal cord in nociception is discussed shortly, although you should remember where this location is from your reading of Block 2.

5.3 The inflammatory response

It is clear that aside from obvious cuts and bruises, tissue damage can be caused by a variety of events such as bacterial and viral attack, chemicals and heat. The injured tissues subsequently release a variety of substances that cause local short-term changes, which are collectively known as an **acute inflammatory response** (acute because the response usually lasts only a matter of hours or, at most, for a few days).

The classic components of inflammation are:

- pain
- heat
- redness
- swelling.

The inflamed area shows these signs because the local blood vessels dilate (vasodilation), thus increasing blood flow into the area and causing it to look red as well as raising the local temperature. The permeability of the capillaries increases too, and an excess of fluid, proteins and cells leaks into the area, which becomes swollen by the addition of these extra materials (Figure 5.6).

An early effect of inflammation is a clotting reaction that blocks surrounding tissue spaces and lymphatic vessels, effectively sealing off the area. (Later this effect may manifest itself as bruising.) Sealing off the area prevents infection spreading to other tissues. Interestingly, the speed with which this action occurs is in proportion to the severity of the tissue damage, so staphylococcal infections such as those caused by the bacterium *Staphylococcus aureus*, which release highly toxic products that cause cell death and abscess formation, are responded to more rapidly than the less virulent streptococcal infections, such as tonsillitis and pneumonia. Hence, streptococcal infections are, in general, more likely to spread around the body and even to cause death than staphylococal pathogens.

Cells of the immune system also contribute to the inflammatory response, and the most significant of these are the mast cells (Figure 5.6). These are manufactured in bone marrow, released into the blood and, within a few hours, they are in the damaged tissues. Their typical lifespan is only 4–5 days, but is shorter if they are triggered into degranulating, where they release granules of irritant chemicals such as histamine, which triggers vasodilation.

Vasodilation also occurs in response to the presence of two neuropeptides – substance P and calcitonin gene-related peptide – which are released from the tips of damaged nociceptors (Figure 5.6). The two peptides also stimulate the degranulation of mast cells, which is one of the ways in which an involvement of the immune system can be triggered in the absence of bacterial infection.

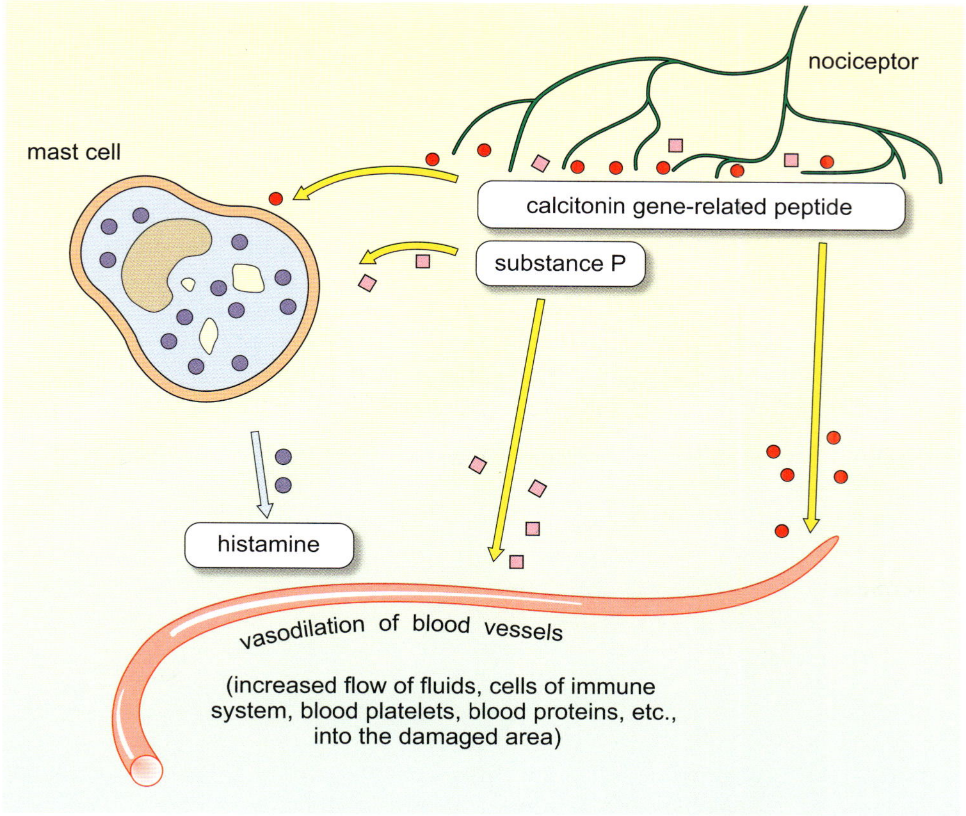

Figure 5.6 Factors triggering the inflammatory response.

Damage to cells (by whatever means) prompts the release of other chemicals, many of which affect the firing of nociceptors. These include prostaglandins, kinins, serotonin (5HT), ATP, acetylcholine (ACh) as well as ions such as potassium (K^+). You already know about some of these chemicals from Table 5.2. A number of these substances are also involved in the inflammation process, as explained in the following sections.

5.3.1 Kinins

Kinins are small peptides with wide-ranging properties that include the ability to cause vasodilation, increase vascular permeability, bring about the contraction of smooth muscle and stimulate the arachidonic acid cascade. The arachidonic acid cascade refers to the production of prostaglandins from arachidonic acid, and it is important in this context because some prostaglandins can sensitise nociceptors.

The best-known kinins are bradykinin and kallidin. There is evidence that as well as helping to initiate the actions mentioned above, bradykinin plays an important role as a mediator of the beneficial cardiovascular effects of the important angiotensin-converting enzyme (ACE) inhibitors, which help to lower blood pressure. Bradykinin is also implicated in allergies and asthma (as a cause) and is a potent stimulator of nociceptors, so it has many roles.

The kininogens are precursor molecules for kinins. There are two forms: high molecular mass kininogen (HK) and low molecular mass kininogen (LK). Molecular mass is discussed in more detail in Block 6 so will learn more about it later on. For the purposes of this block, you just need to recognise that there are two different forms of kininogen.

The process that forms bradykinin in the body is summarised in Figure 5.7. HK circulates in the plasma bound to prekallikrein, which is the precursor chemical to kallikrein (an enzyme that releases bradykinin from HK). Prekallikrein is converted to kallikrein in a variety of ways. In the context of inflammation, the main activator of inactive prekallikrein is Hageman factor, which is itself normally inactive, but it is activated by injury or any other cause of inflammation. The increased vascular permeability that occurs during inflammation allows the various components to leak out of the blood vessels, which activates the Hageman factor. In turn, this effect converts prekallikrein to kallikrein and leads to the generation of bradykinin from HK.

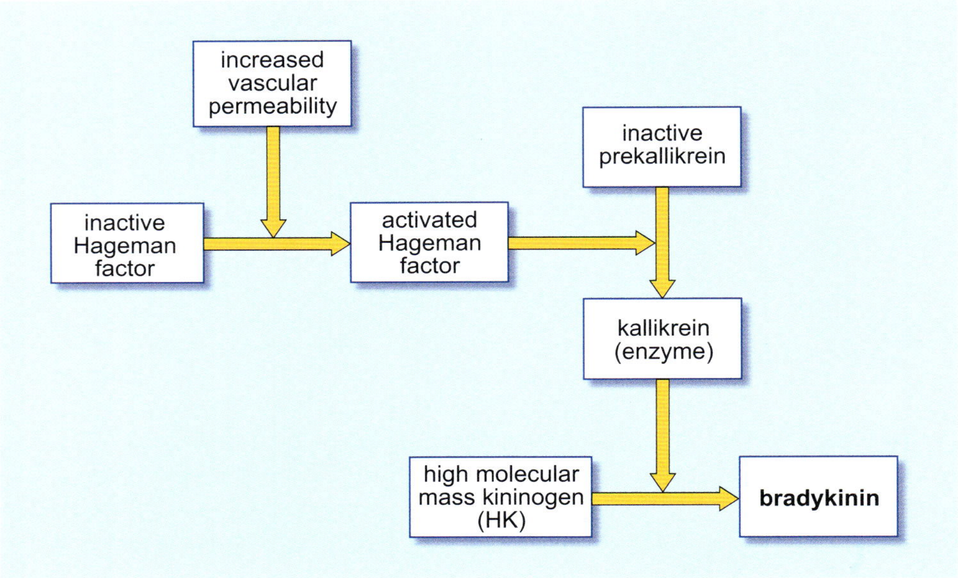

Figure 5.7 The formation of bradykinin.

5.3.2 Prostaglandins

As mentioned earlier, bradykinin and other kinins stimulate the arachidonic acid cascade, giving rise to various prostaglandins. These are extremely potent substances that have many properties: some prostaglandins help protect the body (for example, they help the stomach resist ulcer formation); others contribute to the inflammation process and the accompanying pain sensation. It is important here to remember that they can make nociceptors more sensitive, thereby increasing the pain caused by the action of the bradykinin.

The prostaglandin portion of the arachidonic acid cascade is shown in Figure 5.8. (You do not need to remember these structures; they are shown simply to illustrate how minor changes can have major effects on their biological properties.) As you may recall from Block 2, arachidonic acid is stored within the cell in the form of cell membrane phospholipids. It is released as required by the action of an enzyme, phospholipase A_2.

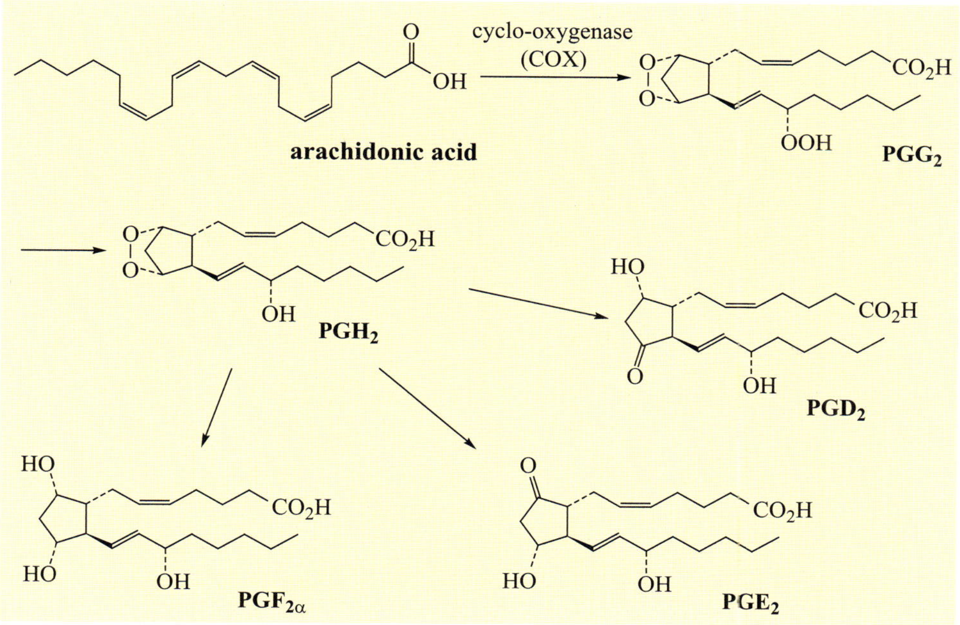

Figure 5.8 The production of prostaglandins from arachidonic acid, known as the arachidonic acid cascade.

The enzyme cyclo-oxygenase (COX) converts arachidonic acid to an intermediate known as prostaglandin PGG_2. This substance is converted by another enzyme to prostaglandin PGH_2. This, in turn, is transformed by three different enzymes into three possible products, each with different properties, PGD_2, PGE_2 and $PGF_{2\alpha}$. These are just a few of the very many metabolites formed from arachidonic acid, hence the term 'arachidonic acid cascade'.

5.4 Nociceptor projections to the brain

Despite the wide range of nociceptors and the stimuli that they respond to, they all enter the spinal cord in the dorsal horn. A cross-section of the spinal cord is shown diagrammatically in Figure 5.9a. The grey matter contains the cell bodies and dendrites of neurons; the white matter contains only the axons of neurons.

Grey matter consists of the motor or ventral horn and the sensory or dorsal horn, which is divided into ten approximately horizontal layers (I–X) known as Rexed's laminae (Figure 5.9b). Aδ and C fibres enter the spinal cord laterally and terminate mainly in lamina I, the marginal layer, and lamina II, also known as the **substantia gelatinosa (SG)**, which is very important in

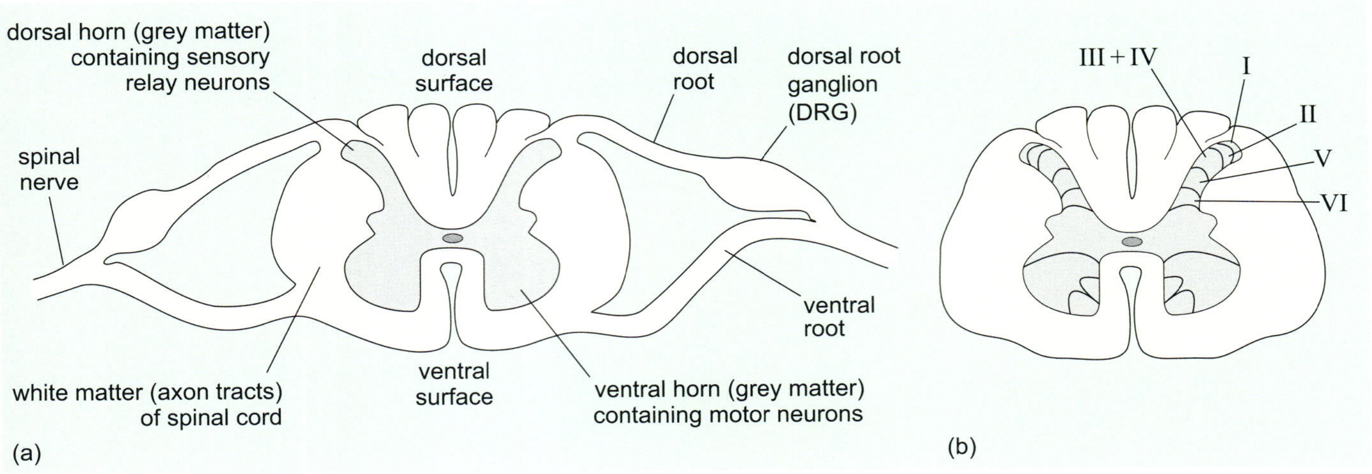

Figure 5.9 (a) Cross-section of the spinal cord. (b) Rexed's laminae I–VI of the dorsal horn. (Note: laminae VII–X are not shown.)

pain transmission. Researchers now recognise a difference between the inner and outer layers of the SG, known as II_i and II_o. Deeper into the spinal cord than the SG are laminae III, IV, V and VI.

Aδ and C fibres branch when they enter the spinal cord. Some branches terminate in lamina I on large neurons (lamina I neurons) that send axons down deeper through the other laminae and then ventrally across the spinal cord to form part of the main pathway carrying pain information to the brain – the **spinothalamic tract (STT)**. This tract ascends to the brain on the *opposite* side of the spinal cord to the afferent input (Figure 5.10) to synapse in the ventral posterior lateral (VPL) and central laminar. From here, projections extend to various cortical regions including the somatosensory cortex (S2) and the cingulate cortex, an area involved in emotion.

■ How does this arrangement of projections compare with the arrangement for sensing touch?

□ For touch, the projections primarily ascend in the dorsal column/medial lemniscus tract where they cross to the opposite side of the body at the level of the medulla after leaving the cuneate and gracile nucleus (Section 2.5).

Some Aδ fibre branches also project to the base of the dorsal horn (lamina VI) to connect to interneurons (forming a link between sensory and motor connections) controlling flexion reflexes. For example, if you stub your toe you will experience an immediate sharp pain followed by a dull throbbing one. The initial sensation is known as 'fast pain' while the throbbing is known as 'slow pain'. The function of the fast pain is to activate flexion reflexes so that a limb is quickly withdrawn from a damaging stimulus. Slow pain, in contrast, may be a means of forcing an individual to keep an injured limb immobile so that healing may occur, and this is mediated by C fibres.

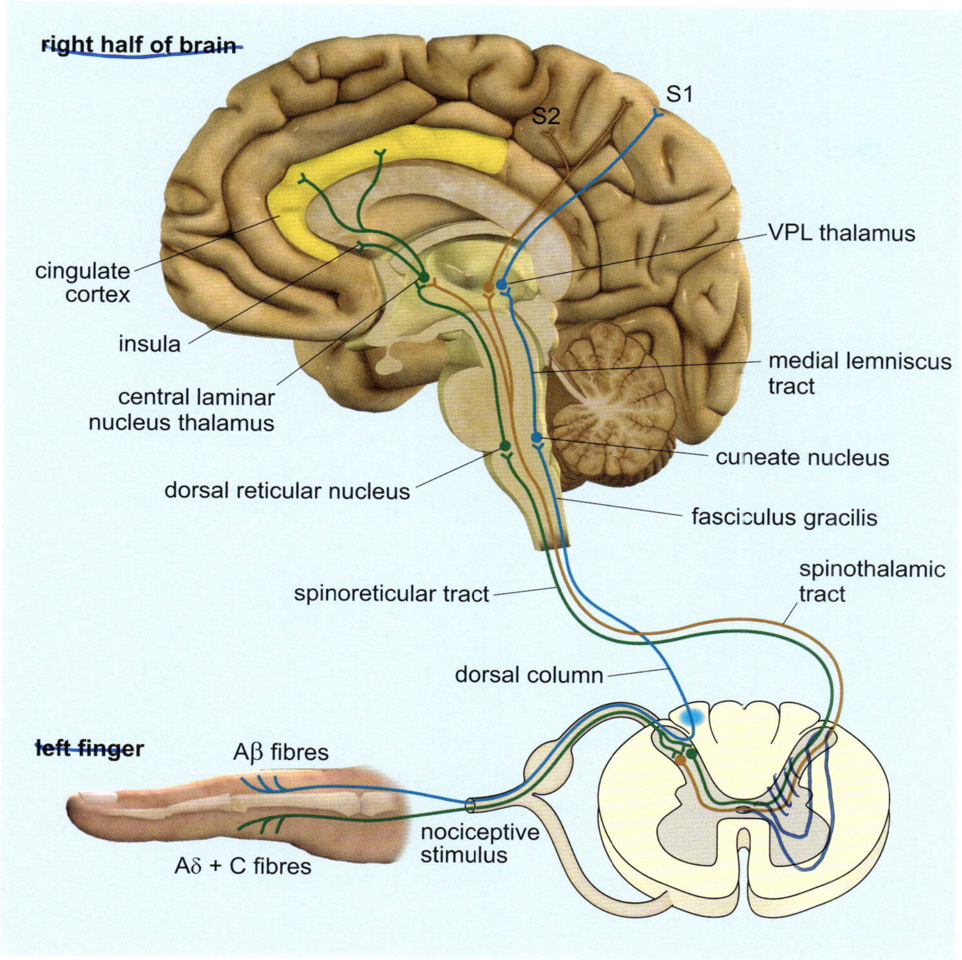

Figure 5.10 The spinothalamic tract is one part of a complex set of pain pathways and is illustrated alongside the route taken by some touch information (dorsal column/medial lemniscus tract).

The majority of lamina I neurons, like the Aδ and C fibres, respond only to tissue-damaging stimuli, although a few respond to innocuous heating or cooling of the skin. Lamina I neurons can be thought of as the 'second-order neurons' of the pain pathway.

You should be aware from Figure 5.10 that the STT is not the only pathway pain information takes to the brain. It can also travel in the spinoreticular pathway as shown in Figure 5.10, or in another pathway known as the spinomesencephalic pathway (not shown). The spinoreticular pathway originates predominantly from laminae VII and VIII of cervical spinal segments and synapses on neurons in the reticular system of the medulla and pons before projecting to the central laminar nucleus of the thalamus. It has both ipsilateral and contralateral components. The spinomesencephalic pathway arises from laminae I and V and travels contralaterally to terminate in the midbrain regions of the superior colliculus and periaqueductal gray.

Additional pain information from the face region travels to the brain in the trigeminal system (also not shown in Figure 5.10, but see Section 2.5).

Nociceptive primary afferents communicate with the second-order neurons using a variety of neurotransmitters, neuromodulators or trophic agents. Principally, however, the main neurotransmitter used is glutamate, which is present in 50% of the terminals that synapse on the spinothalamic neurons that ascend in the STT. Glutamate acts on both ionotropic and metabotropic glutamate receptors, and so has both short- and long-lasting effects.

■ What is the mechanism of activation of ionotropic receptors?

□ It occurs via ligand binding, which immediately triggers a response in the postsynaptic neuron because the ligand binding is linked directly to the opening of ion channels to generate a change in membrane potential.

■ How is this different from the metabotropic receptor?

□ Metabotropic receptors also bind ligands but the difference is that this is not directly linked to the opening of ion channels. Instead, the ligand binding causes further events inside the neuron, such as activation of a G protein (in the case of G-protein metabotropic receptors).

On the other hand, substance P principally exerts its effect by binding to neurokinin 1 receptors, which are G-protein coupled receptors that have long-lasting effects. The spinothalamic tract has been recognised for over a century as the main 'pain pathway' originating in the spinal cord.

Somatosensory perception following neurological damage

The medical condition Brown–Sequard syndrome, which was first recognised in the nineteenth century, gives an insight into the workings of the STT. In this condition the subject has damage to one complete half of the spinal cord but, because the STT ascends the cord on the opposite side to the afferent input, they lose pain (and temperature) sense on the opposite side to the lesion (Figure 5.11).

Cutting the STT surgically on one side of the cord similarly abolishes pain and temperature sense on the opposite side of the body below the cut. However, one of the great surprises in pain research was the discovery that most of the fibres in the STT could be excited by brushing or touching on the skin. They respond to either low-threshold (touch) or high-threshold (noxious) cutaneous stimulation.

This is because the lamina I axons make up only a small fraction of the STT. Most of the axons arise from other neurons, which also have cell bodies in the dorsal horn on the opposite side of the cord but in deeper laminae (usually lamina IV, V or VI). These other neurons receive input synapses from both noxious (Aδ and C) and non-noxious (Aβ) afferents, and have dendrites that project through the dorsal horn into lamina I, where they can make contact with the terminals of the Aδ and C fibres. Aβ sensory fibres make synaptic contacts lower down the dendrites of these deep neurons, as shown in Figure 5.12. Neurons in the spinal cord that receive inputs from both high-

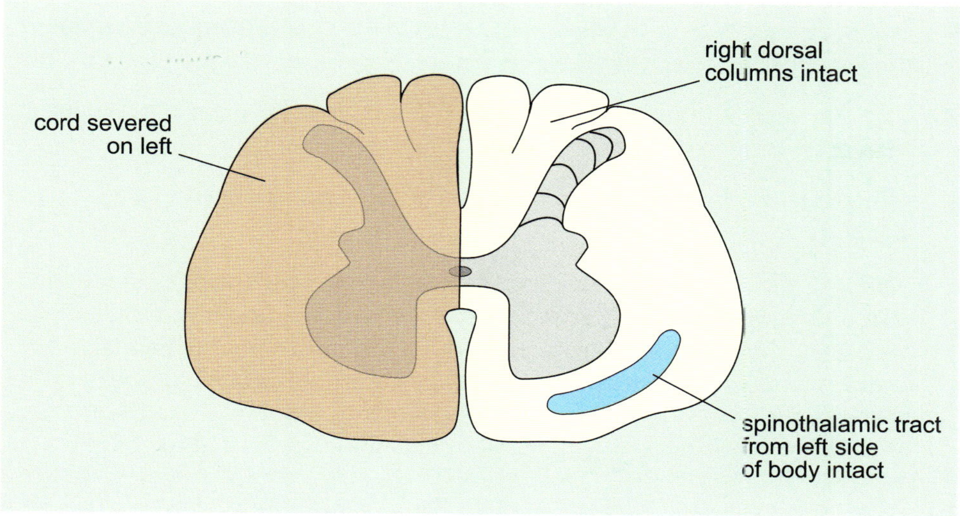

Figure 5.11 People with Brown–Sequard syndrome experience loss of pain and temperature sensation on the side of the body below the lesion, and loss of proprioception on the opposite side of the body below the lesion.

and low-threshold afferents are called **wide dynamic range neurons**. (This name comes from the fact that their dynamic range – the intensities over which they are responsive – is very wide.)

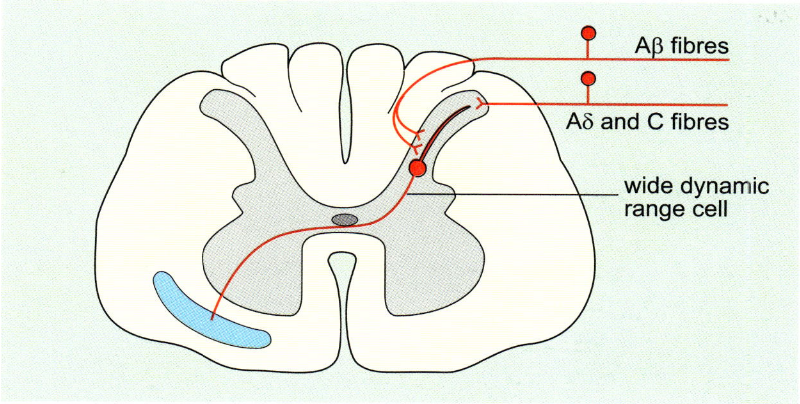

Figure 5.12 Input to wide dynamic range neurons. Aβ fibres synapse on the middle and lower parts of lamina V neuron dendrites; Aδ and C fibres synapse on the extreme tip.

The STT therefore has two kinds of neuron: those that are nociceptor-specific (cell bodies in lamina I) and those that have both nociceptive and non-nociceptive inputs (cell bodies in deeper laminae). The deep neuron projections make up the majority of the STT and these have small receptive fields: small enough to signal the precise location of a stimulus on the skin. The lamina I neurons are very much fewer in number and do not have small enough receptive fields to indicate the precise location of a painful stimulus. The receptive field of a lamina I neuron might, for example, cover the whole of one finger, but we can localise pain specifically to skin beneath an injured fingernail using the receptive fields of the neurons in the deeper laminae.

The fact that most of the neurons in the STT are wide dynamic range presents a fundamental problem.

■ What might this problem be, based on what you have read in this chapter?

□ Suppose there is activity in these wide dynamic range axons. The brain can only know the number of action potentials arriving in the thalamus, not what stimuli caused them. How is the brain to know which type of input (namely the nociceptors or the low-threshold afferents) is activating the neurons?

Suppose the lamina I neurons send an 'alerting' signal to the brain to signify that injury has occurred, but only specify the location on the body surface in a general way. The brain then sends signals down descending axons in the spinal cord, which modulate the output of the deep neurons so that low-threshold inputs to these neurons are suppressed. Then only those wide dynamic range neurons with inputs from nociceptors will be active, and the brain will be able to localise the injury.

The idea that the brain does not simply passively receive input from the spinal cord, but actively modulates the spinal relay neurons to filter and control the signals they send up to the forebrain, has been of major importance in pain research. It was first put forward by Patrick Wall at University College London in the 1960s and was a major step in the development of the important gate-control theory of pain, which is discussed in detail in the next section.

5.5 The gate-control theory of pain

The gate-control theory of pain put forward by Melzack and Wall (1965, 1996) was enormously influential in the development of ideas of how the whole brain, not just the pain system, works. Research in the last two decades has shown that the original theory has several significant errors of detail. Nevertheless, it has led to many new strategies and drugs for pain relief. This section begins by looking at the model itself and the findings that raise questions about its accuracy, before discussing its relevance to pain relief.

5.5.1 Gating pain perception in the spinal cord

The original gate-control theory is shown diagrammatically in Figure 5.13.

In this model, large diameter sensory nerve fibres (Aβ fibres) excite a relay neuron (here called a T cell) which projects up the spinal cord. The T cell activity is felt as pain. The Aβ fibres also excite lamina II neurons, which have short axons that synapse locally, so these lamina II cells are known as interneurons. The lamina II neurons inhibit the T cells, either presynaptically or postsynaptically or both. Small diameter fibres (Aδ and C) excite the T cell,

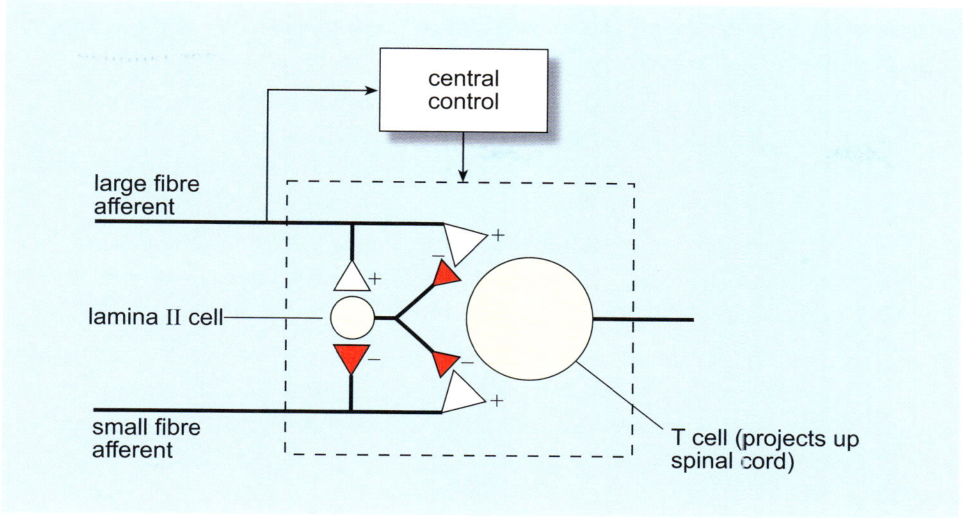

Figure 5.13 The original gate-control theory of pain.

but they inhibit the lamina II neuron. There is also an unspecified 'central control' in the theoretical model that is activated from the large fibre.

Crucial to the gate-control theory is the operation of the lamina II neurons. These constitute the actual 'gate' mechanism in the system. In its simplest form, the theory says that when these neurons are active, the input to the T cell is shut off, the gate is closed, and pain information does not reach the forebrain. Action potentials arriving in large fibre afferents have a dual role on the T cell system. They initially excite the T cells but then, via 'feedforward' inhibition through the lamina II neurons, inhibit them. Thus, the effect of large fibre inputs can only cause transient pain. Activity in small diameter afferents also directly excites the T cells but blocks any lamina II inhibition of the cells. Therefore, the small diameter afferents produce powerful and non-adapting excitation of T cells, and thus severe pain.

5.5.2 Support and criticisms of the gate-control theory

In support of the theory we can identify the T cell as a deep dorsal horn neuron whose projections make up the spinothalamic tract, with excitatory input from both large and small (i.e. wide dynamic range) fibres. But the theory does not predict or explain the presence of two types of STT neuron: wide dynamic range and nociceptor-specific neurons.

It is now known that lamina II neurons may contain the inhibitory transmitter gamma-amino-butyric acid (GABA). These GABA-ergic interneurons can produce presynaptic or postsynaptic inhibition on relay neurons. This also would fit with the gate theory. The theory suggests that lamina II neurons should have low-threshold receptive fields, as they are activated by large diameter sensory fibres also with low-threshold receptive fields. This has been confirmed for some neurons in lamina II. However, the theory predicts that lamina II neurons with low-threshold receptive fields (from large diameter afferents) should also have an inhibitory input from high-threshold (small diameter) afferents. Such neurons have not been found.

Furthermore, it is clear that there are at least two anatomically different types of neuron in lamina II, each with contrasting physiological properties:

- Stalked cells are found in the outer part of lamina II (next to lamina I). Their axons project into lamina I and their dendrites arborise (branch) in laminae II and III. They have nociceptor-specific or wide dynamic range receptive fields.
- Islet cells have axons and dendrites wholly within lamina II and most have only low-threshold receptive fields or wide dynamic range receptive fields. Many contain GABA, which is not found in stalked cells.

So islet cells could fit the role of inhibitory interneurons postulated in the gate theory, except that they do not have the type of receptive fields necessary for an exact fit to the model. However, stalked cells could be excitatory. Finally, interneurons have been found in lamina I, which may be inhibitory or excitatory for the larger relay neurons of lamina I.

Perhaps the most powerful criticism of the gate theory has focused on its prediction that the small fibre input could have two types of synaptic contact: excitatory (onto T cells) and inhibitory (onto lamina II neurons). It is now accepted that all synapses from primary afferent sensory nerve fibres are excitatory, regardless of which type of neuron they contact, so this aspect of the model is clearly incorrect.

In summary, it is clear that anatomically and physiologically the gate theory is a considerable oversimplification of the actual situation in the spinal cord. But is it *functionally* correct? The remainder of this section considers whether the gate-control theory of pain can explain known forms of endogenous analgesia (the body's own natural means of reducing pain) and exogeneous analgesia (such as that administered by a medical doctor).

5.5.3 Pain relief due to gating: testing the theory

Endogenous arousal analgesia

Can the gate theory explain endogenous analgesia seen during intense excitement or arousal, such as under conditions of stress? It can, because the theory includes another input to the spinal cord gate from the 'central control' box (see Figure 5.13). This part of the model was envisaged as a descending control system from the brain to the spinal cord. This prediction was verified by the discovery of neurons in the brainstem reticular formation that send axons down the spinal cord to synapse in the dorsal and ventral horns.

Two groups of reticular neurons in particular appear to be significant in pain control: noradrenalin-containing neurons in the locus coeruleus and adjacent structures in the pons, and serotonin (5HT) containing neurons from the raphe nuclei in the medulla. Some of these descending axons appear to synapse on primary nociceptive afferents, while others synapse on neurons in laminae I and II of the dorsal horn.

During stressful 'fight or flight' situations, the locus coeruleus neurons are active and release noradrenalin (NA) from axon terminals in the substantia gelatinosa. This release has a powerful pain-blocking effect, and drugs that enhance noradrenergic transmission in the spinal cord are powerful analgesics. Thus, descending noradrenergic neurons somehow close the gate in a very effective way. Several mechanisms have been postulated for this, but so far none has been proved. Three of these mechanisms are shown in Figure 5.14.

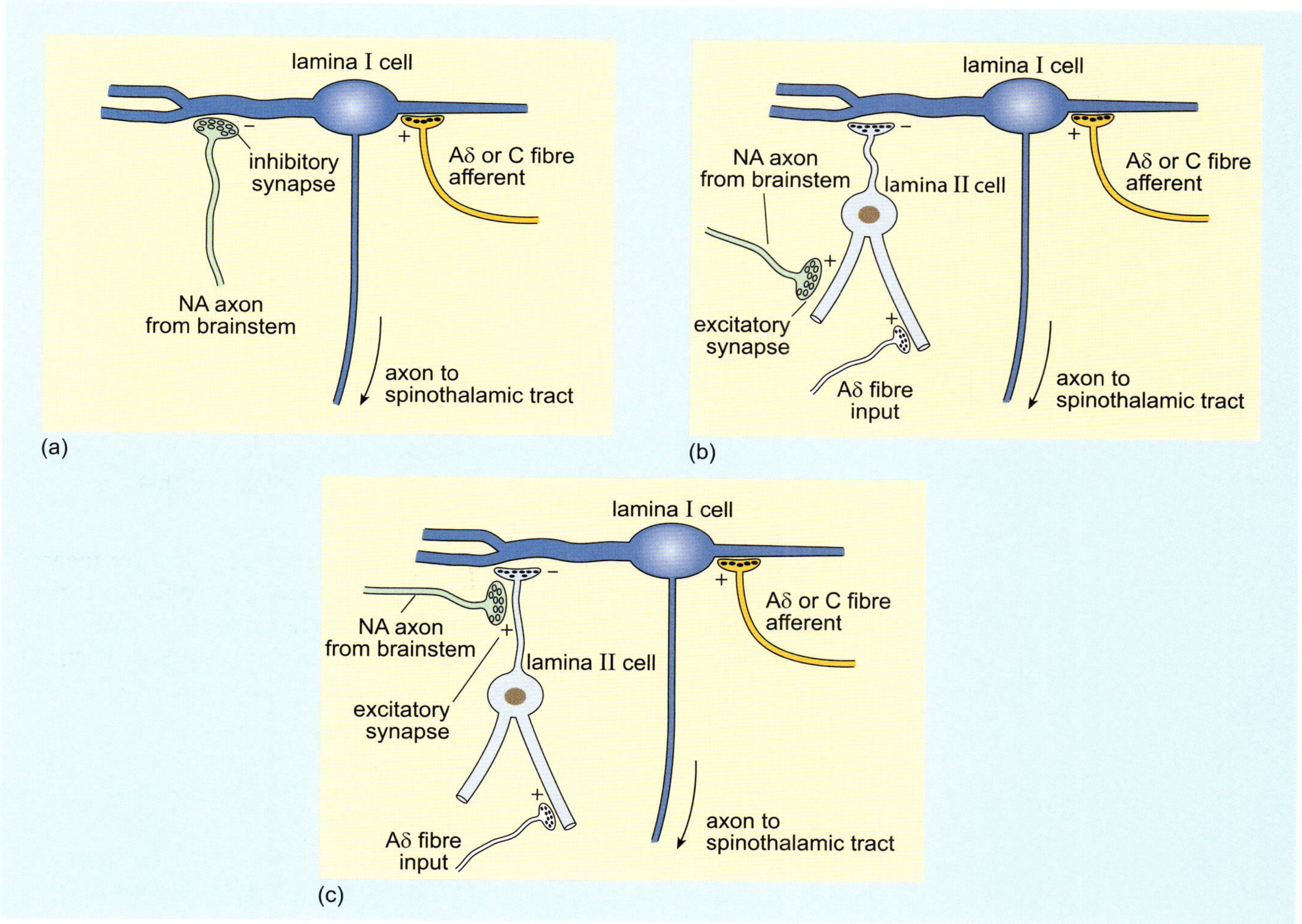

Figure 5.14 Some possible mechanisms of noradrenalin (NA) spinal action: (a) direct postsynaptic inhibition; (b) excitation of inhibitory interneurons; (c) presynaptic excitation of inhibitory interneurons.

The simplest mechanism would be that the NA has a direct postsynaptic inhibitory synapse on lamina I neurons (Figure 5.14a). An alternative suggestion, more in keeping with the known anatomy, is that the NA has an excitatory effect on inhibitory interneurons, such as islet cells (Figure 5.14b). A third possibility, for which there is some evidence, is that NA has a presynaptic excitatory effect on inhibitory interneurons (Figure 5.14c).

In contrast to the situation with NA, the function of the serotonergic descending system from the rostral ventromedial medulla (of which the raphe nucleus is a part) is more difficult to analyse. These neurons also synapse on neurons in laminae I and II, and electrical stimulation of the raphe nuclei produces a powerful analgesia in experimental animals. However, drugs that excite 5HT receptors do not have specific analgesic effects. It has been suggested that the descending 5HT neurons may have a more general inhibitory effect, possibly helping the brain to filter somatosensory input so that it can concentrate on what is important to it at that particular moment. The substance certainly seems to be involved in the initiation of sleep, possibly by lowering somatosensory input to the reticular formation and thus reducing arousal. A complicating factor is that 5HT receptors are found in many places in the dorsal horn, including presynaptically on primary afferents from C fibres.

A further possibility has since become the focus of attention, which is not predicted by the gate-control theory. It is that descending 5HT projections are involved in changes in synaptic connectivity known to occur in the spinal cord after injury (synaptic plasticity) and their restoration to normal after wound healing (Xing et al., 2007). It has been shown that descending 5HT axons undergo plasticity following dorsal root ganglia injury (Ramer, 2012) since these axons increase dramatically in number.

This is important clinically because dorsal root injury leads to severe neuropathic pain in 90% of cases (Berman et al., 1998) and it is one of the most common forms of injury following road traffic accidents (Ramer, 2012). The term 'neuropathic pain' refers to pain that occurs as a result of damage to the nervous system. Thus, further research may well indicate that descending 5HT projection plasticity has the potential to restore lost sensory function and to reduce pain. At the time of writing, a direct link has not yet been made, although it seems a promising area of study.

Endogenous opiates (enkephalins)

Both stalked and islet cells of lamina II may contain peptides called enkephalins, which bind to the same receptors as the classic analgesic drug opium and its derivatives morphine, heroin and codeine (opiate drugs). It is now accepted that morphine and other opiate drugs are analgesic because they mimic the effect of the endogenous enkephalins released by lamina II neurons. However, there are also opioid receptors located presynaptically on the dorsal root ganglia C fibres themselves.

■ What effect would activation of the presynaptic receptors discussed above have on nociception, and why?

□ Activation of these receptors would cause pain relief since blocking Ca^{2+} influx would prevent the release of presynaptic neurotransmitter in the dorsal root ganglia C fibres.

Enkephalins are released together with amino acid transmitters such as GABA, glutamate or glycine when the lamina II neurons are activated. When the enkephalin binds to the enkephalin receptors, the receptors change shape, which activates an intracellular protein (one of the G protein family). This G protein then acts on various metabolic processes in the neuron, for example the sodium pumps that control the resting potential.

Enkephalins and other peptides are often referred to as neuromodulators rather than neurotransmitters. The G protein mechanism of action is called the 'second messenger' system. They do not by themselves initiate action potentials in the neurons but modulate the effect of the primary transmitter in some way, perhaps by amplifying or prolonging its effect. They may also modulate the effect of other transmitters on the neuron. For example, they could enhance the effect of noradrenalin on the neuron by increasing the number or sensitivity of active noradrenalin receptors.

Several other peptides, including substance P, galanin, dynorphin, neurotensin and cholecystokinin, are found in the dorsal horn. Their function is still somewhat obscure. Because some C fibres release substance P together with an amino acid transmitter (glutamate or aspartate), it was initially thought that substance P was the 'pain transmitter'. However, more recent work suggests that all of these peptides work in the same way as the enkephalins; that is, they act as neuromodulators. In several cases it has been shown that more than one peptide is co-released with the main transmitter.

Exogenous analgesia: transcutaneous electrical nerve stimulation

Transcutaneous electrical nerve stimulation (TENS) is a method of pain relief that was actually developed in response to the gate-control theory of pain. Since, in the model, the large fibres excite the lamina II neurons and therefore produce feedforward inhibition of the T cells, one prediction of the theory is that input in large fibres can shut the gate and therefore reduce pain. This is (thought to be) the mechanism of action of TENS.

TENS can be very effective in certain conditions, such as pain during childbirth, when drug intervention is undesirable. TENS machines, now widely available in pharmacies and health stores, excite peripheral sensory nerve fibres by electrical shocks applied through the skin. Electrical stimuli preferentially excite myelinated fibres, so TENS machines are thought to work by activating Aβ fibres and thus block pain by activating inhibitory neurons, as in the gate theory. However, even with TENS the situation is complex, as the most effective treatment appears to be when the electrical stimulation itself is just short of painful. It may be that weak stimulation of Aδ and Aβ fibres releases endorphins (which also act on opioid receptors). These are therefore also pain-suppressing chemicals within the brain.

5.6 Brainstem and forebrain control of pain

In Section 5.4 we described the main ascending pain pathways. We followed this in Section 5.5 with a description of the gate-control theory of pain, which allows the pain pathway to be gated at the level of the spinal cord – preventing pain information reaching the brain. In that section we also discussed the role of the 'central control' in the gate-control theory, focusing specifically on descending monoamine projections from the dorsal raphe and the locus coeruleus. In this section we consider how this descending monoamine modulation of pain could be activated from the brainstem and the descending control of pain from the forebrain.

5.6.1 Brainstem mechanisms

Many spinothalamic tract fibres have branches that project to the reticular formation in the medulla and the brainstem (Figure 5.15). These branches stimulate the neurons in the reticular formation and therefore are thought to underlie the arousal effects of painful stimuli (chronic pain is a common cause of insomnia for example). This pathway underlies this effect because the reticular formation is part of the so-called 'ascending reticular activating system', which is known to modulate level of arousal and therefore sleep.

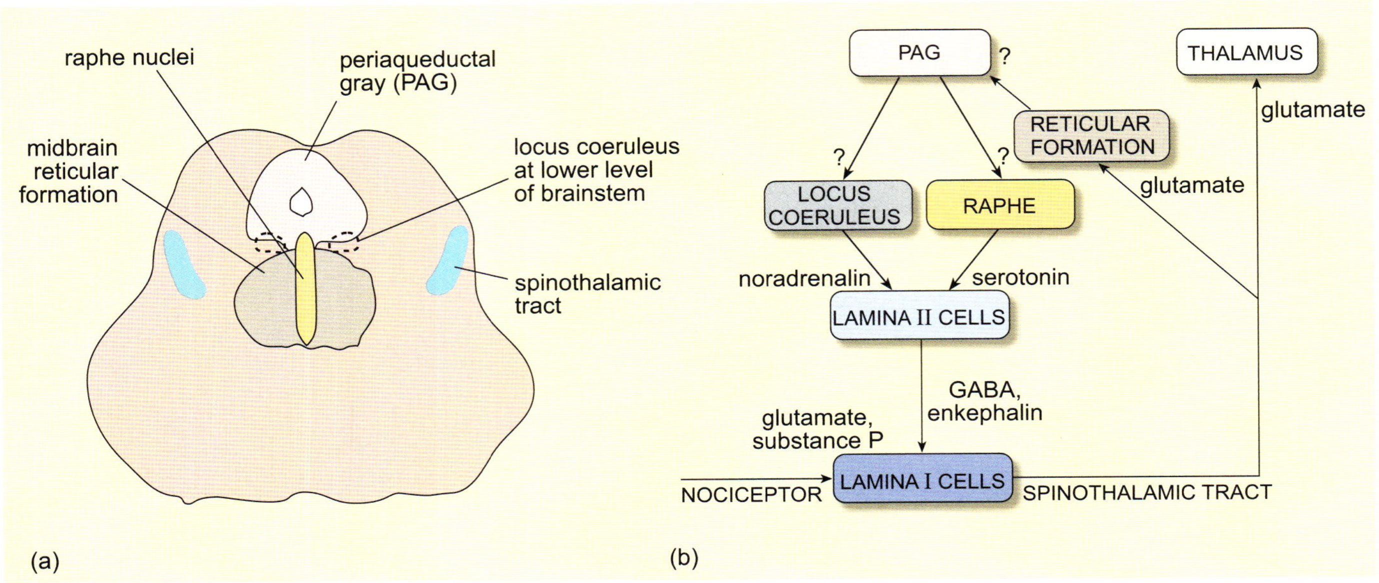

Figure 5.15 (a) Cross-section through the brainstem at the level of the inferior colliculus. (b) Schematic diagram of the spinal cord and brainstem pathways.

Adjacent to the reticular formation in the midbrain is the **periaqueductal gray (PAG)**. This area is an important centre in the descending control of pain. It receives an input from the limbic system, in particular the hypothalamus.

Electrical stimulation of the PAG via implanted microelectrodes can produce powerful analgesia, more powerful than stimulation of either the raphe nuclei or the locus coeruleus, which we discussed in Section 5.5.2 in the context of our functional assessment of the gate-control theory. It is thought that PAG neurons project to the raphe and/or locus coeruleus and activate the amine-containing neurons that in turn project down the spinal cord to block pain transmission. Here, the term 'amine' simply refers to the neurotransmitter group released by these neurons (serotonin and noradrenalin, respectively). Enkephalin-containing neurons are found in the PAG and in other parts of the reticular formation, and in the hypothalamus. You might be interested to know that the euphoric (and addictive) qualities of opiates appear to be due to their effects at the midbrain and hypothalamic opiate receptors rather than at opiate receptors elsewhere in the pain system.

It can be seen from Figure 5.15b that pain-stimulated arousal could be part of a negative feedback pain control system. Activity in the STT generates activity in the PAG, which in turn activates the locus coeruleus and raphe nuclei, and these generate descending inhibition of the STT via the release of noradrenalin and serotonin, respectively. This process would also logically be the mechanism via which serotonergic plasticity can occur in the spinal cord in instances of neuropathic pain following road traffic accidents.

5.6.2 Forebrain mechanisms

Spinothalamic tract fibres actually innervate several thalamic nuclei other than the ventral posterior thalamic nucleus, including the specific somatosensory relay nuclei (the ventrobasal group), and the non-specific 'reticular' nuclei of the thalamus. The question of whether there are nociceptor-specific neurons in the thalamus is, however, controversial. It is known that there is a powerful control system from S1 to the thalamus, and this projection may control and modulate the receptive fields of thalamic neurons.

It is also known that damage to the thalamus caused by a stroke can lead to the so-called thalamic syndrome. Patients feel intense, usually burning or crushing pain from any sort of skin contact with the affected limb. This is a severe form of allodynia, which is neuropathic in origin.

■ What is allodynia?

□ A hypersensitivity to pain such that a previously innocuous stimulus is now felt as painful. You met this term earlier in Section 5.1.

The neurons in the 'classic' somatosensory cortices (Brodmann's areas 3a, 3b, 1 and 2 which covers S1) do not normally respond to stimulation of the nociceptors. However, positron emission tomography (PET) scans have shown that these areas may be needed for the localisation of pain and judgement of its intensity. Nociceptor-specific responses are, however, found in neurons in the mid cingulate gyrus of the cerebral cortex by magnetic resonance imaging (Figure 5.16). PET scans of cerebral blood flow in healthy volunteers reveals that painful heat stimuli produce activation of a number of brain regions. The regions were activated in direct proportion to the intensity of pain that the participants perceived, indicating that sensory dimensions of the pain experience are processed in a highly distributed fashion.

Neurons in the anterior insula (a fold of cortex between the temporal and frontal lobes, see Figure 5.16b) are also activated by noxious stimulation. These two cortical areas (insula and cingulate gyrus) both receive input from the posterior thalamus and both have projections to structures in the limbic system. It is thought that these areas may mediate the 'unpleasant' or 'affective' (emotional) aspect of pain.

Overall, our knowledge of the forebrain mechanisms mediating pain perception is less than our knowledge of the peripheral nociceptors and spinal cord mechanisms. Different aspects of pain may be processed in several cortical and subcortical areas at the same time.

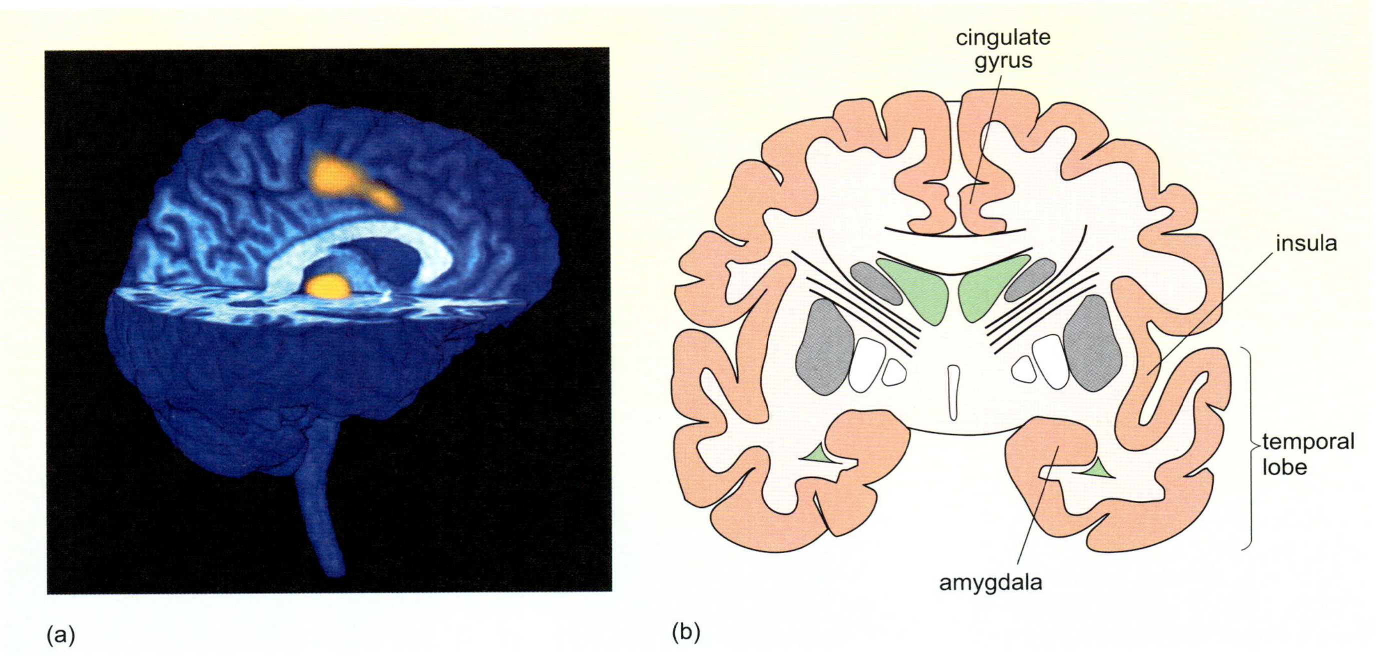

Figure 5.16 (a) Pain intensity-related activation of the mid cingulate cortex (upper orange area) and thalamus (lower orange area), superimposed on a blue MRI image. (b) Vertical cross-section (coronal section) through the brain at the level of the anterior commissure.

Activity 5.2 Core reading

Allow 2 hours

(*Relevant module learning outcomes: KU1, KU4 and KU6*)

Access the core reading associated with this chapter, which is available from the *Block 3 Activities* resource. This reading is an integral part of the module, so you should treat it as you would the module text and devote an adequate amount of time to studying it. You will find questions and guidance on how to approach your reading of this text in the activity.

We have now looked in detail at how the brain processes pain information and mediates our perception of pain. However, this endogenous control over pain is often not sufficient in itself and we require other ways of controlling and relieving it. It is these other interventions that we focus on in Chapter 6.

5.7 Chapter 5 summary and questions

- Pain is vital; without it we quickly become seriously injured. It is not like other sensations; it does not stop when the stimulus is discontinued. It is part of an integrated response to injury and may last until the related wound is healed.
- Pain is detected by nociceptors, specialised peripheral nerve fibres with free endings that specifically detect tissue damage. These endings are sensitised by many chemicals released from injured tissue.
- Nociceptor afferents synapse in the dorsal horn of the spinal cord. The majority of pain signals pass up the spinothalamic tract (STT) on the opposite side of the spinal cord to the afferent input. STT activity may be modulated by descending control from the brainstem and forebrain.
- The gate theory of pain postulates that lamina II neurons of the dorsal horn form a 'gate' which can close and block pain transmission at the spinal cord. Note that this is just a theory of the way in which the pain system functions.
- The gate theory of pain has offered some explanation of arousal analgesia and the actions of opiates. It has also led to the introduction of transcutaneous electrical nerve stimulation (TENS) for pain relief, but has been shown to be an oversimplification, in particular in its explanation of the function of lamina II neurons. There are now known to be several different types of these neurons, and more than one type of spinothalamic relay neuron.

Self-assessment questions

Question 5.1

Describe the main route that pain information takes, from the point of stimulation to the cortex.

Question 5.2

Define the term 'wind-up' and explain its underlying mechanism.

Question 5.3

Explain how the arachidonic acid cascade contributes to enhanced pain following inflammation.

The perception and control of pain

6

> As long as the blood was still running warm from his wound, Agamemnon continued to harry the enemy ranks with spear and sword and boulder. But when the blood staunched and the wound began to dry, he felt a stabbing pain, sharp as the pangs which seize a woman in childbirth.
>
> (*Homer,* The Iliad)

By now you should have noted that pain is in some ways unique from the other senses. For example, suppose you accidentally cut yourself with a knife. The skin and other tissue damaged clearly do not return to a normal state in a few milliseconds. Instead, a single painful stimulus initiates a whole series of irreversible biochemical and physiological processes. Blood clotting cascades are activated to stem the bleeding and the immune system is alerted and sends mast cells into the damaged area. Some of these changes are progressive, and they persist not for milliseconds but for days, weeks, or longer until the wound is finally healed. In other words, unlike the other senses, receptors for tissue damage do not return to their pre-stimulus state after activation, but remain 'switched on' for an indefinite period.

In the last two decades neuroscientists have shown not only that the sensitivity of damage-detecting sensory nerve endings is altered following injury, but also that their synaptic connections inside the central nervous system may be significantly modified and reorganised. That is, they exhibit plasticity. The connectivity and sensitivity of the nerve endings may only return to normal when the wound is completely healed, and even then there can be permanent changes in central connections, just like there can be permanent scar tissue after serious injuries.

Pain is thus part of an integrated response to injury that acts to prevent further injury (at the time and in the future) and to promote healing, and its perception can be highly variable. In this chapter we first examine pain perception and the factors that affect it, looking in more detail at the functions pain serves, before finally considering how we treat it.

6.1 Pain perception

Exactly how pain is experienced depends on many factors. If you are asked to imagine how much pain you would perceive if you accidently cut your finger, you might – quite sensibly – say it would depend on the size of the cut. If you gave this answer you would in fact not necessarily be correct because the relationship between nociception and pain perception is highly complex.

6.1.1 The dissociation between nociception and pain

It is possible for there to be a complete dissociation between the nociceptive stimulus and the perception of pain. In some cases where tissue is damaged, no pain is reported. Alternatively, there can be pain with no obvious nociceptive cause. Generally, this pattern of contrasting dissociations is known as a 'double dissociation' (Figure 6.1), and in the context of the relationship between nociception and pain it can particularly occur when there is a high level of arousal.

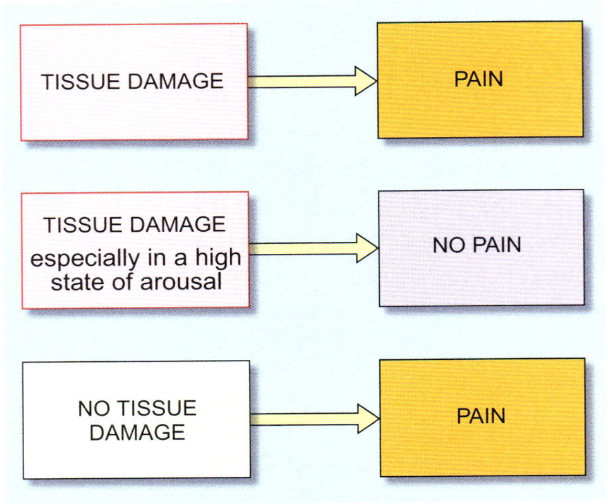

Figure 6.1 The double dissociation of tissue damage and pain.

It has long been known that sports and battle injuries may not be painful at the time. This is well illustrated by an account in Homer's *Iliad*, an epic poem about the Trojan War which was written over 2500 years ago and started this chapter. It describes how Agamemnon (commander of the Greek armies in the war) continued to fight after being wounded.

This description is typical of arousal analgesia, which is probably mediated by the release of endogenous opioid peptides and other chemicals in the brain and spinal cord, such as noradrenalin and serotonin.

Likewise, it is possible for individuals to be experiencing severe chronic pain without any obvious tissue damage. However, this might not be a true dissociation because it could be that there is internal damage and disease. There are certainly a great many cases now where 'pain without injury' would be deemed an incorrect diagnosis because the cause of the pain has been established as neuropathic. Recall that this term describes pain attributed to damage or malfunction of the tissue of the nervous system itself, rather than being due to nociception.

It should be noted, though, that this explanation does not completely account for the problems of the double dissociation of tissue damage and pain. There are still cases where pain is experienced for which no physical correlates can be identified, and there remain a few individuals who, in spite of tissue damage, cannot feel pain even though they have an apparently functional nervous system.

Minor injuries can also cause a lot of pain, so there is no clear link between the severity of tissue damage and pain perceived since some severe injuries may also not be very painful. Pain onset can also be substantially delayed, for example following limb amputations or stroke (Schott, 2001). These variations can pose considerable problems for the clinical treatment of pain, which in the past has focused on removing the physical causes or dealing with the effects experienced.

The dissociation between nociception and pain is perhaps most eloquently exhibited in the case of emotional pain, such as that experienced after the breakdown of a relationship or the death of a loved one. For many years, such pain was considered a poor imitation of the pain caused by physical, noxious stimuli, but the advent of imaging technologies has allowed some interesting insights into so-called psychological pain.

For example, research by Williams et al. (2000) looked at the pain associated with social ostracism. Their studies used a game called 'Cyberball', in which participants throw a virtual ball to what they believe are two other human players represented by animated characters on a computer screen. This virtual game allows some of the participants to be ostracised so that, after they receive the ball once or twice, it is never thrown to them again. The other participants – the 'included' ones – get the ball throws shared out equally between them.

In 2003 this research group demonstrated that when individuals felt ostracised in the game, fMRI scans of their brains showed activation in the anterior cingulate cortex – an area in the frontal lobe associated with the emotional aspects of pain when processing nociceptive information (Eisenberger et al., 2003). Moreover, the administration of painkillers similar to those used for a physical pain resulted in a reduction in activation of this brain region and a reduction in distress caused by the game (DeWall et al., 2010).

Therefore, while the actual nociception experienced may correlate with the pain perceived, this is clearly not always the case, so there must be other factors involved in modulating our experience of pain. The remainder of this section looks briefly at some of them.

6.1.2 Factors affecting pain

The amount of pain can vary in one person at different times of the day, and a person's pain reaction can be influenced by many interrelated factors (Figure 6.2). These various factors are depicted as operating through a 'volume control' or 'gate' mechanism located somewhere in the nociceptive pathway, and this would be the same gate control discussed in Chapter 5.

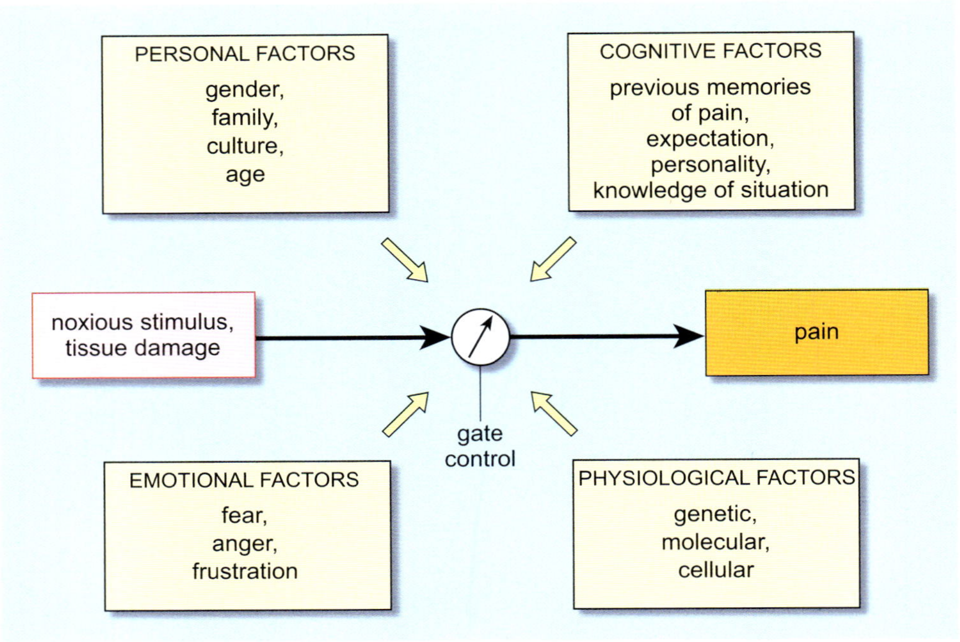

Figure 6.2 Factors influencing the amount of pain experienced in response to a noxious stimulus.

Pain-related expressions vary with personal factors such as the person's age (for example, a child is more likely to cry over a minor graze than an adult) and gender. Average pain thresholds are also known to be different in males and females, with women being more sensitive than men (Fillingim, 2000). Also, as we grow up, our behaviour is shaped by family and cultural attitudes to pain: in some societies people are expected to be stoical, while other cultures may encourage or tolerate more open expression of feelings.

Cognitive factors affecting pain perception include situational factors, namely the interactions between psychological and contextual factors in a given situation. Understanding the source of the pain and the degree of control over the situation can affect how much pain is felt. For example, the pain of childbirth is intense but has 'meaning', unlike the pain of cancer: plus labour pain has an obvious cause, and eases with the delivery of the baby.

Context is also important. For example, soldiers wounded in battle generally complain less of pain from their injuries than a civilian with comparable injuries sustained in a road traffic accident. These variations may reflect differences in how the injury affects the current lifestyle of the individual (the soldier is taken out of the firing line, but the civilian has to worry about loss of earnings, etc.). An individual's personality may also influence how they behave when in pain: for example, extroverted people may complain more about a minor injury, while introverted people tend to 'suffer in silence'.

Pain also provokes a range of emotional responses, which again vary depending on the individual and the circumstances. The experience can cause anxiety, especially if the cause is not known. People debilitated with chronic pain can become frustrated, angry, or depressed. Once again, these reactions tend to vary from person to person and may very often be influenced by social factors as well as biological ones; for example, the amount of family support an individual has. Finally, physiological factors also impact on pain perception, and we explored the physiological basis of pain in Chapter 5.

In summary then, the individual experience of pain is very variable because it depends on so many factors that are unique to an individual. Given that this is the case, it can be difficult to see how pain serves a useful function, although we have argued previously that it does. We explore the function of pain in more detail in the next section.

6.2 The function of pain

When experiencing pain you may have wondered why it is occurring and, at the time, probably did not think that it had any benefit to you. However, pain serves a vital function in maintaining health and shaping our behaviour.

6.2.1 Protective function of pain

The physiologist Sir Charles Sherrington (1906) described pain as the 'psychical adjunct of a protective reflex'. This is a useful statement as it highlights the importance of pain perception. Pain prompts the person to rest the injured part so as to avoid further damage and promote healing. Although the pain is generally regarded as a nuisance, this 'alarm-bell' function is an absolute necessity.

The importance of this mechanism is evident especially in people who are unable to feel pain, such as sometimes occurs in those with conditions like leprosy or diabetes (Block 1). Such individuals tend to experience numerous injuries and develop arthritis because of excessive joint loading. They do not, for example, feel the abdominal pain associated with appendicitis, and so may die from peritonitis. Consequently, such individuals who are unable to feel pain rarely survive long after childhood.

As the example of appendicitis indicates, pain has an important diagnostic function. A patient's description of their discomfort can often be sufficiently informative to lead to a diagnosis. The relevant features can include:

- the severity of the pain (what limitations does it impose on daily life?)
- its timing (constant, intermittent, occurs on walking?)
- its nature (throbbing, burning?)
- its location.

Types of pain that might result from a number of causes are depicted in Figure 6.3, in terms of their severity and duration. The three upper lines represent 'somatic' pains which are pains associated with the body, excluding the face and the body organs. The two lower examples illustrate 'visceral' pains (pains from organs), which typically have a longer, slower time course. Note that sensations from the face and mouth are relayed by the trigeminal nerve, the fifth cranial nerve. Trigeminal neuralgia represents episodes of intense facial pain caused by a disorder of this nerve.

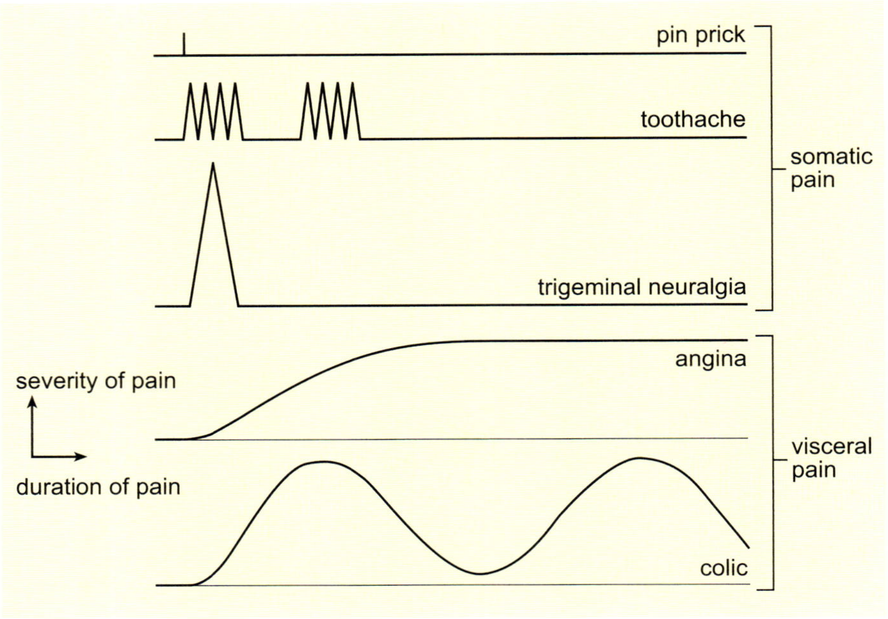

Figure 6.3 Schematic representation of the relative time course and intensity of different types of pain.

However, there are some instances when descriptions of the pain may not directly relate to the site of the actual nociceptor activation. This is called **referred pain**, which is experienced at one location despite arising from nociceptor activation at another location. It occurs when visceral pain – that is, pain arising from nociceptor activation deep within the body in an organ like the stomach, for example – is interpreted as arising from a superficial, cutaneous area. Some examples of referred pain are shown in Figure 6.4.

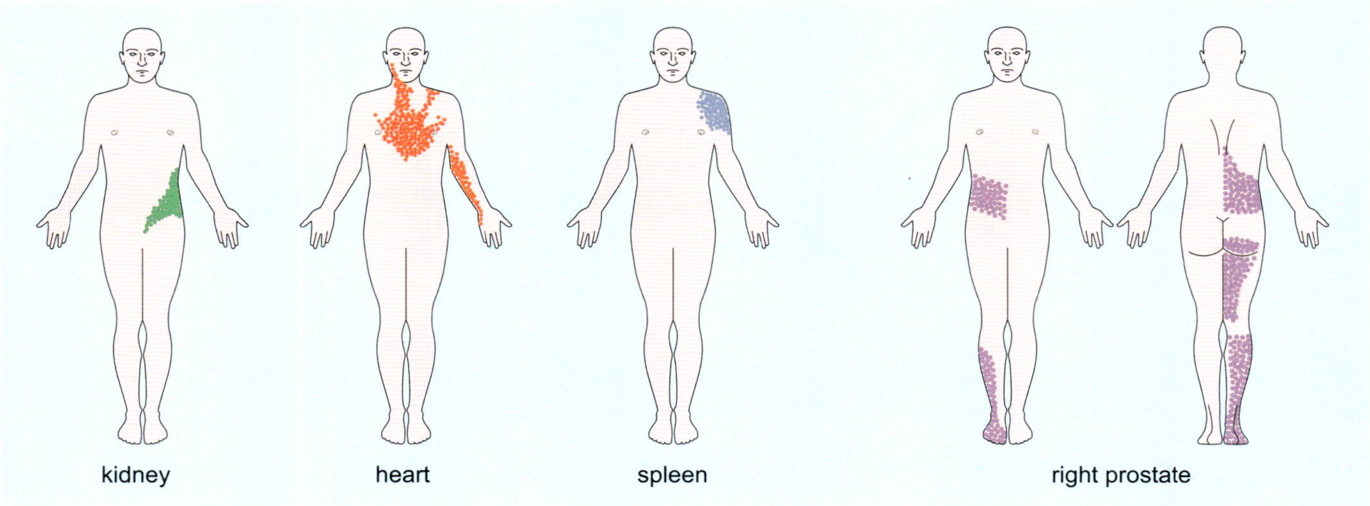

Figure 6.4 Examples of pain arising from a visceral disorder being referred to a cutaneous region (the shaded areas).

The best-known example of referred pain is probably the patient with angina who reports pain in the left arm and shoulder although the site of injury is the heart. This apparent absurdity is not a haphazard association, but one that reflects the developmental origins of the organs concerned and their innervation. The visceral nociceptors synapse with the same second-order neurons in the dorsal horn of the spinal cord as the peripheral nociceptors.

- ■ Why is this physical arrangement of inputs problematic for interpreting the site of stimulation?
- □ It is difficult for the brain to know which input led to the firing of the dorsal horn neurons, and so the location of pain can become confused.

This 'wiring problem' may explain the phenomenon of referred pain. Some neurons in the dorsal horn receive inputs from both skin and internal structures (Figure 6.5). Although each afferent pathway can be activated independently, they converge on neurons in the spinal cord and share a common projection to the brain. Neurons in the brain are therefore unable to distinguish between activity arising in one or other of the peripheral pathways, and any activity is assumed to originate in the more commonly stimulated site on the skin. Referral is always in one direction. We do not normally 'hear from' our internal organs, so when the 'silent' visceral nociceptors are active we interpret the activity as coming from the more familiar peripheral locations (i.e. the skin as in Figure 6.4) and not vice versa.

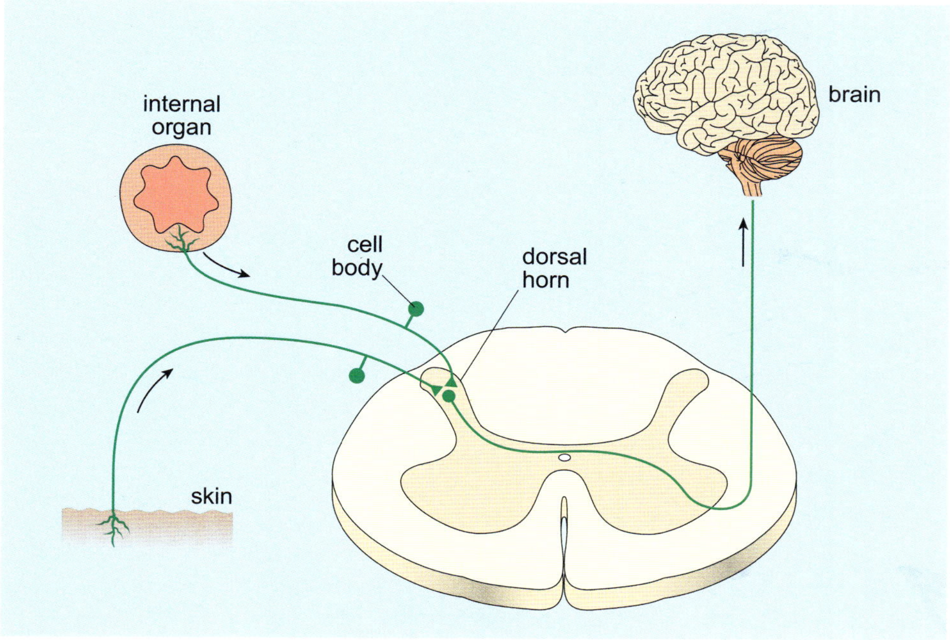

Figure 6.5 A possible neural basis for the phenomenon of referred pain.

However, because associations are made in a consistent way based on these anatomical principles, this apparently displaced pain can still provide the clinician with useful diagnostic information. Additionally, active visceral nociceptors can show reduced activity using the same analgesics (for example, aspirin) as are used to combat pain from peripheral nociceptor activity.

6.2.2 Pain as a learning tool

Pain also necessarily influences learning and shapes behaviour. The consequences of an action are known to either promote or suppress that action, as in the behavioural phenomenon of **instrumental conditioning** (this is the same as 'operant conditioning', which is a term you may have come across). By this process, any action associated with a positive outcome (i.e. pain relief) will be repeated in the future, while an action associated with a negative outcome (pain) will be avoided. The neural processing that supports this psychological phenomenon tries to influence behaviour such that actions that produce pain are avoided, while actions that produce pain relief are taken and, of course, this serves an adaptive function ensuring survival.

Another type of learning, which associates stimuli and outcomes rather than actions and outcomes, is **classical conditioning** (or Pavlovian conditioning). You may be aware of the famous experiment in which the Russian physiologist Ivan Pavlov trained his dog to salivate at the sound of a bell (Pavlov, 1960). He did this by ringing a bell when the dog was presented with food. Eventually, the dog associated the bell with food being brought and salivated at the sound even when there was no food.

This process of classical conditioning may also have a functional purpose since it can help to reduce the experience of pain as in the so-called placebo effect, which is discussed in Section 6.4. In the placebo effect, stimuli such as a doctor's white coat, which is typically seen by a patient in the context of being made to feel better via the administration of medicine, can lead to the experience of feeling better even if no active drug has been given. Such effects are testament to the brain's powerful ability to control pain perception.

In this section you have now read about how pain functions to ensure health and survival. However, it is noteworthy that in both cases the pain concerned is normally most 'useful' when time-locked to the stimulus or tissue damage causing it. For example, it is functional for a child to experience a small pain when they touch a hot pan if it ensures they never do so again. It would be less beneficial if, in that same situation, the child continued to experience pain for many months afterwards, when they were no longer touching the pan and had learned to be more cautious.

In fact, the distinction between functional pain – which is often acute and accompanies tissue damage – and dysfunctional pain – which is often chronic and less clearly linked to tissue damage or the environment – is very important, not least because the treatment of the two types of pain differ. The next section considers why chronic dysfunctional pain may occur, and the interesting example of phantom limb pain.

6.3 Dysfunctional pain

As indicated earlier, not all pain has an adaptive value (like chronic pain, which persists long after the injury or disease has apparently healed). Likewise, the terminal stages of cancer are often associated with severe pain which serves no obvious function. However, one of the most interesting conditions relating to chronic pain is perceived in 'phantom limbs'. In this section we discuss this type of pain, before looking at what pain specialists now believe could offer a neural basis of chronic pain, and how they can use this information to help prevent it in some cases.

6.3.1 Phantom limb pain

The term 'phantom limb pain' refers to the pain that can arise in people who are missing certain body parts (Figure 6.6). The occurrence of this kind of pain is actually quite common, affecting some 60–70% of people with amputations. And the experience is not actually confined to those who have lost limbs: it can include the perception of pain in the breasts, genitalia and even internal organs such as the bladder.

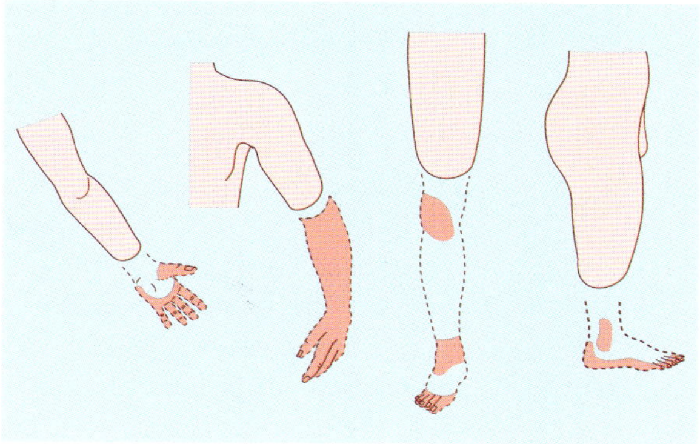

Figure 6.6 Phantom limb pain (shaded regions) experienced by some people with amputed limbs.

A wide range of sensations can be experienced from the missing limb (e.g. cold, hot, wet, sticky, itchy, tingly). It has been suggested that there is a background level of cortical activity in the somatosensory cortex in the absence of any specific sensory input, and it is possible that this activity underlies such sensations. Additionally, after the initial loss of the body part, there are certain tactile stimuli that are particularly prone to misinterpretation.

■ Referring to the somatosensory homunculus (Figure 2.19), explain why a touch to the back of the head might be felt as a touch to a missing arm.

□ The homunculus shows that the areas of the primary somatosensory cortex (S1) receiving input from the head and from the arm lie adjacent to one another. If the person who is missing the arm does not see that they are being touched, it is understandable that they might interpret the signal incorrectly as coming from the much larger area of the cortex that is responsible for receiving sensory input for the missing limb.

Over time these non-painful phantom limb sensations diminish, and it is suggested that this reduction occurs as S1 gradually reorganises itself, reducing the area devoted to the missing part. (The plasticity of the somatosensory homunculus was discussed in Chapter 3 in relation to its perceptual rather than stimulus-bound nature.)

It is also the case that children born without a limb frequently possess a clear image of the presence of that limb. This body image appears to reside in the parietal cortex, particularly the right parietal cortex. The converse experience is that some people with lesions in that part of the cortex reject one of their own limbs, although this more commonly occurs following lesions of the frontal cortex and corpus callosum (Schaefer, 2010). Such people can feel repulsed by their limb 'hanging around them' and some will try to remove it, pushing it out of bed or even requesting its amputation (Box 6.1).

Box 6.1 Alien hand syndrome

Perhaps the most striking illustration of this rare disorder is from the film *Dr Strangelove or: How I Learned to Stop Worrying and Love the Bomb* (1963). In the film, Dr Strangelove experiences loss of ownership of his right hand which, on occasion, grasps his own throat. Although this is a fictional example, there are real cases of alien hand syndrome such as that described by Goldstein in 1908. The woman concerned complained that the hand (in this case her left one) tried to throttle her, or that it would tear off the bedcovers or try to spill a drink she was holding in her other hand.

In each case, the precise characteristics of the alien hand syndrome vary depending on the location of the causative neural damage. For example, people who experience the phenomenon following frontal cortex damage show perseverative (repetitive) movements, while those who experience it following damage to other areas of brain do not.

Although various sensations do reduce over time, the pain that is experienced as originating in a phantom limb does not. This pain can be impossible to treat and is one of the more common causes of chronic pain. Originally it was suspected that this was occasioned by sensory input from the point where the limb is missing, but it now seems more likely that it is attributed to the aberrant activity in nociceptive structures caused by the continued activation of nociceptors. This presents particular problems when treating the pain.

6.3.2 Central sensitisation

If an injury does not heal quickly and continues to be painful, or if pain continues as a consequence of other conditions (e.g. inflammation or toxins released as a result of bacterial or viral attack), then the ongoing input to the dorsal horn neurons can create the problem of 'wind-up'.

Recall from Section 5.1.1 that wind-up refers to an increase in sensitivity, although in that section it was discussed in the context of the nociceptors themselves (also known as 'peripheral sensitisation'). More widely, the term 'central sensitisation' is used to describe the increasing response given by dorsal horn neurons to a steady, continuing excitatory input from nociceptors. It is as though they have a memory of the nociceptive input and subsequently become sensitised to these inputs, and fire more readily. The dorsal horn neurons do, in fact, change in these circumstances: there is an up-regulation of (increase) glutamate neurotransmitter receptors and of the production of neurotransmitters.

There are a number of ways to prevent central sensitisation. For example, in the case of amputations, current practice is to augment general anaesthetic with local analgesia at the site of the amputation. In this way at least the surgical procedures will not in themselves cause wind-up. However, this approach is obviously limited to cases of planned amputations rather than those that arise at the scene of accidents.

An alternative method is to block the *N*-methyl-D-aspartate (NMDA) glutamate receptors on dorsal horn neurons so that they cannot respond to the glutamate released by the nociceptor C fibres. This can be done by procedures such as an epidural or a spinal injection of an appropriate anaesthetic (Figure 6.7).

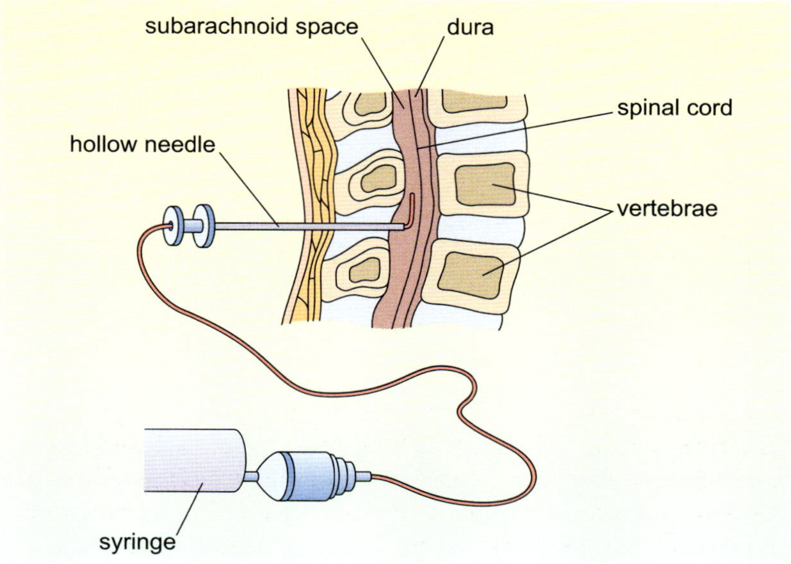

Figure 6.7 Inserting an epidural anaesthetic.

An epidural is particularly well known for being an effective analgesic during childbirth because it allows the mother to remain conscious when a caesarean section is necessary. Its use as an anaesthetic in this circumstance is preferable to a spinal block, where local anaesthetic is injected into the subarachnoid space, producing a complete motor block. With a spinal block, the recipient is not able to move any part of the body below the point of administration. The anaesthetic is not specific, so there will be no messages transmitted in either direction and both motor and sensory fibres are silenced. An epidural, in contrast, reduces motor function but does not remove it completely, which allows the mother to continue to actively labour.

In both of these examples of nociceptor inhibition by medical intervention (i.e. during planned limb amputation and childbirth) the clinical purpose is the same: to prevent the dorsal horn neurons from firing during surgery and to reduce the possibility of wind-up. In discussing these attempts to prevent wind-up, we have ventured into a key topic: the control of pain. Normally this is with the view to reducing it, but where that is not possible the aim is to prevent it increasing. The examples of approaches briefly touched on here are best described as preventive measures, but in the majority of cases such treatment is not feasible because we cannot predict when we will be in pain. The remainder of this chapter is dedicated to treatments aiming to control existing pain.

6.4 Pain control

Pain may be controlled in various ways and by intervention at different levels in the nervous system. The treatment is usually chosen according to the type or severity of pain. Acute pains tend to be managed pharmacologically, with drugs that target specific sites in the nociceptive pathway. For example, Figure 6.8 shows drugs acting on:

- peripheral nociceptors
- afferent fibres (axons)
- synapses in the spinal dorsal horn (and also the spinal nucleus of the trigeminal nerve, which is the sensory nerve supply to the face and mouth)
- higher centres in the CNS (forebrain and brainstem reticular formation).

Chronic pain is now recognised as a distinct entity, rather than merely being an acute pain that has lasted a long time; it is not merely a symptom of disease, but is a problem (syndrome) in its own right. It is associated with depression and feelings of helplessness. Treatments that are effective for acute pains may not be effective for chronic pains.

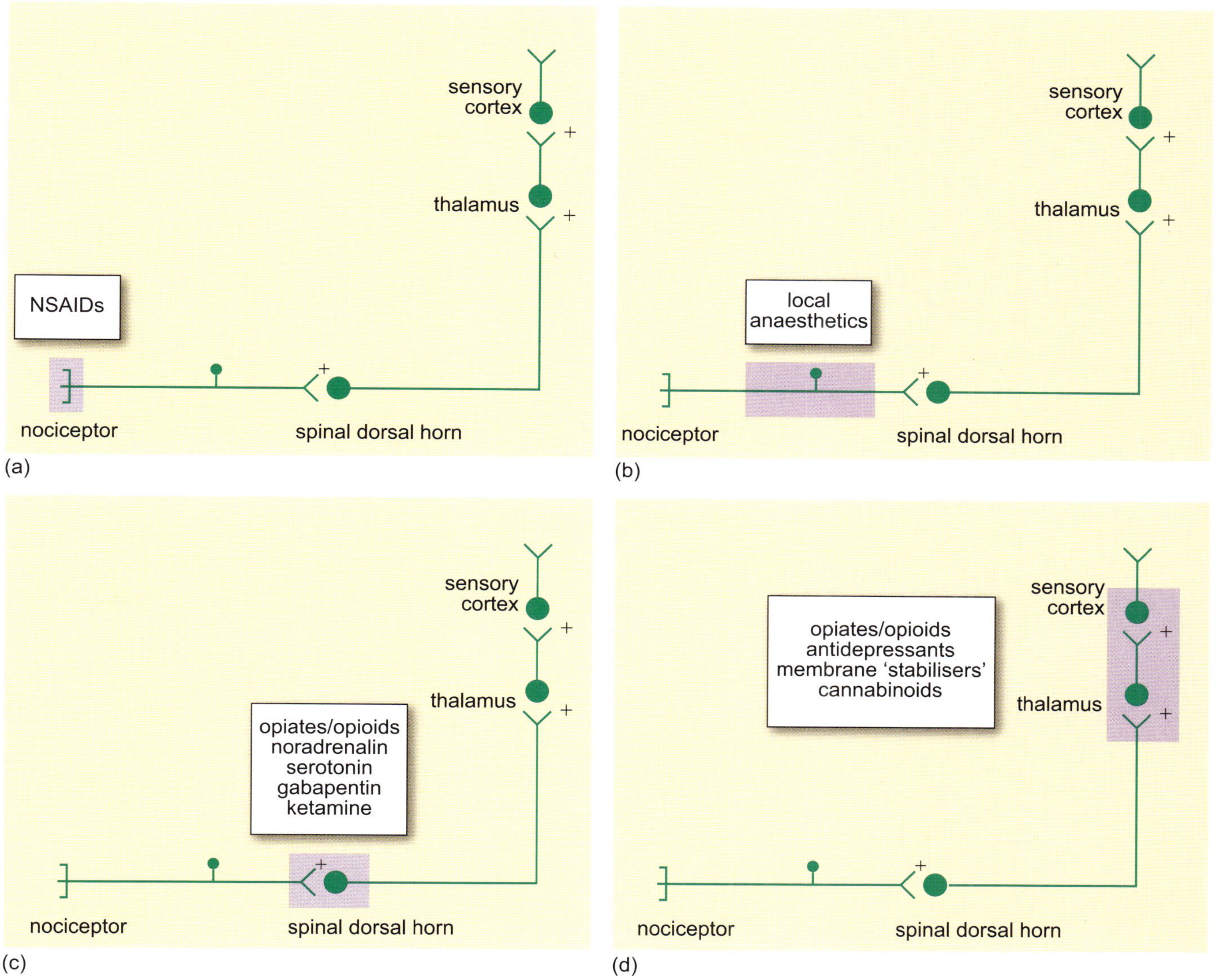

Figure 6.8 Pain control methods by drugs that act on: (a) peripheral nociceptors; (b) afferent fibres; (c) the spinal dorsal horn; (d) higher parts of the central nervous system. Some of the drugs identified are discussed in Section 6.4.1.

As well as pharmacological methods, there are a range of approaches that may be used to treat pain, and some of these are described in Table 6.1. The diversity of the treatments results directly from the range of processing of information from periphery to the brain, and the complex nature of pain perception itself. In this section we cover each of these methods in turn, as well as looking more closely at placebo effects.

Table 6.1 Summary of various methods of pain control.

Method	Description
Pharmacological	use of drugs to block or modify signalling or impulse transmission in the nociceptive pathway
Stimulation	procedures such as TENS, acupuncture and other forms of counterirritation
Surgical	cutting or lesioning of the presumed nociceptive pathway
Pain clinics	multidisciplinary centres specialising in treating chronic pains by a combination of methods
Behavioural therapy	designed to eliminate specific and 'negative' pain-related behaviours and encourage more 'positive' coping strategies
Pain management programmes	a form of behavioural therapy using a multidisciplinary approach to help patients cope with their pain
Complementary and alternative medicine (CAM)	includes acupuncture and hypnotherapy, but also less popular approaches like mirror therapy for people with phantom limb pain

6.4.1 Pain control by drugs

As already suggested, drugs may act at various points in the nociceptive pathway from nociceptors to the brain. Here we explore examples of each of these points in turn.

Drugs that act on nociceptors

Tissue injury provokes a complex response mediated by an inflammatory cascade of chemicals that cause nociceptor sensitisation. A number of analgesic drugs act to prevent this (see Figure 6.8a). The most widely used are the non-steroidal anti-inflammatory drugs (NSAIDs), many of which are available without a prescription. NSAIDS block the enzyme cyclo-oxygenase (COX), which acts on arachidonic acid to synthesise the prostaglandins.

■ What role can prostaglandins have in nociception? (Refer back to Sections 5.1.2 and 5.3.2 if you are not sure.)

□ Prostaglandins are listed in Table 5.2 as being among the substances that can sensitise the nociceptors, ultimately increasing the perception of pain.

Most 'everyday' analgesics (e.g. aspirin and ibuprofen) are in this category. Notable exceptions are paracetamol, which has little or no anti-inflammatory effects, and codeine, which acts in the CNS.

The most common disease involving inflammation pain is arthritis. This is one of the world's most painful diseases, more common than heart disease, cancer or diabetes. To relieve the crippling pain of arthritis, millions of people rely on NSAIDs. The oldest and best known of these is aspirin.

Aspirin used to be the standard against which other NSAIDs were compared but now ibuprofen, which has fewer side effects, has taken on that role. In inhibiting the COX enzyme and relieving pain, anti-inflammatories such as aspirin and ibuprofen (and other newer drugs like naproxen) also prevent the formation of beneficial prostaglandins (such as those that regulate stomach acid production). Consequently, each year one in every 1200 people who take these medications for longer than two months dies as a result of gastrointestinal and renal side effects.

In 1991 it was discovered that there are two cyclo-oxygenase enzymes, called COX-1 and COX-2:

- COX-1 is present all the time and is largely responsible for producing the beneficial prostaglandins
- COX-2 is formed in response to an inflammatory stimulus and is responsible for the painful effects.

This discovery raised the prospect that it might be possible to target just COX-2, and indeed two drugs that are selective COX-2 inhibitors (rofecoxib and celecoxib) became available in the late 1990s. However, rofecoxib was later withdrawn from the market in 2005 because of concerns that it caused an increased risk of heart attack and circulation problems and, at the time of writing, similar concerns are held about celecoxib.

Despite paracetamol (acetaminophen) being a widely available and commonly used analgesic, its mechanisms of action were unknown until very recently. However, in 2011, researchers at Kings College London discovered that the protein TRPA1 is necessary for paracetamol's analgesic effects. You first met TRPA1 in Chapter 3 (Table 3.1), where the protein was described as a thermoresponsive ion channel. It is found co-localised with TRPV1 on some nociceptive neurons.

However, paracetamol does not bind directly to TRPA1, but instead is metabolised into several breakdown products which themselves interact with TRPA1. One of these products is *N*-acetyl-*p*-benzoquinoneimine (NAPQI). Andersson et al. (2011) found that mice without the gene that codes for TRPA1 showed no analgesic effects of paracetamol administration, and DRG neurons cultured from these mice showed no evidence of increased activity as a result of the drug. They then administered NAPQI directly to cultured DRG neurons from mice with the gene and discovered that these neurons showed increased activity. As well as revealing how paracetamol achieves its analgesic effects, this work was groundbreaking because it highlighted the potential for other drugs to be developed to have an action via TRPA1.

Drugs that act on the primary afferent axon

Local anaesthetics such as lignocaine (lidocaine) act by blocking voltage-gated Na^+ channels in the axon membrane (see Figure 6.8b).

■ What effect would blocking voltage-gated Na^+ channels have on axonal transmission, and why?

□ Axonal transmission would effectively be blocked since voltage-gated Na^+ channels are essential for action potential propagation down the axon away from the axon hillock.

Small diameter axons (Aδ and C fibres) are the most susceptible to local anaesthetic block; this is convenient, as nociceptor nerves have small diameter axons. Local anaesthesia is suitable for preventing pain during minor surgery, for example tooth extraction or the removal of an ingrowing toenail, and, as you read in Section 6.3.2, it can also be used during limb surgery and childbirth (spinal and epidural anaesthetics), either alone or as a supplement to a general anaesthetic.

Drugs that act in the central nervous system

The first synapse in the CNS (the spinal dorsal horn or the trigeminal equivalent, the spinal nucleus) is a major site of analgesic drug action (see Figure 6.8c).

- ■ What is the name given to the postsynaptic neurons in the first synapse in the pain pathways?
- □ They are second-order neurons.

The opiates used include a range of drugs of varying analgesic potency, such as codeine, dihydrocodeine, morphine and diamorphine (heroin). These act on various opiate receptors in the CNS, not just at the level of the spinal cord, and principally inhibit transmission in the nociceptive pathways. The drugs' actions are quite complex, as they can act both on interneurons in the spinal cord and on the main projection neurons. Tramadol is a widely used analgesic that acts on opiate receptors and via the monoaminergic pathways (here these are serotonin and noradrenalin).

In addition to actions in the spinal cord, opiates also act in the forebrain to alter mood and to produce euphoria (see Figure 6.8d). The patient may still feel the pain, but it does not bother them. Furthermore, opiate analgesia has the unfortunate side effect of causing severe itching, as mentioned in Chapter 5 and discussed further in Box 6.2.

Box 6.2 Dissociating opiate mechanisms of itch and pain

As discussed in Section 5.2, itch (puriception) and pain were thought to coexist in an antagonistic relationship, hence the reason why scratching (a potentially painful action) reduces the itch sensation temporarily. This relationship was also thought to be why masking pain using opioids could induce the itch (since dampening one sensation enhances the other). However, researchers have discovered that morphine-induced scratching is independent of morphine-induced analgesia, and being able to relate different molecular mechanisms to each phenomenon opens up the possibility of developing new opioid analgesics that do not induce puritus.

For example, Liu et al. (2011), working at the Center for the Study of Itch at Washington University in St Louis, showed that when they increased the dose of morphine administered to mice by approximately threefold, the analgesic effect increased by 81% whereas the scratching behaviour they observed in response to the morphine increased only slightly. They went on to demonstrate that morphine-induced pain relief occurs via the activation of μ-opioid receptor MOR1, while the itching induced by morphine occurs via the activation of a different form of the μ-opioid receptor, MOR1D.

MOR1D has the ability to form a molecule made up of two non-identical repeat units, known as a heterodimer, with the GRPR. The GRPR was previously thought to form the labelled line code for itch in the spinal cord. The formation of the heterodimer between MOR1D and the GRPR confers additional properties to the GRPR, which enables exogenously administered morphine to activate the receptor and create the sensation of itch. Thus, finding exogenous opiates that would activate MOR1 without activating MOR1D could create a functional analgesic that would not have the undesirable side effect of causing intense itching.

A development that has improved the delivery of effective analgesia in hospitals is patient-controlled analgesia (PCA). Here, the patient takes charge of their analgesic needs, rather than having to call for a nurse or wait for the routine ward round. The drug is contained in a reservoir which is linked to the patient via an intravenous line. The patient can press a button to receive a small dose of analgesic when they want it. To avoid overdoses, the PCA device is set so that it will not deliver another dose until a pre-set interval has passed ('lock-out').

Portable PCA devices are now available in the form of 'syringe-drivers' which slowly deliver a drug dose over a period of time. Such devices can be used in patients who cannot take oral medications and for whom repeated injections are not appropriate. A syringe-driver can allow a patient to receive analgesia while at home rather than in hospital – an important consideration for terminally ill people. For patients unable to cope with attached devices, implantable drug-delivery systems are available. Another way of administering strong analgesics, such as the opiate fentanyl, is via adhesive skin patches, which contain enough drug for about three days of therapy.

Cannabinoids (cannabis and derivatives) are reported to have analgesic effects, but the evidence in humans is mainly anecdotal and their use is controversial. They are mild hallucinogens and exert their effects by acting on specific receptors in the CNS. At the time of writing, cannabis is a Class B controlled drug in the UK. (Although the government downgraded it to Class C for a time on the advice of scientific advisers, they subsequently followed public opinion and reconsidered the classification restoring it to B again in 2009.)

A recent review of a number of clinical trials concluded that cannabinoids give about the same level of pain relief as codeine for acute post-operative pain. Another study reported that the cannabis derivative dronabinol and the synthetic cannabinoid nabilone are useful antiemetics (i.e. prevent vomiting and nausea) in patients receiving chemotherapy.

For chronic neuropathic pain, gabapentin is reported to be an effective drug. Examples of its application are post-herpetic neuralgia and diabetic neuropathy. The drug mimics the action of the inhibitory transmitter GABA but may have additional analgesic actions. Anticonvulsant ('membrane stabilising') drugs such as carbamazepine, lamotrigine and phenytoin can also be effective for treating neuropathic pains such as trigeminal neuralgia. They have various actions, such as blocking Na^+ channels in neuronal membranes and acting as GABA agonists.

Tricyclic antidepressants such as amitriptyline and dothiepin are also used in treating neuropathic pains. In addition to their effects on mood, they seem to have some analgesic action that may be due to increased availability of the amines serotonin and noradrenalin, both of which are implicated in descending 'anti-nociceptive' pathways originating in the brainstem. Similar effects are obtained with the selective serotonin reuptake inhibitors (SSRIs), which increase synaptic levels of serotonin.

Finally, ketamine has been used as a veterinary anaesthetic for several decades, but it can be used to relieve pain through its effect in blocking the *N*-methyl-D-aspartate (NMDA) receptors in dorsal horn neurons that are now recognised as playing a major role in the development of chronic pain. Glucocorticoids such as dexamethasone and prednisolone can be used along with analgesics as part of a pain control regimen. They are not analgesics but, as corticosteroids, they have powerful anti-inflammatory effects and reduce the tissue swelling (oedema) that often contributes to the pain.

6.4.2 Stimulation methods

Stimulation techniques may be applied either to peripheral nerves, where they operate as inhibitory controls (e.g. TENS and acupuncture), or to parts of the CNS via implanted electrodes (descending controls), as shown in Figure 6.9. In the latter case, this should bring to mind that unspecified 'central control' box in the gate-control theory from Chapter 5.

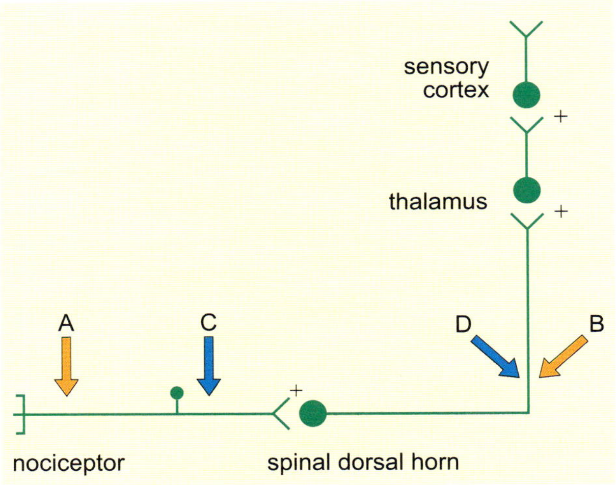

Figure 6.9 Site of action for pain control by stimulation methods (orange arrows) and neurosurgery (blue arrows): (A) TENS; (B) spinal cord stimulation; (C) peripheral nerve lesioning; (D) lesioning spinal cord pathways (e.g. cordotomy).

Stimulation of spinal cord pathways can be achieved by means of an electrode placed over the spinal cord within the vertebral canal. It is obviously an invasive procedure, but is reported to be effective in relieving visceral pains, especially angina. The electrode may be temporarily inserted through the skin into the epidural space, or can be permanently placed by a spinal operation.

6.4.3 Surgery

Many neurosurgical procedures have been derived for interrupting the presumed 'pain pathway' at some point in the peripheral or central nervous system (see Figure 6.9). Traditional 'open' surgical approaches such as cordotomy, where the surgeon operates through a fairly large incision, are less common today. Instead, neurolytic techniques may be used to block peripheral nerve pathways with phenol or alcohol injection, or the neural pathway can be lesioned with a thermal probe (either heating – called 'thermocoagulation' – or cooling – 'cryotherapy') during minimally invasive 'keyhole' operations. These procedures are often used in treating cases of trigeminal neuralgia that fail to respond to drug therapy.

Note that surgical intervention can also occur successfully in the anterior cingulate cortex (Lawson et al., 2009) for the relief of chronic pain, where patients receiving this surgery report that they still feel the pain but that it is not unpleasant or bothersome. This highlights the importance of considering pain as a perceptual phenomenon with emotional components additional to the sensory nociceptive response. An approach that builds directly on this view is discussed next.

6.4.4 Pain clinics and behavioural therapy

Pain clinics provide a multidisciplinary approach to pain management. They allow all aspects of the patient's pain (physical, emotional, behavioural, social) to be treated at the same time. They are staffed by a team of pain specialists from various health care backgrounds, and the combined expertise allows a more coordinated approach.

According to Dolin et al. (1996), the aim of pain clinics is to:

- decrease the subjective level of pain
- enable the patient to be more active
- reduce drug intake
- improve quality of life, and enable a return to work
- reduce the load on health care resources.

As already discussed in this chapter, an individual's behaviour tends to be influenced by experience, particularly via instrumental conditioning. That is, if a particular action has a favourable outcome (e.g. a reward), the action is likely to be repeated, and if an action results in something unpleasant (e.g. punishment), it is less likely to be repeated.

As already mentioned, acute pain causes an individual to rest the injured part. However, if the pain persists, the person may receive more attention from the family and be allowed to rest. In addition, they may be able to avoid work and other things that they do not want to do. These actions are viewed as negative coping strategies because the behaviour will persist as long as the pain. It is known to lead to feelings of helplessness, dependency, isolation and depression.

Positive coping strategies, on the other hand, can include activities such as exercise, increased mobility, and social encounters, which can all have beneficial effects on the amount of pain the person perceives as stemming from the injured part. The aims of behavioural therapy are to encourage positive coping strategies and move someone out of negative approaches. This is actually much the same as for the pain clinic, except that targeted behavioural therapy is often used to deal with patients who may not have had success with the multifaceted approach of the pain clinic.

The behavioural therapy approaches are designed more specifically to alter the patient's attitude, to be more positive and to raise their self-esteem. They can also involve more specific behavioural strategies, such as cognitive therapy to encourage more positive thinking, coping skills such as relaxation techniques, and hypnosis.

6.4.5 Pain management programmes

Despite the success of pain clinics, chronic pain is still very common. Pain management programmes use a multidisciplinary approach to help patients cope with their pain. The main aim is to improve the quality of life, rather than trying to reduce the level of pain, hence the name pain *management*. Pain relief is not neglected, but it is often not the primary focus.

The basic approach of these programmes is to educate patients so that they are better informed about the causes of their pain and to reduce their consumption of analgesics. This is desirable because some drugs can become addictive (such as opiates), or they can have other unintended side effects. Patients are treated in groups comprising people at different stages in the programme. Thus, those just starting the programme can learn from fellow patients how it works, and can directly see the benefits of participating.

The patients are active in developing a programme that suits their own needs and are supported by an expert team of specialists, often including pain consultants, psychologists, pain nurses, physiotherapists and occupational therapists. Alternative and complementary therapists can also contribute to the programme, and we explore the role of these specialists next.

6.4.6 Complementary and alternative medicine

Complementary and alternative medicine (CAM) includes acupuncture, aromatherapy, chiropractic, homeopathy, massage and reflexology. Over the course of a year, CAM treatments are used by around 20% of the UK population and the popularity of this approach is even greater in France and Germany, where 50% and 60% of the population respectively have used it.

People use CAM for 'positive reasons' (for example, the 'high-touch, low-tech' approach is perceived as 'holistic' or 'natural') or 'negative reasons' (such as dissatisfaction with conventional health care methods). Some CAM techniques are very popular, but there is little hard evidence that they work. Often, reports of efficacy are anecdotal or opinions, rather than being based on rigorous clinical trials. Although some individual studies may suggest a beneficial effect (see Linde et al., 1996, which found positive effects in the use of the herbal remedy St John's wort as a treatment for mild depression), the evidence is less impressive when it is put under the scrutiny of a systematic review. There is also potential for a contribution from a placebo response as a result of classical conditioning. In other words, the methods are not consistently effective.

In addition to these common CAM approaches, there is a technique known as 'mirror therapy', which is used for individuals who have phantom limb pain, although arguments continue about its efficacy. It relies on the multisensory nature of proprioception and requires patients to attempt repeated movements of the amputated limb while watching a mirror image of the movement of their equivalent, intact limb. The mirror therapy is rationalised to be efficacious because the visual sensory input overrides the nociceptive sensation, thus the brain manages to filter out any apparent painful inputs from a limb that is not there. In one study the technique was argued to be 100% effective in reducing self-reports of pain in the amputated limb (Chan et al., 2007).

Finally, PET scans show that the adverse aspects of pain (the unpleasant emotional experience associated with pain) are generated by activity in the anterior cingulate cortex. If activity in this area can be silenced, as has been possible in some experiments using hypnosis, then application of a painful stimulus loses its power to cause distress despite being 'felt'.

6.4.7 Placebo effects

No account of pain treatment is complete without some consideration of the placebo effect, whereby patients derive beneficial outcomes from treatment without having actually received any direct pharmaceutical intervention. This approach has gained a bad reputation over the years, mainly because it is often associated with quackery. However, it can be a very powerful adjunct to pain therapy.

The placebo effect is influenced by the mode of delivery: an injected placebo is more effective than a pill; large pills are more effective than small ones. Melzack and Wall (1996) established that its efficacy seems to rely on the patient's expectation, such that if they believe the treatment is going to work, it probably will. It is for this reason that methods of pain relief need to be assessed in what are known as double-blind randomised controlled trials.

In such trials, patients are randomly assigned to one of two groups: an active drug group who receive the drug or treatment being assessed, or a placebo group who are administered a non-harmful alternative with no direct health benefits. Furthermore, both the patients and the experimenters collecting the data are 'blind' to which substance has been administered to which group. At the end of the trial, both groups tend to show some reduction in symptoms. However, in order to demonstrate the efficacy of the active agent or drug, it must perform significantly better than the placebo.

There is evidence that the placebo effect is stronger in some people than in others. Voudouris et al. (1989) studied the mechanism of the placebo effect by testing the ability of an 'analgesic cream' to reduce experimentally induced pain. Their subjects were initially tested with and without the cream to assess placebo responses. Some participants received painful (electrical) stimuli to their arm as the first condition. The cream was then applied and the stimuli repeated. Unknown to the participants, the stimulus intensity was reduced, so they now felt only a tingle. Then the cream was reapplied, but this time the stimulus intensity was increased to the original level. Remarkably, the participants reported a lower level of pain than in the first test.

Other work showed that this placebo analgesia did not work if the participants were made aware that the stimulus levels had been manipulated during the experiment, supporting Melzack and Wall's suggestion that the placebo response relies on the participant's expectation (1996). A placebo does not work if the patient does not know it has been given, or it is given under general anaesthesia.

Activity 6.1 Pain and pain relief

Allow 1 hour

(*Relevant module learning outcomes: KU1 and KU2*)

Now is a good time to complete this activity, which is available from the *Block 3 Activities* resource on the module website. Here, you have a chance to review the gate-control theory and to extend your knowledge of the mechanisms of pain relief.

6.5 Concluding remarks on nociception and pain

In Chapter 5 you read about the signalling of noxious stimuli by a range of mechanisms, including mechanical, chemical and thermal, and how the body's inflammatory response leads to a prolonged reaction to noxious events (rather unlike other sensory systems, where sensation stops with the end of the signal).

Then, in Chapter 6 you explored the clinical treatment of pain via a variety of therapies, ranging from drugs to behaviour therapy, and discovered that pain is not always linked clearly to the signal, as in the double dissociation of nociception and pain. Also, you saw that the complexity of the CNS pathways involved in pain perception enables humans to learn about pain in the forms of classical and instrumental conditioning, and how this learning can be functional. For example, classical conditioning can lead to the generation of a placebo effect, where no active substance needs to be given to a patient to create pain relief. Similarly, pain as a negative reinforcement prevents an action being repeated in the future, which is an example of instrumental conditioning.

6.6 Chapter 6 summary and questions

- Although most pain arises from an obvious injury or disease, the amount of pain felt often bears no relation to the (apparent) extent of the injury. Pain is a complex emotional experience and can be affected by a wide range of corporeal and external factors.
- Pain is a necessary phenomenon. It has survival and evolutionary value.
- Pain can be considered as acute or chronic, depending on the sensation perceived and the length of time over which it is experienced. The function of chronic pain is unclear, and its effective control is considerably more challenging.
- Pain can arise from limbs that are no longer present. Other sensations are also possible such as itching and feelings of hot or cold. Mirror therapy is a controversial therapy that has been used with reported success in some studies to treat phantom limb pain although its efficacy is still contested.
- Dorsal horn neurons can exhibit a form of wind-up which is known as central sensitisation. This refers to an enhancement in their responding to continued steady input from nociceptors.
- Pain treatment can take a variety of forms, both pharmacological and psychological, depending on its nature, duration and location. Where pain cannot be removed, treatment is geared towards helping patients to live with their pain, rather than allowing it to dominate their lives.

Self-assessment questions

Question 6.1

Not all pain is dysfunctional. Explain why pain may have adaptive value.

Question 6.2

Describe the physiological mechanism that underlies phantom limb pain.

Question 6.3

Despite the fact that NSAIDs are commonly used anti-inflammatory drugs, every year one in 1200 people dies from using them over a prolonged period of time. What causes these deaths at a molecular level, and how might it be possible to prevent them?

Question 6.4

Not all clinical treatment of pain requires drug administration. Explain why this is.

Block 3 conclusion

You have now reached the end of this block on somatosensation, the first sense that you have explored in detail in this module. At this point there are some key concepts that we hope you will take forward to the remaining blocks.

The mechanisms and systems involved in this sense are very complex and our knowledge of them is far from complete. Often this means that there are no perfect treatments for clinical conditions and occasionally there are new discoveries that mean the textbooks have to be rewritten. So, you should not feel too disappointed if you have reached this point and still have unanswered questions about somatosensation.

Despite the fact that this block focused on somatosensation, you should have noticed that it was impossible not to draw on the contribution of other sensory systems, such as those providing visual or vestibular information, because these senses work together to provide our unified experience of the world. Thus, no sensory system can be understood in isolation.

Block 4 Hearing and Balance

Eleanor Dommett with Elizabeth Parvin, Mandy Dyson,
Jonathan Ashmore, Robert Fettiplace, Carole Hackney, Chris Darwin,
David Baguley, Don McFerran, David Furness and Rollin Stott

Learning outcomes

You should be able to do the following once you have completed this block. Note that the information in brackets indicates which module learning outcome(s) each block outcome relates to.

- Define and use, or recognise definitions and applications of, each of the **bold** terms in the text. (KU1)
- Describe the structure and function of the outer, middle and inner ear in hearing. (KU2)
- Explain how information about the frequency, intensity and location of sound may be coded for in the auditory system. (KU1)
- Describe the ascending auditory pathway and the function of the main nuclei involved. (KU4)
- Describe the basic principles of psychophysics and how it may be used to investigate hearing. (KU1 and CS4)
- Explain the difference between intensity and loudness and between frequency and pitch. (KU1)
- Describe the main causes of hearing impairments and the methods used to treat individuals with impaired hearing. (KU5 and KU6)
- Describe the structure and function of the main components of the vestibular system. (KU2)
- Describe the main causes of vestibular impairments and the methods used to treat such impairments. (KU5 and KU6)
- Describe examples of interactions between the auditory and/or vestibular system and other sensory systems. (KU1)

Introduction to hearing and balance

1

> The inside of my head began to resound like the inside of an old fridge hooked up to a half-blown amplifier ... skeins of sound punctuated every now and then by clanks, zizzles, and whistles ... It was deafening in there. A fight, a riot.
>
> *(Nick Coleman, 2012)*

When we try to understand one of our senses we often think in terms of what it would be like to live without it. In the above quotation, music journalist Nick Coleman talks about the constant noise that developed after he lost his hearing in one ear, illustrating that hearing impairment, like other sensory conditions, can take many forms. Indeed, various types of hearing loss and impairment, some of which you will read about in this block, affect around 280 million people worldwide (WHO, 2006) and so represent a significant health problem. These sensory deficits not only have direct effects on an individual's perception but also affect their psychological wellbeing, as quality of life can be dramatically reduced as a result.

In order to gain an understanding of just how much humans and other animals rely on sound stimuli, and therefore their sense of hearing, you need to consider what information is gained from this sense.

■ Spend a few minutes thinking about the kind of sounds that you hear regularly and can instantly recognise.

□ There are all sorts of examples you might have considered, such as the sound of a doorbell, keys in your pocket or a familiar voice.

Indeed, humans and other animals are often able to differentiate between very similar noises. For example, my dog only sits up when my partner's car pulls into the driveway and not any other car. Continuing with the car example, the sound of a car can provide us with lots of useful information, such as whether it is nearby or at a distance and whether it is moving away or towards us. It can also tell us if there is a problem with the car, as any change from the expected sound is often noticed by the owner and prompts a trip to the garage.

Just from this one set of examples you can probably appreciate that sounds in our environment create an extremely rich tapestry of audible information, and that our sense of hearing allows us to navigate and understand the world we live in. Beyond this basic means of navigation and understanding, sound is, of course, also often critical to our enjoyment of the world, through interacting with other people with speech, or listening to music.

This block begins by looking at the signal responsible for hearing, i.e. the sound wave, before moving on to describe how the ear senses the sound wave and how the brain perceives sounds. It then considers the types of hearing impairment that commonly arise and how they may be treated. However, you might have noticed that this block is not simply entitled 'Hearing' but rather

'Hearing and Balance', therefore you will also be studying the sense of balance. This sense is one that many of us take for granted but, in fact, it requires a considerable amount of sensory input from multiple sensory systems.

You have already learned in Block 3 about proprioception, which is one of the systems important for balance. In this block you will read about the role of the vestibular system, which provides the brain with a sense of spatial awareness and allows us to perceive linear and rotational acceleration. The other system that is critical for balance is vision, and although that topic is not explored in detail here (because it is the focus of Block 5), we do consider how the vestibular system interacts with vision to maintain balance.

You may be wondering why information on balance, or more specifically the vestibular system, is being combined with hearing. Recall from Block 1 that the two systems both have their sensory receptors in the inner ear, albeit in different regions. Moreover, they have very similar receptors and mechanisms of transduction. Finally, sensory disorders associated with deficits in one system may produce symptoms associated with the other. For example, vestibular disorders may include symptoms of hearing loss and individuals with hearing loss may experience balance problems. Therefore, much of what you read about hearing and its impairment (Chapters 1–6 of this block) is also relevant to the vestibular system (Chapter 7).

Sound: the signal

2

The word 'sound' can have two meanings. It can be used to describe the signal, when we talk about sound waves, or it can be used to describe the perception. This chapter looks at the signal in preparation for the later chapters, which consider the perception of sound.

2.1 What is sound?

As you may recall from Block 1, sound is a longitudinal pressure wave. The idea of sound being a wave is probably quite familiar to you but what is perhaps less familiar is how exactly simple waves can form the complex and rich sounds that we hear in everyday life – a topic you touched on in Activity 2.1 of Block 1. Consideration of both simple and complex waves is necessary because, while our environment is almost exclusively full of complex sounds, our auditory system is capable of breaking these down into simple sound waves for processing. Therefore, by understanding how simple waves form complex sounds, you gain some insight into how the auditory system may reverse this process: breaking up complex sounds into simple waves.

When we talk about a sound wave, we are essentially referring to the regular movement of air particles caused by the vibration of an object. For example, a tuning fork produces a simple sound wave if its prongs are squeezed together and then released. The oscillation of the prongs causes movement of the air close to their surfaces, and the air molecules alternately bunch together and move apart. When the molecules bunch together, local air pressure increases and when they are moved apart, it decreases.

Because the tuning fork is vibrating regularly, the result is a repeating pattern of compression and rarefaction, as shown in Figure 2.1a. If the increases and decreases in air pressure are plotted at some fixed moment in time, they would show a pattern similar to Figure 2.1b, with a wavelength of λ (lambda). This is the distance between two identical points in the cycle of compression and rarefaction. If the vibrations are instead plotted at some fixed point in space, they would show a pattern similar to Figure 2.1c, with a period (i.e. the time taken to complete one full cycle) of T.

Both Figures 2.1b and 2.1c have the same shape, which is known as 'sinusoidal' because it is the same as the shape obtained if sin θ is plotted versus θ. It represents the simplest kind of wave and, in the case of sound, a 'pure' tone.

Study note

If you are not familiar with the sine function, please refer to the *Study Companion*.

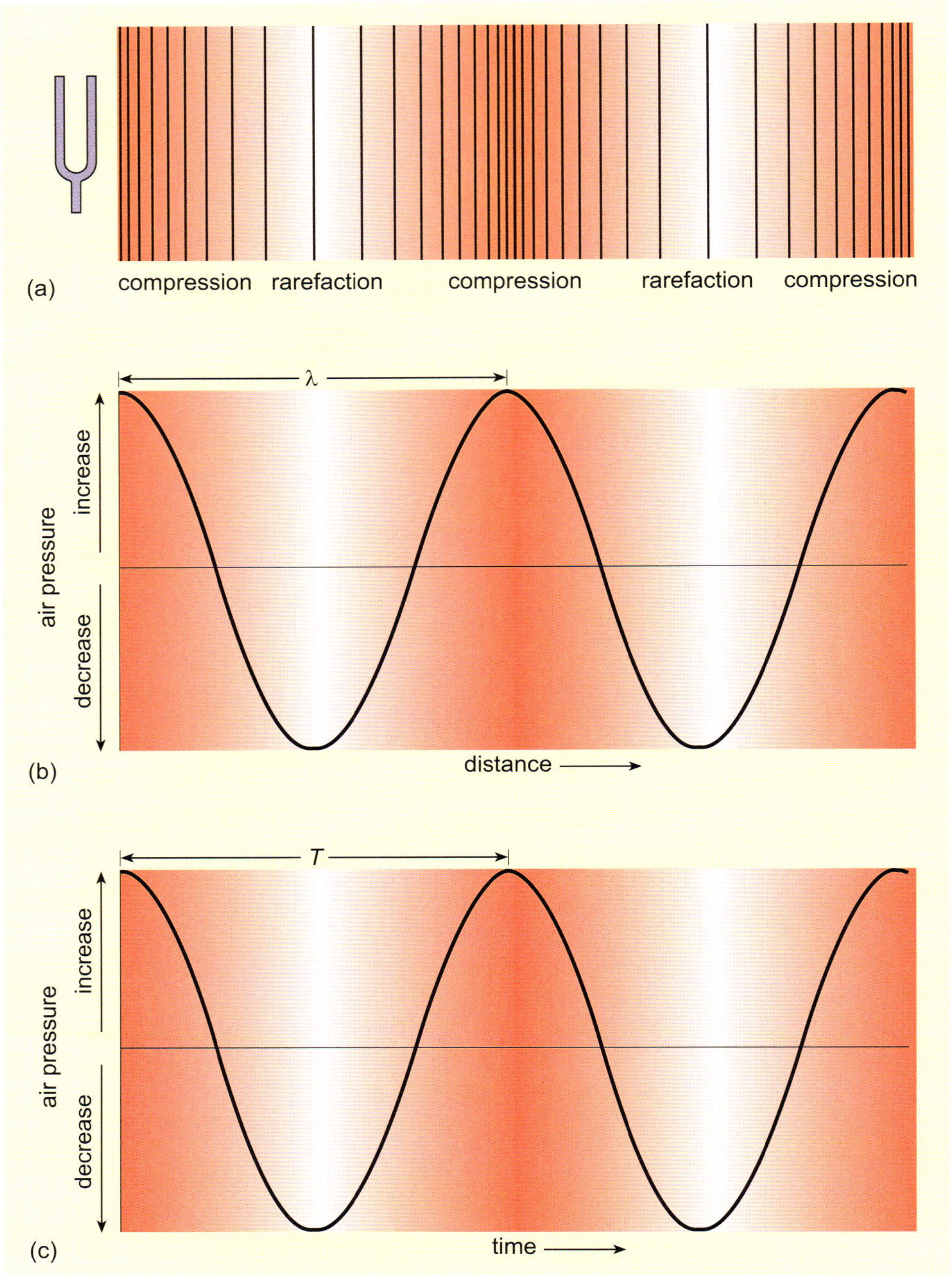

Figure 2.1 (a) Vibrations of a tuning fork produce compression and rarefaction in local air pressure. (b) A plot of the change in pressure (from atmospheric pressure) versus distance at a given time. (c) A plot of the change in pressure versus time at a particular location.

Having revisited the way in which sound waves can arise through the vibration of air particles resulting from the movement of an object, we can look at the characteristics of sound waves. There are three important aspects to consider: frequency, phase and amplitude.

2.1.1 Frequency

In Block 1 Box 2.1 you learned how wavelength, frequency and period are related.

■ Use Figure 2.2 to estimate these three quantities for the sound wave shown. The speed of sound in air can be taken as 343 m s^{-1}.

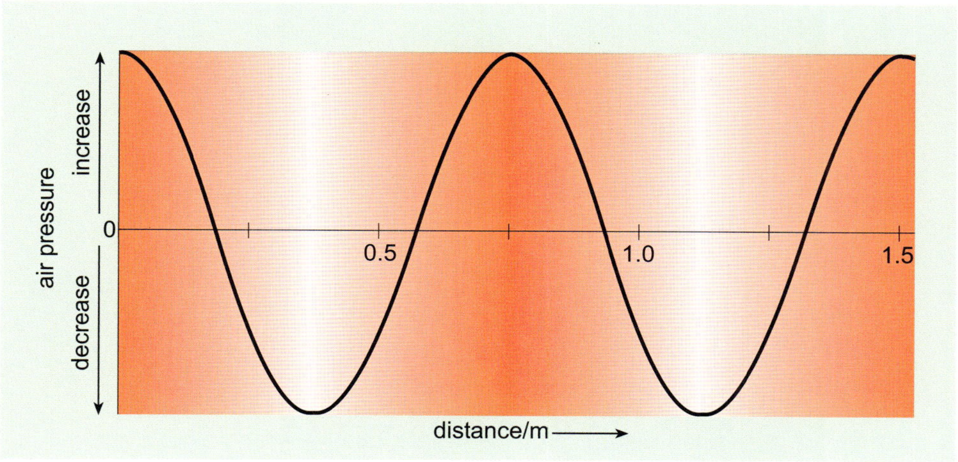

Figure 2.2 Plot of the change in pressure (from atmospheric pressure) versus distance at a given time for a pure sound wave.

□ The wavelength is 0.75 m. You can read this from the graph as the distance between two peaks or two troughs. The frequency, *f*, in hertz (Hz), can be calculated from the following equation, which you met in Block 1 (Equation 2.3):

$$f = \frac{c}{\lambda}$$

So the frequency is 343 m s^{-1}/0.75 m = 457 Hz.

The period is equal to 1/frequency and therefore is 1/457 Hz = 0.0022 seconds, or 2.2 ms.

Sound waves do not tend to be characterised or distinguished between by their wavelength. Rather, they are often characterised and differentiated according to their frequency. This is the rate at which peaks (or troughs) pass a given point. Figure 2.3 shows how a change in frequency affects the appearance of a waveform plotted against time. The period is longer in the bottom trace compared with the top one, so the bottom trace has a lower frequency (i.e. fewer cycles per second) than the top one.

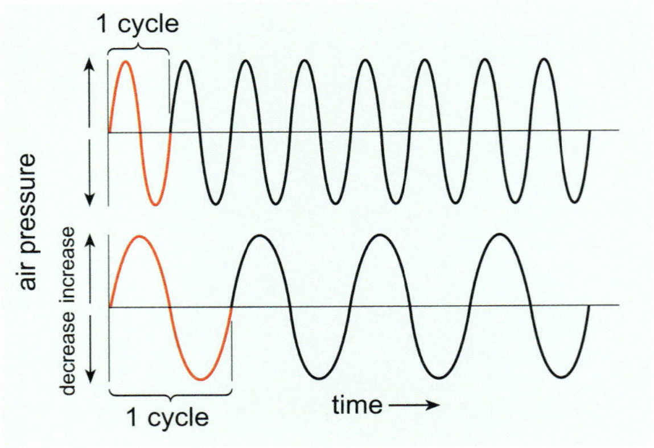

Figure 2.3 Two sound waves of different frequency.

■ Recall from Block 1 Chapter 2 how frequency relates to the pitch of the sound we perceive.

□ Normally, high-frequency sounds are perceived as having a high pitch while low-frequency sounds are perceived as having a low pitch. However, this relationship is not a simple one, as you will learn in Chapter 5.

The range of human hearing is normally from about 20 Hz to 20 000 Hz (or 20 kHz) in young people, but the top of the range decreases with increasing age. Sounds with frequencies below 20 Hz are known as infrasonic, and those with frequencies above 20 kHz are ultrasonic. There are many natural sounds that are classed as ultrasonic or infrasonic, such as the communication signals of dolphins and bats, which therefore cannot be heard by humans. To give you a musical context, the note called middle C on a piano has a pitch corresponding to a frequency of 262 Hz. Similarly, the highest note a female singer is capable of reaching has a pitch corresponding to a frequency of about 1000 Hz and the lowest note a male singer can reach corresponds to a frequency of around 55 Hz.

2.1.2 Phase

Another distinguishing feature of a sound wave is shown in Figure 2.4. Both waves depicted have the same frequency and size, yet they are not identical. The difference is that the waveforms start at different points in their cycles. This is known as a difference in **phase**. In the top trace the waveform starts at the mid-point of the *y*-axis (i.e. zero difference between the air pressure near the wave and general atmospheric pressure) and decreases, while in the bottom trace it starts at zero and increases.

The quantity we use to specify differences in phase between waves is number of degrees but it could also be the number of radians: 360° is one full cycle and is equivalent to 2π radians, so the two waves in Figure 2.4 are 180°, or π radians, out of phase. Waves of the same phase are said to be 'in phase'.

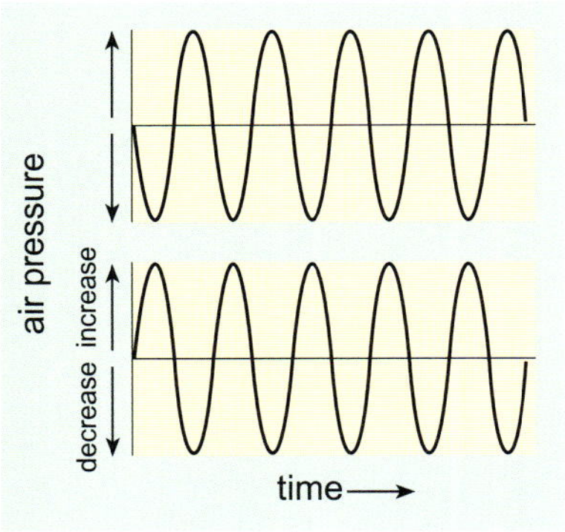

Figure 2.4 Two sinusoidal waves of different phase.

Study note

If you are not familiar with radians and degrees, and the relationship between them, please refer to the *Study Companion*.

- ■ If two sound waves differ in phase by 360°, are they in phase or out of phase?
- □ They are in phase because the peaks and troughs still occur at the same point even though they are one full cycle apart.

Unlike the frequency of a sound wave, phase does not directly relate to a particular perceptual feature such as pitch. However, phase information is important in sound localisation, which is discussed in Chapter 4.

2.1.3 Amplitude and intensity

Another characteristic of sound waves that may be used to compare them is how big they are – their amplitude. The two waves in Figure 2.5 have the same frequency and are in phase with each other but look different. The lower wave has greater amplitude than the upper one. The difference in amplitude between two waves can be quantified by measuring and comparing the height of the peaks.

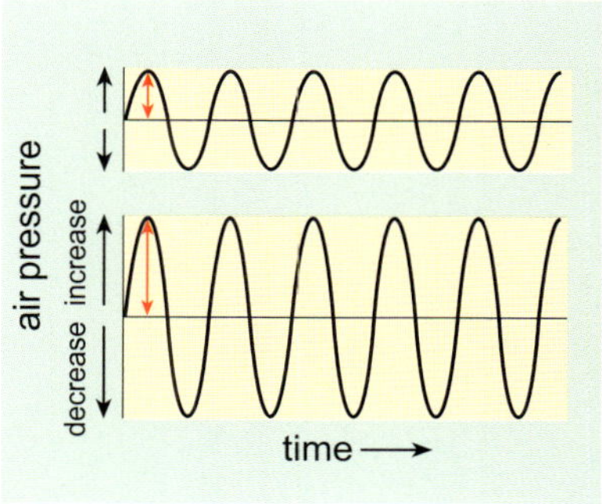

Figure 2.5 Two sound waves of different amplitude, as indicated by the red arrows.

Differences in amplitude of auditory signals arise from the amount of displacement of the vibrating object. So, the amplitude of a sound wave produced by a tuning fork depends on the amplitude of the vibrations of the prongs. This, in turn, is determined by the force with which the prongs are 'twanged': the more force used, the greater the vibrations of the prongs and the greater the amplitude of the wave produced.

The amplitude of a sound wave is a major determinant of how loud or soft we perceive a sound to be. Furthermore, measuring the quietest sound we are able to hear may also be useful in determining the presence of a hearing impairment, so it is a very useful property to understand. Therefore, we now spend a little time considering the different ways information relating to amplitude can be measured and handled.

Measuring amplitude and intensity

The amplitude of a sound wave is expressed in terms of pressure, for which the SI unit is the pascal (Pa). It is measured relative to atmospheric pressure, and is often so small that the micropascal (μPa) is used. Although the majority of medical instruments used to test hearing record pressure measurements, and therefore measure amplitude, it is more common to talk about sound intensity when describing how loud something is, for which the SI unit is watts per unit area (typically, $W\ m^{-2}$).

Study note

If you are not familiar with these SI units and prefixes, please refer to the *Study Companion*.

However, for any wave, intensity and amplitude are related such that the intensity is directly proportional to the amplitude squared:

$$I \propto P^2 \qquad \text{(Eqn 2.1)}$$

where I is the intensity measured in watts per unit area, and P is the pressure or amplitude relative to atmospheric pressure, measured in pascal.

Our auditory system operates over an enormous range of intensity. If we were to assign 1 unit of intensity to the smallest value that can be detected by the human ear, then the loudest sound that we could tolerate is 100 000 000 000 000 (10^{14}) units.

- ■ What is the term used to describe the range of intensities over which a sensory system may respond?
- □ It is the 'dynamic range' of the system.

The dynamic range of our auditory system is so large that it becomes impossible to work with in practical situations (imagine trying to plot a graph from 1 to 10^{14} in ten-unit steps!). Scientists have attempted to overcome this problem by describing intensities relative to one another. To understand how this is done, we need to introduce another unit that is used to measure intensity – the bel, or more commonly, the decibel (dB, one-tenth of a bel). The decibel is the logarithm of the ratio of two intensities I_1 and I_2.

Study note

If you are not familiar with how to use logarithms, please refer to the *Study Companion*. Note that if you have not used logarithms before you should first read through this section in the companion with the aim of understanding the basic principles, rather than trying to grasp the detail of the calculations and formulae.

The ratio of two intensities expressed in decibels is:

$$\text{dB} = 10 \log_{10} (I_1/I_2) \qquad \text{(Eqn 2.2)}$$

where intensity I_1 is being compared with intensity I_2. If I_1 is larger than I_2 then the ratio in dB is positive; if I_1 is smaller than I_2 then the ratio is negative (because the log of a number less than 1 is negative). From now on, since we are only concerned with logs to the base 10 in this block, we shall drop the subscript 10. So if I_1 is equal to 10^{14} (i.e. the top of our dynamic range) and I_2 is equal to 1 (the bottom of the range), then:

$$\begin{aligned} 10\log(10^{14}/1) &= 10\log 10^{14} \\ &= 10 \times 14 \\ &= 140\,\text{dB} \end{aligned}$$

The dynamic range of the auditory system can now be expressed in terms of decibels, yielding a much more convenient array of numbers to work with. The original interval scale of intensities ranging from 1 to 10^{14} has been reduced to a new interval scale of 0–140 dB by transforming intensity units into dB using logarithms.

Sometimes, as already mentioned in the case of instruments used to test hearing, measurements are made of the amplitude (that is the change in pressure, P), rather than the intensity of a sound. However, these measurements can still be expressed in dB because $I \propto P^2$. Therefore, it follows that:

$$\begin{aligned} \text{relative intensity in dB} &= 10\log(I_1/I_2) \\ &= 10\log(P_1/P_2)^2 \\ &= 20\log(P_1/P_2) \qquad \text{(Eqn 2.3)} \end{aligned}$$

Setting standards for comparison

It is important to remember that the decibel is the ratio of two quantities. This means that saying something has an intensity or amplitude of 60 dB is meaningless without additional information. This statement does not indicate whether the intensity is 60 dB above the most intense sound you can tolerate, 60 dB below the lowest sound you can hear, 60 dB above the sound that your friend can hear, or anything else.

When talking about the level of a sound we therefore need a **reference pressure (P_0)** or **reference intensity (I_0)**. The hypothetical reference intensity used in the example above was 1 unit of intensity. The reference intensity commonly used in the study of acoustics is 10^{-12} W m^{-2}, which is the lowest intensity of a 1000 Hz tone that an average young adult can detect, and corresponds to a pressure of 20 μPa. When decibels are expressed relative to this reference pressure, they are described in terms of sound pressure level (SPL). Hence a sound of 60 dB SPL is 60 dB above the reference level of 20 μPa. When decibels are expressed relative to 10^{-12} W m^{-2} they are described in terms of intensity level. Thus, 'level' refers to a dB measure. Table 2.1 gives some typical values of sound intensity level in dB SPL.

Table 2.1 Intensity levels for some familiar sounds.

Sound	Intensity/dB SPL
Jet at take-off (generally above the pain threshold)	140
Loud rock music	120
Gunshot	100
Door slamming	80
Normal conversation	60
Muffled conversation	40
Soft whisper at 1.5 m from source	30
Virtual silence	10
Threshold of hearing	0

■ If the pressure level of a sound is 20 μPa (which is also the standard reference pressure used in acoustics), calculate its intensity level in dB SPL. (*Hint*: you may need to refer back to Equation 2.3.)

□ As shown in Equation 2.3, the relative intensity in dB is calculated as 20 log (P_1/P_2). In this example, the pressure level of the sound is 20 μPa (i.e. P_1), and the comparison pressure is also 20 μPa (P_2), as that is the standard reference pressure, so:

$$\begin{aligned}\text{relative intensity in dB SPL} &= 20\ \log(20/20)\\ &= 20\ \log 1\\ &= 20 \times 0\\ &= 0\end{aligned}$$

In other words, 20 μPa (or 10^{-12} W m^{-2}) corresponds to an SPL of 0 dB and the threshold of hearing shown in Table 2.1.

You should note that doubling the amplitude of a sound does not double its sound pressure level but increases it by 6 dB. So, if we have a sound with an SPL of 20 dB and we double its amplitude, the sound pressure level does not double to 40 dB. Rather, the SPL increases from 20 to 26 dB, as follows.

If the pressure level of a sound is 200 μPa, then:

$$\begin{aligned}\text{dB SPL} &= 20\ \log(200/20)\\ &= 20\ \log 10\\ &= 20 \times 1\\ &= 20\end{aligned}$$

If the pressure level of the sound is doubled to 400 μPa, then:

$$\begin{aligned} \text{dB SPL} &= 20 \log(400/20) \\ &= 20 \log 20 \\ &= 20 \times 1.3 \\ &= 26 \end{aligned}$$

We have already mentioned that a wave's amplitude is a major determinant of perceived loudness. However, as you will see in Chapter 5, factors such as frequency also affect our experience of loudness. For now, having looked at simple waves, the next section considers how these are relevant and useful in the study of complex sounds.

2.2 Intermediate chapter summary

- Sound is a longitudinal pressure wave that is produced by the motion or vibration of an object.
- Pure tones are composed of single sinusoidal waves and can be characterised or compared by their wavelength but more commonly by their frequency, amplitude and phase.
- Pure tones are commonly used in laboratories investigating sound and hearing, but the reality is that these sounds are almost unnaturally simple in comparison with commonly encountered sounds in real life.
- The intensity of a sound is proportional to the square of its amplitude (pressure change). The decibel scale is used to describe the relative amplitude or intensity of a sound. Sound levels are usually compared with the threshold of hearing of the normal ear and the amplitude is measured in decibels relative to a standard sound pressure level (dB SPL).

2.3 From simple waves to real, complex sounds

As stated at the start of this chapter, while our environment contains mostly complex sounds, our auditory system largely works with simple sound waves, and therefore it is useful to understand how these differ from and relate to each other. We therefore begin this section by outlining how real, complex sounds differ from 'theoretical' pure sound waves. In fact, they differ in two key ways:

- The waveforms of 'real' sounds are more complex than pure ones, as the sound is rarely a sinusoidal wave at one single frequency.
- The amplitude of the sound reduces with time or with distance from the source; a property referred to as 'attenuation'.

Each of these ideas is discussed in the sections that follow.

2.3.1 Complex waveforms

Look closely at the different waveforms in Figure 2.6.

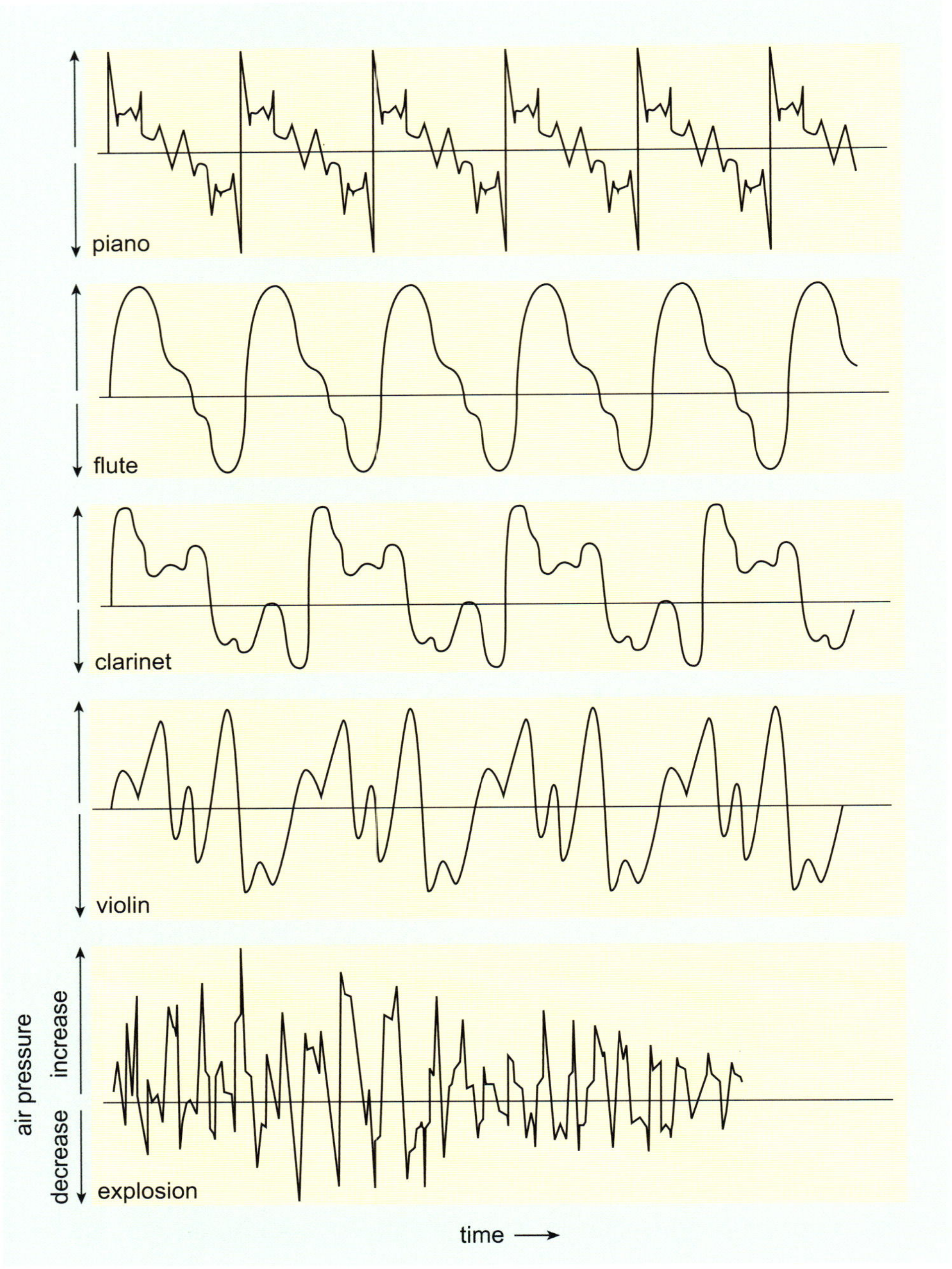

Figure 2.6 The sound waves produced by various sources.

- ■ The musical instruments all produce the same continuous single note. What do you notice about these waveforms?
- □ The first thing you probably notice is that, although the instruments are all playing the same musical note, the waveforms are very different. They are clearly not the simple sinusoidal waveforms that you saw in Section 2.1.
- ■ How is the waveform from the explosion different from all the others?
- □ All the other waveforms repeat at regular intervals because they are playing the same basic note, and as such producing vibrations at the same frequency. By contrast, the explosion waveform is not regularly repeating, meaning that the sound source is not vibrating regularly.

We focus on the regularly repeating, or **periodic**, waveforms from the musical instruments. Their complicated shapes result from the addition of different frequencies that are related to the basic note they are all playing.
To see how this can come about, you need to understand a type of wave called a **standing wave**, which is described in Box 2.1.

Box 2.1 Standing waves

The type of wave considered in Block 1 and at the start of this chapter is known as a **travelling wave**, because its energy is transferred from one place to another. However, waves that are confined in some way are termed standing waves, and need to be considered in different terms.

Consider a wave travelling along a string, like one produced by wiggling one end of a skipping rope in a periodic fashion. If the other end of the string is free then the wave simply travels in one direction, but if the other is fixed then the wave is reflected back along the string. So now there are two travelling waves, of the same frequency and wavelength, moving in opposite directions along the string.

At any one point along the string, according to the superposition of waves (see Activity 2.1 in Block 1), the resultant displacement of the string is the sum of the two displacements. For example, Figure 2.7a shows the two waves (the red and blue lines) travelling in opposite directions along a string, and Figures 2.7b–d show the resultant displacement of these waves (the purple line) at times t_1–t_3.

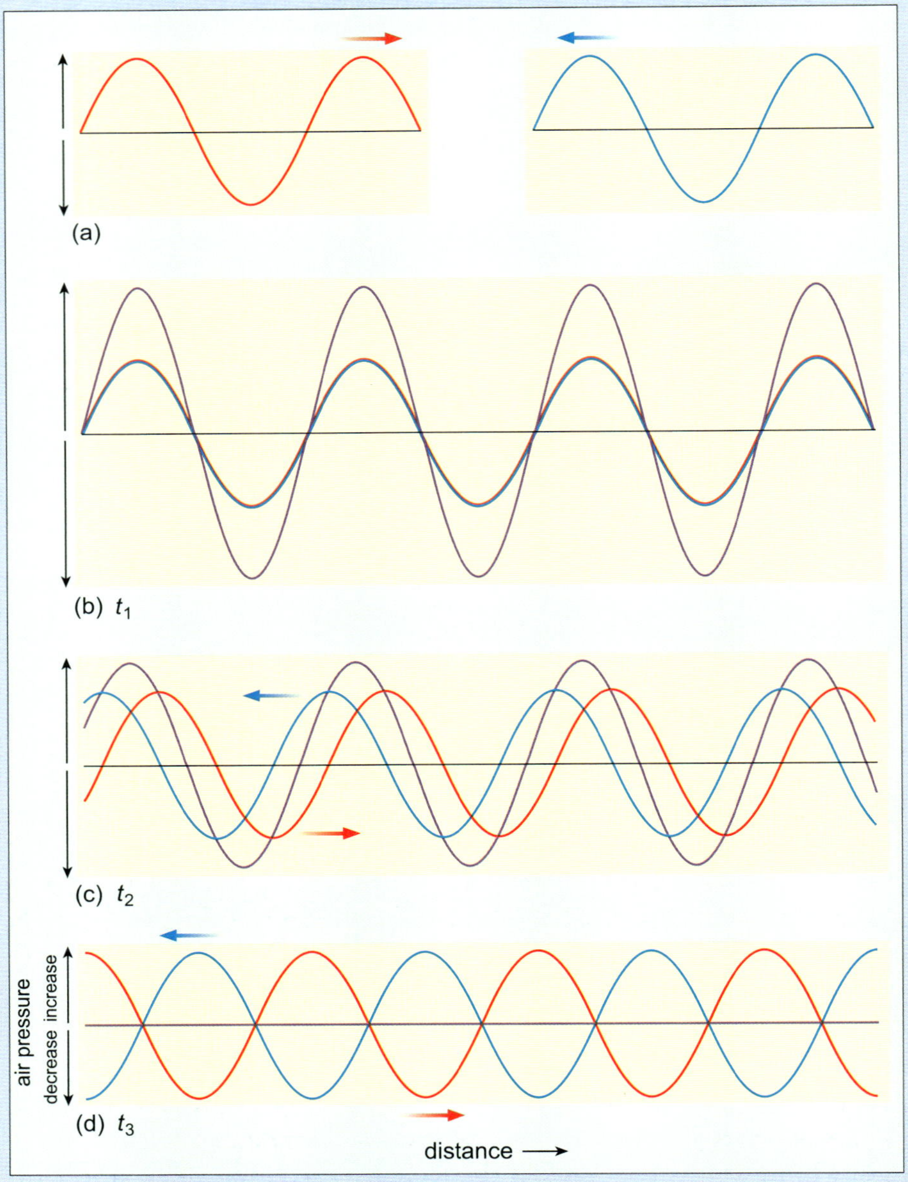

Figure 2.7 (a) Identical travelling waves (red and blue), travelling in opposite directions along a string. (b)–(d) The positions of the waves and their superposition (purple) at times t_1–t_3.

If you were to continue to plot the displacement at subsequent times, you would obtain the repeating cycle shown in Figure 2.8 (after t_5, the cycle would continue). This is a standing wave; there are fixed positions along the waveform where the displacement is zero. These positions are called nodes. The points in between where the wave's amplitude reaches a maximum are known as anti-nodes.

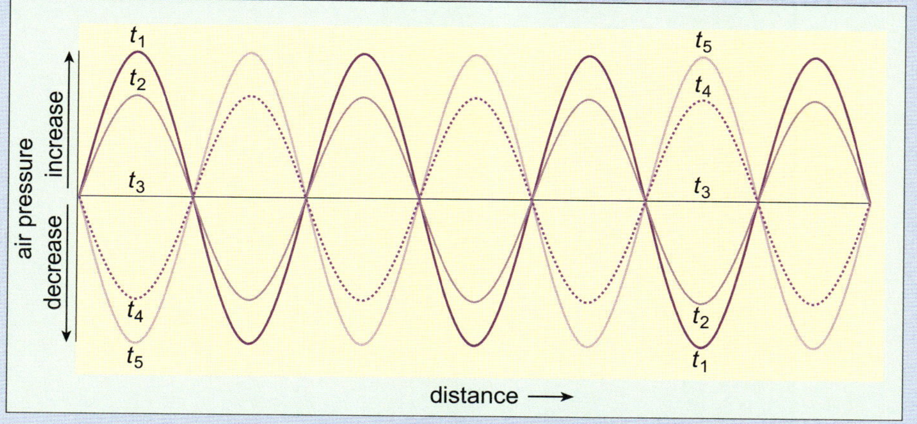

Figure 2.8 Variation in wave displacement for times t_1–t_5.

■ All standing waves have a well-defined wavelength. How many wavelengths are shown in Figure 2.8?

□ The wavelength of a standing wave is twice the distance between adjacent nodes (or anti-nodes), so there are 3½ wavelengths shown in the figure.

Standing waves occur when some special requirements are placed on the wave. These are known as boundary conditions. A good example is the case of the sound wave produced by a violin or other string instrument. In that case, one boundary condition is that the ends of the string, because they are fixed, must be nodes. The other boundary condition is that any point where the string is plucked, or drawn by the bow, must be an anti-node.

Imagine a violin or guitar string that is plucked in the middle (Figure 2.9a). This action sets up a standing wave on the string (Figure 2.9b). The ends of the string are fixed, so according to the boundary conditions defined in Box 2.1 they must be nodes, while the middle is plucked, and so must be an anti-node. Given the wavelength (λ) is twice the distance between adjacent nodes, this produces a standing wave with a wavelength equal to twice the length of the string. The resulting sound is the basic note that the instrument is playing, and is known as the **fundamental frequency**.

Considering the boundary condition explained above, the standing waves shown in Figures 2.9d and 2.9f are also possible if the string is plucked in the middle because they contain an anti-node in the middle of the string and nodes at either end. By contrast, the standing waves shown in Figures 2.9c and 2.9e have a node at the central point and therefore could not be produced if the string is plucked in the middle.

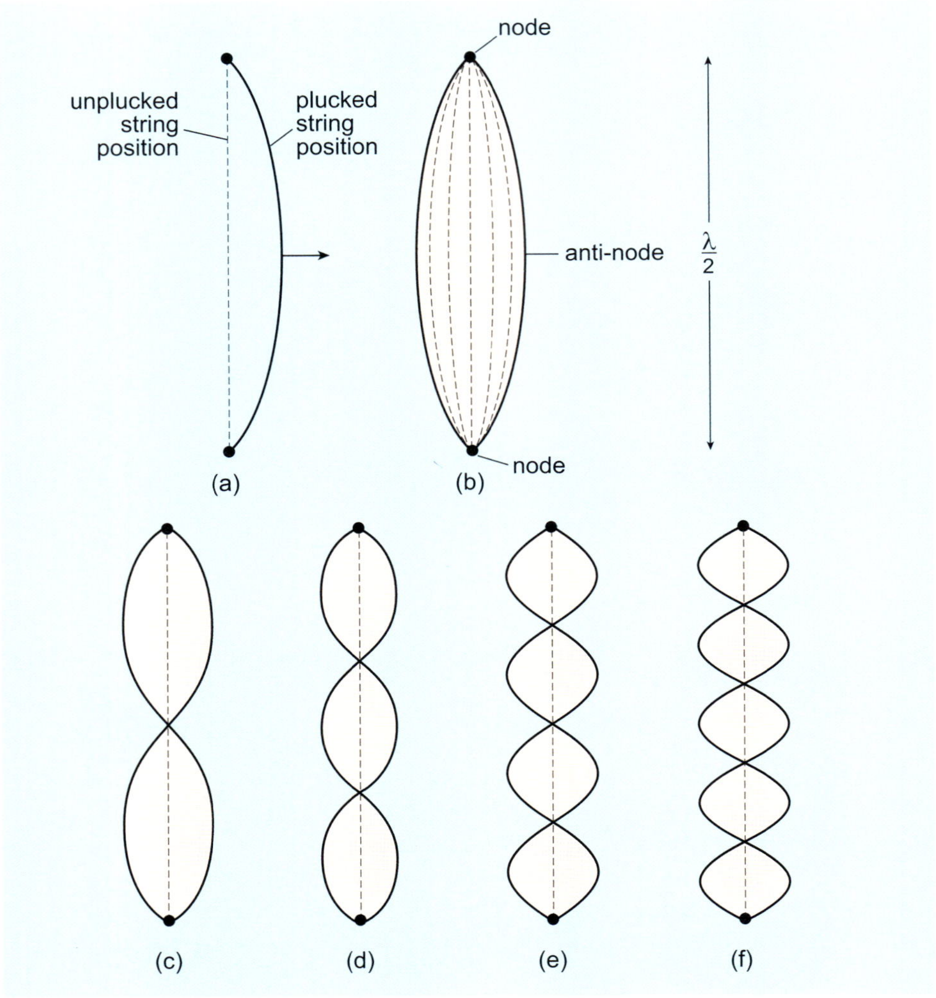

Figure 2.9 A string plucked in the centre (a) gives rise to a standing wave (b) with a node at both ends and an anti-node in the middle. Figures (c)–(f) show some other possible standing waves in a string.

- ■ If the length of the string is L, the wavelength of the standing wave shown in Figure 2.9b is $2L$. How do the wavelengths of the standing waves in 2.9d and 2.9f relate to the length of the string?

- □ In Figure 2.9d the wavelength is 2/3 of the length of the string, or $2L/3$; in Figure 2.9f the wavelength is $2L/5$.

So the notes produced by plucking the middle of the violin string (Figures 2.9b, 2.9d and 2.9f) have wavelengths in the ratio 1 : 1/3 : 1/5 and, since frequency is proportional to 1/wavelength, the notes' frequencies are in the ratio 1 : 3 : 5. The shorter wavelength notes are higher multiples of the fundamental frequency. These higher notes are known as **harmonics**.

All harmonics have frequencies that are multiples of the fundamental frequency. However, the amplitude of the higher harmonics tends to be less than that of the fundamental frequency. The harmonics that are not produced by plucking the violin string in the middle (e.g. Figures 2.9c and 2.9e) are those with frequencies that are two or four times the fundamental frequency (and so on).

2.3.2 Combining fundamental and harmonic frequencies

The sound wave produced by an instrument is the sum of the fundamental frequency and the different harmonics that are produced. Different instruments produce different harmonics, and therefore give rise to the distinctive waveforms shown in Figure 2.6.

If the frequencies of the sound waves are related to each other by a simple ratio, for example 2 : 3 or 2 : 4, the combined sound will be different from the sound of the fundamental frequency alone but still be pleasant. By contrast, if the frequencies are not related by a simple ratio, the effects can be quite discordant.

Figure 2.10 shows how waves of two different frequencies and amplitudes can be added together to give an overall waveform.

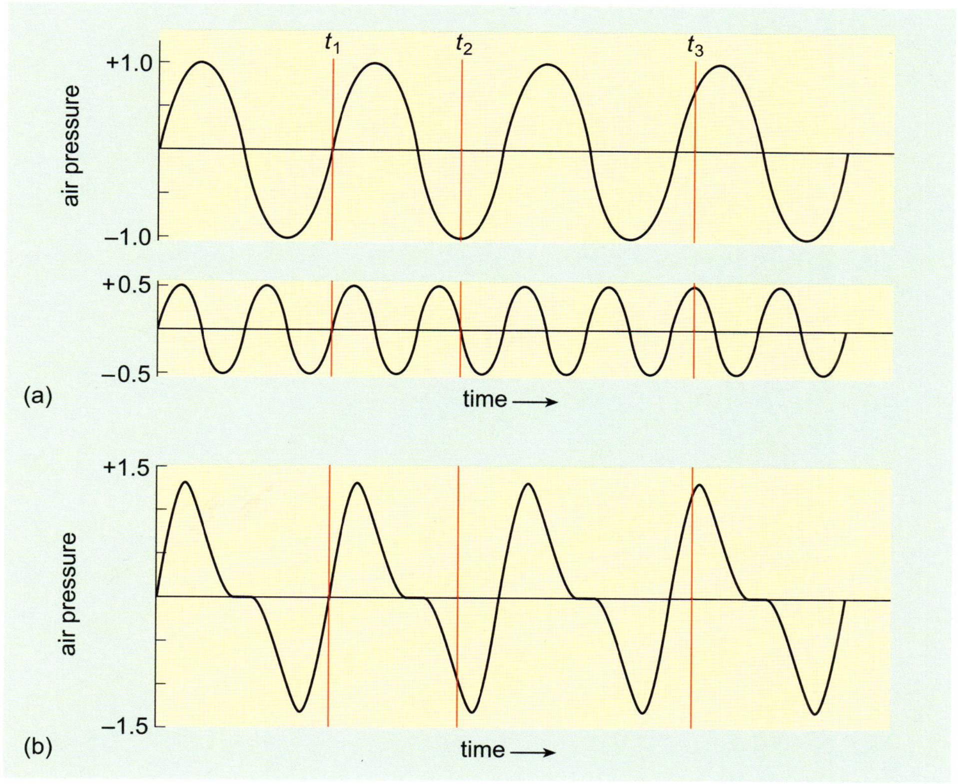

Figure 2.10 (a) Two waveforms, one with an amplitude twice that of the other but half the frequency; (b) the resultant superposition of these waves.

In Figure 2.10a, the amplitude of the lower frequency wave, shown at the top of the panel, is twice that of the higher frequency wave at the bottom of the panel, as might be found for a fundamental frequency and its harmonic frequency, respectively. At any point in time we can measure the pressure due to each of the waves from the graph. So, at time t_1 in the figure, both waveforms have a pressure value of 0. Therefore, if the two waves are added together at time t_1, the value of their sum is 0. At time t_2, the value of the upper wave is –1 and that of the lower is 0. So, if they are added together at this point in time, the overall pressure would be $-1 + 0 = -1$.

- ■ What would the value of the resultant wave be at time t_3?
- □ At time t_3 the value of the upper wave is 0.7 and the value of the lower wave is 0.5, so by adding them together we get $0.7 + 0.5 = 1.2$.

Figure 2.10b therefore shows that the addition of just two simple sound waves can generate a complex waveform. If this process continues with many waves being added together, waveforms such as the sawtooth wave may be produced. This wave can be generated by adding together a number of simple sound waves corresponding to the fundamental frequency and its harmonic frequencies, as shown in Figure 2.11. In this case, the fundamental frequency is 100 Hz and the harmonics would be multiples of this (e.g. 200 Hz, 300 Hz, 400 Hz, and so on). If this process was taken to the *n*th degree by adding an infinite number of harmonics, the waveform shown at the bottom of the figure would be produced.

Thus, complex sounds within our environment are made up of a number of different waves added together. However, as well as adding waves together, it is also possible to decompose a complex wave into its component simple waves. This decomposition is highly relevant to hearing because it is suggested that the cochlea itself carries out such a process, albeit one that may be limited, especially at higher frequencies.

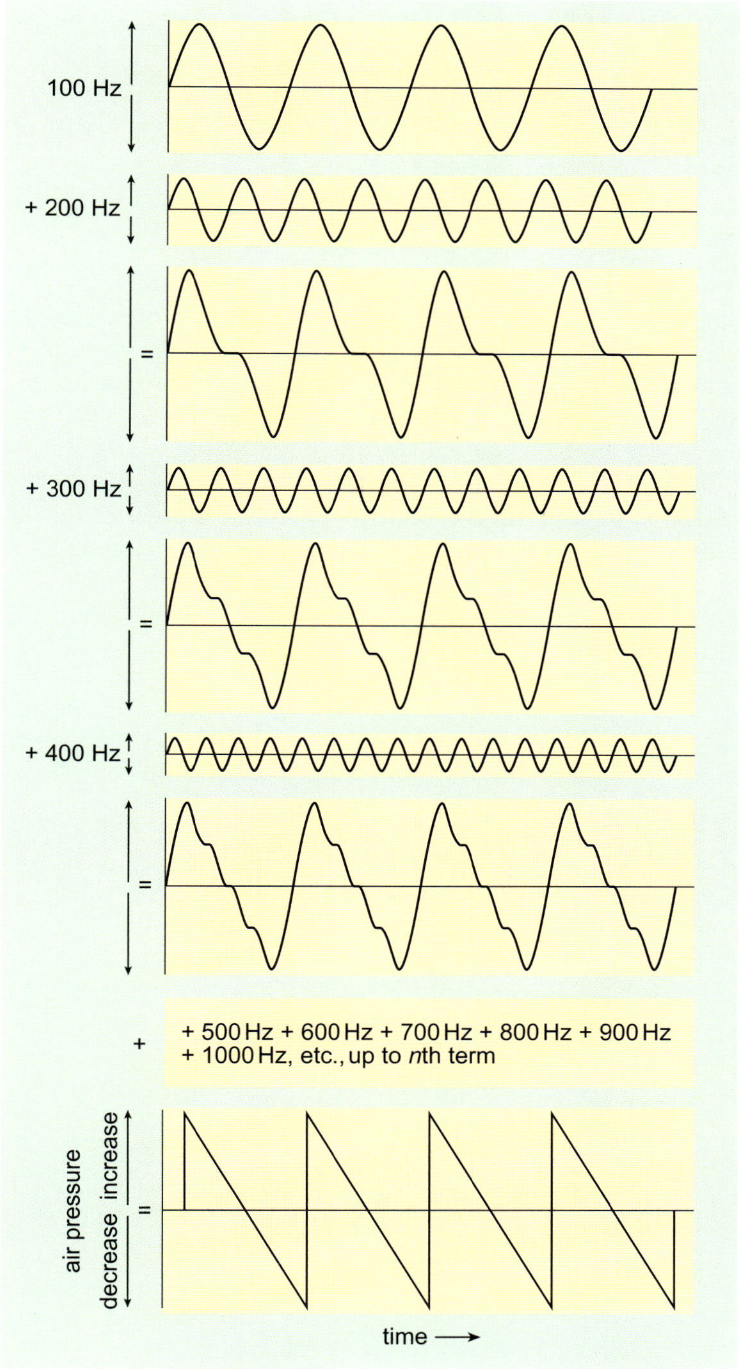

Figure 2.11 The synthesis of a sawtooth wave. The bottom trace shows the waveform after the addition of an infinite number of harmonic frequencies to the fundamental frequency.

2.3.3 Deconstructing complex waveforms

The process of breaking down a waveform into its component frequencies is known as **Fourier analysis**, after its inventor Joseph Fourier (see Box 2.2). Indeed, the constituent frequencies are referred to as the **Fourier spectrum** (or frequency spectrum). This spectrum can be displayed graphically with the amplitude of each component represented on the vertical axis and frequency on the horizontal axis.

Figure 2.12 shows this sort of graphical representation for a periodic waveform such as the sawtooth wave shown in Figure 2.11. A vertical line is drawn at the frequencies where a component wave is present in the overall signal, with the height of the line proportional to the amplitude of that wave. In this case, because the complex wave is periodic, the only frequencies present are multiples of the fundamental and so the graph displays a series of 'spikes' that reduce in amplitude with increasing frequency, as is expected with increasing harmonic number. The component sinusoidal waves for the mathematical series of a periodic waveform is known as a **Fourier series**. However, if it is an aperiodic (i.e. non-repeating) waveform, such as the explosion in Figure 2.6, the equivalent series is a continuous function referred to as a **Fourier transform**.

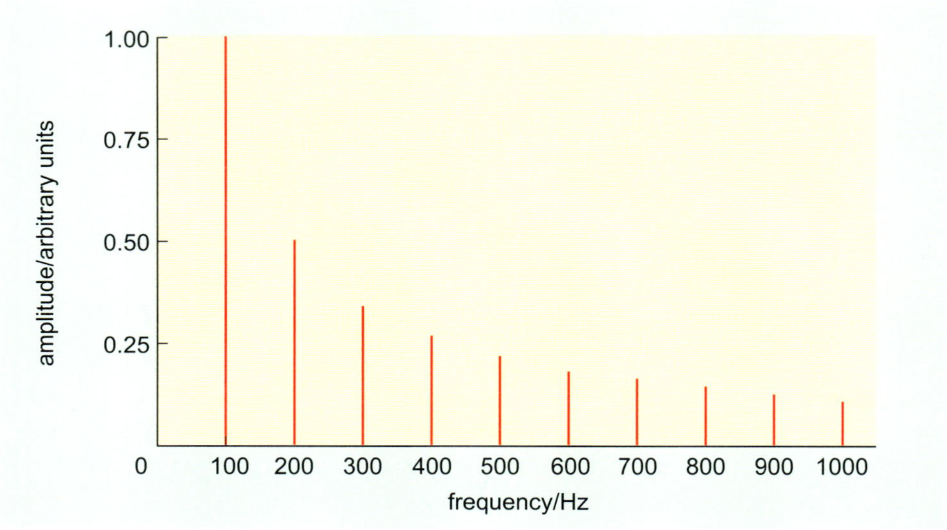

Figure 2.12 The first ten component waves of a sawtooth wave.

Fourier analysis is also important in vision but in a rather different way, as you will learn in Block 5. For now, however, you should complete Activity 2.1 to help consolidate your understanding of the ideas discussed in this section.

Box 2.2 Joseph Fourier

Baron Jean-Baptiste-Joseph Fourier (Figure 2.13) was born in Auxerre, France. As well as becoming highly educated in mathematics, he became involved with the military and through this he came to accompany the Emperor of France, Napoleon Bonaparte, on his Egyptian expedition in 1798. Fourier showed such aptitude for various administrative duties that he was often tasked with political and diplomatic assignments, which he completed with success. Throughout this period he was also contributing mathematical papers to the scientific community.

Figure 2.13 The mathematician and military diplomat Joseph Fourier.

When Britain gained power over Egypt in 1801, Fourier returned to his former position as a Professor of Analysis in Paris. Despite Napoleon bestowing more official duties upon him shortly after his return, by 1807 Fourier had written his theory of heat conduction, which depended on the essential idea of analysing the temperature distribution into spatially sinusoidal components. He put forward the idea that any function can be thought of as a mixture of different frequencies and, despite some opposition at the time, we now routinely refer to the mixture of frequencies in a sound as the Fourier spectrum.

When Napoleon abdicated in 1814, Fourier was placed in an awkward position because King Louis XVIII did not look favourably on old associates of the outgoing Emperor. However, Fourier managed to survive further changes of regime before he entered a full-time life of science and scientific administration. He died, following repeated heart problems, in 1830.

(Adapted from Bracewell, 1986, pp. 462–4)

Activity 2.1 Complex waves and Fourier analysis

Allow 20 minutes

(*Relevant module learning outcomes: KU1 and PS1*)

Now would be a good time to complete this activity, which is available from the *Block 4 Activities* resource on the module website. The activity allows you to examine the composition of complex waveforms, and further illustrates the concept of a Fourier analysis.

Now that the idea of a Fourier spectrum has been introduced, you should read Box 2.3, which outlines a number of types of filter that can be used to affect the Fourier spectrum.

Box 2.3 Filters and the Fourier spectrum

The use of filters is very common: they turn up in sound and vision as well as in other fields such as electronics and communications. The idea of a filter is to remove some of the frequencies in a signal and allow others to pass through. Unsurprisingly, this affects the Fourier spectrum.

There are four important classes of filter, and they are described below and illustrated in Figure 2.14. In each case in the diagram, plot (i) represents the unfiltered Fourier spectrum and plot (ii) is the spectrum that results once the filter (the dashed line) has been applied. However, in practice, filters are rarely perfect, and the solid red line indicates the range of frequencies that might typically pass through such filters.

- A low-pass filter (Figure 2.14a) allows low frequencies through, as its name suggests, but rejects high frequencies.
- A high-pass filter (Figure 2.14b) does the opposite to a low-pass filter: high frequencies are retained and low ones are lost.
- A band-pass filter (Figure 2.14c) allows a limited range (or band) of frequencies through. This range depends on the lower and upper limits of the band. Band-pass filters are very relevant to hearing, as they may be used in hearing aids.
- A notch or band-stop filter (Figure 2.14d) is the opposite of a band-pass filter: it cuts off frequencies in a certain range and allows the frequencies above and below the band to pass through. (Excessive levels of music are thought to impair the function of the ear such that it acts like a band-stop filter with a central frequency of around 2 kHz.)

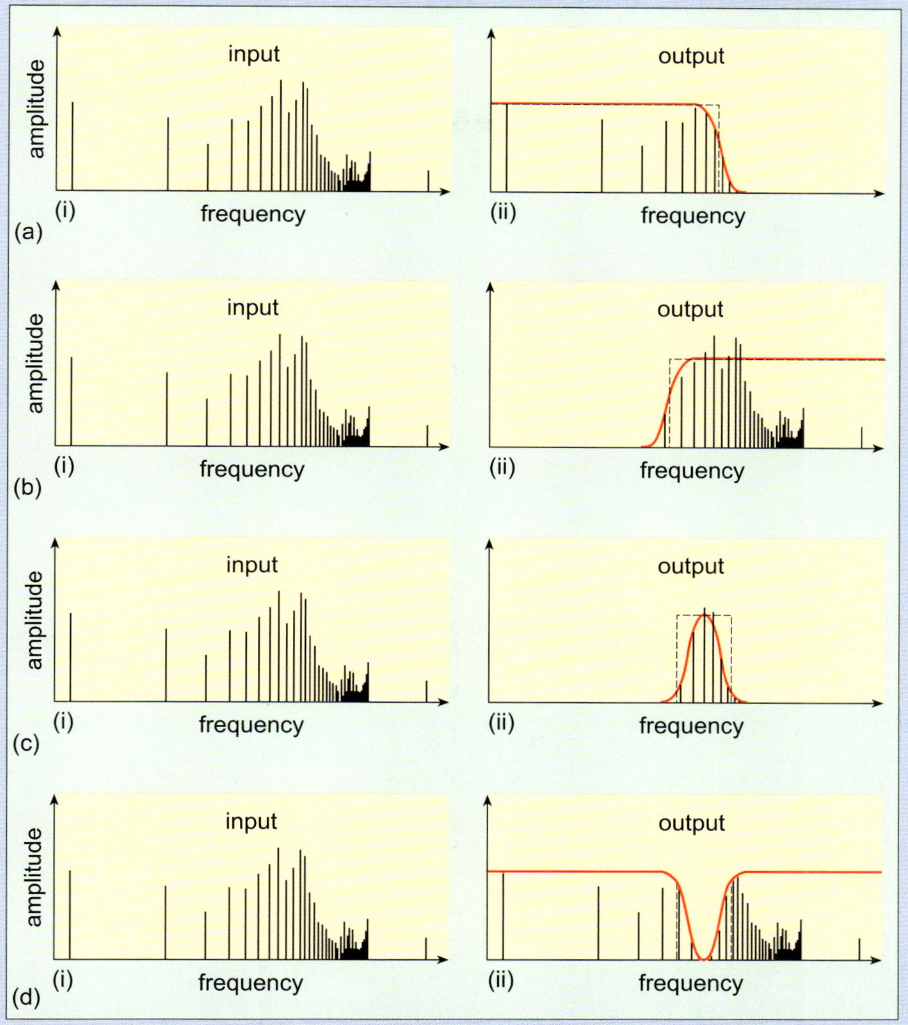

Figure 2.14 The effect of applying different classes of filter to a Fourier spectrum: (a) low-pass; (b) high-pass; (c) band-pass; (d) notch, or band-stop. The dashed line represents the boundaries of the filter and the solid red line the range of frequencies that might actually pass through it.

2.3.4 Reduction in intensity

As stated at the start of this section, real, complex sounds typically show attenuation (a reduction in intensity over time). Sounds reduce in intensity as the vibrational energy in the source dissipates. This fact is evident in the notes produced by many musical instruments, for example when a drummer hits the drum and then removes the drum stick, or the pianist takes their hand off the key and the string inside the piano gradually stops vibrating.

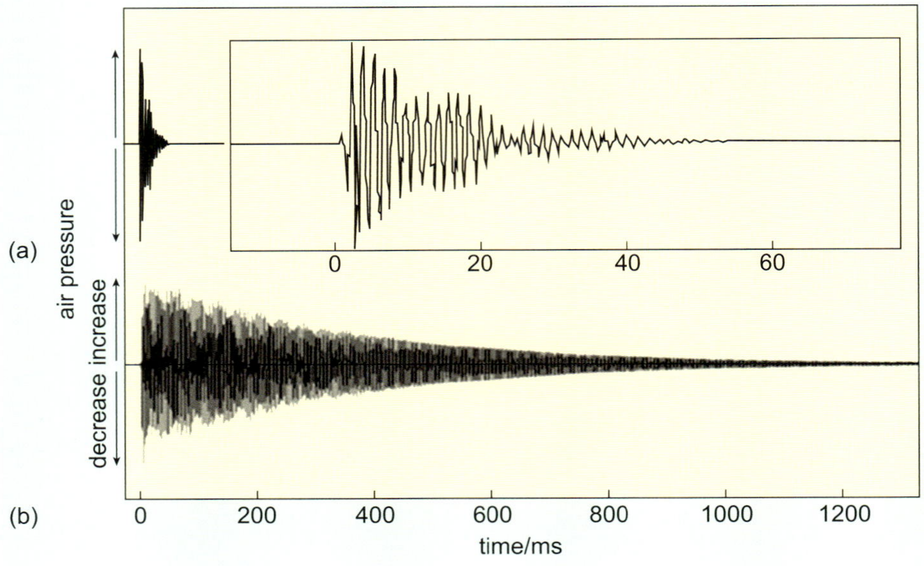

Figure 2.15 Example of (a) a rapidly decaying sound from a castanet (enlarged in inset) and (b) a slowly decaying sound from a glockenspiel.

The way in which sounds reduce in intensity varies enormously, with some sounds finishing almost as soon as they have begun and others carrying on for much longer. This idea is clearly displayed in Figure 2.15, which plots the decay of the sound from a castanet, which tends towards no change in air pressure in around 50 ms, and a glockenspiel, which attenuates towards zero displacement much more gradually in more than 1200 ms.

Another situation in which sound intensity decreases is when the distance between the sound source and the observer increases. Sound spreads out from the source so that there is less intensity per unit area at greater distances. Figure 2.16 shows an example of a piper playing the bagpipes in the open air, so the sound waves travel uniformly outwards in all directions. Because the area of a sphere increases with r^2, where r is the radius, the intensity of the sound reduces as r^2 increases. This means that increasing the distance by a factor of two decreases the intensity of the sound by a factor of four.

In reality, this decrease in intensity with $1/r^2$ is only true where the waves spread in all directions; for directional waves (e.g. a wave in a pipe), the reduction in intensity can be much more gradual. And if sounds did not become attenuated when the vibration of the source reduced or with distance from the source, our environment would be full of a complex din of noises.

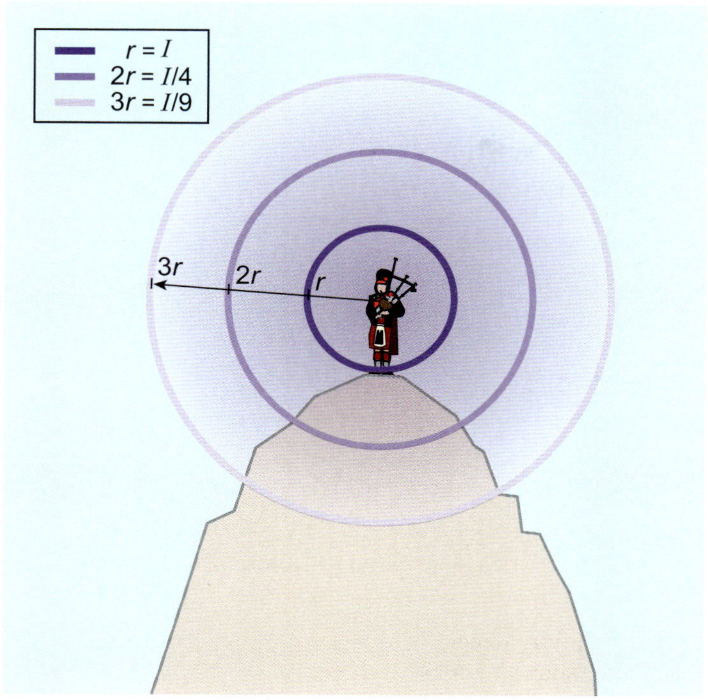

Figure 2.16 When sound waves spread out in all directions from a source, their intensity reduces in a way that is proportional to $1/\text{radius}^2$.

Activity 2.2 Intensity and distance

Allow 10 minutes

(*Relevant module learning outcomes: KU1 and PS1*)

Now would be a good time to complete this activity, which you can access from the *Block 4 Activities* resource on the module website. It provides a further example of how sounds become less intense with distance from their source.

2.4 Sound propagation in other media

This chapter has focused on sound propagation through air, but sound can also travel through various other media. The speed of a sound wave, that is to say the speed with which sound energy can be transferred from one point to another, varies between different media and depends on the density of the medium and on its ability to be deformed. This should not be confused with the speed of motion of the constituent particles in the medium, which is invariably much less than the speed of propagation of the wave.

Table 2.2 gives the speed of sound in various materials. From the data you can see that it is greater in liquids than in gases, and greater still in (most) solids. Note also that the temperature in air and water is included, as the speed is temperature-dependent.

Table 2.2 The speed of sound in different materials.

Substance	Speed of sound/m s^{-1}	Temperature/K
Air	343	293
Water	1480	293
Soft tissue	1540	–
Bone	4080	–

Study note

You first met the kelvin (K) as a unit of temperature in Block 2. There is further information about this unit in the *Study Companion*.

In the next chapter you will learn about the structure and function of the ear and how the signal moves from air to the fluids within the inner ear.

2.5 Chapter 2 summary and questions

- Real, everyday sounds differ from pure sounds because they rarely consist of a single simple wave. For periodic waveforms they consist of the fundamental frequency and harmonics of this. The component waves can be revealed by carrying out a Fourier analysis to provide the Fourier spectrum. The cochlea may perform a similar analysis.
- Real sounds differ from complex sounds because they are typically reduced in intensity with time and distance from the source.
- Sound waves can travel through a variety of media, although the speed at which they travel varies depending on the medium.

Self-assessment questions

Question 2.1

What is the approximate wavelength of the note corresponding to middle C (262 Hz) in (a) air and (b) water? (*Hint*: you need to use the information in Table 2.2 to answer this question.)

Question 2.2

How many decibels correspond to a reduction in intensity by a factor of two?

Question 2.3

Many musical instruments consist of some sort of pipe or tube. It is possible to set up standing waves in tubes, and the harmonics produced depend on whether or not the tube is open at both ends or closed at one end. In a tube which is open at one end (such as an organ pipe) there must be a node at the closed end and an anti-node at the open end. Sketch diagrams of the fundamental frequency and the first two harmonics of the standing waves set up in a tube which is open at one end.

Sound reception: the ear

3

The auditory system must accomplish three basic tasks to hear a sound.

- First, it must deliver the acoustic stimulus to the receptors.
- Second, it must transduce the stimulus, turning pressure changes into electrical signals.
- Third, it must process these electrical signals so that they can efficiently indicate the qualities of the sound such as frequency, intensity and location.

How the auditory system accomplishes these tasks is the subject of much of the rest of this block. In this chapter we confine ourselves to the first two tasks by examining the sequence of events from initial receipt of the signal to transduction, beginning with a description of the basic structure of the ear.

The human ear can be divided by both anatomical position and function into three fairly distinct components:

- the **outer ear**, which is responsible for gathering sound energy and funnelling it inwards
- the **middle ear**, which acts as a mechanical transformer
- the fluid-filled **inner ear**, where the sensory receptors or **hair cells** are located within the **cochlea**, and transduction occurs (Figure 3.1).

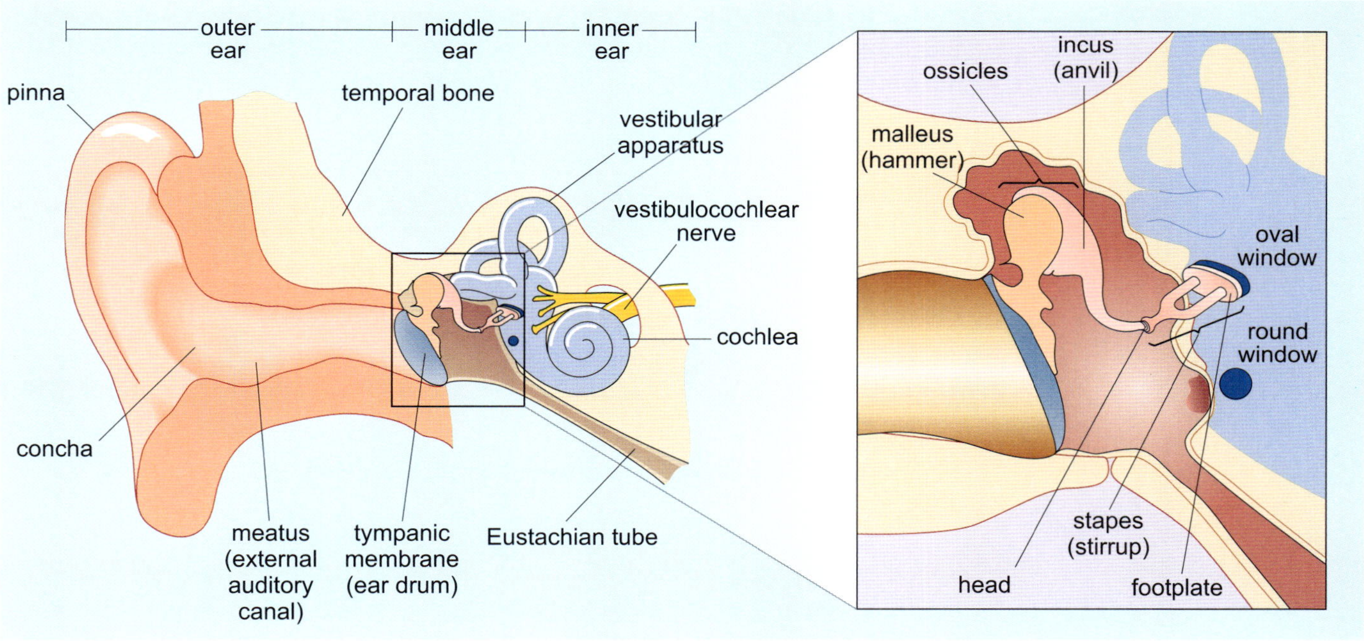

Figure 3.1 The human ear showing the outer, middle and inner ear.

Normally when we hear a sound it is a physical disturbance transmitted through air, which passes through the outer and middle ear and enters the inner ear structures. Here it is detected, assuming it is intense enough and of the right frequency. However, if you tap with your finger the temporal bone, which you can feel just behind your outer ear, you can hear the percussive sound transmitted directly to your inner ear. In this case, sound is said to be transmitted by **bone conduction**. This simple test is one of those used to identify whether hearing losses come about because sound is not being transmitted properly through the outer and middle ear to the inner ear, or whether it is the inner ear itself that is working incorrectly.

As a functional entity, these three main components of the ear constitute the **peripheral auditory system**. The effectiveness of the transmission in each component of the ear is determined by three mechanisms, each of them under central nervous system (CNS) control.

- The outer ear can be oriented towards (or away from) a sound by movement of the head, and thus the intensity of sound entering the auditory system can be controlled by the individual's behaviour.
- The middle ear, responsible for transmitting sound to the inner ear, contains two muscles that control the sound passing through.
- The inner ear itself also receives a signal from the brain (via the efferent system) that can control the sensitivity of the hair cells that act as sensory receptors.

These three control mechanisms are shown schematically in Figure 3.2. The descending control from the CNS acts both to limit and, if necessary, enhance the sound stimulus reaching the sensory receptors of the inner ear such that the optimum level of stimulus is maintained in a given situation.

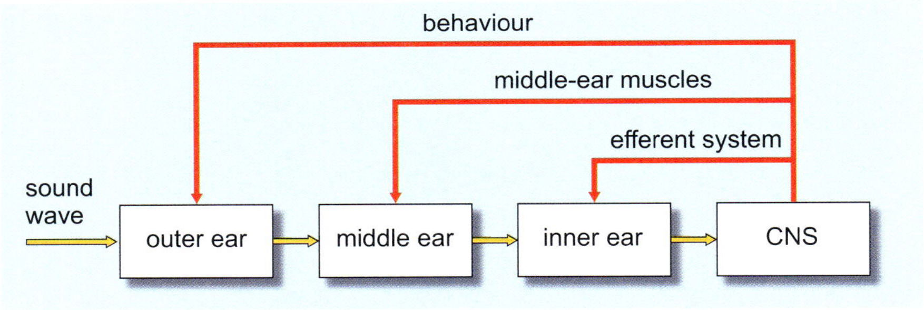

Figure 3.2 The components of the mammalian ear, and how they are affected by the CNS.

Together, the three components of the peripheral auditory system determine the information sent along the cochlear nerve, which forms the cochlear portion of the vestibulocochlear nerve or VIIIth (eighth) cranial nerve to the brain. We now look at the structure and function of each component in turn, beginning with the outer ear.

3.1 The outer ear

The outer ear includes the visible flap or **pinna** (also referred to as the auricle), the funnel-like inner portion called the **concha**, and the **meatus** or external auditory canal (see Figure 3.1).

The pinnae have two important functions: funnelling and localising sound. The funnelling of sound needs little explanation as it simply refers to channelling sound waves into the concha and meatus – something you can enhance by cupping your hand around your ear.

The localisation of sound (i.e. determining the position of its source) and the role of the pinnae are considered in detail in Chapter 4, so only a brief explanation is provided here. Some animals can move their pinnae to orientate towards a sound, supporting localisation. By contrast, in humans, with a relatively static pinna, the acoustic shielding effect of the head between the two ears and the dispersal of the sound around the head provides the major clue for the brain to work out where a sound is coming from. Clues about the elevation of a sound source are also provided by the reflection of sounds from the curved surfaces of individual pinnae. These clues can be used to establish the horizontal and vertical localisation of sound, respectively.

■ How would the immobile pinnae affect how we localise a sound source?

□ Unlike animals with mobile pinnae, we must reposition our head in order to aim our ears at a sound source.

From the pinnae, sound waves travel into the concha and meatus. This arrangement effectively creates a tube with the pinna end open and the other end closed by the **tympanic membrane** or ear drum, which closes off the meatus at the junction to the middle ear. This shape means that the outer ear acts as a closed-tube resonator, which enhances sounds in a specific and useful range of frequencies (see Box 3.1).

Box 3.1 The outer-ear resonator function

In Section 2.3.1 you learned about standing waves on a string and it was explained that the harmonics produced in the wave account for the characteristic sounds that arise from different string instruments. You should also have sketched the possible standing waves that could be set up in a tube that is open at one end (such as an organ pipe) for your answer to Question 2.3 in the previous chapter. These are examples of the kind of standing waves produced in many musical instruments, but they are also representative of waves that are possible in the outer ear because it is essentially a tube which is closed at one end and open at the other.

Look back at the answer to Question 2.3, which shows three different standing waves set up in an open tube.

- How do the wavelengths of these waves relate to the length of the tube, L?

- If the length of the tube is L then the wavelength of the fundamental frequency must be $4L$ because the closed end is a node and the open end is an anti-node, and the wavelength is always twice the distance between adjacent nodes (or anti-nodes). The wavelengths of the other two standing waves are $4L/3$ and $4L/5$, respectively.

The ear is not a musical instrument, so why do the wavelengths and frequencies matter for the outer ear? The answer is that the anatomy of the outer ear makes it behave as a resonator; frequencies of incoming sound waves that match the frequencies of possible standing waves within the outer ear are amplified, so there is a larger signal reaching the middle ear.

The fundamental frequency of an incoming signal that has a wavelength equal to four times the length of the tube formed by the outer ear will be the frequency at which the ear is most sensitive. The length of the 'tube' in the outer ear is approximately 25 mm, so we can estimate this fundamental frequency (f) to have a wavelength (λ), of 100 mm, or 0.1 m. The speed of sound (c) in air at body temperature (approximately 40 °C) is about 355 m s^{-1}, so, as $c = \lambda f$, the frequency is:

$$
\begin{aligned}
f &= 355\ \text{m s}^{-1} \\
&= 3550\ \text{Hz} \\
&= 3.55\ \text{kHz}
\end{aligned}
$$

Because the outer ear is not a perfect tube this is only an approximate calculation, but it indicates that hearing is boosted for incoming sounds with a frequency in the region of 2 to 5 kHz – just the range of many of the sounds we hear in everyday life, including some speech information.

When sound waves reach the thin and pliable tympanic membrane, the compressions and rarefactions of air caused by the sound wave push and pull at the membrane, moving it inwards and outwards at the same frequency as the pressure variations in the incoming wave. It is this vibration that ultimately leads to the perception of sound. The higher the frequency of the sound, the faster the membrane vibrates. Additionally, the greater the amplitude of the sound waves, the greater the deflection of the membrane.

It should also be noted that the outer ear protects the tympanic membrane against foreign bodies and changes in humidity and temperature, although neither of these functions is discussed further in this block.

3.2 The middle ear

The middle ear is a cavity interposed between the tympanic membrane and the membranous **oval window** that opens into the cochlea of the inner ear (see

Figure 3.1). This region contains (moist) air: its communication with the pharynx in the throat region through the **Eustachian tube** allows the pressure on either side of the tympanic membrane to be equalised to atmospheric pressure. If you have ever experienced your ears popping as you go up in an aeroplane this is because the atmospheric pressure drops as the plane gains altitude and the pressure in the middle ear pushes the tympanic membrane out, creating the popping sensation.

The middle ear on each side of the head contains three bones forming a chain, called the ossicles (derived from the Latin for bone, *os*). These are the smallest bones in the body and function to transmit the vibrations caused by auditory stimulation at the tympanic membrane to the inner ear. The bones are called the **malleus** (Latin for 'hammer'), the **incus** ('anvil') and the **stapes** ('stirrup'). The ossicle attached to the tympanic membrane is the malleus, which forms a rigid connection with the incus. The incus provides a flexible connection with the stapes. The flat bottom portion of the stapes, the **footplate**, is connected to the oval window. The axis of rotation of the ossicles runs through the point where the malleus and incus are fused together (Figure 3.3).

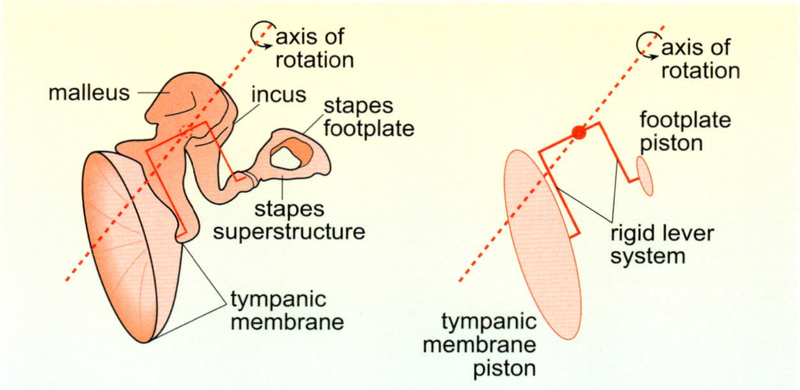

Figure 3.3 Illustrative and schematic representations of the structure of the middle ear.

In response to sound input, the inward–outward movement of the tympanic membrane displaces the malleus and incus and the action of these two bones alternately drives the stapes deeper into the oval window and retracts it, resulting in a cyclical movement of the fluid within the inner ear. But why must sound be transmitted via the ossicles and not simply transferred directly?

The reason is that the middle ear cavity is *air*-filled, while the inner ear is *fluid*-filled. The passage of sound information from the outer to the inner ear involves a boundary between these media and therefore a change in **acoustic impedance** (see Box 3.2). For example, if you have tried talking to someone who is under water, you may have observed that sound does not travel efficiently across an air–water interface. In fact, the vast majority of sound energy at an air–fluid boundary is reflected back within the air rather than passing through the water.

Box 3.2 Acoustic impedance

If we had no outer or middle ear, and the oval window of the inner ear was directly exposed to sound waves transmitted through the air, only 0.1% of the sound energy entering the ear would be transmitted through to the cochlea and the other 99.9% would be reflected. Consequently, our hearing would be much less sensitive (about –30 dB). The reason for this is that the inner ear is filled with fluid and therefore has much greater acoustic impedance than air.

Acoustic impedance is a measure of how readily the particles of the conducting medium can be displaced by the sound waves, which is much more difficult for water than for air. The acoustic impedance is equal to the ratio of the sound pressure to the flow velocity of the particles of the transmitting medium. (It is analogous to electrical impedance (resistance), which is the ratio of voltage to current flow.) This quality is not easy to measure, but the acoustic impedance (Z) can also be shown to be equal to the product of the density of the medium (ρ) and the speed of sound in the medium (c). So

$$Z = \rho c \qquad \text{(Eqn 3.1)}$$

Table 3.1 shows the acoustic impedance of air, water and bone.

Table 3.1 The values of density, speed of sound and acoustic impedance for air, water and bone.

Medium	Density at 20 °C/ kg m^{-3}	Speed of sound/ m s^{-1}	Acoustic impedance/ kg m^{-2} s^{-1}
Air*	1.20	343	4.11×10^2
Water	998	1480	1.47×10^6
Bone*	2000	2800	5.60×10^6

*These values are approximate because bone varies in composition and air varies in moisture content.

At an interface between one medium and another, the amount of sound reflected, and hence the amount transmitted, is determined by the difference between the two acoustic impedances. The equation to calculate the percentage of the intensity reflected at an interface is

$$\text{percentage reflection/\%} = \left(\frac{Z_1 - Z_2}{Z_1 + Z_2}\right)^2 \times 100 \qquad \text{(Eqn 3.2)}$$

where Z_1 and Z_2 are the acoustic impedances of the two media.

■ Use this equation to confirm that the figures given in Table 3.1 for reflection at a water–air interface are correct.

□ In this case

$$\text{percentage reflection/\%} = \left(\frac{1.47 \times 10^6 - 4.11 \times 10^2}{1.47 \times 10^6 + 4.11 \times 10^2}\right)^2 \times 100$$

$$= 99.9\%$$

This value shows that almost all of the sound would be reflected back and explains why, when swimming underwater in a pool, you can only hear ambient sounds from around the pool very faintly because there is very little transmission of sound into the water. Sounds made inside the water though are loud.

3.2.1 Overcoming acoustic impedance

If sound waves were to impinge directly on the oval window, the tympanic membrane would barely move, because of acoustic impedance in the different media in the ear. The main function of the middle ear is to compensate for this change in impedance. There are two main mechanisms that allow the middle ear to do this: area ratios and ossicular lever action.

Area ratios

Measurements show that the area of the tympanic membrane that vibrates in response to high-intensity sound is 55 mm^2. The footplate, which makes contact with the oval window, has an area of only about 3.2 mm^2, meaning that the area of the tympanic membrane is 17 times that of the footplate. So, if all the force exerted on the tympanic membrane is transferred to the footplate, the pressure (the force per unit area) must be 17 times greater at the footplate because it is smaller than the membrane. (One rather painful demonstration of this principle is to compare the pressure exerted on your toe by someone stepping on it wearing a stiletto-heel shoe compared with the pressure that exerted by the same person wearing a training shoe.)

Ossicular lever action

The second way in which the ossicles transfer the force from the tympanic membrane to the footplate is through a lever action. The simplest lever to imagine is that of a children's see-saw. The pivot point, or fulcrum, is the centre of the see-saw, and the two ends where children sit move up and down depending on the forces applied to them, and are level if equal forces are applied equidistant to the fulcrum. If, as an adult, you have ever tried to balance a see-saw with a child on the other end you will know that if you sit at the same distance from the fulcrum as the child on the opposite end, you risk the child's end shooting upwards, because the force you apply is greater. To avoid this effect, you need to sit nearer to the fulcrum.

This example illustrates that lever action can be considered in terms of the distance from the fulcrum and the force applied, such that the product of force and distance at one end must equal the product of force and distance at the other end. Figure 3.4 shows the malleus and incus can form a lever around a fulcrum where they fuse. The length of the malleus corresponds to D_1, the distance between the applied force ($F_{applied}$) and the fulcrum. The length of the incus corresponds to D_2, the distance between the fulcrum and the resultant force ($F_{resultant}$).

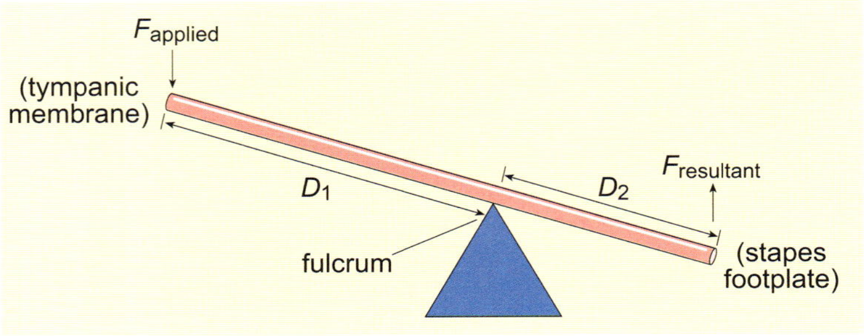

Figure 3.4 The lever action of the middle ear.

The force applied at the tympanic membrane, shown by a downward arrow in Figure 3.4, is transmitted to the malleus and acts over the length of this bone (D_1). The product of this force and distance must be equal to the product of the resultant force applied by the footplate to the oval window (shown as an upward arrow in this figure) and the length of the incus (D_2), as follows:

$$F_{applied} \times D_1 = F_{resultant} \times D_2 \qquad \text{(Eqn 3.3)}$$

Using this equation, it is possible to deduce that if D_2 is less than D_1, the resultant force will be greater than the applied force. This is, in fact, the case in the middle ear as the incus is shorter than the malleus, the former being around 7.0 mm long and the latter being about 8.5 mm long.

Equation 3.3 can be rearranged to give the factor by which the applied force is multiplied to produce the resultant force:

$$F_{resultant} = \frac{D_1}{D_2} \times F_{applied} \qquad \text{(Eqn 3.4)}$$

Which results in:

$$\begin{aligned} F_{resultant} &= \frac{8.5}{7.0} \times F_{applied} \\ &= 1.2 \times F_{applied} \end{aligned}$$

Therefore, the force applied to the malleus by the tympanic membrane is multiplied by a factor of 1.2 to produce a greater force, which is transmitted to the oval window and consequently the cochlea.

The combined effect of the ossicular mechanisms

Together, the two mechanisms described above can enhance the sound pressure at the cochlea over that of the tympanic membrane by a factor of 20 (17×1.2). Using Equation 2.3 it is possible to calculate that this 20-fold increase in pressure is in effect an increase of 26 dB. Therefore, without the middle ear, the efficiency of sound transmission into the inner ear would drop and the sensitivity to sound would be reduced. This situation occurs when the middle ear is prevented from working properly, for example, when it becomes filled with mucous fluid during an infection.

This value of 26 dB is hard to verify precisely in humans, but it can be studied in animals. Figure 3.5 shows data collected from the middle ear of a cat (Nedzelnitsky, 1980); specifically, the measured ratio of the pressure at the tympanic membrane (P_T) to that at the entrance to the cochlea (P_C) over the audible frequency range of the animal. Because of the differences in human and feline anatomy, it was predicted that the sound pressure at the cochlea should be 80 times that at the tympanic membrane (i.e. 38 dB greater). The real data shows, however, that this theoretically predicted value is too high, and the middle ear actually only enhances the signal by about 25 times (or 28 dB). It also shows that this enhancement is frequency-dependent.

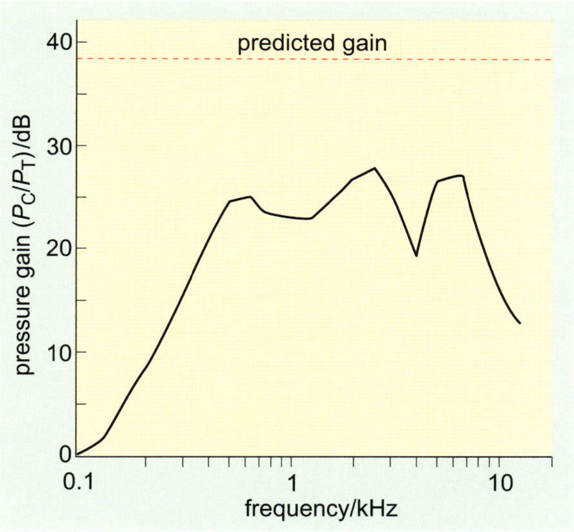

Figure 3.5 Middle-ear pressure gain for a cat across a range of audible frequencies.

Study note

Like a number of other graphs in this module, Figure 3.5 uses a logarithmic scale, which allows clear presentation of data over a very large scale. You have previously seen such a scale in Figure 2.8 in Block 3, and further information is available in the *Study Companion*.

The reasons why the amount of pressure gain is frequency-dependent are complex. However, the following factors are thought to be critical:

- The linkage between the ossicles is flexible, and at low frequencies the coupling between the malleus and incus and between the incus and the stapes becomes imperfect. Thus at low frequencies, the pressure gain will fall towards the value of 0 dB, which would be expected if no middle-ear structures were present.
- The ossicles have a finite mass. At higher frequencies the inertial mass of the ossicles (and of the tympanic membrane) become significant, and the ossicles will not follow rapid changes in sound pressure faithfully. In this regime also, the pressure gain will therefore be reduced.

3.2.2 The protective function of the middle ear

As well as compensating for a difference in acoustic impedance, the middle ear has a protective role because it is the site of the **middle-ear reflex**. This reflex involves the simultaneous contraction of two muscles: the **tensor tympani muscle**, attached to the malleus near the centre of the tympanic membrane, and the **stapedius muscle**, attached to the stapes near the attachment to the incus.

Contraction of the tensor tympani muscle results in an inward pull on the tympanic membrane, which reduces the motion of the membrane in response to sound stimulation. Contraction of the stapedius muscle pulls the stapes towards the tympanic membrane. Therefore, when simultaneous contraction of both muscles occurs, the effect is to lock the ossicles, preventing their free movement. This removes any impedance compensation provided by the middle ear and reduces the transfer of sound energy to the inner ear.

The middle-ear reflex is activated when loud sounds are presented to the ear (i.e. when sound levels exceed about 70 dB SPL). The process thus protects against loud sounds, although because of the time taken to contract the muscles (typically at least 40 ms), the reflex does not protect against short, percussive stimuli, such as gunshot noises. There is some evidence that the middle-ear reflex is also activated during speaking and other vocalisation: this prevents you being deafened by the sound of your own voice.

So far you have learned about the outer and middle ear, the former of which can enhance certain frequencies and both of which are concerned with the faithful transmission of the sound wave to the inner ear, where transduction occurs. As the site of transduction, the inner ear requires more detailed consideration and this is the focus of the next section.

3.3 The inner ear

The inner ear can be divided into three parts: the semicircular canals, the vestibule and the cochlea (Figure 3.6), all of which are located in the temporal bone. The semicircular canals and the vestibule affect the sense of balance and are not concerned with hearing, so they are discussed in Chapter 7 of this block. However, the cochlea (Latin for 'snail'), and what goes on inside it,

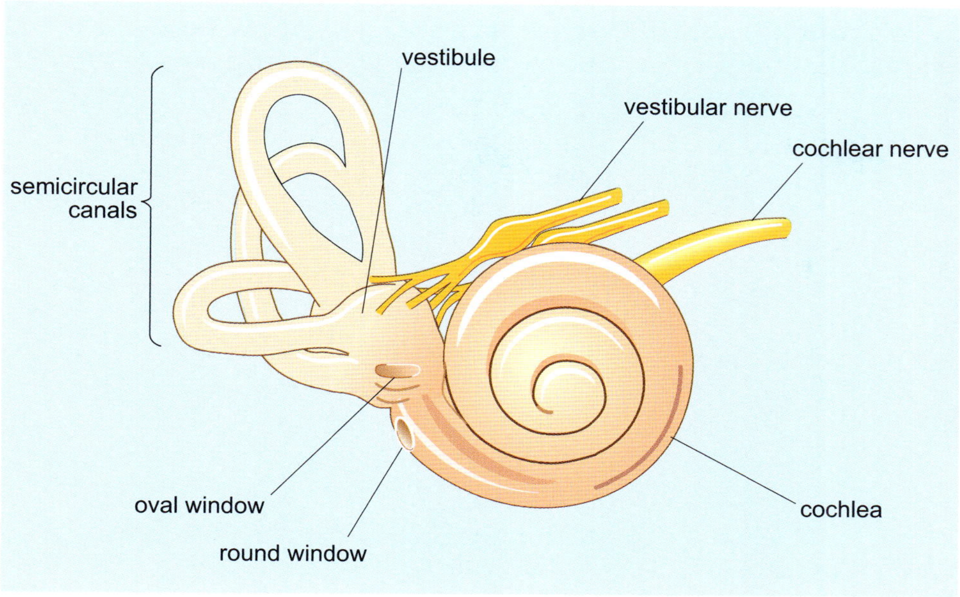

Figure 3.6 Structure of the inner ear, showing the semicircular canals, the vestibule and the cochlea.

provides the key to understanding many aspects of auditory perception, and is therefore covered here in some detail.

3.3.1 The gross anatomy of the cochlea

The cochlea has a spiral shape resembling the shell of a snail (Figure 3.7a). You can approximate the structure of the cochlea by wrapping a drinking straw two-and-a-half times around the tip of a sharpened pencil. The hollow tube, represented by the straw, has walls made of bone and the central pillar of the cochlea, represented by the pencil, is a conical bony structure called the **modiolus**. The cochlea's hollow tube is about 32 mm long and 2 mm in diameter in humans. In other mammals, the length varies from about 10 mm in a mouse to about 60 mm in some species of whale.

The structure of the cochlea can be shown schematically as if unravelled for ease of understanding (Figure 3.7b). The tube is divided into three chambers:

- the **scala vestibuli**
- the **scala media** (or cochlear duct)
- the **scala tympani**.

The three scalae wrap around inside the cochlea like a spiral staircase (*scala* is Latin for 'stairway'). The scala vestibuli forms the upper chamber, and at the base of this chamber is the oval window. The lowermost of the three chambers is the scala tympani. It too has an aperture, the **round window**, which is closed by an elastic membrane. The scala media separates the other two chambers along most of their length. The start of the cochlea, where the oval and round windows are located, is known as the basal end or base, while the other end, the inner tip of the spiral, is known as the apical end or apex.

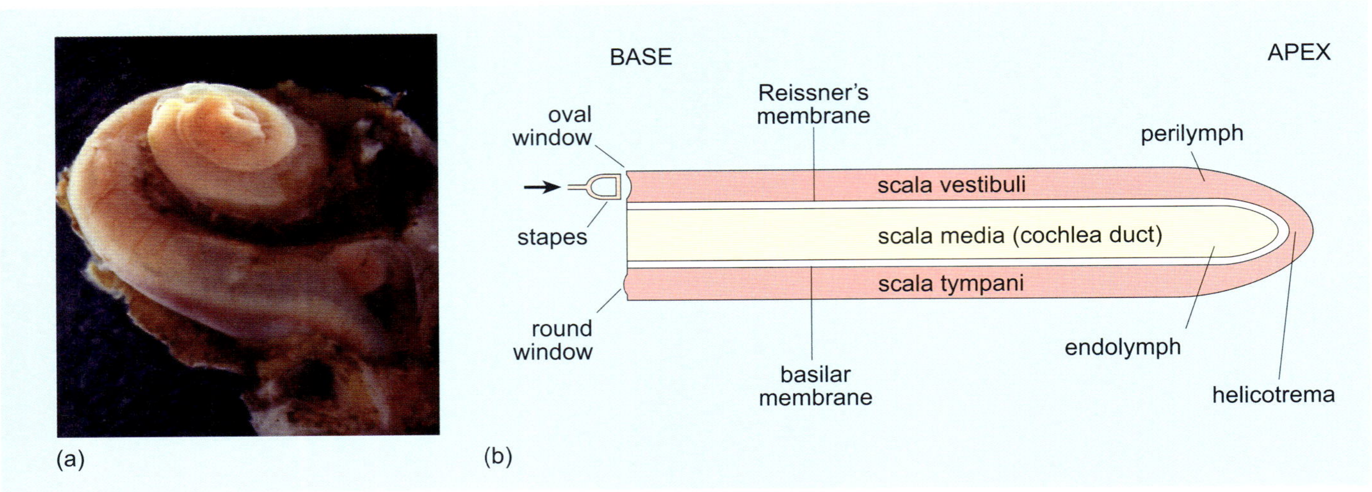

Figure 3.7 (a) Coiled cochlea of a human fetus at 5 months' gestation (magnification ×40). (b) Diagrammatic representation of the three scalae of the cochlea (uncoiled).

The scala vestibuli and the scala tympani communicate with one another via the **helicotrema**, an opening in the cochlear duct at the apex that allows the pressures in the two scalae to equalise. Both scala vestibuli and scala tympani are filled with the same fluid, known as **perilymph**. This has essentially the same composition as the extracellular fluid bathing most of the nervous system. In contrast, the scala media is filled with **endolymph**, which has very high potassium and low sodium concentrations, and is therefore similar in composition to intracellular fluid. More information about the fluids within the inner ear is provided in Box 3.3.

Box 3.3 Fluids of the inner ear

The fluids within the inner ear are critical in maintaining the correct physiological state of the cells of the cochlea. However, for the physics of sound propagation, they can be treated as though they have the physical properties of pure water. Recall that the fluid in the scalae vestibuli and tympani is perilymph. This is a solution with the same composition as cerebrospinal fluid (CSF) and extracellular fluid found outside the cells. The principal ion is sodium (Na^+). Perilymph is derived from blood plasma and arises from the capillary circulation around the cochlea.

The endolymph fluid within the scala media is different from the perilymph in its composition. The principal ion is potassium (K^+), but the solution also contains low calcium (Ca^{2+}) concentrations (typically 20 mM). It is thus closer in composition to intracellular solutions. The source of the endolymph in the scala media is a transport epithelium tissue, the stria vascularis, which is located on the lateral wall of the cochlear duct. The surfaces of the cells that surround and face into the scala media are linked by cell–cell tight junctions, meaning that the membranes of cells join together to form a virtually impermeable barrier, which prevents fluid within the scala media from readily diffusing out. The stria vascularis (as its name suggests) has a rich vascular blood supply that is responsible for supplying the high metabolic demands of the epithelium.

Study note

Block 2 used the unit mol l^{-1} for concentration. Here we use M, which is another way of denoting concentration. If you are unfamiliar with how this unit functions, please refer to the *Study Companion*.

Figure 3.8 shows a cross-section of the cochlea, revealing the three chambers that run along its length. Between the scala vestibuli and the scala media there is a fine boundary called **Reissner's membrane**, and between the scala tympani and scala media there is the **basilar membrane**. This membrane is acellular and mainly composed of collagen fibres, and it provides the support structure for the hair cells that act as receptors within the ear. These two membranes and the scala media divide the cochlea into upper and lower compartments: the scala vestibuli and scala tympani, respectively.

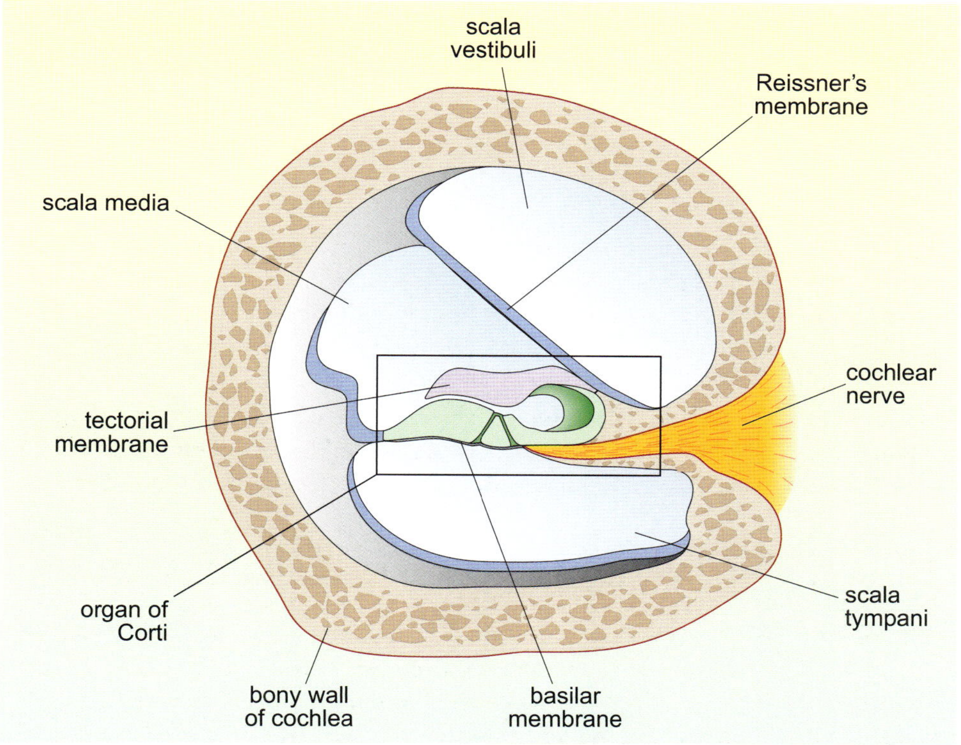

Figure 3.8 Cross-section of the cochlea.

Although these two compartments in the cochlea are freely connected at the apex by the helicotrema, rapid pressure changes produced in the scala vestibuli by movement of the stapes footplate act across the basilar membrane, rather than through the helicotrema. Lying on top of the basilar membrane within the scala media is the organ of Corti (which is discussed in the next section) and hanging over this organ is the **tectorial membrane**: an acellular matrix of collagen and specialised protein fibrils. The collective term for the partitions of the scala media (i.e. the organ of Corti, the basilar membrane and the tectorial membrane) is the **cochlear partition**.

3.3.2 Components of the cochlear partition

The **organ of Corti**, named after its discoverer, Alfonso Corti, is shown in detail in Figure 3.9. It is the primary auditory receptor structure and houses the hair cells that respond to incoming sound stimuli. These hair cells are mechanoreceptors, much like those you learned about in Block 3. However, there are also some notable differences between auditory mechanoreceptors and those involved in somatosensation. For example, auditory receptors are not capable of producing an action potential and therefore only produce a receptor potential. Action potentials are instead first produced in the axons of the neurons forming the cochlear nerve, which are the first-order neurons.

Additionally, as their name suggests, each mechanoreceptor in the organ of Corti has about 100 hair-like **stereocilia** extending from a structure at the apical end of the cell called the cuticular plate. The plate provides a strong structural anchoring for the stereocilia. It is at the stereocilia that transduction occurs. Transduction is discussed further in the next section, but for now we consider the hair cells and their connections in more detail.

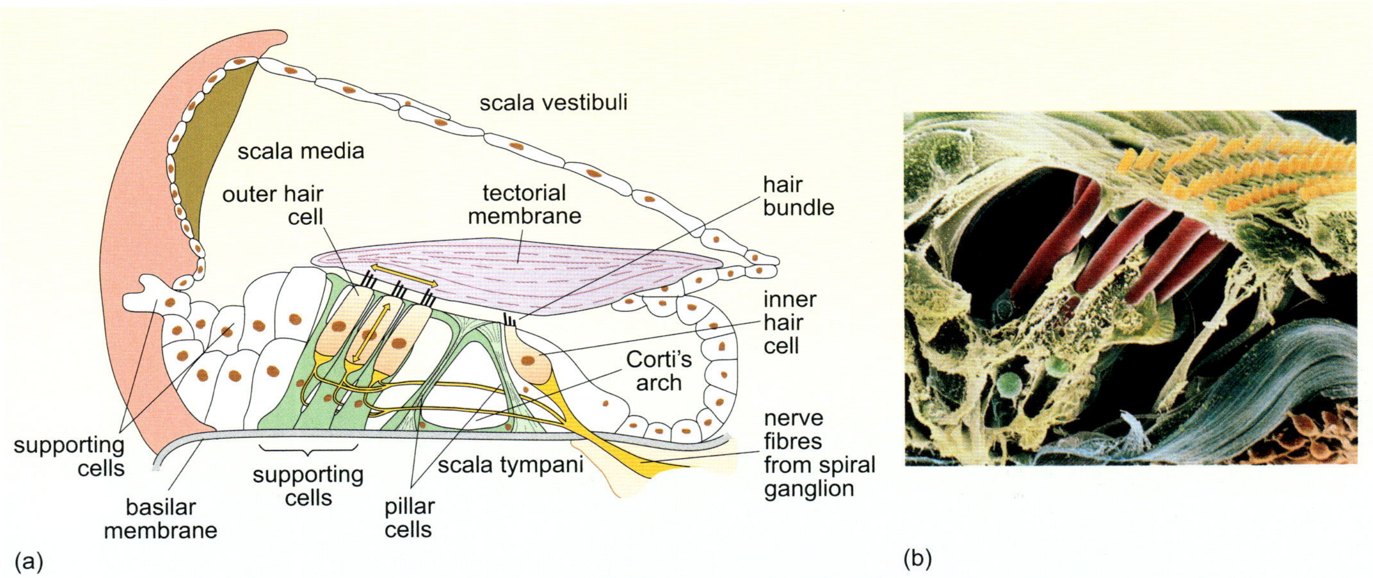

Figure 3.9 The organ of Corti: (a) schematic cross-section; (b) coloured scanning electron micrograph showing four rows of hair cells that are supported by pillar cells (magnification ×600).

You can see from Figure 3.9 that there are two types of hair cells: **outer hair cells** and **inner hair cells**, which are separated by a rigid inverted V-shaped structure known as **Corti's arch**. The human cochlea contains about 3500 inner hair cells and about 12 000 outer hair cells, distributed in rows along its length. They are structured as shown in Figure 3.10. You will learn about the role of the kinocilium and tip links, which are also shown in the figure, later on in this chapter. For now it is sufficient to say that the kinocilium is the tallest of the stereocilia and the tip links connect adjacent stereocilia.

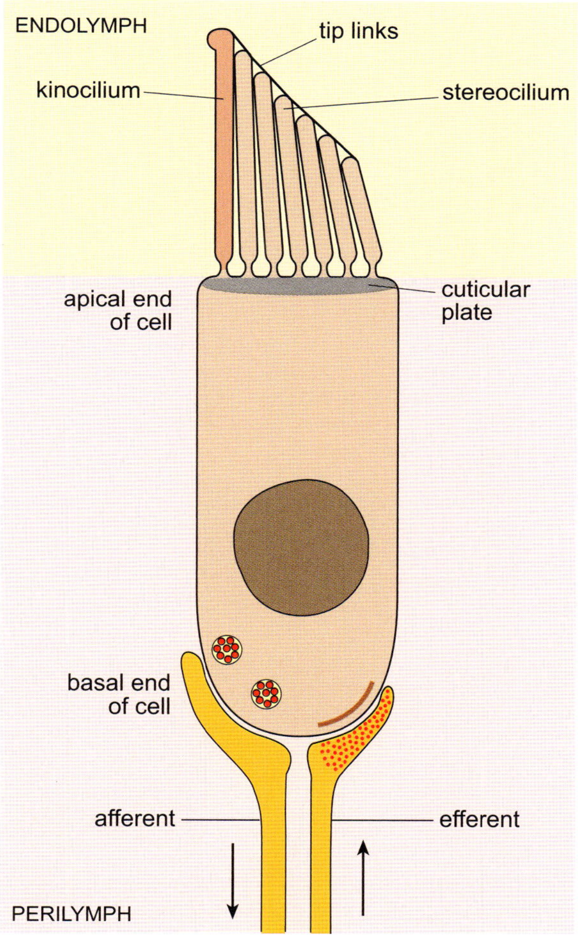

Figure 3.10 The structure of a hair cell.

The outer hair cells have their apical end, and therefore their stereocilia, embedded in the overlying tectorial membrane. By contrast, stereocilia of inner hair cells fall just short of the tectorial membrane. It is widely accepted that the inner hair cells are the primary sensory cells of the cochlea, while the function of the outer hair cells is less well understood and is thought to relate to the regulation of cochlear sensitivity and frequency selectivity.

The two types of hair cell make contact with two different kinds of neuron, both of which have their cell bodies in the spiral ganglion (or cochlear ganglion) located within the modiolus, and their axons within the cochlear nerve (Figure 3.11). The inner hair cells synapse with Type I neurons called radial fibres while the outer hair cells synapse with Type II neurons called outer spiral fibres. Each inner hair cell synapses with up to 20 radial fibres and each outer spiral fibre contacts up to 10 outer hair cells. This innervation pattern means that the vast majority of the afferent fibres (up to 95%) in the cochlear nerve carry signals from the inner, rather than the outer, hair cells.

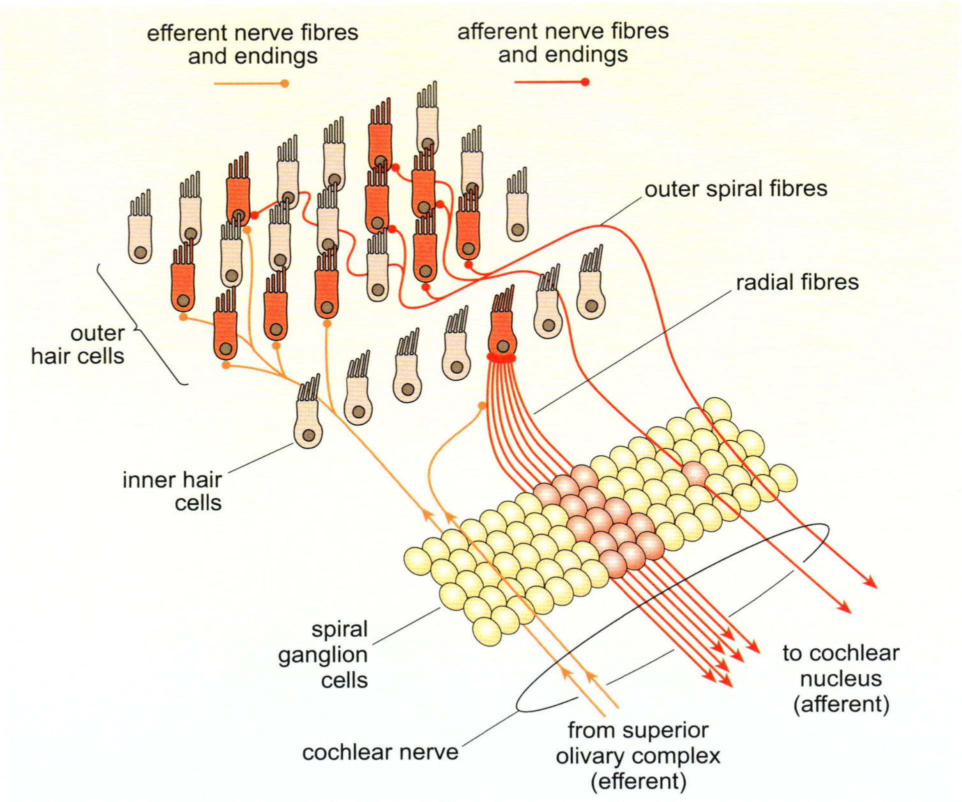

Figure 3.11 Innervation of the organ of Corti. Afferent neurons have their cell bodies within the spiral ganglion.

The axons of the Type I neurons that contact the inner hair cells are thicker than those of the outer spiral fibres and are myelinated. It is the former type from which microelectrode recordings are usually obtained in laboratory investigations.

- ■ What is the consequence of these Type I axons being thicker and myelinated?
- □ Both of these factors allow action potentials to be conducted more quickly.

In fact, very little is known about what the unmyelinated axons of the Type II neurons signal to the brain because it is so difficult to record from them. The only recordings that have been made suggest that they just respond to very loud sounds. By contrast, the outer hair cells are known to *receive* efferent innervation via the cochlear nerve from the superior olivary complex in the

olivocochlear bundle, and are part of a fast motor feedback system that modifies the mechanics of the basilar membrane (i.e. a system of descending control).

The olivocochlear bundle also contains some axons that innervate the Type I dendrites rather than the inner hair cells themselves. Stimulation of the olivocochlear bundle reduces firing in the cochlear nerve, mainly by dampening the amplification produced by the outer hair cells (see Section 3.5). In other words, sound signals in the cochlear nerve result in feedback via the olivocochlear bundle, which reduces cochlear sensitivity in a frequency-specific way. This feedback loop probably helps to protect the ear from very loud sounds, but takes several milliseconds to operate because numerous synapses are involved.

3.4 Intermediate chapter summary

- The human ear is made up of the outer, middle and inner ear. The outer ear consists of the pinna, the concha and meatus and is closed off by the tympanic membrane. The middle ear is air-filled and contains the ossicles. The inner ear is fluid-filled and contains the cochlea, the semicircular canals and the vestibule.
- Sound in the external environment is channelled into the meatus by the pinna and impinges on the tympanic membrane, causing it to vibrate.
- These vibrations are transmitted to the middle ear ossicles, which act to compensate for the differences in acoustic impedance as the sound moves from an air-filled chamber to a fluid-filled chamber. They also function in preventing damage to the inner ear by very loud sounds via the middle-ear reflex.
- The cochlea has three compartments: the scala tympani, the scala vestibuli and the scala media. Inside the scala media is the organ of Corti, which contains hair cells – the sensory mechanoreceptors for hearing.
- Both the inner and outer hair cells form synapses with different types of neurons in the cochlear nerve. The outer hair cells also receive descending input.

3.5 Mechanoelectrical transduction

As mentioned in Section 3.3, the stereocilia are the site of mechanoelectrical transduction in hair cells. In order for transduction to occur, the stereocilia must be subjected to a mechanical force. From what you have read so far, you know that the pressure of a sound wave is transmitted through the outer ear to the middle ear. The footplate, moving with a piston-like action, then makes direct contact with the oval window, conveying the pressure to the inner ear and, in particular, to the scala vestibuli.

When the footplate pushes the oval window, the liquid in the scala vestibuli is displaced. If the membranes inside the cochlea were rigid then the increase in fluid pressure at the oval window would displace the fluid up the scala vestibuli, through the helicotrema and down the scala tympani, causing the round window to bulge out.

This is actually a fairly accurate description of what happens, except that the membranes inside the cochlea are not rigid. As a consequence, the increase in pressure in the cochlear fluid caused by the inward movement of the footplate also displaces fluid in the direction of the cochlear partition, which is deflected downwards. This deflection in turn causes the elastic basilar membrane to move down, it also increases the pressure within the scala tympani. The enhanced pressure in the scala tympani displaces a fluid mass that contributes to outward bowing of the round window. When the stapes pulls back, the process is reversed and the basilar membrane moves up and the round window bows inwards. In other words, each cycle of a sound stimulus evokes a complete cycle of up-and-down movement of the basilar membrane.

Given that the hair cells are located on the basilar membrane, as the membrane moves, the stereocilia of the hair cells are subjected to a force that causes deflection and therefore transduction. For the outer hair cells, this deflection occurs because the tectorial membrane makes direct contact with the tips of the stereocilia and, as the basilar membrane moves, the corresponding section of tectorial membrane shears radially over the hair cells, deflecting their stereocilia. For the inner hair cells, the tips of the stereocilia do not quite make direct contact with the tectorial membrane but similar deflection is brought about by the flow of fluids (specifically, endolymph) around the stereocilia.

Study note

You first read about shearing forces in Block 3 Chapter 2.

It is clear from the above description that movement of the basilar membrane is a necessary prerequisite for transduction to occur. Therefore, we now look in detail at how motion is set up in the basilar membrane, before focusing on the changes this causes in the hair cells.

3.5.1 Movement of the basilar membrane

The movement of the basilar membrane and surrounding fluid in response to a sound wave effectively creates a force on both the fluid in the cochlea and on the membrane. The way the fluid responds depends on its inertia (its tendency to resist a change in motion). The way the membrane responds depends on its stiffness. Both of these responses differ along the length of the basilar membrane. The membrane is wider at its apex compared with the base by a factor of about five and it decreases in stiffness from base to apex, the base being around 100 times stiffer (Figure 3.12). The inertial resistance of the fluid alters along the length, becoming greater with increasing distance from the oval window.

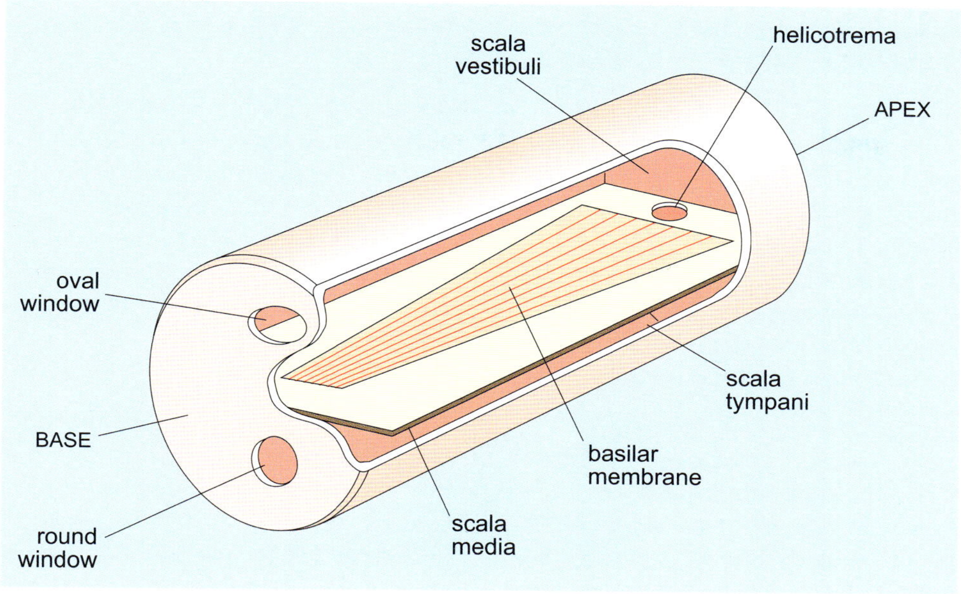

Figure 3.12 Schematic representation of the basilar membrane (cochlea uncoiled) showing the variation in width along its length.

When a sound wave enters the cochlea it attempts to move along the path of least resistance, which partially depends on the conditions in the cochlear fluid and the basilar membrane. To complicate matters further, the inertial resistance in the fluid is frequency-dependent in such a way that higher frequencies are more affected than low frequencies. This difference means that the path of least resistance for a high-frequency sound wave is shorter (Figure 3.13, route A), such that it remains closer to the base than for a low-frequency sound wave, which travels nearer to the apex (Figure 3.13, route B).

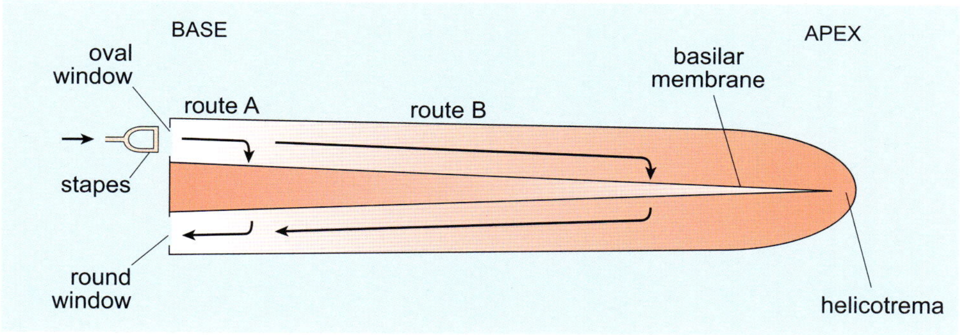

Figure 3.13 The different forces acting on the cochlea vary along its length with darker regions here showing greater forces. High-frequency sounds are more affected by the inertial resistance of the fluid so travel less distance (route A) in contrast to low-frequency sounds (route B).

Stimulation by a pure tone results in a complex movement of the membrane. If the membrane were uniform, the fluctuating pressure difference between the scala vestibuli and the scala tympani caused by the sound would move the entire membrane up and down with similar excursions at all points. However, because of the variation in width and stiffness along its length, various parts of the membrane do not oscillate in phase.

Over a complete cycle of sound each segment of the membrane undergoes a single cycle of vibration but at any point in time some parts are moving upwards and some parts are moving downwards. The overall pattern of movement of the membrane is best described as a travelling wave (see Box 2.1) because the energy of the wave travels from the base to the apex of the membrane. This effect was directly observed by von Bekesy (1947), who evoked movement of the human basilar membrane post-mortem by applying very intense sound stimuli while observing the membrane under a microscope – work that won him a Nobel Prize in 1961.

You can visualise the motion of a travelling wave if you imagine a wave that travels along a piece of ribbon if you hold one end in your hand and give it a flick. The flick might produce a waveform of the sort shown in Figure 3.14a. However, Figure 3.14b represents a more realistic representation of the wave on the basilar membrane because the basilar membrane is attached at its edges and is displaced in response to sound in a transverse (crosswise) direction as well as a longitudinal direction.

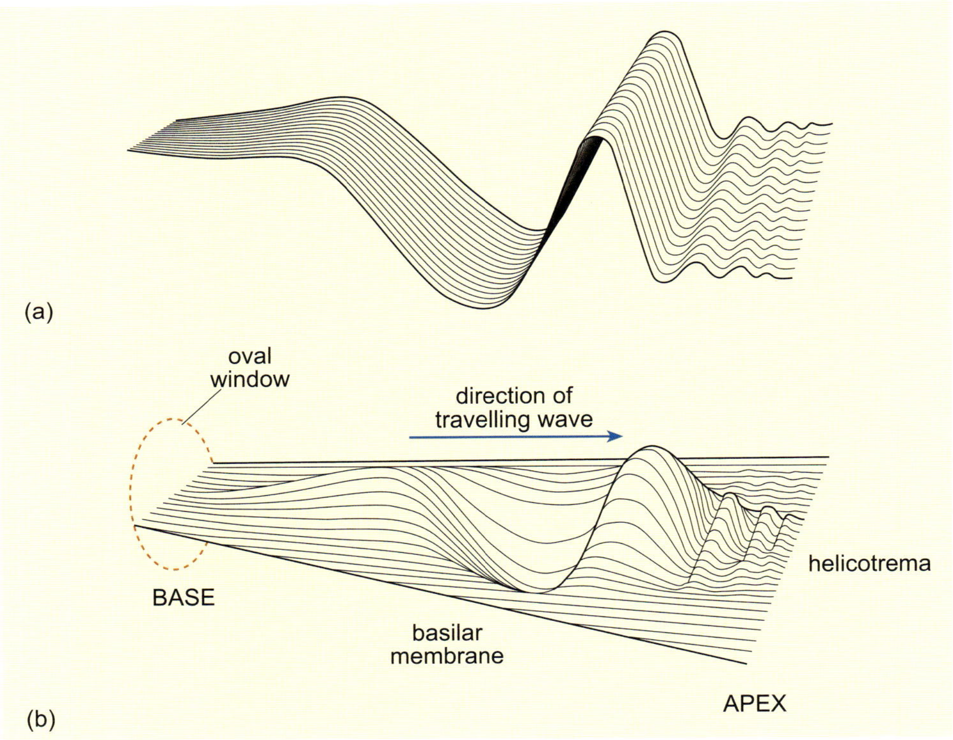

Figure 3.14 (a) The waveform resulting from flicking a ribbon. (b) A more realistic representation of the same waveform in the basilar membrane, with linear and transverse displacement.

■ What do you notice about the change in amplitude of the wave as it travels along the membrane?

□ As it travels, the wave reaches a peak in amplitude which then rapidly falls. The amplitude of the wave is therefore greatest at a particular location on the membrane.

The travelling wave, then, is a unique moving waveform whose point of maximal displacement traces out a specific set of locations. The shape momentarily described by the set of these locations along the basilar membrane is called the envelope of the travelling wave (Figure 3.15). The point along the basilar membrane where the wave, and hence the envelope, reaches a peak differs for each frequency. In other words, each point along the basilar membrane that is set in motion vibrates at the same frequency as the sound impinging on the ear, but *different frequency* sounds cause a *peak* in the wave at *different* positions on the basilar membrane (Figure 3.16a).

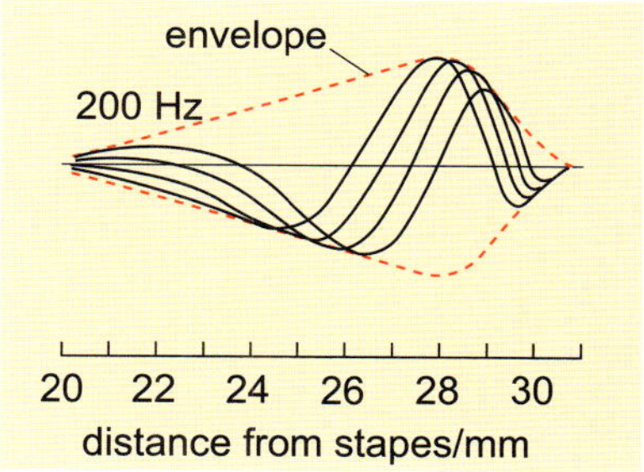

Figure 3.15 The envelope formed by a 200 Hz tone.

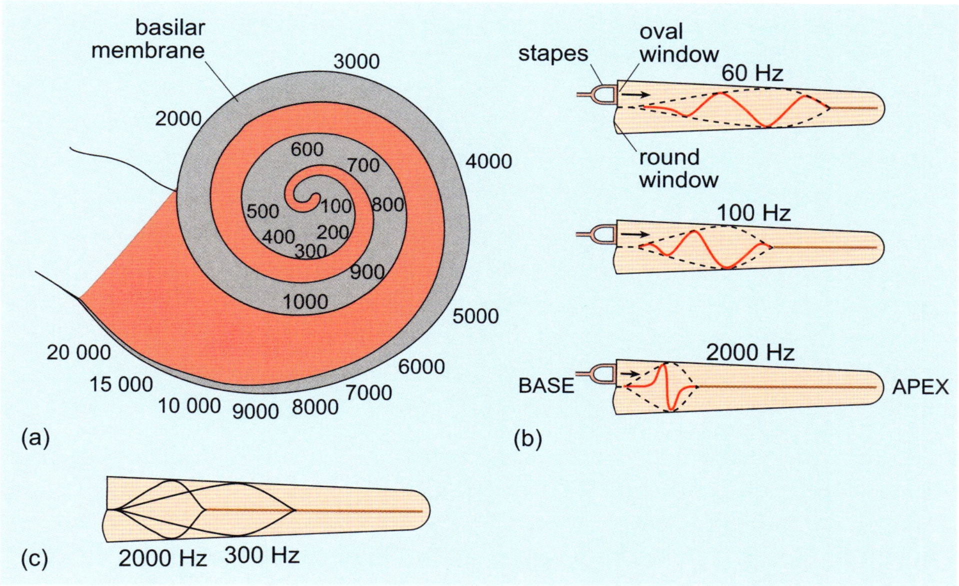

Figure 3.16 (a) Schematic map of frequency representation in hertz on the basilar membrane. (b) Examples of envelopes formed in the membrane for waves of 60 Hz, 100 Hz and 2000 Hz. (c) Displacement envelopes in response to a signal composed of two waves of 300 Hz and 2000 Hz.

Figure 3.16b shows examples of envelopes that would occur in the membrane for stimuli of three different frequencies. One instantaneous waveform is shown for each frequency.

■ What do you notice about the point of maximum displacement for each frequency in Figure 3.16b?

□ For the lowest frequency (60 Hz) the maximum displacement is near the apical end; for the highest frequency (2000 Hz) the maximum displacement is near the base; the intermediate frequency (100 Hz) has maximal displacement between the two.

Therefore, high-frequency sounds cause a small region of the basilar membrane near the stapes to move, while low frequencies cause almost the entire membrane to move. The travelling wave always travels from base to apex, and how far towards the apex it travels depends on the frequency of stimulation, lower frequencies travelling further as suggested earlier in this section. If the sound impinging on the ear was more complex – say, consisting of frequencies of 300 Hz and 2000 Hz – each frequency would create a maximum displacement at a different point along the basilar membrane, as shown in Figure 3.16c.

Analysis of the movement

The separation of a complex signal into two different points of maximal displacement along the membrane, corresponding to the simple waves of which the complex signal is composed, means that the basilar membrane is performing a type of frequency (Fourier) analysis much like that described in Section 2.3.3. The basilar membrane displacement provides useful information about the frequency of the sound impinging on the ear by acting like a series of band-pass filters. Each section of the membrane responds to a small range of frequencies. It does not respond to frequencies that are present in the sound but fall outside the range of frequencies of that section.

The conversion of sound frequency to coding as position of excitation is referred to as a **tonotopic mapping**. It should be noted that while the cochlea is sometimes considered a biological Fourier analyser because of the response properties of the basilar membrane, this is a slight oversimplification because the real situation is more complex for a number of reasons, including the amplification action of the outer hair cells, which is discussed in Section 3.6.

The filter characteristics of the basilar membrane have been studied using an advanced technique called the Mössbauer effect. Figure 3.17 shows the results of such a study by Robles et al. (1986). The data was collected by presenting different frequency sounds to the inner ear of a chinchilla and then measuring the level of each tone that is required to displace the basilar membrane by a fixed amount (1.9×10^{-8} m). Measurements were taken at a particular point on the basilar membrane.

- ■ From Figure 3.17, estimate the frequency of the tone that required the lowest sound level to displace the basilar membrane by the set amount.
- □ Approximately 8000 Hz (in fact, it is 8350 Hz, or 8.35 kHz).

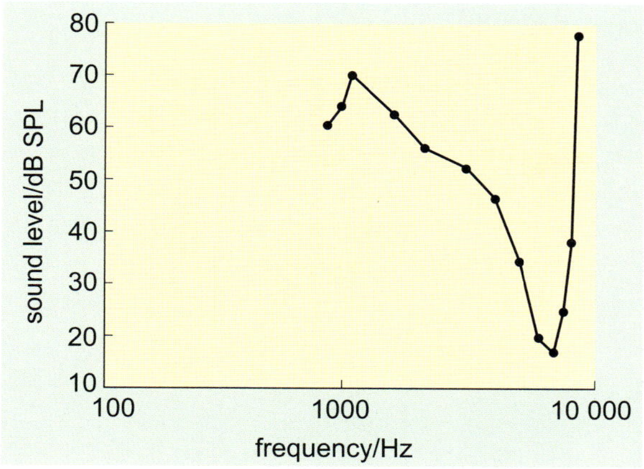

Figure 3.17 The sound level required to maintain the basilar membrane of a chinchilla at a constant displacement as a function of the frequency of the tonal input (based on Robles et al., 1986).

This frequency is known as the **characteristic frequency (CF)** – also referred to as the critical or central frequency – of that part of the membrane because it is most sensitive to (or tuned to) frequencies in the region of 8 kHz. For frequencies above and below 8.35 kHz, the tone had to be more intense in order to vibrate the membrane to the same extent. This particular point on the membrane therefore acts as a band-pass filter, in that it responds maximally to tones of 8.35 kHz but shows very little response to tones that are higher or lower than this.

The motion of the basilar membrane also provides information about the temporal pattern of acoustic stimulation. It takes longer for a low-frequency stimulus to reach its point of maximum displacement on the membrane than it does a high-frequency stimulus.

■ Why is this so?

□ High-frequency stimuli cause maximal displacement of the membrane near the basal end, whereas low frequencies cause maximal displacement at the apical end. If sound always travels from base to apex, it takes longer for the wave to travel to reach the apex (see Figure 3.16b).

Finally, the mechanics of the basilar membrane provide information regarding the level of acoustic stimulation. The greater the stimulus level, the greater the amount of basilar membrane displacement. Therefore, more intense signals cause greater membrane displacement at a particular point than less intense stimuli.

We have now established that the vibration patterns of the basilar membrane can provide information on the frequency, timing and intensity of an incoming sound wave. However, for this information to be of use, it must be faithfully transmitted to the stereocilia of the hair cells where it can be turned into a neural signal.

3.5.2 Movement of the stereocilia

Recall that movement of the stereocilia results from the shearing force set up by the tectorial membrane (outer hair cells) or surrounding fluid flow (inner hair cells) as the basilar membrane vibrates in response to a sound wave. Figure 3.18 shows how the displacement of the two membranes during vibration causes them to pivot about *different* hinging points and therefore creates this shearing force, which is transduced by outer hair cells into electrical energy. Similar displacement would be found with forces resulting from fluid flow in inner hair cells.

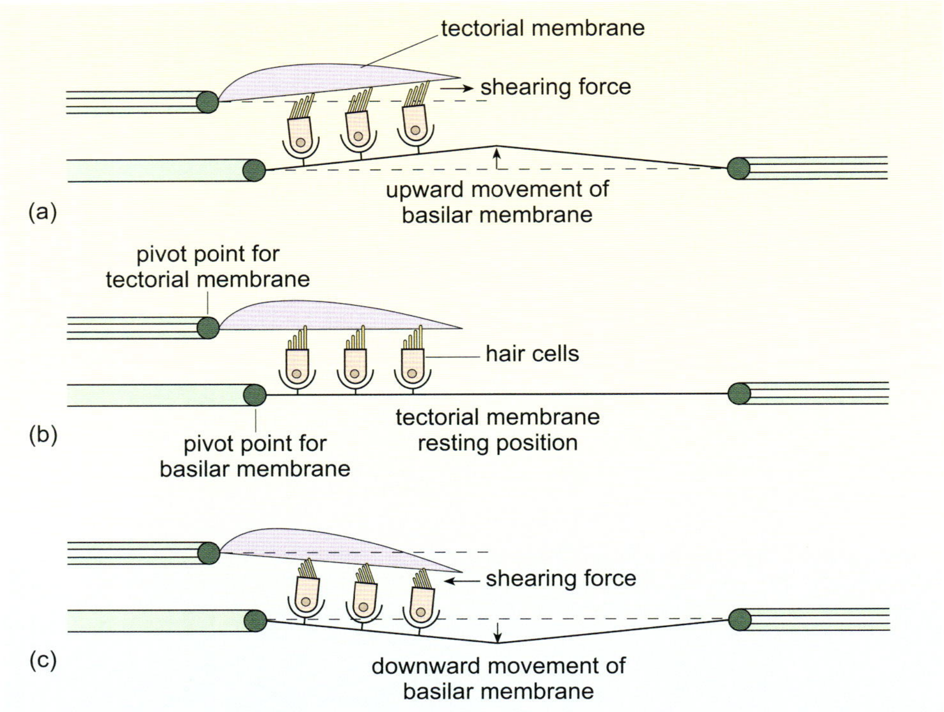

Figure 3.18 (a) Shearing force resulting from displacement of the basilar membrane towards the scala vestibuli. (b) Relationship between outer hair cells and tectorial membrane with no stimulation. (c) Shearing forces in the direction opposite to that shown in (a) after displacement in the opposite direction.

In order for transduction to occur, the permeability of the hair cell membrane must change. Many other sensory receptors, such as photoreceptors and olfactory neurons, employ second messengers in the transduction process that act to open ion channels. This is not true for hair cells as the rapidity with which they respond to stimuli makes this impossible. For example, the highest frequency humans can hear is 20 kHz and the localisation of sound sources requires resolution of time differences in the order of 10 μs. Therefore, in order to deal with the frequencies of biologically relevant stimuli, transduction must be rapid and ion channels must be opened directly.

It is now known that the shearing force causes tension in the filamentous connections called **tip links** that join the distal ends of neighbouring stereocilia, which you first saw in Figure 3.10. This tension results in the opening of mechanically-gated ion channels located at the tip of the stereocilia. This is believed to occur because each tip link is attached at one end or both ends to the molecular gates of one or a few channels (Figure 3.19).

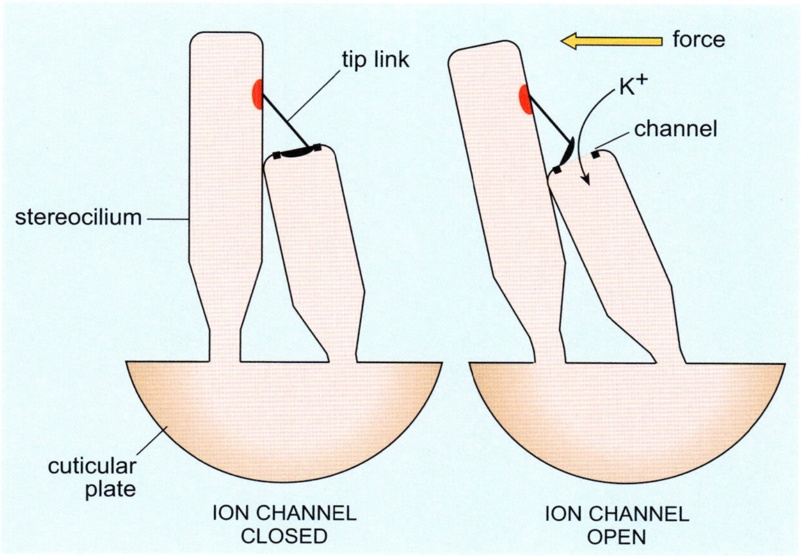

Figure 3.19 Mechanism of mechanoelectrical transduction. When a force is applied to the stereocilia, the tension in the tip links can cause ion channels to open.

Opening the ion channels in the hair cell's membrane allows ions to flow through these channels, altering the cell's membrane potential (this is the electrical response). So, in response to a mechanical stimulus, there is an influx of ions into the cell, which disturbs the resting potential of the cell membrane and drives it to a new level: the receptor potential. The channels are relatively non-selective about which ions they allow to pass through them. However, recall from Box 3.3 that potassium is plentiful in the endolymph. The stereocilia of the hair cells are bathed in endolymph, whereas the basal region of the hair cell is bathed in perilymph, which is relatively low in potassium. So, once the channels are opened, potassium ions flow into the hair cell.

■ How does this situation differ from what happens in most other cells?

□ In most cells, the flow of potassium ions down their concentration gradient is outwards because there is a higher concentration of potassium inside the cell than in the surrounding medium.

In fact, when the stereocilia of a hair cell are displaced by a mechanical stimulus (Figure 3.20b), its response depends on the direction and magnitude of the stimulus. In an unstimulated cell about 15% of the ion channels are open. As a result, the cell's resting potential (about −50 mV) is determined, in part, by the inward flow of current. A positive stimulus that displaces the stereocilia towards the kinocilium (the tallest stereocilium) opens additional channels and the resultant influx of positive ions depolarises the cell by as much as tens of millivolts. A negative stimulus that displaces the stereocilia away from the kinocilium shuts the channels that are open at rest and hyperpolarises the cell. The resulting change in receptor potential is illustrated in Figure 3.20c, while Figure 3.20d shows that a small displacement in a certain direction can trigger a significant rise in receptor potential, representing about 90% (the shaded area) or the response range of the cell.

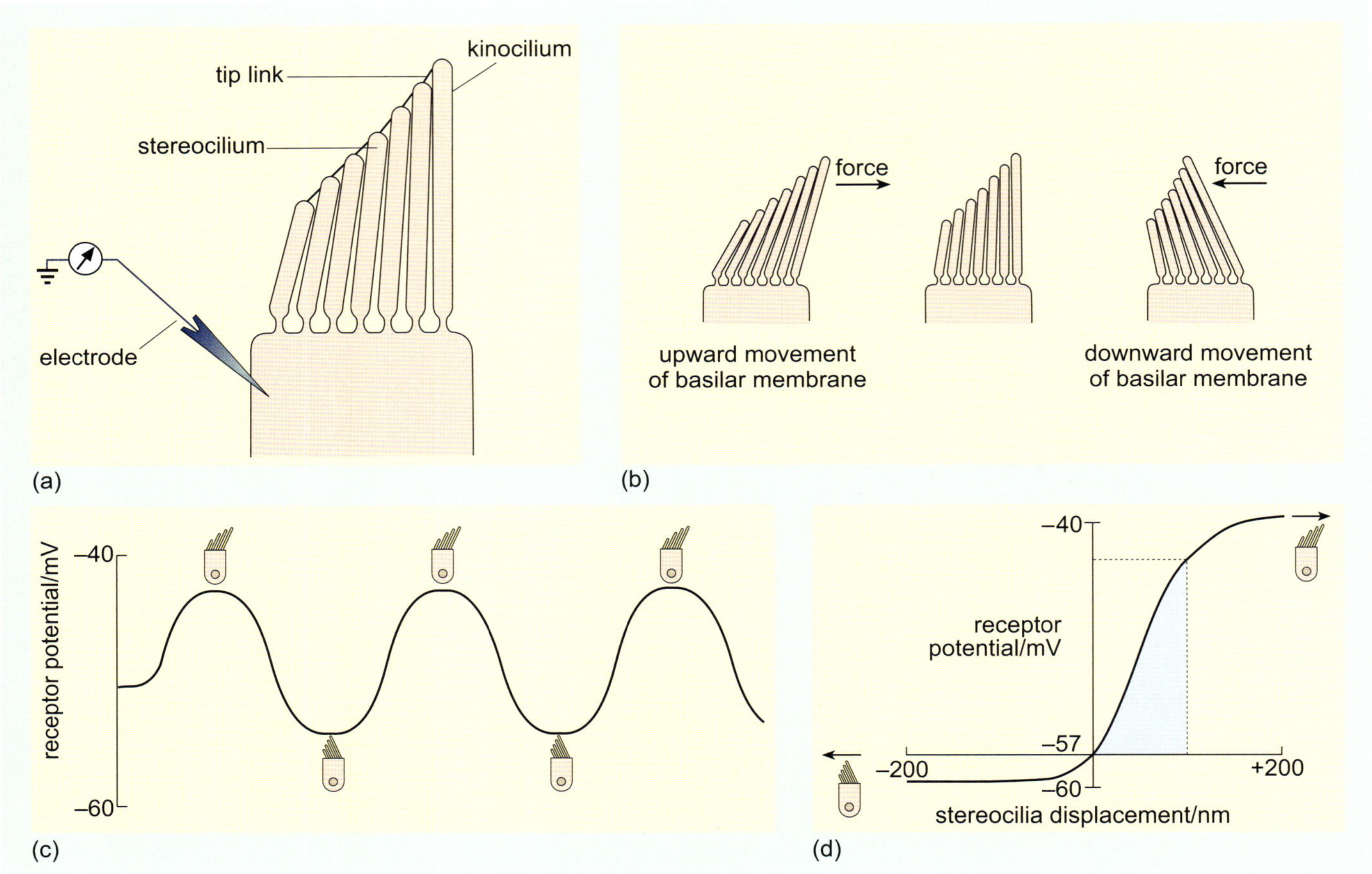

Figure 3.20 (a) Schematic diagram of a hair cell with an electrode inserted into its cytoplasm, enabling receptor potentials to be recorded. (b) Mechanical force causes deflection in the stereocilia which produce (c) an oscillatory receptor potential. (d) The relationship between stereocilia displacement and cell receptor potential.

This directional sensitivity of the cells, their arrangement on the organ of Corti and the hypothesised motion of the components within the organ of Corti in response to a stimulus mean that an upward movement of the basilar membrane leads to depolarisation of the cells, whereas a downward deflection elicits hyperpolarisation. Therefore, as the basilar membrane moves in response to the incoming sound wave, the hair cell receptor potential can oscillate at the same frequency as the incoming signal. However, at frequencies above 1000 Hz this oscillatory pattern is lost and instead the hair cell becomes effectively depolarised for the entire duration of the stimulus with what is known as a **summating potential** (Figure 3.21).

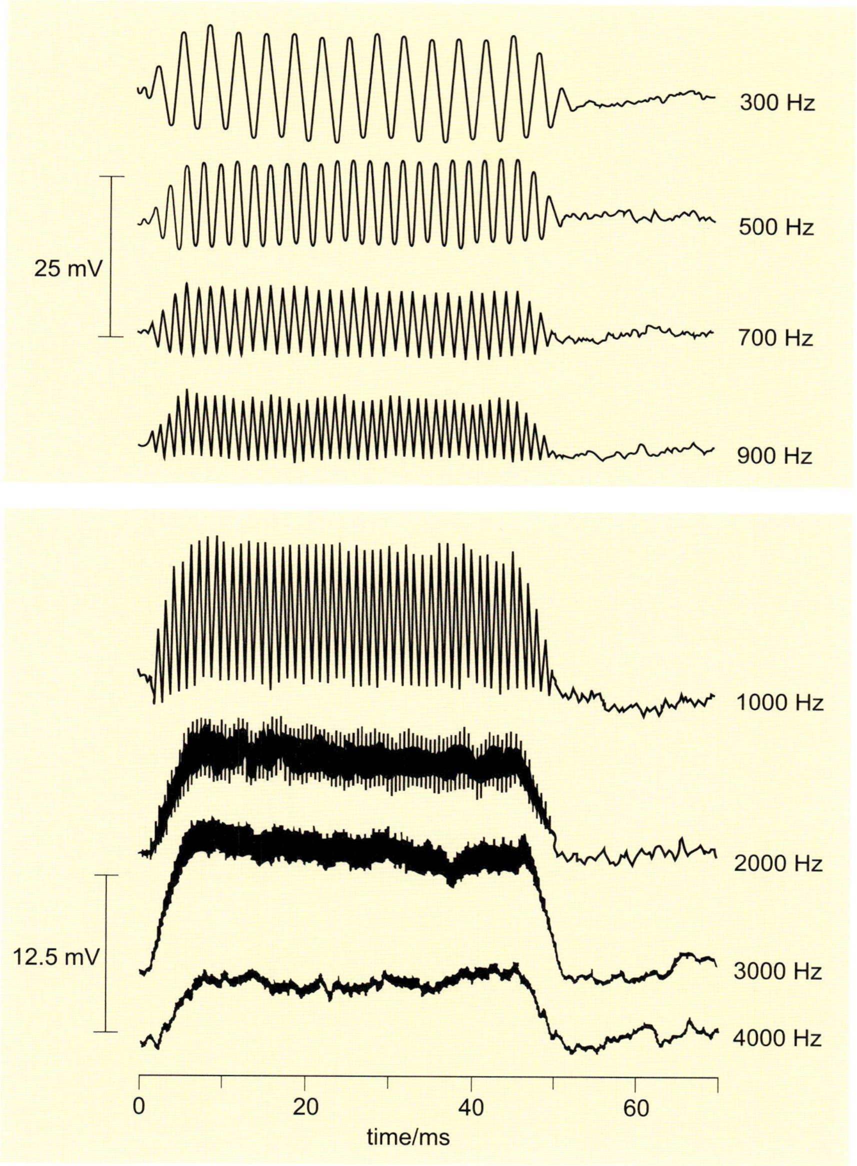

Figure 3.21 As sound frequency increases, the hair cell receptor potential switches from an oscillatory potential to a sustained depolarisation referred to as a summating potential.

The receptor potential of a hair cell is graded, such that as the stimulus amplitude increases, the receptor potential grows increasingly larger, up to a maximal point of saturation. The relationship between a deflection of the stereocilia and the resulting electrical response is S-shaped, as shown in Figure 3.20d. This results in a high degree of sensitivity. A small displacement of only 100 nm (100×10^{-9} m) represents 90% of the response range of the hair cell (shaded part). Deflection of a hair cell by the width of a hydrogen atom is enough to make the cell respond.

Unlike the mechanoreceptors you studied in Block 3, and as you read here in Section 3.3.2, hair cells are not capable of producing an action potential, and therefore the receptor potential created by stereocilia displacement triggers the release of a neurotransmitter into the synapse. This chemical acts on afferent neurons which, given sufficient stimulation, can produce an action potential. This synapse is the focus of the next section.

3.5.3 Neurotransmitter actions

In order to achieve the temporal precision necessary for transmitting information to the afferent neurons, hair cells contain a specialised presynaptic structure called a **synaptic ribbon**. This is comprised of organelles that tether a large number of synaptic vesicles to the hair cell's presynaptic active zone, or the zone where neurotransmitter can be released from. In the mouse cochlea this ribbon has been shown to contain as many as 200 synaptic vesicles (Nouvian et al., 2006).

It is believed that ribbon synapses stabilise a larger-than-normal pool of readily releasable neurotransmitter (as opposed to recycling or reserve pools – see Box 3.4), which allows the synchronised release of multiple vesicles. This action is not possible in the absence of the synaptic ribbon. The actual molecular make-up of the ribbon is still under investigation but, at present, it is thought that there are key differences in the synaptic proteins found at these synapses in contrast to those found at conventional synapses.

In addition to the ability to release large amounts of neurotransmitter in a synchronised manner, another feature of the hair cell synapses that aids temporal resolution of the signal is the proximity of the presynaptic Ca^{2+} channels to the Ca^{2+} sensors of exocytosis. Recall from Block 2 that Ca^{2+} influx causes release of the neurotransmitter by exocytosis from the presynaptic terminal. In hair cells the sensor is so close to the Ca^{2+} channels (which are opened following the depolarisation of the cell due to an increased K^+ concentration) that levels of calcium rising and falling can be detected in a microsecond range, and thus neurotransmitter release is modulated rapidly (Moser et al., 2006). The specialised features of these synapses are shown in Figure 3.22.

Recall from the previous blocks that there are a number of different neurotransmitters. Hair cells are known to release glutamate, which normally has an excitatory effect. Once the glutamate has been released, it is able to bind to postsynaptic receptors on the afferent neuron to exert its effect. Research has demonstrated that glutamate binds to a particular type of ionotropic receptor called the α-amino-3-hydroxy-5-methyl-4-isoxazolepropionic acid receptor, more commonly known as the AMPA receptor (Glowatzki et al., 2008).

Although the ribbon synapse is capable of releasing a large amount of glutamate, the actual amount released depends on the size of the receptor potential and therefore the deflection of the stereocilia. Because around 15% of the ion channels are open in the absence of deflection, some neurotransmitter leaks out and causes spontaneous firing of action potentials in the afferent neuron.

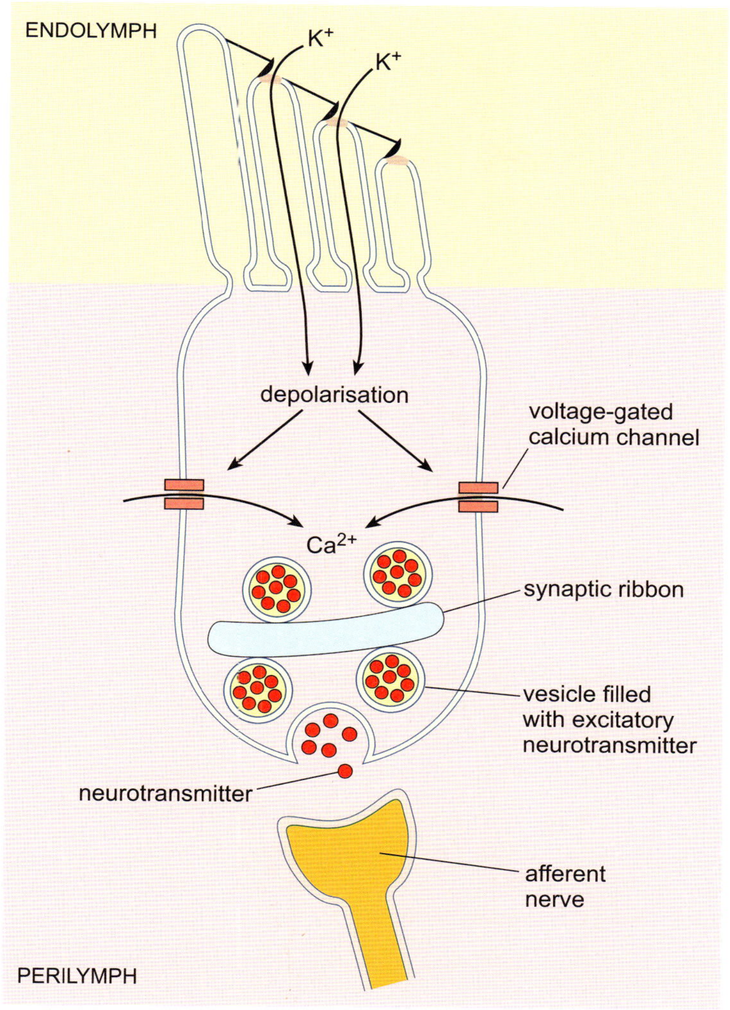

Figure 3.22 Action of neurotransmitter in synapses. Entry of potassium ions depolarises the hair cell, which opens voltage-gated calcium channels. Incoming calcium ions further depolarise the cell and lead to the release of neurotransmitter from the vesicles of the synaptic ribbon.

In the presence of a sound stimulus, depolarisation of the hair cell releases more glutamate, which results in increased glutamate binding to the AMPA receptor. This causes an increase in the discharge rate of action potentials in the afferent neuron above the spontaneous rate (excitation). By contrast, a decrease in glutamate binding to the AMPA receptor causes a decrease in the discharge rate of action potentials below the spontaneous discharge rate (inhibition), as illustrated in Figure 3.23.

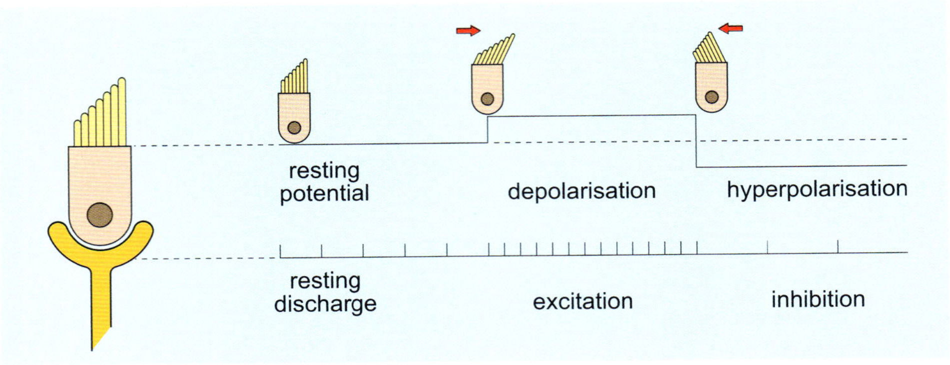

Figure 3.23 In unstimulated hair cells there is a low level of spontaneous firing in the axons of the cochlear nerve. When the cell is stimulated, depolarisation results in an increase in firing (excitation) while hyperpolarisation results in a decrease in firing (inhibition).

You read above that receptor potential can oscillate in a manner that reflects the incoming sound wave for stimuli up to 1000 Hz. For frequencies up to this amount the receptor potential modulates neurotransmitter release and therefore the firing of the afferent neuron is in synchrony with the sound wave. This is known as **phase locking**, as the action potentials occur preferentially at one point in the cycle. At frequencies over 1000 Hz the phase locking is lost and firing in the afferent neuron just increases above the spontaneous rate.

Box 3.4 Pools of neurotransmitter

In the 1960s, scientists studying the release of acetylcholine in cats proposed that neurons contain two different pools of neurotransmitter: one that is readily released and one that is not (Birks and MacIntosh, 1961). However, later research revealed that not all of the readily releasable pool was equally releasable, suggesting that it is more appropriate to think of neurotransmitter as being in three distinct pools within a neuron (Zucker and Regehr, 2002). These pools are described below, using the terminology of Rizzoli and Betz (2005).

The readily releasable pool

This pool consists of immediately available vesicles of neurotransmitter that are docked to the presynaptic membrane primed for release within 1 second of stimulation. The pool is normally a small proportion of the overall amount of neurotransmitter (1–2%) and may be rapidly depleted within just a few milliseconds of depolarisation.

The recycling pool

This pool consists of vesicles of neurotransmitter scattered within the presynaptic terminal and makes up about 10–20% of the available neurotransmitter, and appears to be released during moderate stimulation. Release occurs within a few seconds.

The reserve pool

This pool makes up the bulk of neurotransmitter available (80–90%) and is contained within vesicles sited away from the presynaptic membrane. Release from these vesicles will only occur during extremely intense stimulation after tens of seconds or even minutes.

As well as mediating neurotransmitter release, calcium also has another function: it opens potassium channels, called calcium-activated potassium channels, in the basal region of the cell.

- ■ Given that the basal end of the cell is surrounded by perilymph, would you expect potassium to move into or out of the cell when these channels open?
- □ Potassium ions would leave the hair cells because the perilymph outside the hair cells is low in potassium.

The effect of this movement of potassium ions is to repolarise the hair cell.

Note that the efferent connections to hair cells are mediated by acetylcholine, which predominantly exerts an inhibitory response through either metabotropic or ionotropic receptors.

3.5.4 Hair cell adaptation

As you learned in Block 1, adaptation is a critical feature of sensory systems and hearing is no exception to this. In fact, there are two different mechanisms of adaptation that ensure the receptor potential diminishes rapidly when hair cell bundle deflection is maintained, that is, when the stimulus no longer changes. Both of these mechanisms are triggered by calcium and take place over different timescales.

Fast adaptation occurs in the sub-millisecond range in mammals, and is believed to be due to calcium acting directly on the ion channels to close them or counteracting their activity in some way (Fettiplace and Hackney, 2006).

Slightly more is known about the slower adaptation mechanism, which is thought to depend on the association between two proteins: myosin and actin. Actin is a highly conserved and abundant protein found in cells. There are a number of other proteins capable of binding to actin, of which those in the myosin family are one type. Myosin is connected to the actin backbone of the stereocilia and controls the tension in the tip links, and therefore the force applied to the mechanically-gated ion channel.

When the stereocilia are at rest – that is, not deflected – this tension means that the majority of K^+ channels are closed (Figure 3.24a). When there is a deflection of the stereocilia, the tension in the tip links increases and the channels are opened, allowing an influx of K^+ (Figure 3.24b). However, if this deflection is sustained, Ca^{2+} binds to the myosin, causing it to dissociate from the actin backbone. This allows it to slip down the backbone, like the rungs of a ladder, therefore reducing the tension on the tip link and the mechanically-gated ion channels, which can then close (Figure 3.24c).

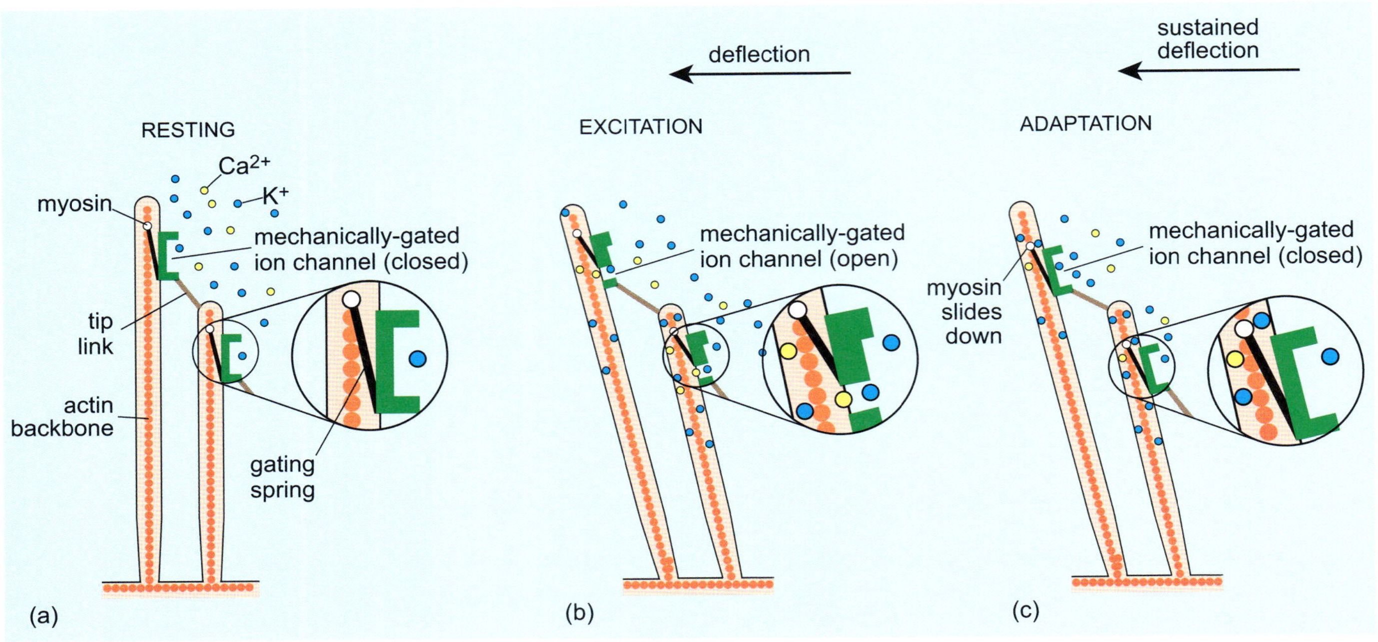

Figure 3.24 The actin–myosin binding (a) at rest and (b) during deflection of the stereocilia. (c) Calcium-dependent dissociation of the two molecules, producing adaptation to the stimulus.

3.5.5 Hair cell tuning

We have shown that when a certain frequency of sound stimulates a point on the basilar membrane, this boundary responds by moving, and the hair cells at that site are stimulated by the force that this movement creates. Groups of hair cells therefore only respond if certain frequencies are present in the sound, as shown in Figure 3.25. Here, the 4 kHz component of a travelling sound wave results in a peak forming at position B, which displaces the stereocilia of the local hair cells and ultimately generates an action potential in the auditory neuron.

The frequency sensitivity of a hair cell can be displayed as a tuning curve. To construct a tuning curve, recordings are taken from the axons in the cochlear nerve that synapse with individual hair cells while the subject is exposed to pure tone stimuli of various frequencies. For each frequency, the intensity of the stimulus is adjusted until the firing of the neuron reaches a predefined level. The tuning curve is then the graph of sound intensity against stimulus frequency (Figure 3.26).

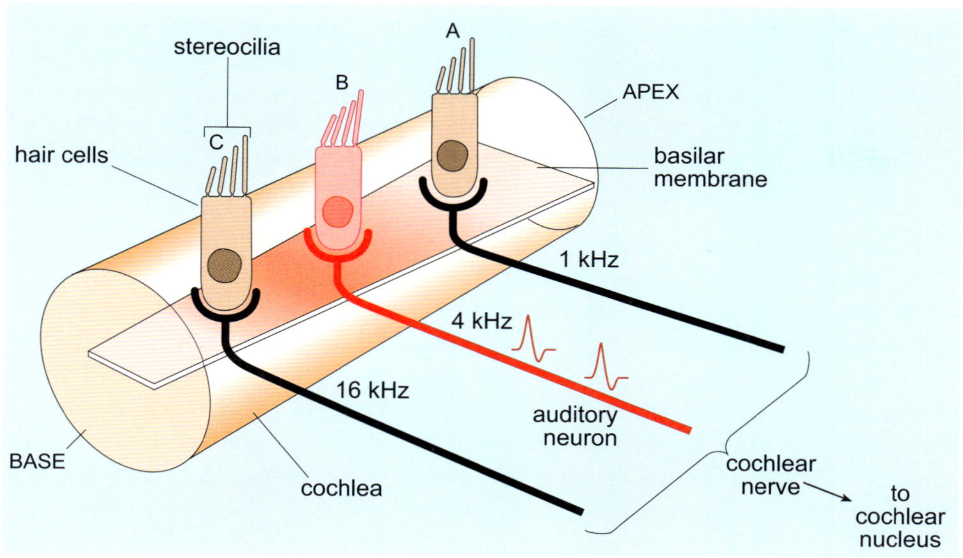

Figure 3.25 Schematic representation of a specific component frequency of a sound causing a particular group of hair cells to fire.

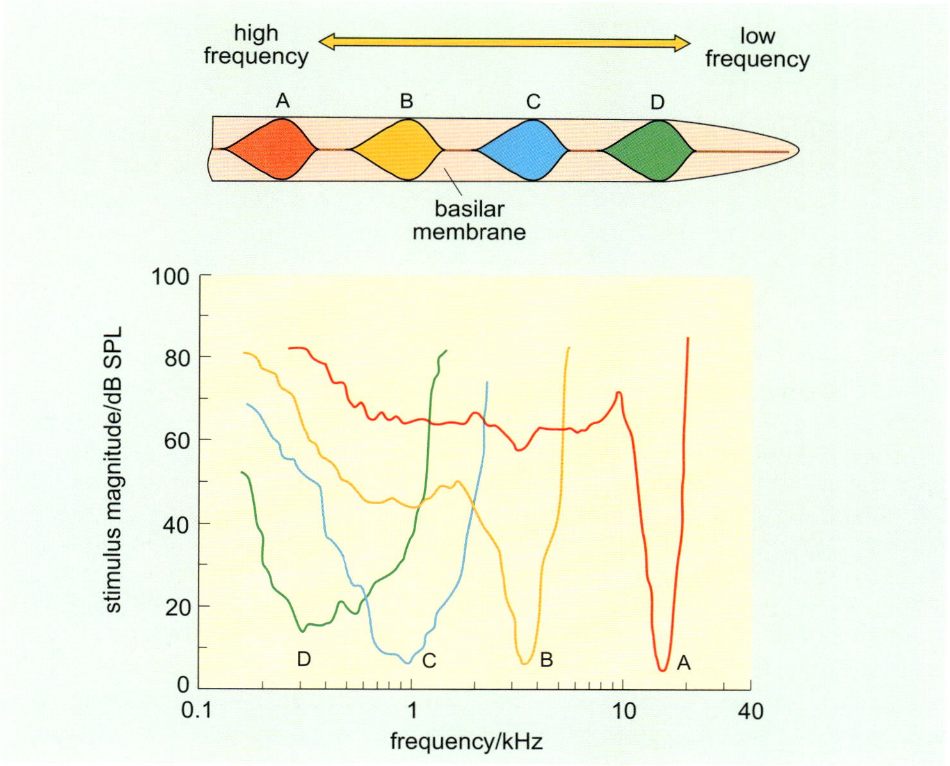

Figure 3.26 Tuning curves of specific afferent neurons corresponding to different positions (A–D) on the basilar membrane.

Tuning curves for these axons, and therefore the corresponding hair cells, are characteristically V-shaped. The tip (i.e. lowest point) of the V represents the frequency to which the cell is most sensitive – the characteristic frequency – as a sound of this frequency will elicit a response from the cell even when it is of very low intensity. Sounds of greater or lesser frequency require higher intensity to excite the cell.

By examining the firing of individual neurons in response to various frequencies, researchers have discovered an interesting phenomenon called two-tone suppression. This effect can be demonstrated by recording from a neuron within the cochlear nerve while presenting a sound of the characteristic frequency for that neuron at an intensity that just elicits a response, and then adding a second sound. The second sound is chosen to fall just outside the tuning curve for that neuron and therefore is a slightly higher or lower frequency and is presented at a greater intensity. For example, if recording from neuron C in Figure 3.26, the first tone would be at the characteristic frequency of 1 kHz and presented at a low intensity (e.g. 8 dB SPL). The second tone could then be just outside the tuning curve, for example a 3 kHz tone at 50 dB SPL. When the second tone is added, the firing rate of the neuron is reduced.

■ Thinking back to Block 2 Chapter 3, which mechanism could underlie inhibition of the neuron when a neighbouring frequency is applied?

□ Lateral inhibition could be a suitable candidate here.

In fact, although this form of inhibition would result in a similar phenomenon, the mechanism underlying two-tone suppression is related to the mechanics of the basilar membrane (and not neural mechanisms as is the case in lateral inhibition). However, this interesting observation illustrates that, even in the absence of a neural mechanism between neighbouring neurons, it is possible for interactions to occur.

3.6 Outer hair cells: the cochlear amplifier

The great majority of neurons that carry information from the cochlea to higher levels of the auditory system connect to the inner hair cells. Thus most, if not all, information about sounds is conveyed to the brain via the inner hair cells.

Given that the outer hair cells greatly outnumber the inner hair cells, it seems paradoxical that most cochlear output is derived in this way. However, research suggests that outer hair cells do play an important role in the transduction process. Early experiments demonstrated that in the absence of outer hair cells the hearing threshold was increased by around 50 dB (Ryan and Dallos, 1975) and that the amplification they provided was mechanical (Mountain, 1980).

Later research suggested that the presence of a motor protein allowed the outer hair cells to contract and elongate, in response to changes in membrane potential. The changes in motor protein length could oppose the viscous forces (due to the surrounding fluid and cells of the organ of Corti) that act on the cochlear partition. These viscous forces tend to damp down local excitation of the cochlear partition. With viscous forces removed, each section of the cochlear duct can act as a virtually undamped resonator, with a larger and more frequency-specific response to an appropriately matched tone. Following this discovery, the outer hair cells are sometimes said to constitute a cochlear amplifier by enhancing the effect on the inner hair cells and creating a bigger response in the cochlear nerve (Dallos, 2008).

In addition to having a role in amplification, experiments examining the impact of the loss of the outer hair cells have also indicated a change in frequency selectivity. Figure 3.27 shows an example frequency selectivity curve for an axon within the cochlear nerve in an intact cochlea (the solid line) and another for when the outer hair cells are lost through damage (the dashed line). The curve for the intact cochlea shows a tip, corresponding to the characteristic frequency for that axon, where the intensity needed to elicit a response is very small. When the outer hair cells are damaged, the tip is effectively lost so that frequency selectivity is impaired. Additionally, the lowest point in the curve for the damaged cochlea moves to the left, and therefore towards lower frequencies. The topic of hearing impairment is discussed in Chapter 6.

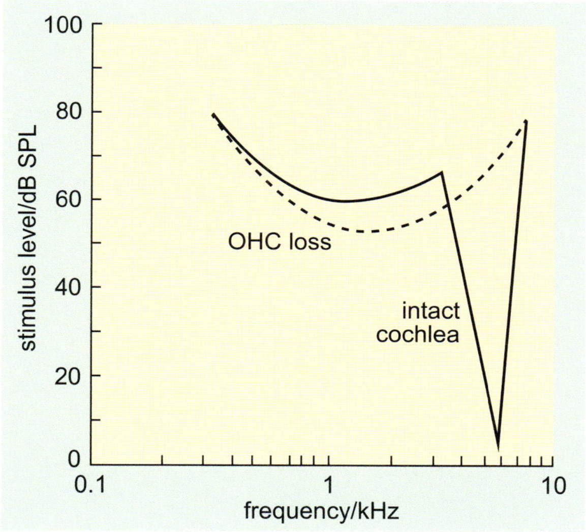

Figure 3.27 Frequency tuning curves for an axon in the cochlear nerve contacting an intact cochlea and one in which the outer hair cells (OHC) are severely damaged.

3.7 Chapter 3 summary and questions

- Motion along the basilar membrane is described as a travelling wave. High-frequency sounds cause greatest vibration near the base of the membrane, and low frequencies cause greatest vibration near the apex.
- This vibration results in displacement of the organ of Corti and movement of the hair cells against the tectorial membrane or because of surrounding fluid forces.

- Displacement of the stereocilia towards the kinocilium results in an influx of K^+ ions and a depolarisation of the hair cell. Displacement of stereocilia away from the kinocilium results in hyperpolarisation of the hair cell by closing the K^+ channels that are normally open at rest.
- Depolarisation of the hair cell allows Ca^{2+} ions to enter the cell, leading to the release of the neurotransmitter glutamate from the presynaptic terminals on the hair cell. These terminals have distinct structural features to allow high temporal resolution of signalling.
- Glutamate binds to the afferent neuron, resulting in an increase or a decrease in the level of firing from the low level of spontaneous activity.
- Outer hair cells, which vastly outnumber inner hair cells, help amplify vibrations of the basilar membrane and therefore act as a cochlear amplifier.

Self-assessment questions

Question 3.1

Describe the two ways in which the middle ear compensates for acoustic-impedance differences as sound is transmitted to the inner ear.

Question 3.2

What is a travelling wave in the context of the response of the basilar membrane to an incoming sound signal?

Question 3.3

Describe the method used to determine the characteristic frequency of a single axon within the cochlear nerve.

Question 3.4

What features of the hair cell allow it to respond with high temporal precision?

Neural processing of auditory information 4

So far in this block you have learned about the basic properties of sound waves, and how these are transduced into an electrical signal in hair cells. These signals can result in action potentials in the neurons that form the cochlear nerve, enabling the transmission of information to the brain.

This chapter considers how key information about the frequency, intensity and location of sound can be extracted from the signal and transmitted to the higher regions of the brain. Although the cochlea is the site of transduction and the first point in this pathway, it is also responsible for a significant amount of information extraction and, therefore, we begin by looking at how information is coded in the cochlea.

4.1 Information processing in the cochlea

Chapter 3 described the role of the basilar membrane in the transduction of sound information by examining the displacement of the membrane in response to the incoming sound wave. Specifically, we highlighted the way in which the position of the maximum movement along the membrane (and the amount of movement) provides critical information about the frequency and intensity of the sound stimulus. In this section we consider further how the cochlea processes this information.

4.1.1 Frequency extraction by place code

You now know that each hair cell exists in a localised region of the cochlea, and that the neurons that make up the cochlear nerve contacting a hair cell may fire action potentials in response to movement of the basilar membrane at that location. This means that the response of any given neuron should reflect the characteristic frequency of the hair cell activated, and therefore the frequency selectivity of the location on the basilar membrane from which it comes. In other words, the neurons that belong to the cochlear nerve preserve the frequency selectivity found along the basilar membrane.

Axons on the outside of the cochlear nerve bundle (those that innervate the basal hair cells) have high characteristic frequencies, whereas those towards the middle of the nerve bundle, which innervate the apex of the cochlea, have low characteristic frequencies. Thus, it is thought that each place or location within the cochlear nerve responds 'best' to a particular frequency.

The axons within the nerve are spatially arranged to correspond directly to their basilar membrane origin. This way of determining frequency is known as the place theory and gives rise to the **place code**. The arrangement is known as **tonotopic organisation**, which can be defined as the orderly spatial arrangement of neural elements corresponding to the separation of different frequencies. Functionally, tonotopic organisation allows the input frequency to be determined according to which axon within the cochlear nerve discharges with the greatest relative firing rate. However, such an organisation model is not limited to the cochlear nerve, and in fact is found at all higher levels of the auditory system, up to and including the auditory cortex.

There are several ways in which the frequency selectivity of individual axons within the cochlear nerve can be determined. One is to present a single axon with a wide range of stimuli of different frequencies but identical intensity. The graph generated when responses to the stimuli are plotted against the frequency of each stimulus is called an **iso-intensity contour**. Figure 4.1a shows a number of such contours for a single neuron in the cochlear nerve (Rose et al., 1971), where the number of action potentials can be seen to vary with frequency for four stimulus intensities. In each case, the more spikes that are generated at a given frequency, the more sensitive the axon is at that particular frequency.

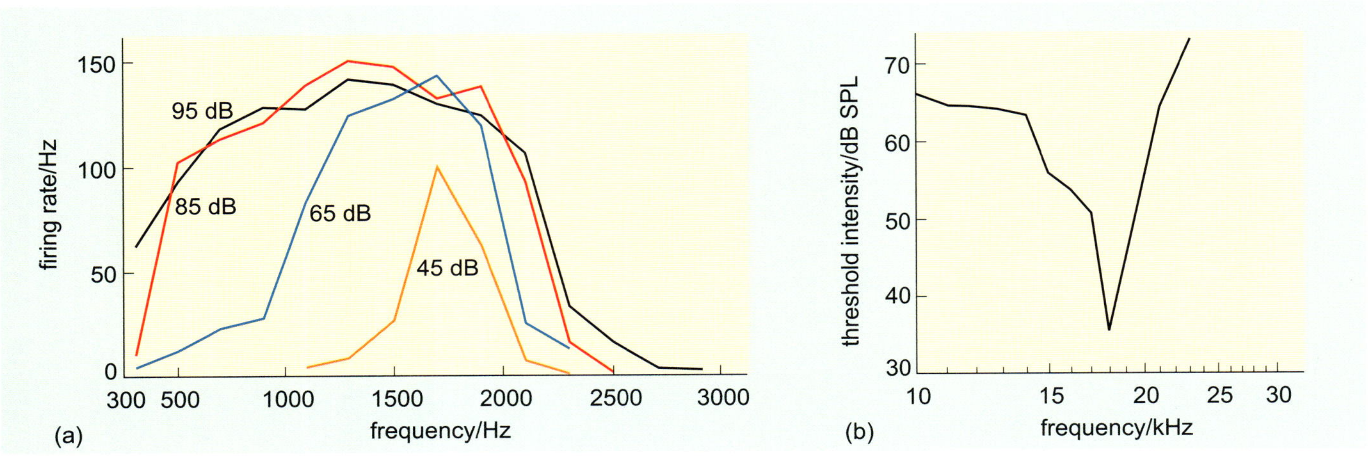

Figure 4.1 (a) Four iso-intensity contours for a single axon in the cochlear nerve. (b) Tuning curve for an axon in the cochlear nerve of a guinea pig.

- ■ What do you notice about the shape of the different contours?
- □ The higher the intensity of the stimulus, the broader the contour.
- ■ What does the data indicate about the frequency selectivity of the axon?
- □ At lower intensities, the neuron responds maximally to a narrow range of frequencies but, as the intensity of the signal increases, the range of frequencies to which the axon responds increases (i.e. the axon shows lower frequency selectivity at high intensities).

A second way of displaying the tuning characteristics of a single axon is to generate a tuning curve. This is done in a similar way to the tuning curves of hair cells, namely readings are taken from axons in the cochlear nerve while the ear is exposed to a series of pure tones, in order to determine the intensity required to generate a predetermined level of neural firing (see Section 3.5.5). However, in this case, the predefined level of firing is the onset of firing, because the aim is to find the intensity of each different frequency that elicits a response (the threshold intensity). Figure 4.1b is a tuning curve for a single axon within the cochlear nerve of a guinea pig, showing how the threshold intensity for that axon varies with the stimulus frequency (Goldstein, 1999).

■ What is the characteristic frequency of this particular neuron?

□ About 18 kHz. The intensity of the stimulus needed to elicit a response is lower here than for any other frequency (less than 40 dB SPL).

You can see that the high frequency side of the curve in Figure 4.1b is very steep, whereas the low frequency side is less steep and may have a long, low-frequency tail.

■ What does this pattern indicate?

□ It means that neurons are unlikely to respond to many frequencies higher than their characteristic frequency even when the intensity of the signal is very high. (At a frequency of about 23 kHz, the intensity of the signal needs to be about 70 dB to elicit a response.) For frequencies below the characteristic frequency, the intensity of the signal needed to elicit a response is not quite so high and there is a broader range of frequencies to which the axon will respond.

Masking effects and place theory

Some of the evidence for place theory comes from psychophysics experiments on the phenomenon of **masking**. This effect is basically when one sound 'drowns out' another, but is technically defined as the rise in threshold of one stimulus (test stimulus) due to the presence of another (masker) stimulus.

A typical masking experiment is detailed in Box 4.1, and these kinds of experiments have established that a signal is most easily masked by a sound of similar frequency to the signal. This discovery led to the idea that our ability to separate the components of a complex sound depends on the frequency-resolving power of the basilar membrane. It also led to the idea that masking reflects the limits of frequency selectivity and provides a way to quantify it.

In fact, many masking effects can be explained in a very simplified way by analysing the interaction of displacement patterns in response to sound on the basilar membrane. For example, Figure 4.2 shows the vibration patterns on the basilar membrane caused by three tones of 400 Hz, 800 Hz and 1000 Hz.

The vibration pattern of the 800 Hz tone (which is shaded) almost totally overlaps that for the higher frequency 1000 Hz tone, but there is less overlap with the 800 Hz and 400 Hz tones. You might therefore (correctly) expect that the 800 Hz tone masks the 1000 Hz tone more effectively than the 400 Hz tone. The fact that masking spreads upwards in frequency more than downwards is consistent with the asymmetry seen in basilar membrane vibration patterns, and therefore also in the tuning curves of cochlear nerve axons. This masking phenomenon, therefore, supports the place code mechanism of frequency tuning on the basilar membrane.

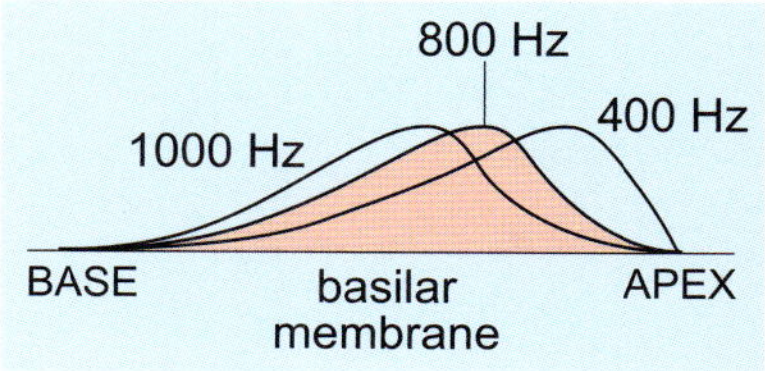

Figure 4.2 Vibration patterns on the basilar membrane caused by 400, 800 and 1000 Hz tones.

Masking has also been used to determine tuning curves. A low-intensity pure test tone is presented throughout the experiment and a series of masking pure tones are then presented, one at a time, with the test tone. The level of each masking tone is reduced until the test tone is just audible. Each masking tone, because it is a pure tone, will cause vibration mainly at one point on the basilar membrane. If the masking tone is the same as, or of similar frequency to, the test tone it will mask it more effectively than a masking tone of a different frequency.

The results of this kind of masking experiment are shown in Figure 4.3, which depicts three test tones (their frequencies are indicated by the arrows on the *x*-axis) and the tuning curves for the masking tones used to disguise them. The traces show what we would expect according to the place theory of frequency coding on the basilar membrane: when the masking tone is the same frequency as the test tone, it does not need to be very intense in order to mask the test tone. However, when the masking tone differs in frequency from the test tone, higher intensities are required to mask the test tone.

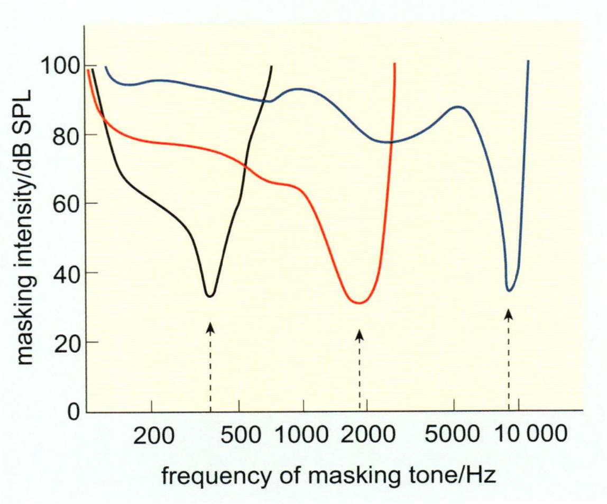

Figure 4.3 Three tuning curves generated using the masking method described in the text. The arrows show the frequency of three different test tones.

Box 4.1 A masking experiment

The procedure for a masking experiment is shown in Figure 4.4. First, the threshold for hearing is determined across a range of frequencies (the small arrows in Figure 4.4a). Then, a masking stimulus is presented at a particular place along the frequency scale (the large arrow in Figure 4.4b) and, while the masking stimulus is present, the thresholds for all frequencies are redetermined.

The masking stimulus used can be a pure tone or, more commonly, white noise. A band-limited white-noise stimulus is simply one that contains a band of frequencies with equal sound pressure at each frequency.

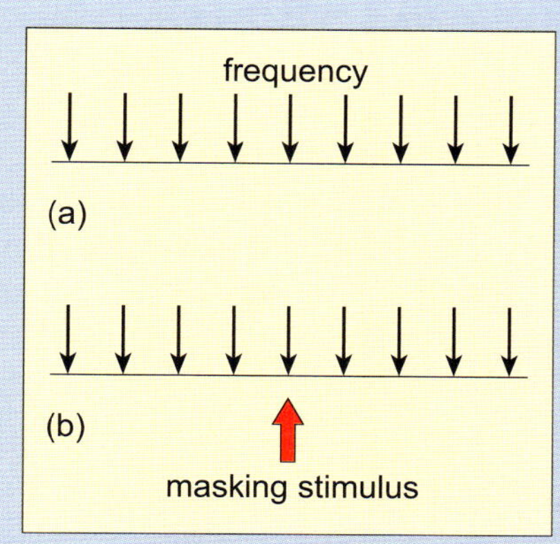

Figure 4.4 The procedure for a masking experiment. (a) The threshold for hearing is determined across a range of frequencies (small arrows). (b) The threshold is redetermined at each frequency in the presence of a masking stimulus (large arrow).

When thresholds are measured in the presence of a masking noise, the original values are raised. Figure 4.5 shows the results of an experiment using a band of noise 90 Hz wide centred at 410 Hz.

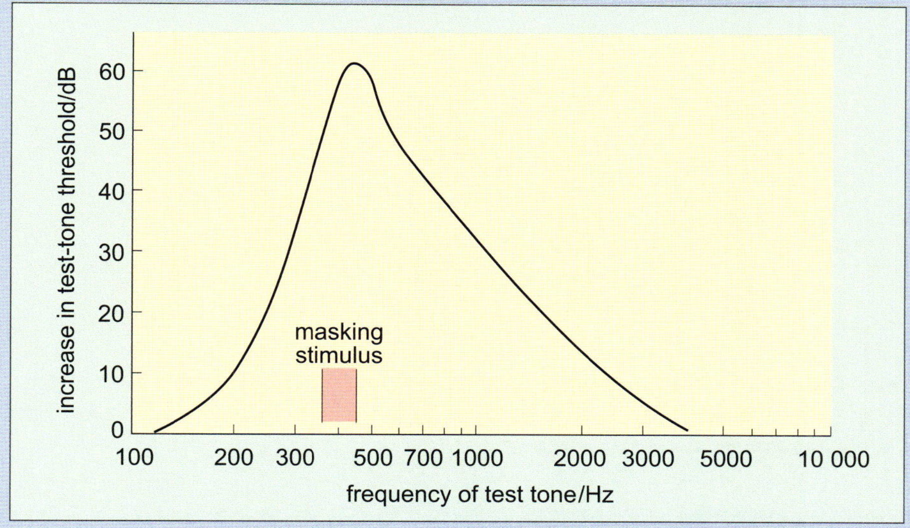

Figure 4.5 Results of a masking experiment, indicating the amount that the threshold is raised in the presence of a masking noise.

There are two things to note about the results. First, the threshold increases most for frequencies near those in the masking tone (by approximately 60 dB above the original reading for the frequency in the middle of the masking band). Second, the curve is not symmetrical; the masking effect spreads more to high frequencies than to low frequencies. So, lower frequencies mask higher-frequency sounds much more effectively than the reverse.

4.1.2 Frequency extraction by temporal code

Although the evidence for place coding of frequency information is compelling, there is a question about whether the tuning curves obtained from axons in the cochlear nerve provide a mechanism for frequency discrimination that is fine enough to account for behavioural data. People can detect remarkably small differences in frequency, which are likely to be smaller than the width of the band-pass filters effectively provided by the hair cells distributed along the basilar membrane.

What accounts for this ability? Wever and Bray (1930) proposed that in response to a pure tone, the vibration of the basilar membrane matches the input frequency. They further suggested that the hair cells respond in such a way that the temporal pattern of basilar membrane vibration is reproduced in the firing pattern of the neuron. As you read in Chapter 3, hair cells are well equipped to release neurotransmitter in a manner that faithfully represents the incoming signal and to modulate afferent neuron firing accordingly, such that their response is locked to a certain point (e.g. the peak) in the stimulus (Figure 4.6). By phase locking in this way, the response pattern of the neuron would accurately reflect the frequency of the sound wave. This is called the **temporal code**.

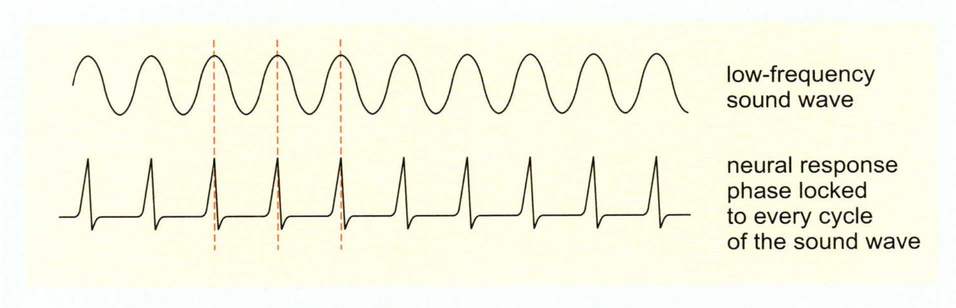

Figure 4.6 The temporal code for frequency information: firing of the neuron (bottom trace) is phase locked to the same point in every cycle of the pure tone stimulus (top trace).

This idea is attractive and there is evidence that it occurs, but only at low frequencies.

■ Thinking back to Chapter 3, suggest why phase locking of afferent neuron firing does not occur beyond 1 kHz.

□ The hair cell cannot produce an oscillating or a periodic receptor potential beyond this level, but rather a summating potential occurs. Given that the hair cell is responsible for modulating the firing of the afferent neuron, a lack of oscillation in the receptor potential prevents this information being transmitted to the afferent neuron. Additionally, even if the hair cell were able to transmit this information, neurons cannot fire above 1 kHz because of the refractory period.

In fact, afferent neurons cannot maintain sustained firing above a few hundred hertz of stimulus frequency. This realisation led Wever and Bray (1930) to propose the operation of a **volley principle**, as illustrated in Figure 4.7. Here, the frequency of the sound wave depicted is too high for a single neuron to fire on every cycle. According to the volley principle, each of the six neurons measured fires in phase at a certain point in the cycle, although it does not respond to *every* cycle. If the responses of all neurons are then combined, as may happen further up in the auditory system, then information regarding signal frequency is preserved as the combined response (the bottom trace in the figure) is sufficient to reproduce the frequency of the incoming signal.

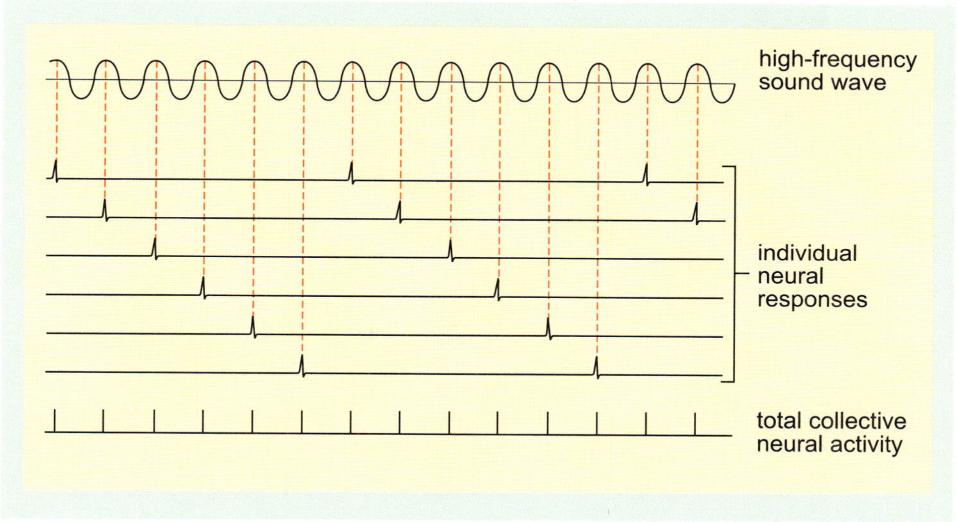

Figure 4.7 The volley principle: the ensemble of axon responses shown at the bottom of the figure has a pattern of firing that corresponds to the frequency of the input sound wave at the top.

Using this principle, it is possible to phase lock to sustained signals with frequencies up to 1 kHz (2–3 volleys per cycle, i.e. 2–3 neurons working together) thereby enhancing the transmission of information about stimulus frequency. However, to encode frequencies of 20 kHz would require around 70 neurons working together and evidence suggests that the volley mechanism breaks down completely by 3–5 kHz (10 volleys per cycle; ~10 neurons working together) when the variability inherent in neural firing becomes too great for such fine patterns to be resolved, and the frequency coding fails.

Researchers now believe that the mechanism used to encode frequency is actually dependent on the particular frequency being encoded. Below 50 Hz, it appears that frequency is encoded solely using temporal code because at such low levels there is a broad pattern of vibration on the basilar membrane, which would make place code inaccurate. Temporal code continues to operate effectively for frequencies up to 1000 kHz, while place code solely enables coding of frequencies above 3000 Hz. Intermediate frequencies can be coded for by both mechanisms.

Note that temporal coding is also of particular importance when the incoming sound is intense enough to saturate the neural firing rate. Neurons of many characteristic frequencies will respond to an intense signal because it will be above the threshold even for those with characteristic frequencies that are different from the signal frequency (although they will respond less vigorously). However, frequency information will still be encoded in the temporal firing pattern of all stimulated neurons. As with tonotopic organisation, phase locking is also found in central auditory structures and therefore allows frequency extraction throughout the auditory system.

The information provided from the frequency analysis performed by the cochlea is summarised quite neatly by the concept of the 'excitation pattern' – the profile of activity across frequency. This can be expressed in terms of activation of cochlear nerve axons with a range of characteristic frequencies, or psychophysically (as in Figure 4.5). The importance of the frequency analysis performed by the cochlea cannot be underestimated because it underlies most of our auditory abilities, including the detection of pitch, loudness and sound quality, speech sound discrimination, and localisation.

4.1.3 Intensity coding by firing rate

As with frequency information, stimulus intensity may also be encoded in two ways. The first of these is according to the firing rates of neurons.

Intensity is assumed to be encoded by an increase in discharge rate of action potentials within the cochlear nerve. As the stimulus gets more intense, the basilar membrane vibrates with greater amplitude, causing the membrane potential of activated hair cells to be more depolarised. In turn, these hair cells release more glutamate, causing the afferent neurons that synapse onto the hair cells to fire at a greater rate.

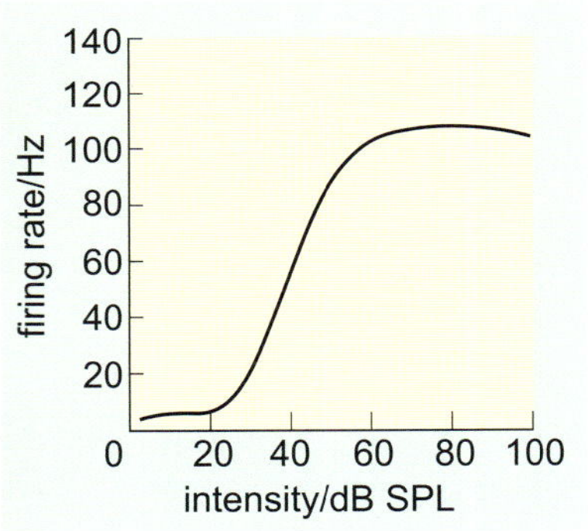

Figure 4.8 Intensity response function for a single neuron in the cochlear nerve.

However, for single neurons the discharge rate increases only for a relatively small range of sound pressure levels. Figure 4.8 shows the results of recordings from a neuron in the cochlear nerve in response to a stimulus of increasing intensity. The stimulus is a pure tone at the characteristic frequency of the neuron. As the intensity of the stimulus increases, so does the number of action potentials generated per second.

- ■ What does the figure show about the responses of the neuron as a function of the sound level of the stimulus?
- □ The threshold of the neuron is about 25 dB SPL and the cell responds maximally to all sounds greater than about 60 dB SPL.

For this neuron, a change in response with intensity only occurs over the dynamic range of about 40 dB, after which it no longer responds to increases in sound level with an increased firing rate: the neuron is said to be saturated. Given then that humans are sensitive to a 140 dB dynamic range, it is clear that one neuron cannot respond over this entire scale. However, if intensity is determined by the discharge rate of a number of neurons with different response thresholds, then a large dynamic range can be accommodated.

For example, the most sensitive neurons have response thresholds of about 0 dB SPL and characteristically have high rates of spontaneous activity. They produce saturating responses for stimulation at moderate intensities, about 40 dB SPL. At the opposite extreme, some afferent neurons display less spontaneous activity and much higher thresholds, and give graded responses to intensities of stimulation in excess of 100 dB SPL.

While combining information from neurons with different dynamic ranges is possible, another mechanism has been suggested. Wen et al. (2009) demonstrated that the dynamic range of neurons forming the cochlear nerve of a cat could adapt to a continuous sound signal by effectively shifting their dynamic range to centre on the probable sound intensity. The researchers do not think that this mechanism alone can account for the full range of intensity sensitivity, but suggest that it may at least contribute.

4.1.4 Intensity coding by number of neurons

In addition to an increase in the firing rate of neurons with differing dynamic ranges, the inclusion of discharges from many neurons whose characteristic frequencies are different from those of the stimulus may also help to account for the wide dynamic range of the ear. As the intensity of a sound increases, the amplitude of vibration of the basilar membrane rises, which results in neurons either side of those with the characteristic frequency being activated. Thus, a pattern of excitation is produced in the cochlear nerve such that neurons with a characteristic frequency close to the input frequency fire more strongly than those whose characteristic frequency is slightly removed from that of the incoming signal.

Figure 4.9 shows a pattern of neural excitation along the basilar membrane that may be produced by a pure tone of 80 dB SPL (solid line). Assuming that the neurons most excited by this stimulus are firing at a maximum rate – that is, they are saturated – any increase in intensity of the stimulus will not result in an increase in the firing rate of these neurons. However, the neurons with a characteristic frequency either higher or lower than the stimulus frequency are not firing at their maximum level. Therefore, increasing the stimulus level causes an increase in the firing rate of these neurons, broadening the excitation pattern (dashed line).

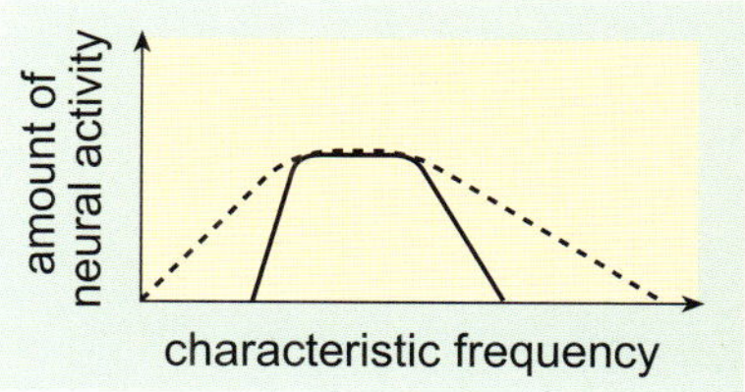

Figure 4.9 An increase in stimulus intensity causes more neurons to fire as those with a characteristic frequency just above or below the stimulus frequency respond in addition to those most sensitive to the stimulus frequency.

Thus, intensity could be encoded by how broad the excitation pattern may be to a given stimulus. Indeed, this is thought to be the case, however, the presentation of masking stimuli that would affect the edges of the excitation pattern only has a small effect on intensity discrimination, confirming that this is not the only mechanism used for coding intensity.

4.2 Intermediate chapter summary

- The cochlea extracts information about the frequency and intensity of an incoming sound signal.
- Frequency can be coded in two different ways: place code, which relies on tonotopic organisation; and temporal code, which relies on phase locking.

- The method of frequency coding used in the cochlea depends on the frequency of the stimulus, with lower frequencies using temporal code and higher frequencies relying on place code.
- Intensity can be coded for by firing rate and number of neurons firing in the cochlear nerve.

4.3 Information processing beyond the cochlea

So far, we have considered the anatomy of the peripheral auditory system and how the basic attributes of sound are coded in that context. However, a great deal of additional processing takes place in the neural centres that lie in the auditory brainstem and cerebral cortex. Because the perception of certain features of sound such as localisation are binaural – that is, they depend on the interaction of information arriving at the two ears – we need to study the central auditory structures, where information from both ears is integrated. This section therefore deals with processing in the **central auditory system**, which consists of the structures that are outlined in the next section.

4.3.1 The ascending auditory pathway

Almost all neurons with axons in the cochlear nerve synapse on neurons within the cochlear nuclear complex in the brainstem. The relationship between the cochlear nuclear complex and higher auditory structures is shown in Figure 4.10. This figure is highly schematic and simplified, showing only the main tracts and nuclei involved in auditory processing.

Once axons leave the cochlear nuclear complex, most cross over to the contralateral side of the brain. This means that most of the auditory information processed by each half of the brain comes from the ear on the other side of the head. This arrangement is similar to touch information, which, as you may recall from Block 3 Chapter 2, crosses the midline after leaving the brainstem structures.

Both crossed and uncrossed projections from the cochlear nuclei synapse in the area of the brainstem called the **superior olivary complex**. This is the first place in the ascending pathway to receive information from both ears. Neural impulses are then transmitted from the superior olivary complex to the **inferior colliculus** in the midbrain through and/or around the lateral lemniscus (some synapse in the lateral lemniscus, but most pass directly through it). From there, the signal is passed to the **medial geniculate nucleus** in the thalamus and finally to the **auditory cortex**.

Now that you have an overview of the route auditory information takes from the cochlea to the brain, we next consider the processing of sound information at each structure in turn, beginning with the cochlear nuclear complex.

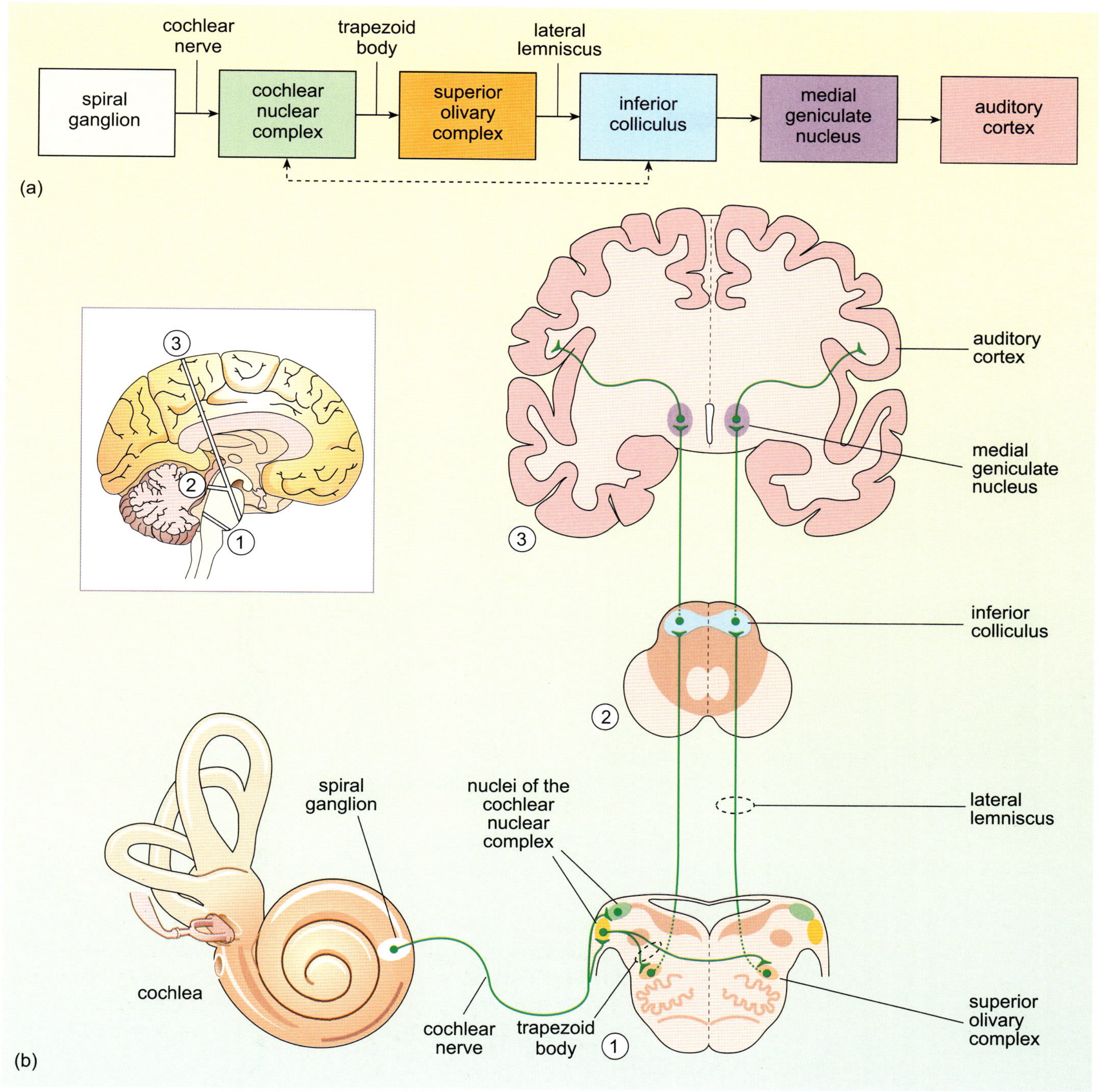

Figure 4.10 The main anatomical stages in the ascending auditory pathway from the cochlea to the auditory cortex shown: (a) schematically and (b) through cross-sections of the brain.

4.3.2 The cochlear nuclear complex

The cochlear nuclear complex can be divided into three major cochlear nuclei: anteroventral, posteroventral and dorsal. As the cochlear nerve enters this nuclear complex it divides into two main branches. One branch innervates the anteroventral cochlear nucleus (AVCN) and the other innervates both the posteroventral (PVCN) and dorsal cochlear nuclei (DCN) (Figure 4.11). Each region preserves the tonotopic map set up in the cochlea, as illustrated by the paths taken by the high-frequency and low-frequency information in Figure 4.11b.

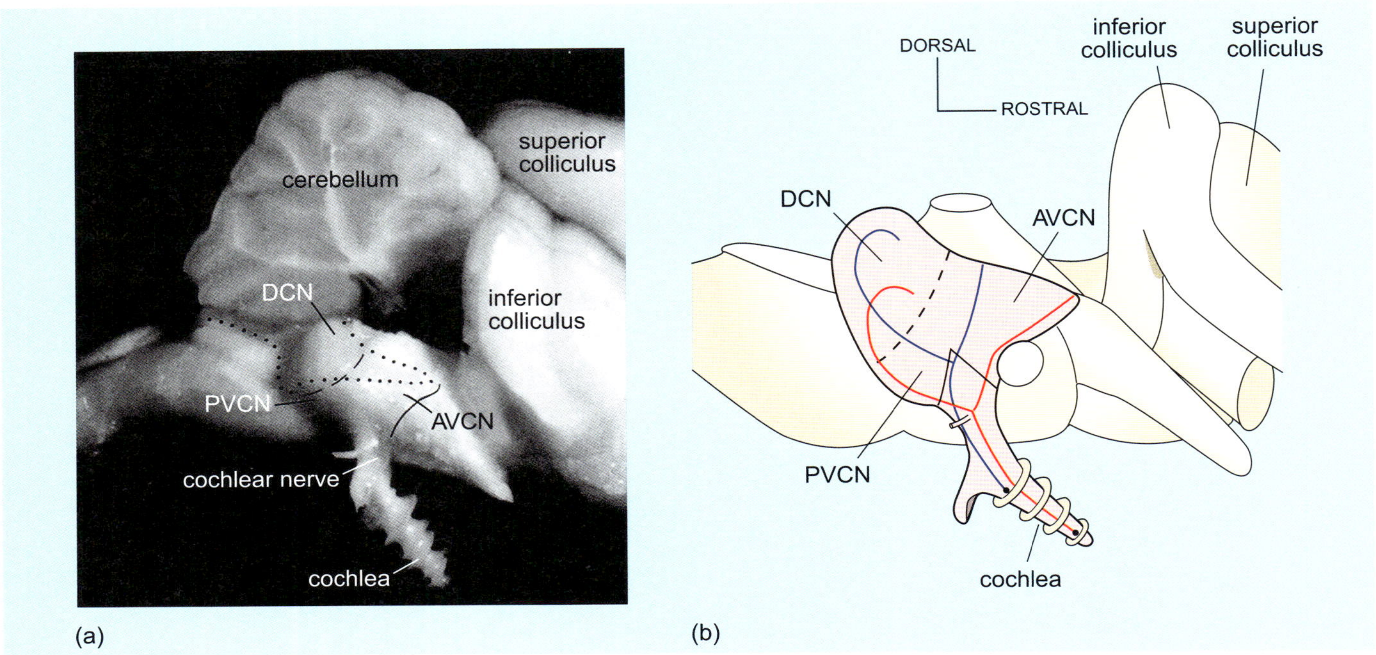

Figure 4.11 (a) Lateral view of the cochlear nuclear complex and adjacent structures in a rodent brain. (b) Diagram of the same view showing how high-frequency (blue) and low-frequency (red) information carried in cochlear nerve axons branches on entry to the complex.

The cochlear nuclei contain a number of different neuronal types, which can be identified by their structure. Specifically, these are described as 'bushy', 'stellate', 'octopus' and 'fusiform'. These different neurons display responses that are more complex than those found in the incoming cochlear nerve. This is not just a result of the distinct patterns of afferent input to the different types of neuron but also because inhibitory inputs from other types of neurons within the complex (or from higher up the pathway) influence their responses.

Several different firing patterns are found to occur in response to the same tonal stimulus as a result of this interplay between excitation and inhibition. This idea is shown in Figure 4.12a, which shows the overall response recorded from the cochlear nerve axons to a stimulus presentation (indicated by the black bar), and the responses of the individual cell types to the same stimulus (Figure 4.12b–e).

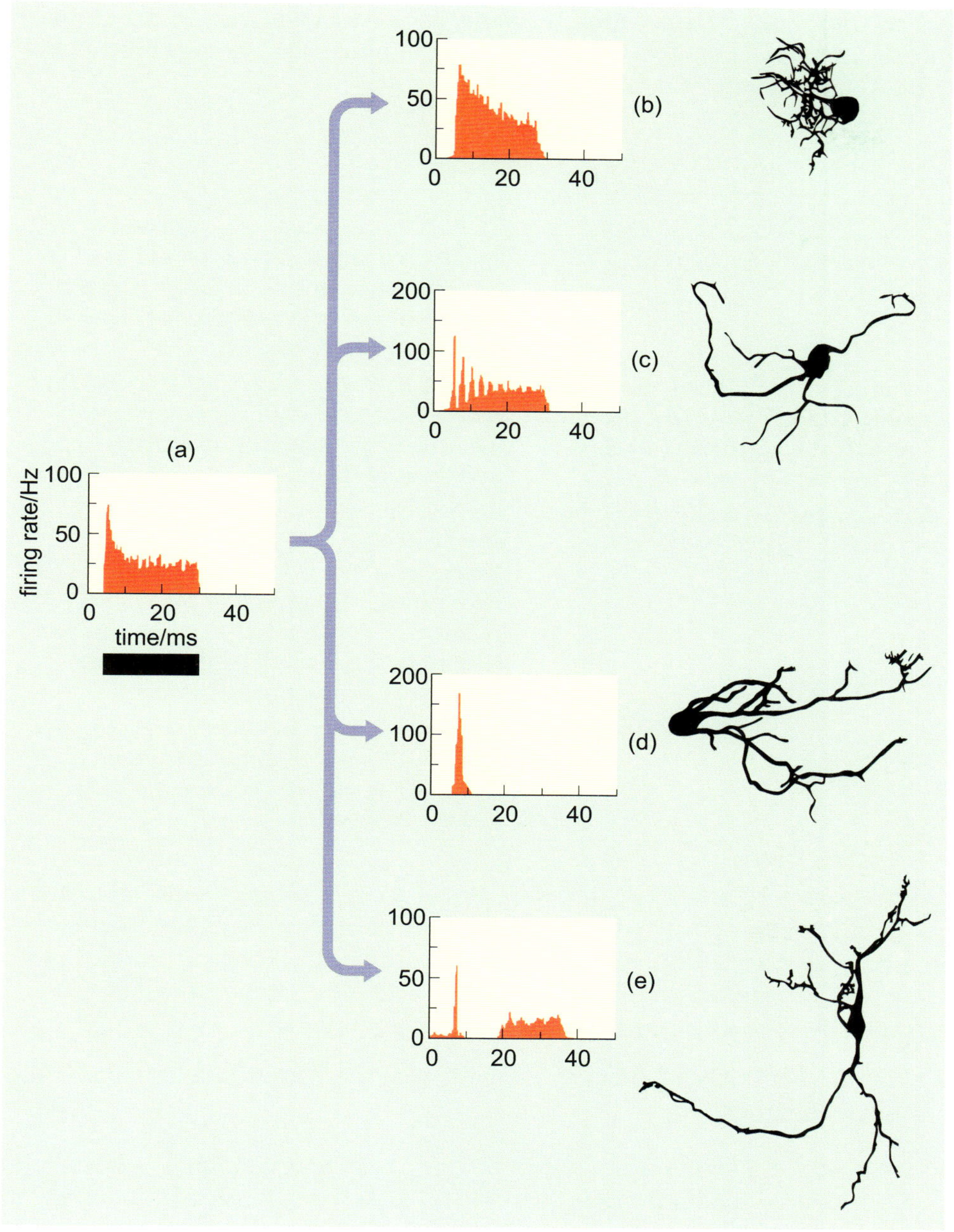

Figure 4.12 (a) Overall response recorded from the cochlear nerve axons to a stimulus presentation. (b)–(e) Respective responses of individual bushy cells, stellate cells, octopus cells and fusiform cells.

The plots reveal:

- primary-like responses by bushy cells in the AVCN
- regularly timed spikes by stellate cells in the PVCN
- onset responses by octopus cells in the PVCN
- build-up responses by fusiform cells in the DCN (which show a reduction in firing after the initial burst and then a subsequent build-up).

In line with these different firing patterns, each type of neuron in the cochlear nuclear complex is thought to be linked to the processing of a specific aspect of the sound stimulus (Table 4.1).

Table 4.1 Differences between the neuron types in the cochlear nuclear complex.

Cochlear nuclei	Cell type	Structural features	Responses
Ventral (AVCN/PVCN)	stellate (chopper)	star-like with several symmetrical dendrites	fire at very regular rates over a large dynamic range despite slight variations in stimulus frequency, indicative of a role in processing sound intensity
	bushy	single, stout, branched primary dendrite receiving input from only a few afferent fibres, creating a large efficient synapse called the 'end bulb of Held'	firing is locked to that of the afferent input and in some case sharpened as adjacent frequencies are inhibited, indicating a role in processing frequency
PVCN	octopus	long, thick dendrites typically extending from one side of the cell body	firing at the onset of a specific frequency or frequency range at higher amplitudes, indicating a role in extracting timing information; also project to midbrain auditory nuclei involved in motor reactions, leading to suggestion that they may be involved in acoustic startle responses
DCN	fusiform (pyramidal)	layered organisation similar to cerebellar cortex	display excitatory and inhibitory responses to a broad range of stimulus frequency; spatial firing pattern indicates a role in vertical localisation

From Figure 4.12 and Table 4.1, you should recognise that sound information is carefully organised at the level of the cochlear nuclear complex to allow parallel processing of information relating to frequency, intensity and location. Moreover, in some cases the information is actually 'sharpened up' to make perceptually relevant features such as onset more salient.

■ From your study of Block 2, suggest what mechanism might underlie this sharpening up.

□ Lateral inhibition.

Indeed, many neurons in the cochlear nuclear complex have been found to experience this phenomenon. The signal that enters the complex is therefore modified before being sent to the next structure in the ascending pathway: the superior olivary complex.

4.3.3 The superior olivary complex

Recall from Figure 4.10 that this structure is the first point in the ascending auditory pathway where binaural comparisons can be made because information from both ears is available to the same neurons. Such comparisons are critical for the localisation of sound. Therefore, Sections 4.3.4 and 4.3.5 focus on how the superior olivary complex processes the incoming signal to allow the localisation of a sound.

In fact, there are two distinct mechanisms for localising sound and they are carried out by particular regions of this complex: the medial superior olivary (MSO) nuclei and the lateral superior olivary (LSO) nuclei. The MSO nuclei rely on time differences in the sound signal reaching both ears, while the LSO nuclei monitor differences in intensity between the two ears. These factors are discussed in the sections that follow.

4.3.4 Interaural time delays

The average distance between human ears is about 20 cm.

■ The speed of sound in air is about 343 m s^{-1}, which means that it will travel 343 metres in one second. How long does it take a sound wave to travel the distance between the human ears?

□ If sound travels 343 m in one second, and speed is calculated as the distance travelled divided by the time taken:

$$\text{time} = \frac{\text{distance}}{\text{speed}} = \frac{0.2\ \text{m}}{343\ \text{m s}^{-1}} = 0.0058\ \text{s}$$

So it takes about 0.6 ms for the it to travel the distance between the ears.

Therefore, from the calculation above, if a sudden noise comes perpendicularly from the right of your head, it will reach your right ear 0.6 ms before it reaches your left ear. For a sound coming from directly in front of you, there will be no delay, and at angles in between, the delay will be between 0 and 0.6 ms. Thus, there is a simple relationship connecting the location of the sound source and the interaural delay.

Neurons in the MSO nuclei can detect interaural time delays in the signals they receive from the left and right cochlear nuclear complex using a mechanism involving a series of delay lines and coincidence detectors. This idea was first put forward by Jeffress (1948) and research has since shown that these MSO neurons are excited by inputs from both cochlear nuclear complexes.

Consider Figure 4.13, for example. Here, sound reaches the left ear and hence the left cochlear nucleus first, resulting in the generation of action potentials that are relayed to neurons in the MSO nuclei (Figure 4.13a). A fraction of a millisecond later, sound reaches the right ear, initiating activity in the right cochlear nucleus (Figure 4.13b). By this time, however, the impulses travelling from the left cochlear nucleus have travelled further along the axon (which is the delay line). Impulses from both ears reach coincidence at, in this case, olivary neuron 3, which then fires an action potential (Figure 4.13c).

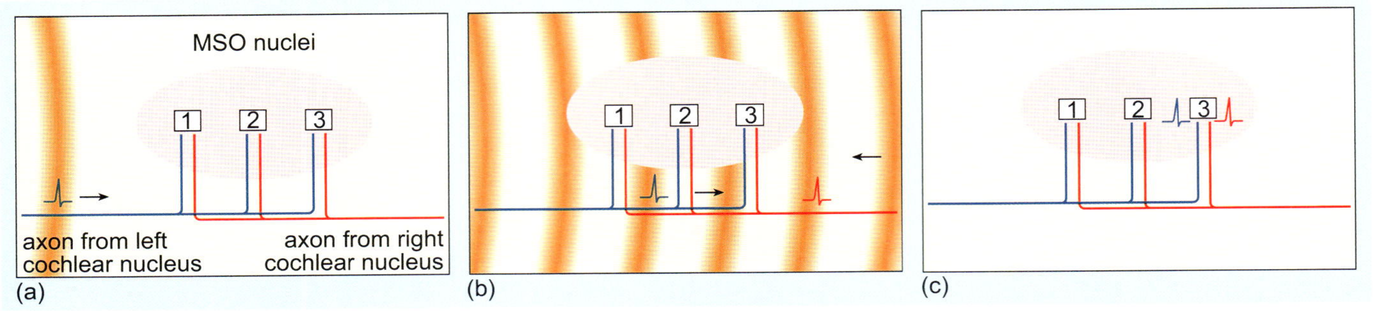

Figure 4.13 Delay lines and coincidence detection in the MSO nuclei.

- According to this illustration, if the sound were directly in front of the person, which of the MSO neurons would fire?

- Neuron 2, because the time it would take the action potential to travel from the left and the right cochlear nuclei would be the same and coincidence would occur in the midline MSO nuclei.

You can see from this example that the auditory system can extract information about the location of a sound source by attending to which neuron in the MSO fires in response to the sound. This is because these neurons only fire if inputs from both ears summate at a given location, and different neurons fire in response to different delays. However, this method cannot be used for detecting the location of a continuous tone because such a signal is always present at both ears, and if we don't hear the onset of a sound then our auditory system cannot determine the initial difference in arrival times at the two ears. Therefore, in order to localise a continuous tone, the auditory system has to use a different kind of temporal information.

Recall that neurons are capable of phase locking to a sound stimulus such that they fire at characteristic points or phase angles along the sound wave. For example, a neuron may fire at the peak of the sound wave, although it may not fire every time the wave reaches this position. In both ears, impulses produced by neurons tuned to the same frequency will lock to the same phase angle, e.g. the peak. But, depending when the signals reach the ears, the train of impulses generated in one ear may be delayed relative to the impulse train generated in the other ear.

Imagine you are exposed to a 400 Hz sound coming from the right (Figure 4.14a). At this frequency the wavelength is about 85 cm, which is more than the 20 cm distance between your ears. After a given peak in the sound wave (point 1 in the diagram) passes your right ear, you must wait 0.6 ms, the time it takes the sound to travel 20 cm, before detecting the *same* peak in your left ear. Because the wavelength of the sound wave is much longer than the distance between your ears, you can reliably use the interaural delay in peaks in the wave to determine sound location without the risk of your brain confusing the peaks at points 0 and 2 with the one at point 1.

However, if the wavelength was smaller than the distance between your ears, the same point but several cycles further along might be inadvertently compared, and the location of the sound misperceived as coming from directly

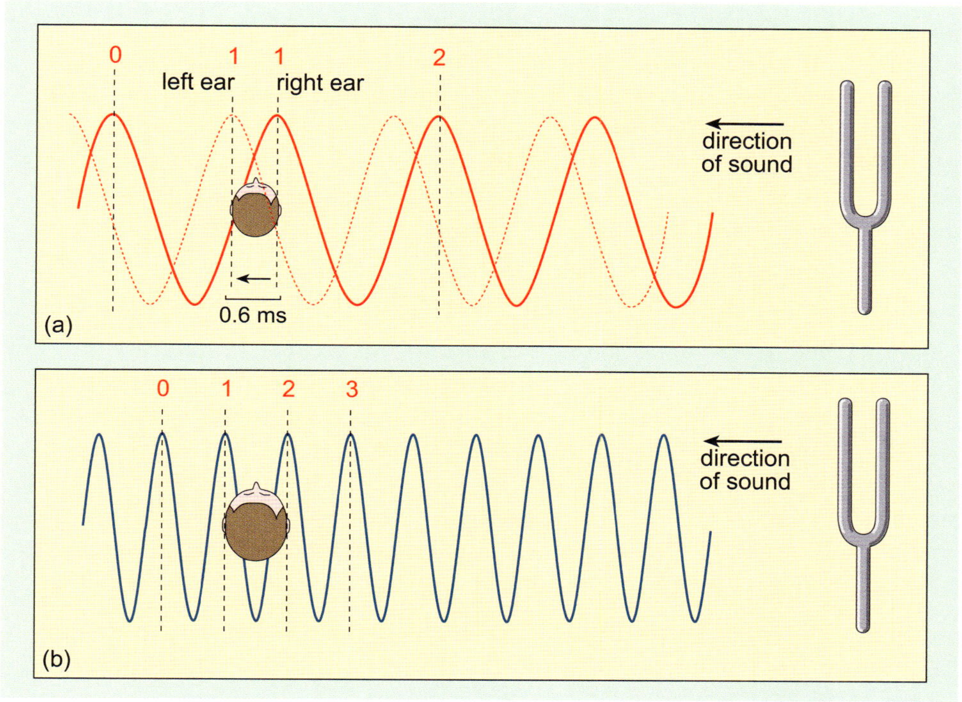

Figure 4.14 Locating different sound wavelengths. (a) A signal from the right results in peak 1 arriving at the right ear 0.6 ms before arriving at the left. Because the wavelength is more than twice the head diameter, no confusion is caused by the other peaks. (b) A signal from the right with a wavelength shorter than the head diameter causes the location of the source to be incorrectly perceived as being directly in front.

in front of you (Figure 4.14b). Clearly, the peaks detected at the ears are different (labelled 1 and 2 in the figure) but as far as the brain is concerned, there would be no phase difference and the sound would be perceived as coming from the front. Such problems are known as **phase ambiguities** and occur with continuous tones of frequencies above about 1500 Hz. In fact, even with sounds of frequency as low as 750 Hz we can be confused about the location of the source.

Note that a 1500 Hz tone will result in a peak appearing at each ear simultaneously, as shown in Figure 4.14b. A 750 Hz tone has half that frequency, hence twice the wavelength so, peak-to-peak, would cover two head widths. In other words, on a person's head, one ear would be at a peak when the other was at a trough of the wave. The brain has no information to indicate which feature is leading, the trough or the peak. Depending on which is leading, the sound is either coming from the right, or the complete opposite, the left! This problem is easily solved by turning the head from side to side. The ear that was lagging will 'catch up' with the leading ear as it turns towards the sound source. This indicates which ear was leading, and hence the sound direction.

Head movement can resolve ambiguities effectively until the sound wavelength is equal to the head width (at about 1500 Hz), but beyond this frequency phase differences cannot be interpreted effectively. For this reason, comparisons of interaural time delays can only be made for continuous tones at relatively low frequencies in humans, in the range of 20–1500 Hz. For high frequencies (over 2000 Hz), we have to use another mechanism to locate sounds – the difference in interaural intensity.

4.3.5 Interaural intensity differences

Neurons in the LSO nuclei can detect binaural differences in intensity. For any sound, there is a direct relationship between the direction that the sound comes from and the extent to which the intensity of the sound at the two ears differs. If the sound comes perpendicularly from the right of the listener, it will be lower in intensity in the left ear. If it comes from directly in front, the intensity at the two ears will be the same. With sound coming from intermediate directions between these points, there are intermediate intensity differences.

Intensity differences between the ears can result from two factors: variation in the distance the sound must travel to the two ears, and differences in the degree to which the head casts a 'sound shadow'. This shadow results from diffraction, or the process of the sound wave dispersing around the head. The amount of diffraction, and therefore the size of the sound shadow, is dependent on the wavelength of the sound stimulus relative to the width of the head: wavelengths shorter than the width of the head will incur greater diffraction of the sound wave. The greater the level of diffraction, the greater the sound shadow cast by the head and the greater the level of difference between the ears.

Low-frequency sounds have wavelengths that are long compared with the width of the head. The sound therefore disperses very well around the head and there is very little sound shadow cast. By contrast, high-frequency sounds have wavelengths that are comparatively shorter, which cast a significant sound shadow (Figure 4.15).

■ What would be the effect on intensity differences at each ear of the sound shadows cast by the head for low- and high-frequency sounds? What does this mean for the likelihood of using interaural intensity differences to localise such sounds?

□ For low frequencies, the sound shadow cast by the head would cause a minimal difference in the intensity of sound at the two ears and so there would be little scope for using interaural intensity differences in order to localise the sound. For high frequencies, the sound shadow cast by the head would cause a significant difference in the intensity of the sound at the two ears and so the use of interaural intensity differences would be possible. In fact, interaural differences in intensity are negligible at low frequencies, but may be as large as 20 dB at high frequencies.

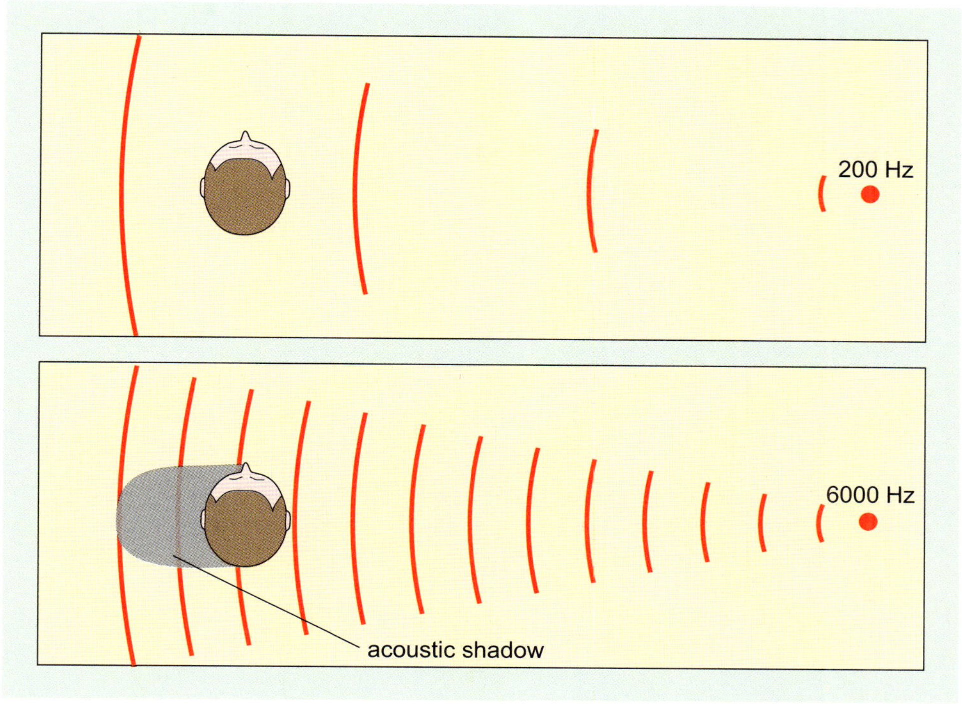

Figure 4.15 The effect of frequency on the size of acoustic shadow.

The LSO neurons receive an excitatory input as a result of sounds on the same side of the head as each nucleus, but are inhibited by sounds on the other side. This results in the response being strongest when the sound is loudest in the ear on the same side and weakest when the intensity is the same in both ears, as happens when the sound is situated along the midline. Note that this cannot be the only mechanism we use for locating high-frequency sounds because we could not use it to determine whether a sound was directly in front, behind or even overhead. In fact, the shape of our pinnae provides this important information, which is discussed next.

4.3.6 Additional localisation cues

In Chapter 2 you learned that sound intensity decreases with distance from the source, and this factor serves as another cue for localising sound because it allows us to judge the distance to the source.

■ The sound of a door slamming has an intensity level of 80 dB SPL when you are standing 1 m from it. What intensity level (in dB SPL) would you experience if you are 2 m and then 4 m from the source?

□ As you learned in Section 2.3.4, the intensity of a sound decreases with $1/\text{distance}^2$ as you move away from the source. This means that increasing the distance by a factor of two decreases the intensity of the sound by a factor of four. The change in decibels can be calculated using the equation:

$$\text{change in dB} = 10 \log\left(\frac{1}{4}\right)$$
$$= -6 \text{ dB}$$

So the new intensity level at a distance of 2 m is (80 – 6) dB = 74 dB SPL. At a distance of 4 m, the intensity is reduced by another factor of 4, so the level is 68 dB SPL.

Study note

For the mathematically minded: if we did the same calculation using pressure levels we would get the same result because the pressure, which depends on the square root of the intensity, would drop off as 1/distance and would therefore reduce by a factor of 2 at 2 m. Using Equation 2.3, this would also give a reduction of 6 dB.

A second cue relates to the frequency of a sound. When a sound travels over a distance, the high-frequency components attenuate to a greater extent than the low-frequency components. This means that sounds that are further away tend to be richer in low frequencies and are perceived as duller than they would be otherwise. To use this kind of localisation cue it is necessary to be familiar with the sound and therefore to perceive how dull it appears.

Finally, the location processing we have discussed is applicable to the horizontal plane only but we are also able to localise sounds in the vertical plane. Much of our ability to do this is due to the shape of the outer ear, in particular the pinna. The pinnae provide a monaural cue to localisation. The bumps and ridges on the pinnae produce reflections, and delays between the direct path and the reflected path make vertical localisation possible.

Vertical localisation is seriously impaired if the convolutions of the pinnae are damaged. Research by Hofman et al. (1998) involved putting moulds into the outer ear to alter the curves of the pinna and therefore its reflections. They found that doing so dramatically impaired the localisation of vertical sound sources. However, accurate performance was regained over time, indicating that the participants had relearned how to localise sound with their 'new' ears.

Activity 4.1 Sound localisation

Allow 20 minutes

(*Relevant module learning outcomes: KU1 and PS1*)

Now would be a good time to complete this online activity, which is available from the *Block 4 Activities* resource on the module website. It allows you to adjust the characteristics of sound waves to illustrate the use of interaural phase and intensity differences to localise a sound source, and the impact of the sound shadow on waves of various frequencies.

4.3.7 The inferior colliculus

The next part of interest in the ascending pathway of the central auditory system is the inferior colliculus (plural, colliculi). These structures are visible as the rear pair of four bumps located on the dorsal surface of the midbrain (Figure 4.16). Axons from the auditory brainstem nuclei carry information on frequency, intensity and localisation to the inferior colliculi via the lateral lemniscus. Each inferior colliculus consists of a central nucleus and an external region composed of a dorsal cortex and a lateral nucleus.

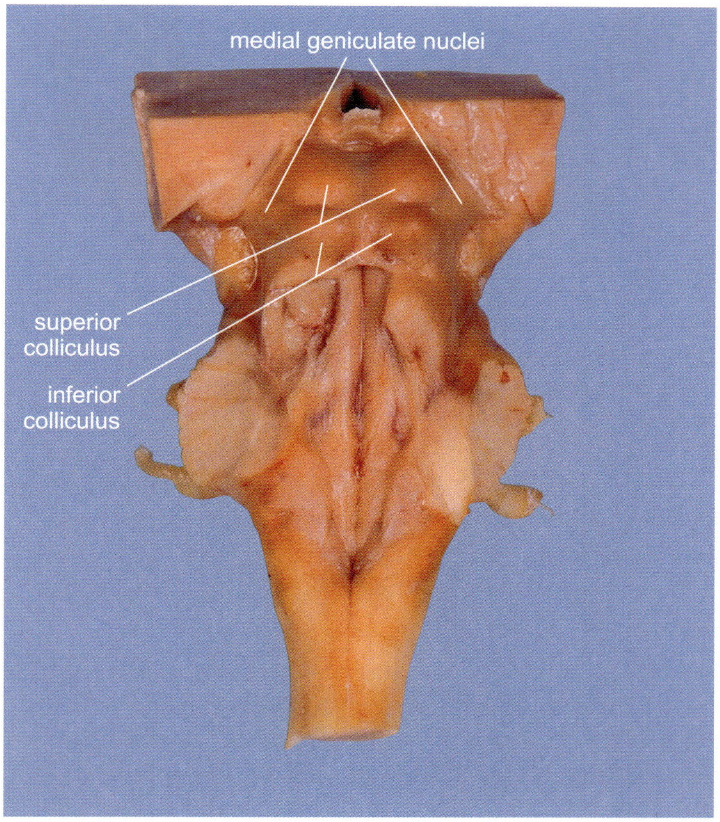

Figure 4.16 A dissection of the human brainstem and diencephalon viewed from the dorsal surface to show the locations of the inferior and superior colliculi and medial geniculate nuclei in relation to the thalamus.

Neurons in the central nucleus are arranged in **isofrequency layers**, such that the neurons within each layer exhibit similar characteristic frequencies. Figure 4.17a shows that high-frequency layers are found towards the midline, while low-frequency layers are towards the lateral edge, again preserving the tonotopic organisation found in other regions. Similarly, Figure 4.17b shows another map relating to sound intensity thresholds for the 20 kHz isofrequency layer in the central nucleus of a mouse. The numbers on the left-hand map correspond to the threshold levels in dB SPL, which are represented as coloured contours on the right. For this layer (and each one shown in Figure 4.17a), neurons in the centre of the layer are the most sensitive, with concentric rings of neurons with similar thresholds and decreasing sensitivities occurring towards the edges. This distribution pattern means that sound intensity can be related to the spread of excitation.

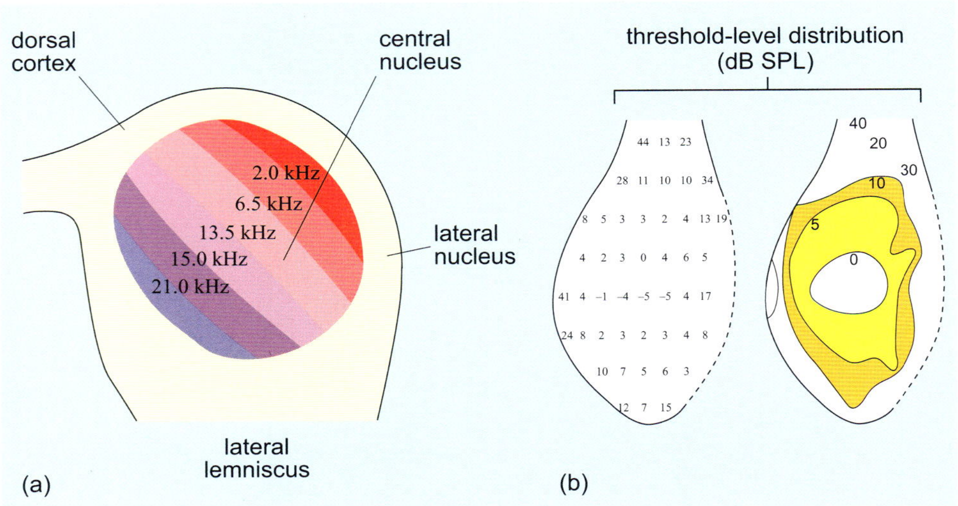

Figure 4.17 (a) Isofrequency layers in the inferior colliculus of a cat. (b) Two representations of the tone-response thresholds found in the 20 kHz isofrequency layer of a mouse.

Many neurons in the inferior colliculus also follow time-varying signals when either the frequency or the intensity is being modulated. Different neurons respond best to different rates or amplitudes of modulation, and these responses also appear to be mapped from the medial (low rate of change) to lateral (high rate of change) inferior colliculus.

The maps described above are only some of those found so far, but are useful for illustrating that precise patterns of activity are set up in response to a particular complex sound. This results in a pattern of neural output being sent on to the next stage of the pathway that relates specifically to that sound; in fact, in the medial geniculate nucleus, neurons have been found that respond only to particular complex sounds such as the mew of a kitten. It seems, therefore, that the intersecting maps in the inferior colliculus extract the features required for sound pattern categorisation by the forebrain.

As would be expected for a structure receiving information on the localisation of sound, neurons in the inferior colliculus also make responses relating to the position of sounds in space. In barn owls a 3D space map for sound location has been found in the avian equivalent of the inferior colliculus. In mammals, however, the signals are sent on to the superior colliculus where the visual space map appears to align with the auditory space map.

As well as building on the processing of lower regions of the central auditory system, the inferior colliculi are directly involved in a number of sound-related behaviours, particularly auditory-motor responses such as those that change the tension of the middle ear muscles to protect the inner ear from loud sound. They also send projections to motor nuclei in the pons and cerebellum, which contribute to turning the head and eyes in response to sounds. Furthermore, the inferior colliculi are the origin of descending pathways to the periolivary region (a region that partially surrounds the superior olivary complex) and the cochlear nuclei, and can affect cochlear responses by influencing the olivocochlear bundle feedback loop discussed in Chapter 3.

4.3.8 The medial geniculate nucleus

The medial geniculate nuclei are labelled in Figure 4.16, and each is a rounded protruberance on the surface of the thalamus. They comprised three major subdivisions: the ventral, dorsal and medial nuclei.

The ventral nucleus is sometimes referred to as the principal nucleus, and it is here that the majority of information arrives from the inferior colliculus. This nucleus maintains the tonotopic organisation present in the inferior colliculus such that neurons with the same characteristic frequency are arranged within the same layer, and it is constructed as stacked layers that represent successive frequencies. The level of processing within the medial geniculate nucleus appears similar to those at lower levels, in that the neurons are tuned to specific frequencies and most are sensitive to information from either ear. Sensitivity to the location cues of interaural time and intensity differences is also maintained by neurons of the principal nucleus, which is perhaps unsurprising when you consider that it is this nucleus that projects to the primary auditory cortex.

In contrast to the principal nucleus, the dorsal division is not tonotopically organised. The neurons within it respond to a broad range of frequencies, many only to complex sounds.

The medial division receives inputs from somatosensory, vestibular and visual sources (including the superior colliculus) as well as the inferior colliculus, and the neurons within it respond to one or more of these sensory modalities. The dorsal division projects to the non-primary auditory areas that surround the primary auditory cortex, while the medial division projects diffusely to auditory areas of the cortex and to adjacent cortical fields.

4.3.9 The primary auditory cortex

The auditory cortex occupies the dorsal surface of the temporal lobe (Figure 4.18) with the ascending projection from the medial geniculate nucleus innervating the primary auditory cortex or ‘A1’, which corresponds to Brodmann’s areas 41 and 42. This region, like those projecting to it, contains a tonotopic map with neurons tuned to low frequencies in the rostral portion, while those responsive to high-frequency sounds are found in the caudal portion (Figure 4.18 inset).

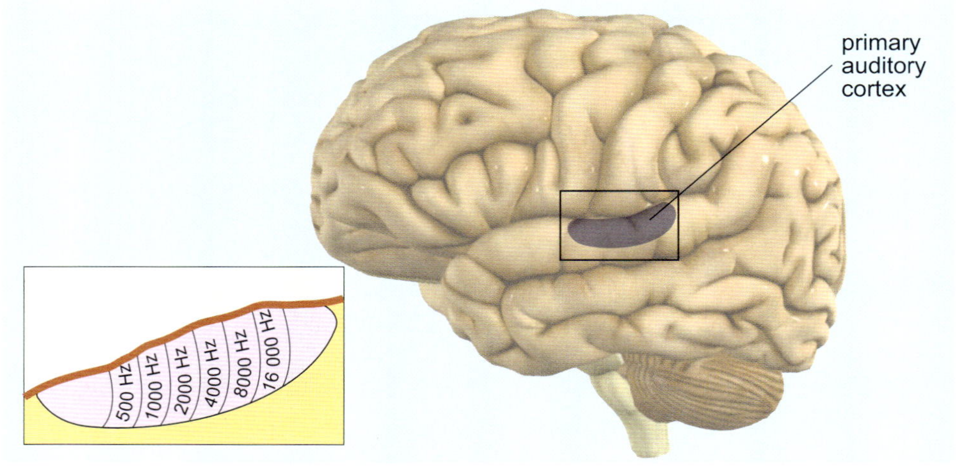

Figure 4.18 The location of the primary auditory cortex, A1. The inset gives an indication of the tonotopic organisation of A1, showing the position of the isofrequency bands responding to different characteristic frequencies.

In addition to this tonotopic map there is also a functional banding relating to binaural stimulation. This arises because A1 neurons show two different types of response to binaural interaction:

- the first is summation, with neurons being excited by stimuli to both ears
- the second is suppression, with neurons being excited by sounds in one ear but inhibited by sounds in the other.

Bands of neurons that show excitation–excitation (EE) responses alternate with bands showing excitation–inhibition (EI) responses, and run approximately at right angles to the isofrequency layers (Figure 4.19). This arrangement means that A1 is divided into columns responsive to every audible frequency and type of interaural interaction.

Much of what researchers believed to be true about A1 stems from our knowledge of the primary visual cortex (V1), which is very well understood by comparison. As you will learn in Block 5, V1 shows sensitivity to particular stimulus features that are not found in subcortical visual areas and, as such, it was expected that A1 would show similar sensitivity. While there do appear to be clusters of A1 neurons with similar response properties (but currently unknown functional significance), most A1 neurons show sensitivity to frequency, intensity and location in much the same way as subcortical structures. Additionally, many years of research have led researchers to recognise that there are no standard basic stimuli which A1 neurons are particularly sensitive to, as might be expected from the comparison with V1.

One reason put forward for this discrepancy between the functioning of the primary auditory and the visual cortices is that the pathway to A1 travels through more brain regions than the pathway to V1 and so by the time auditory information reaches A1, it is already processed beyond the level found in V1 (King and Nelken, 2009). Furthermore, Nelken et al. (2003) suggest that the inferior colliculus is in fact the auditory equivalent of V1, and it is here that much of the interesting features of a sound are extracted.

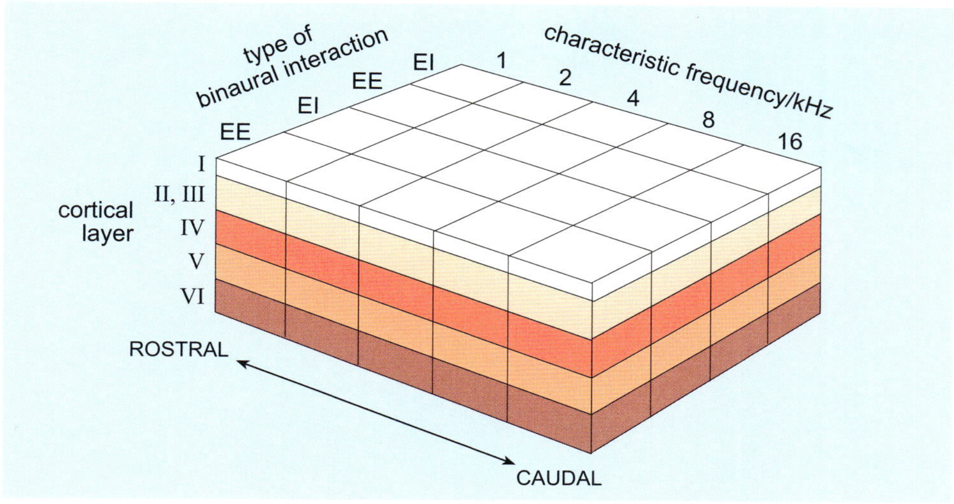

Figure 4.19 Model of a block of A1 showing isofrequency bands and alternating bands of binaural excitation–excitation (EE) and excitation–inhibition (EI) response, running at right angles to each other.

If we assume that the number of relay structures is important, it is possible to deduce the visual equivalent to A1, which may help researchers draw parallels between the two sensory systems and direct their research based on what is known about visual processing. Using this method, A1 is the fifth structure from the receptor cells (cochlear nucleus → superior olivary complex → inferior colliculus → medial geniculate nucleus → A1), and an equivalent structure in the visual pathway is the inferotemporal cortex (Tanaka, 1996).

In support of this approach, the two structures do appear to show processing similarities. For example, the inferotemporal cortex responds to complex visual features and A1 neurons respond to specific combinations of auditory components, and as such may be processing complex features. Nelkon (2004) suggests that the role of A1 is to analyse auditory scenes where individual sounds must be represented in the context of a complex auditory scene, in other words, within a mixture of sounds. It is proposed that A1 organises the features of sounds extracted elsewhere into objects, and exactly how this is done may depend on how many objects are present. This means that if there is only one sound stimulus present, as is often the case in experimental paradigms, coding can be quite simple. By contrast, if there is a mixture of sounds present, coding of features may be more complex.

4.3.10 Beyond the primary auditory cortex

Auditory processing does not just end in the primary auditory cortex. In fact, there are two main pathways that extend from this region to other cortical areas, which are depicted in Figure 4.20.

The first stream is the anteroventral stream, which extends to the superior temporal region in the temporal lobe and is believed to be involved in processing information about what a stimulus is. It has therefore been labelled the 'what' pathway. The second stream is the posterodorsal stream, which extends to the posterior parietal cortex. This stream is likely to be involved in processing spatial information and has therefore been labelled the 'where' pathway. These pathways both make connections with regions of the prefrontal cortex (the ventrolateral prefrontal cortex VLPFC for the 'what' stream and the dorsolateral prefrontal cortex DLPFC in the case of the 'where' stream), which is a brain structure linked to higher cognitive functions such as attention.

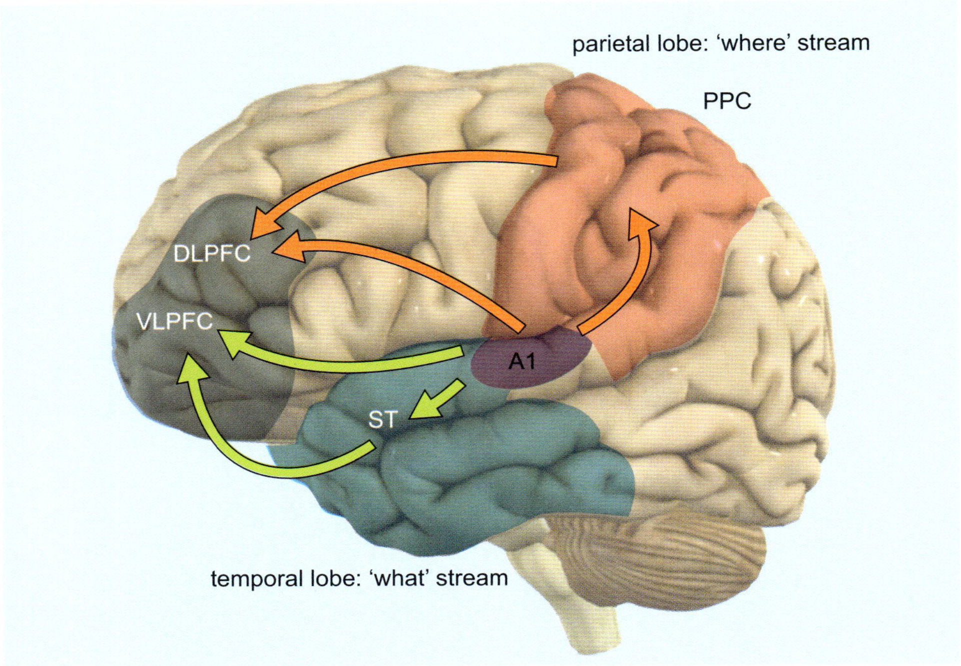

Figure 4.20 Beyond A1, auditory information travels in the anteroventral 'what' stream, which extends into the superior temporal region (ST) and then the ventrolateral prefrontal cortex (VLPFC), and the posterodorsal 'where' stream, which extends up to the posteroparietal cortex (PPC) before projecting to the dorsolateral prefrontal cortex (DLPFC).

In reality, these two divisions are likely to be an oversimplification, and certainly the functions attributed to them are likely to extend beyond that suggested by the 'what' and 'where' labels. However, the division has provided a useful framework for understanding speech perception and brain damage. Additionally, it aids further comparison with the visual system, which has also been divided into 'what' and 'where' pathways.

4.3.11 The descending auditory pathway

The auditory cortex makes descending projections to the medial geniculate nuclei, the inferior colliculi and even the brainstem auditory nuclei. This **descending auditory pathway** modulates signal processing from the cortex right down to the cochlea. It has been suggested that this descending control allows the cortex to make the thalamus function as an adaptive filter, favouring the transmission of some signals over others. Attention level and anticipation of signals can also modulate thalamic processing. One remarkable property of hearing is its capacity to follow a signal of interest among many others. It seems likely that the descending pathway plays a key role in this type of signal detection.

4.4 Chapter 4 summary and questions

- Localisation requires the integration of information from both ears, and therefore is coded for in the superior olivary complex using interaural time or intensity differences.
- The inferior colliculus has a series of intersecting maps that allow complex feature extraction.
- The medial geniculate nucleus maintains the complexity of the inferior colliculus in its principal nucleus but also receives inputs from somatosensory, vestibular and visual sources to its medial nucleus.
- Specific stimulus characteristics that activate the primary auditory cortex (A1) have remained elusive and it is now thought that this structure processes complex sound features analogous to the inferotemporal cortex in visual processing.
- Beyond A1, auditory information is transmitted to a number of other cortical areas through the 'what' and 'where' streams.

Self-assessment questions

Question 4.1

Describe in detail how the movement of the basilar membrane provides the brain with information about:

(a) a signal's frequency

(b) its intensity.

Question 4.2

Where in the higher auditory centres does the binaural processing of information begin? What is the nature of the information used that enables us to localise sounds? How does the operation of excitatory and inhibitory inputs enable the auditory system to use this information?

Hearing the world

5

You have now learned how sound information is transduced and how key features of the sound wave are extracted at various points in the ascending auditory pathway. However, to really make sense of sound perception, we must go beyond objective measures of sound waves such as intensity and frequency and consider how these quantities relate to the subjective experience of sound.

The first part of this chapter examines how this can be done, focusing on the field of psychophysics. We then discuss how loudness and pitch are experienced before looking at the processes underlying the perception of specific auditory information in speech and music.

5.1 Psychophysics of hearing

Recall from Block 3 that psychophysics can be used to measure and quantify sensation, usually for the purpose of understanding the process of perception.

■ What are the main approaches used in psychophysics to investigate sensation?

□ Measurements of the smallest or lowest level detected (threshold), and of the participant's ability to distinguish between stimuli (discrimination). It may also involve asking the individual about their experience of the stimulus.

Of particular interest in this block are the measurements of threshold and discrimination, which are covered in some detail. Although we focus on investigating these measures in isolation from other stimuli, you should note that the methods discussed are commonly used in masking experiments (see Box 4.1). Therefore we can also measure threshold and discrimination in the presence of masking stimuli.

5.1.1 Measuring threshold

When psychophysicists attempt to measure sensory thresholds they often refer to the **absolute threshold** (or absolute limen), meaning the smallest value of a stimulus that the participant can detect. The concept of an absolute threshold assumes there is a precise point that, when reached, the stimulus becomes *just* perceptible: when the stimulus is one unit weaker than this level, it is not detected. If this were the case then some form of hypothetical graph, like the one shown in Figure 5.1, would be the result. Here, the *y*-axis shows the participant's response to whether or not they can detect sound stimuli of increasing intensity, which is 0% (or 'no') until an absolute threshold of 14 dB SPL is reached.

Two methods can be used to establish if this is what happens, the first of which is the **method of limits**. This process involves gradually changing a property of an undetectable stimulus until it becomes possible for the participant to detect it.

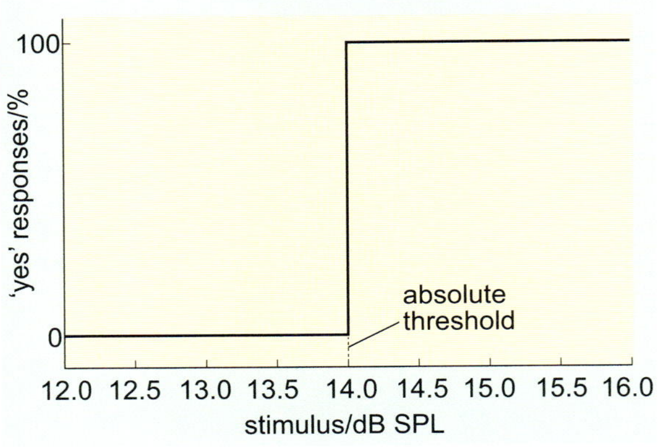

Figure 5.1 A hypothetical graph linking stimulus intensity to absolute threshold.

- For a sound stimulus, what characteristics could you adjust as you move from undetectable to detectable?

- You could alter the frequency or the intensity of the sound wave.

The results from a hypothetical method of limits study are shown in Table 5.1, where the intensity of the signal was gradually increased from 12.0 to 17.0 dB SPL. The participant's response to each stimulus is listed under 'Trial 1'. Only when the stimulus was 14 dB SPL did they indicate that they could hear the stimulus. The threshold for hearing the stimulus therefore lies somewhere between 13.5 and 14.0 dB SPL. However, when the experiment was repeated another three times with the same participant (trials 2–4), the responses were not the same as for the first trial.

Table 5.1 Results from a hypothetical method of limits study.

Stimulus/ db SPL	Trial 1	Trial 2	Trial 3	Trial 4	Detection/%
12.0	no	no	no	no	0
12.5	no	no	no	no	0
13.0	no	no	no	no	0
13.5	no	no	yes	no	25
14.0	yes	no	yes	no	50
14.5	yes	yes	yes	no	75
15.0	yes	yes	yes	yes	100
15.5	yes	yes	yes	yes	100
16.0	yes	yes	yes	yes	100
16.5	yes	yes	yes	yes	100
17.0	yes	yes	yes	yes	100

- ■ Looking at Table 5.1, at which intensities does the participant consistently (100% of trials) not detect the stimulus?
- □ The participant fails to detect the stimulus on every occasion at intensities up to and including 13.0 dB SPL.
- ■ At which intensities does the participant consistently (100% of trials) detect the stimulus?
- □ They always detect the stimulus at intensities of 15 dB SPL and above.

Between 13 and 15 dB SPL, responses varied and were heard in only a certain percentage of the trials: stimuli at a level of 14.5 dB SPL were heard in 75% of trials, whereas a stimulus level of 13.5 dB SPL was heard in only 25% of trials. There are a number of reasons why responses may differ. For example, the actual thresholds can change from trial to trial, the participant's attention may also vary, or there may be a different amount of extraneous 'noise'. If we plot the percentage of stimuli detected during all trials against stimulus intensity we get a graph similar to that shown in Figure 5.2 – a smooth s-shaped curve known as a psychometric function. It is usual to define the absolute threshold as that corresponding to 50% detection on the psychometric function. In this particular example, the threshold for the participant corresponds to a signal intensity of 14.0 dB SPL.

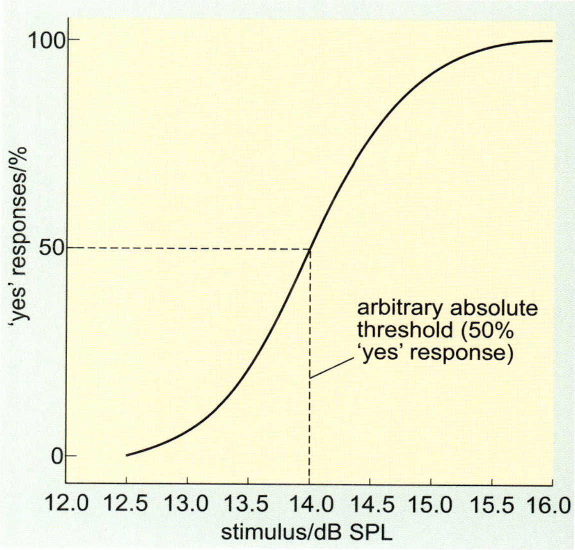

Figure 5.2 A typical psychometric threshold function.

Although very useful, the method of limits is open to various sources of bias and error. One of its drawbacks is that the change in stimulus (increase or decrease) is orderly and regular. Therefore, at any point the participant knows what to expect next, and this could produce biased results.

This problem is overcome by an approach called the **method of constant stimuli**, which uses a set of stimuli decided prior to the test. This method is similar to that described above but has two advantages.

- Stimulus presentation is randomised so that the participant cannot anticipate the nature of the next stimulus.
- The experimenter can estimate any bias of the participant by including 'catch' or 'blank' trials. That is, occasionally the experimenter presents no stimulus to the participant. Their proportion of 'yes' and 'no' responses to these trials will indicate any bias.

As with the method of limits, this experimental approach results in a similar curve of psychometric function, and the absolute threshold of the stimulus value again corresponds to the stimulus detected in 50% of the trials.

5.1.2 Measuring discrimination

As well as measuring absolute thresholds, psychophysicists are also interested in whether the participant can detect a *difference* between two stimuli. You already have experience of attempting to answer this question when you completed Activity 2.1 in Block 3, which examined the two-point touch discrimination threshold. Fundamentally, this area of psychophysics attempts to answer the question: 'How different must two stimuli be from each other in order to detect them as different stimuli?'

The smallest detectable difference between two stimuli is called a **difference threshold** (or difference limen). This is the variation in magnitude between two stimuli – usually a standard (S) and a comparison stimulus (T) – that is detected 50% of the time. The magnitude of this difference specifies the difference threshold; that is, the amount of change in a stimulus necessary to produce a **just-noticeable difference (JND)** in sensation. If the magnitude of a stimulus, say a sound, is 100 dB SPL, and the sound has to be increased to 110 dB SPL in order to be perceived as different, then the JND equals 10 dB.

The measurement of a JND can be made using either of the classical methods discussed above. A psychometric function similar to that shown in Figure 5.2 is generated, except that the horizontal axis is ΔI (the increment in intensity that, when added to the stimulus intensity, I, produces a JND, or the smallest detectable increment). The difference threshold can be deduced from the resulting curve: it is the ΔI that is appropriate to the standard (S) used. For another value of S, a different psychometric function is generated, and a different ΔI derived. By measuring the ΔI for a large number of standards, you can develop a function that describes how the JND changes for different levels of stimulation.

Pioneering work on the relationship between ΔI and S was done by the German physiologist Ernst Weber in the 1830s. Weber found that the increment in stimulation required for a JND was proportional to the size of the stimulus. In other words, the participant could tell the difference between a 100 g standard and a 105 g comparison weight, but not differentiate between the standard weight and a comparison weight that was less than 5 g heavier. By contrast, the JND for a 200 g weight was found to be 10 g. Thus, as the magnitude of the stimulus increases, so does the size of the JND.

Research on a number of senses, including hearing, has shown that the JND is greater for larger standard stimuli and that, over a fairly big range of intensities, the ratio of JND to the standard stimulus is constant such that:

$$\Delta I/S = K \qquad \text{(Eqn 5.1)}$$

This is called **Weber's law**, which states that the bigger the stimulus, the bigger the increment needed for a change to be detectable. K is called the Weber fraction, and applying the equation to our example of lifted weights we find that for a 100 g standard (S), the smallest stimulus change perceivable is 5 g (ΔI), so K = 5 g/100 g = 0.05.

■ According to the information above, what does K equal for a 200 g weight?

□ K = 10 g/200 g = 0.05.

Therefore, the Weber fraction is constant. What this means is that if I increases, ΔI must increase correspondingly.

Although Weber's law holds for most stimuli, there are some instances in which it does not that are relevant to hearing:

- At high sound intensities, discrimination, as measured by the Weber fraction ($\Delta I/I$), improves for pure tones and therefore does not remain constant. For example, for a 1000 Hz tone, the difference threshold ranges from 1.5 dB at 20 dB SPL to 0.3 dB at 80 dB SPL.
- The difference threshold for the frequency of a sound increases as the stimulus intensity decreases. In other words, as the intensity of the sound reduces, it is more difficult to detect it as being different from other sounds close to it in frequency.

Activity 5.1 Measuring just-noticeable differences

Allow 30 minutes

(*Relevant module learning outcomes: KU1, CS2, PS1 and PS2*)

Now is a good time to complete this activity, which is available from the *Block 4 Activities* resource on the module website. In it, you will measure your JND using eight different frequencies as your standard stimulus. If you have someone who can help you with this activity by completing the test, you might like to try first collecting data from your volunteer using the method of limits (by presenting the stimuli in a set order) and then using the method of constant stimuli (where you present the stimuli in a random order).

Now that you have learned about the methods used to assess perception of a stimulus, and tried them out for yourself, we next examine how loudness, pitch and timbre are perceived. These are subjective features of sound. However, loudness and pitch are most closely linked to the objective measures of intensity and frequency, respectively, therefore you already have some knowledge of them. For example, you know that the range of intensity and therefore loudness that we can hear is quite substantial. By contrast, timbre is the characteristic quality of sounds produced by a particular voice or instrument, which you may currently know less about.

5.2 Perception of loudness

The **loudness** of an auditory stimulus is a psychological, not physical attribute of the stimulus. This quality is the subjective experience of intensity but we are not equally sensitive to sounds of all frequencies, so perceived loudness of a tone in fact depends on frequency as well as intensity. Two sounds can have the same physical sound pressure levels but if they are of different frequencies, they are often perceived as having different loudness.

5.2.1 Sensitivity to different frequencies

In Section 5.1.1 you learned that the absolute threshold is the smallest value of a stimulus that a participant can detect. In order to investigate perceptual capabilities, it is useful to generate an absolute threshold curve, which in the case of sound relates the frequency of a signal to the intensity at which it can be detected by the ear. This relationship can be plotted in an audibility curve. In order to generate this curve, you would determine the intensity level required for a listener to detect the presence of a simple sinusoidal wave at each of many frequencies, and then plot these data as in Figure 5.3. Any sounds that fall below the curve on your plot would be below the listener's auditory threshold, and therefore inaudible.

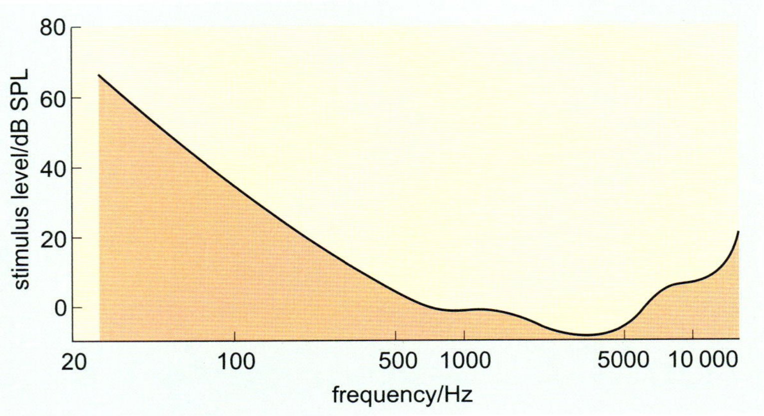

Figure 5.3 Human auditory thresholds as a function of signal frequency.

■ From the graph, describe the relationship between signal frequency and the threshold of audibility of a signal.

□ Auditory thresholds are lowest for tones around 3000 Hz and increase for tones of higher and lower frequency.

This means that the listener in this experiment is most sensitive to tones with frequencies around 3000 Hz, with sensitivities decreasing for tones that are either higher or lower in frequency. This is typical of human auditory thresholds.

■ Why might humans be more sensitive to stimuli around 3000 Hz?

□ The human outer ear acts as an open-tube resonator, boosting signals of 2000–5000 Hz.

There are very high and very low frequencies to which, no matter how intense the stimulus, the auditory system is insensitive. These limits define the boundaries of the auditory system's sensitivity to frequency.

Figure 5.3 is representative of characteristic auditory thresholds for young people. As we grow older, we become less sensitive to stimuli of all frequencies, but hearing loss is greater for high-frequency tones. This is because high frequencies stimulate the basal end of the basilar membrane, which is, in fact, stimulated by all frequencies to some extent. This results in hair cells in this region having a greater potential for becoming 'worn out'.

Activity 5.2 Plotting an audibility curve

Allow 30 minutes

(*Relevant module learning outcomes: KU1, CS2, PS1 and PS2*)

Now would be a good time to complete this activity, which is available from the *Block 4 Activities* resource on the module website. In it, you will hear seven different pure tones at ten intensities and record your information about what you can and can't hear, before plotting this data as an audibility curve.

5.2.2 Measuring loudness

To measure loudness we have to relate the subjective quality of loudness to a physical quantity, such as sound pressure level. One way of doing this is to generate a plot of **equal loudness contours**. Here, a 1000 Hz tone is set to a specific intensity and then the sound levels of other tones of different frequency that are equal in loudness to the 1000 Hz tone are determined.

For example, a participant may be presented with a 1000 Hz standard tone at 60 dB SPL and then asked to manipulate the intensity of a 2000 Hz tone until it matches the loudness of the 1000 Hz tone. The same 1000 Hz tone would then be compared with a 3000 Hz tone, and the intensity manipulated until it matched the 1000 Hz tone in loudness. In this way, the intensity of tones at a variety of frequencies could be obtained so that all tones matched the loudness of the 60 dB SPL, 1000 Hz tone. These intensities are then plotted as a function of frequency to generate equal loudness contours (Figure 5.4).

The unit that is used to describe or measure the loudness of a signal is known as a phon. The loudness in phons is the level in dB SPL of an equally loud 1000 Hz tone. So all tones judged equal in loudness to a 40 dB SPL, 1000 Hz tone have a loudness of 40 phons. The tones presented at levels such that they are equal in loudness to a 70 dB SPL, 1000 Hz tone all have loudness levels of 70 phons, and so on. In theory, a 1000 Hz tone that was just inaudible would lie on the 0 dB line and therefore on a 0 phon contour. However, in practice the average person's hearing is not quite so good and their cut-off point is just slightly more intense than this; hence instead the threshold for hearing is marked with a dashed line that does not quite dip all the way to 0 dB at 1000 Hz.

You might have noticed in Figure 5.4 that the intensity drops below 0 dB for this hearing threshold contour at around 3000 Hz, and wondered how this is possible. However, remember that the sound pressure level is the ratio of one pressure to a reference pressure, in this case the pressure of the 1000 Hz tone that is just inaudible. Therefore, this contour indicates that the 3000 Hz tone becomes audible at a lower intensity than the 1000 Hz tone. This is in line with the previous discussion about the actions of the outer ear as an open tube resonator.

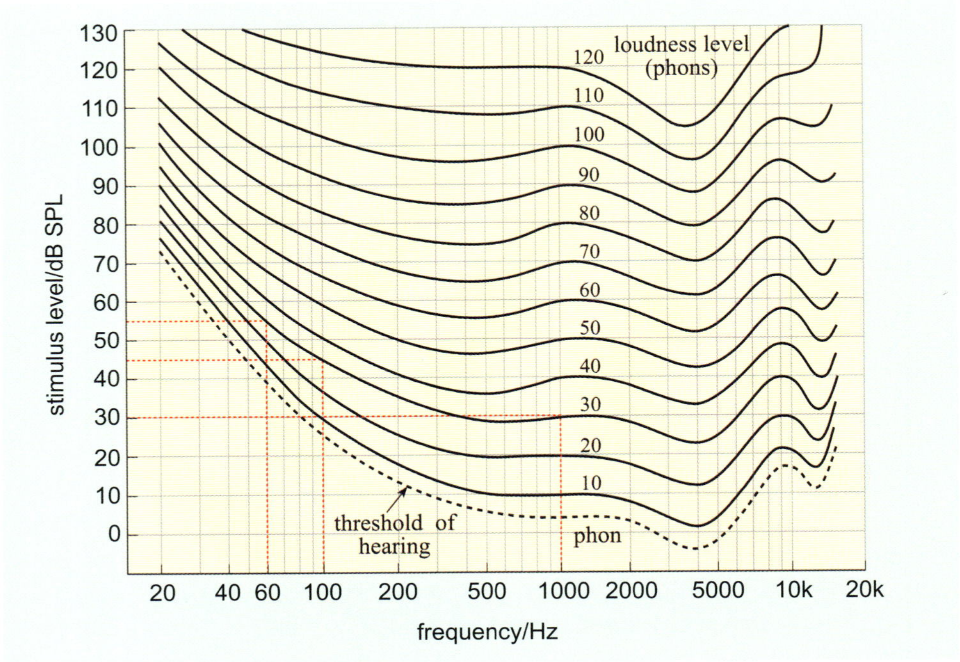

Figure 5.4 Equal loudness contours showing the sound intensities required at different frequencies to produce sounds that appear equally loud. The red dotted lines indicate points of comparison discussed in the text.

Look at the contour labelled '30' in the figure. Any signal with a frequency and intensity on this contour sounds just as loud as any other sound on the contour, although the frequency and intensity of the two sounds will differ. So, for example, a 60 Hz tone at a 55 dB intensity level and a 100 Hz tone at 45 dB both sound as loud as a 1000 Hz tone at 30 dB, and all have a loudness level of 30 phons. Because we are not equally sensitive to sounds at different frequencies, for a sound to remain at 30 phons it would generally require a higher than 30 dB intensity as the frequency shifts away from 1000 Hz, with the exception of the frequency range mentioned above where we are more sensitive.

■ What do you notice about the contours as the loudness level increases from 0 to 120 phons?

□ The contours change in shape and become much flatter.

What this indicates is that at high intensity levels, the frequency of a sound becomes less important in the perception of loudness. Look at the 120 phon contour: in order to sound equally loud, a 60 Hz, a 300 Hz and a 1000 Hz tone need to differ only by a maximum of 7 dB in intensity (127 dB SPL, 121 dB SPL and 120 dB SPL, respectively). This contrasts with the 30 phon contour where, in order to sound equally loud, the three tones differ by as much as 25 dB. This in effect means that we are relatively more sensitive to low-frequency tones than to high-frequency tones at big loudness levels. Below about 70 phons, low-frequency tones generally require a significantly higher intensity to achieve comparable loudness with higher frequency tones. This is especially true for sounds with frequencies below about 1000 Hz.

Because of the relationship between intensity and loudness, complex sounds that are identical in frequency may sound different because of variations in loudness. You might have experienced this if you listen to voices heard from a loudspeaker at full volume. Because we are more sensitive to low-frequency sounds at high loudness levels, they will seem to have much greater low-frequency components, giving them a 'boomy' sound. Similarly, musical recordings made at high volume and then played softly often seem to be lacking in the bass range. This is because at low-intensity levels we are relatively less sensitive to low-frequency tones and so the music sounds 'tinny'. Many music systems compensate for this effect by having a 'loudness' switch which adds extra bass at low volume levels.

5.2.3 Loudness, adaptation and fatigue

As you know, a common property of all sensory systems is that when exposed to a stimulus of sufficient duration and intensity, the responsiveness of the system changes. You have already read about the possible cellular mechanisms of hair cell adaptation in Section 3.5.4, and such changes may have an effect on perception.

Hood (1950, 1972) made a distinction between two types of changes in responsiveness that may occur: **auditory adaptation** and **auditory fatigue**. The central tenet of auditory adaptation is equilibration. This means that the receptor reduces its response to a sustained stimulus such that the energy used to respond matches the energy available to sustain it. The psychological effect of this is a perceived drop in loudness during the first few minutes of stimulus presentation. Adaptation, and therefore changes, to loudness perception can also occur as a consequence of pathological changes (see Box 5.1).

Box 5.1 Pathological adaptation

Rapid decreases in responsiveness to a stimulus can occur in response to any pathological change that results in abnormal metabolic processes in the cochlea or cochlear nerve; for example, the presence of a tumour pressing on the nerve. Indeed, the detection of such rapid changes can be used in the diagnosis of such hearing problems.

Individuals with pathological adaptation can be identified by their responsiveness to interrupted and continuous tones. For people without this kind of hearing loss, the threshold for sounds will be similar, irrespective of whether they are presented as a continuous or an interrupted tone. However, where there are abnormalities in metabolic processes, the threshold for a continuous tone is considerably higher than for an interrupted tone as adaptation has rapidly occurred. Fatigue can be ruled out by interrupting the continuous tone, at which point the threshold returns to normal.

By contrast, auditory fatigue arises as a result of the presentation of a stimulus in excess of that normally required to achieve a sustained response. It can be detected by measuring the threshold for a particular frequency before and after a fatiguing stimulus, and manifests itself as a temporary threshold shift.

5.3 Perception of pitch

As well as loudness, the other most obvious characteristic of a periodic sound is its **pitch**. Pitch is a subjective dimension of hearing that is most closely related to the frequency of a pure tone. High-frequency tones are perceived as being of high pitch, while low-frequency tones are said to be of low pitch. The relationship between pitch and frequency is, however, not a simple one. This section briefly considers the perception of pure tones, which is arguably more straightforward, before moving on to look at the perception of pitch in complex sounds.

5.3.1 Pitch and pure tones

The perception of the pitch of a pure tone is largely based on the frequency of the tone, therefore it should be possible to explain features of pitch perception by examining the coding of frequency information.

■ What are the two mechanisms for coding frequency information in the cochlea?

□ Temporal code and place code. Temporal code relies on phase locking while place code relies on tonotopic mapping along the basilar membrane.

Unfortunately, both of these coding mechanisms appear to fall short in fully explaining the features of pitch perception. For example, it is known that sound level (intensity) has some impact on pitch perception. For tones below 2000 Hz the perceived pitch decreases with increasing intensity, but this trend is reversed for tones above 4000 Hz. The variation can be as much as 5% differences in pitch perception with intensity changes, although there is considerable individual variation in the impact of intensity (Moore, 2012).

Researchers have shown that low-frequency tones (around 1000 Hz) shift their excitation of the basilar membrane towards the basal end with increasing stimulus intensity.

■ Considering place coding, what impact would you expect this shift to have on perceived frequency and therefore pitch? How does this relate to the changes outlined above for tones below 2000 Hz?

□ The basal end of the membrane is associated with higher frequency sounds and so you would expect a higher frequency to be detected, and therefore a higher pitch perceived. This is the opposite of what was found for tones below 2000 Hz, which actually showed a decrease in perceived pitch with increasing intensity.

In fact, researchers have also found that frequency of firing is not sufficiently affected by sound intensity to explain the shift in perception and, as such, temporal code also cannot explain these shifts. At the time of writing, there is no generally accepted explanation of them.

Shifts in pitch with intensity are not the only feature of pitch perception that is not fully explained by the mechanisms of frequency coding. The JND for pitch perception is another such feature, and is typically very small, with a pitch of just 1002 Hz being distinguishable from that of 1000 Hz when presented at a moderate intensity of 60–70 dB SPL (Moore, 2012). This difference is too small to be explained by place coding because the change perceived would correspond to such minute shifts in the basilar membrane vibration that there would be no difference in the afferent neuron firing.

However, temporal code can account for the very small JND measures for pitch perception and it is noteworthy that the amount of differentiation gets considerably larger for tones above 5000 Hz: the point at which phase locking breaks down and therefore at which temporal code can no longer operate. However, given that phase locking does break down at 5000 Hz, temporal code cannot explain how the perception of pitch can occur for sounds above this frequency (although the majority of musical instruments and the human voice rarely exceed this level).

5.3.2 Pitch and complex sounds

Almost all sounds that give a perception of pitch are produced by waves that are periodic. They consist of a fundamental frequency and various harmonics.

- ■ What is the relationship between fundamental and harmonic frequencies?
- □ All harmonics have frequencies that are multiples of the fundamental frequency. For example, if the fundamental frequency was 100 Hz, the second, third and fourth harmonics would be 200 Hz, 300 Hz and 400 Hz, respectively.

The perceived pitch of a periodic complex sound is close to the pitch of the fundamental frequency. Because of this, it was explained as being the point at which vibration of the basilar membrane was greatest and, as such, perception relied on place coding on the membrane. However, work by Seebeck in 1841 revealed a problem with this theory. He demonstrated that even when the fundamental frequency was missing from the complex sound, the pitch perception was largely unchanged. (You can experience this for yourself in Activity 5.3 at the end of this section.)

Despite this setback, an explanation of pitch based on place code was not completely disregarded. Instead, it was suggested that the inner ear effectively reintroduces the fundamental frequency by distorting the basilar membrane in such a way that displacement occurs at the frequency corresponding to the difference between two harmonics. Given that all harmonics are multiples of the fundamental frequency, this would mean any two consecutive harmonics could result in displacement of the membrane at the position associated with the fundamental frequency. Nevertheless, evidence for this distortion was lacking. In addition, masking experiments (see Box 4.1) confirmed Seebeck's findings that pitch perception is unchanged even when the fundamental frequency is masked.

After place code was disregarded as a means of explaining the pitch perception of complex sounds, Schouten (1940) suggested that such perception was dependent on the time intervals between peaks associated with unresolved harmonics – a temporal theory. When these harmonics combine they create a sound that appears to 'beat'. A beat is shown in Figure 5.5, in which a 1000 Hz wave (upper panel) is added to a 1100 Hz wave (middle panel) to give a new and complex periodic waveform. It is known that the cochlear nerve firing reflects the rate of beating, therefore it was suggested that the brain could use this information to detect pitch. This argument was considered all the more convincing because the rate of beating of a mixture of consecutive harmonics is in fact that of the fundamental frequency.

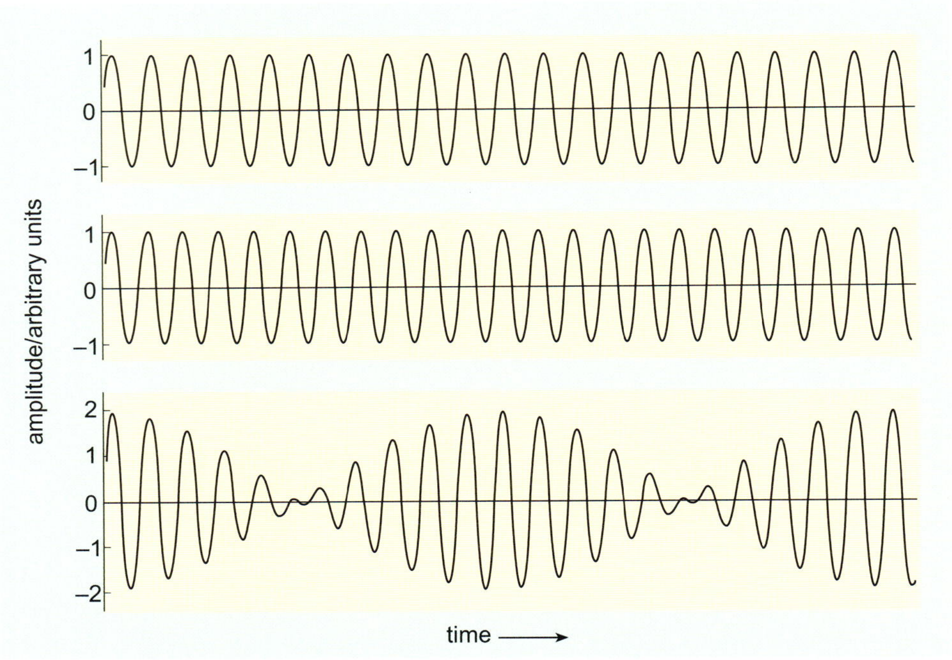

Figure 5.5 When a 1000 Hz wave (upper panel) is added to a 1100 Hz wave (middle panel), the result (lower panel) is a complex periodic waveform.

One of the main problems with Schouten's theory was that we are actually not very good at perceiving pitch when the harmonics are unresolved (namely they cannot be separated out and individuals identified); we are much better at detecting them when the frequencies are fully resolved into their individual sinusoidal waves. A theory more in line with this fact was put forward by Goldstein (1973) and can be considered as a pattern-recognition theory of pitch perception. He suggested that the brain resolves the individual frequencies and then, using pattern recognition, works out the best-fitting harmonic series and takes the fundamental frequency as the pitch. It is important to note that these two theories are not mutually exclusive.

It is possible that we have two mechanisms for pitch perception: a temporal mechanism for unresolved frequencies and a pattern-recognition mechanism for resolved frequencies. Indeed, there have been a number of attempts to combine both theories into one model (e.g. Moore, 2012).

Activity 5.3 From pitch to beats

Allow 30 minutes

(*Relevant module learning outcomes: KU1 and PS1*)

Now is a good time to complete this activity, which is available from the *Block 4 Activities* resource on the module website. It combines a number of concepts which you have been reading about in this chapter, such as the relationship between loudness and pitch as a function of signal intensity and frequency, the effect on pitch of masking, and the way in which the pitch of a complex sound is determined by harmonics. It also provides demonstrations of monaural and binaural beating.

5.3.3 Absolute and relative pitch

Before leaving the topic of pitch perception we briefly consider a phenomenon known as **absolute pitch**. Someone is said to have absolute pitch if they are able to identify the pitch of a tone presented in isolation, or to produce a specified pitch without any external reference (Levitin and Rogers, 2005). Absolute pitch is sometimes referred to as 'perfect pitch', but we have chosen not to use this term because it implies excellent acuity when, in reality, people with absolute pitch still make errors in judging this quality. Absolute pitch is distinct from **relative pitch**, which refers to the ability to identify or produce musical intervals or relations between pitches using an external reference.

If you have previously come across the concept of absolute pitch, you may be wondering why it is discussed here and not in the later section on music. Certainly, absolute pitch is often considered a mark of musicianship, but it is not needed in most musical tasks. Exactly how absolute pitch develops is unknown, although there is a consensus that there must be a period of learning of tones. It is also likely that there is a critical period for this learning because absolute pitch is normally acquired below the age of nine (Levitin and Rogers, 2005). In support of this idea, individuals with disorders associated with a developmental delay, such as Williams' syndrome, develop absolute pitch later on.

Studies of the neural basis of absolute pitch have revealed that, in fact, it does not appear to relate to differences in perception, and activation of auditory structures is no different from that found in people with relative pitch. Instead, there are differences in the activation of the posterior dorsolateral frontal cortex – an area involved in learning – and researchers now believe that absolute pitch is a labelling ability, rather than a perceptual ability (Levitin and Rogers, 2005). This description means that people with absolute pitch can label different pitches in much the same way as the majority of people can label colours, for example.

How this labelling ability arises is unclear. An argument can be made for a genetic predisposition of pitch memory, which is necessary for absolute pitch. A strong pitch memory would allow the detection of subtle pitch changes, for example in voices, which could help in detecting anger, pleasure, stress and illness – all of which may infer an evolutionary advantage. However, it is presumed that some kind of learning must also take place to ascribe the labels initially. Furthermore, even with a genetic predisposition, absolute pitch may not arise if learning supports interval (i.e. relative pitch) training rather than pitch-and-label-association training.

5.4 Perception of timbre

The **timbre** of a sound is a more complex percept than loudness or pitch. Both of the latter can be considered uni-dimensional in that it is possible to rank sounds of increasing pitch and loudness along a continuum from, for example, very low or quiet to very high or loud. By contrast, timbre can be considered a multidimensional characteristic of sound: there is no single dimension to relate the different quality of sound to. For example, 'mellow' and 'shrill' sounds cannot be ranked along a single dimension.

Research by Plomp and colleagues throughout the 1960s and 1970s (see Plomp, 1970, 1976; Plomp et al., 1967, 1969) reveals that timbre appears to be partly determined by the relative amplitudes of the different harmonics; that is, which frequency regions have more energy. However, Schouten (1968) suggested a number of other factors are likely to play a role in identifying particular sound qualities, including:

- temporal structure of the sound, including onset and decay
- whether the sound is periodic or not
- what the surrounding sounds are like.

So far in this chapter we have looked at the methods that may be used to understand perception and how features such as loudness are perceived. In the remainder of this chapter we consider the perception of two particular types of stimulus: music and speech. In the former we look at how pitch and timbre are perceived and touch on other features that may be important in perception. However, for the latter, we consider models of perception rather than the perception of specific features such as pitch. In both cases you will build upon your knowledge of the neural processing of sound by looking at how different brain regions are involved in processing these two classes of stimuli.

5.5 Intermediate chapter summary

- Psychophysics has contributed a significant amount to our understanding of hearing, utilising a number of methods to estimate discrimination abilities and absolute thresholds.
- The perception of loudness is closely related to the intensity of the sound but it can also be affected by sound frequency.

- The perception of pitch is closely related to the frequency of the sound but it can also be affected by sound intensity. Neither place code nor temporal code can fully explain pitch perception alone, although temporal code may be sufficient for many relevant sounds.
- For complex sounds, the perceived pitch is normally close to the fundamental frequency.
- The timbre of the sound is a more complex percept than loudness or pitch and it can be affected by a number of features of the sound, including relative amplitude of the different frequencies and the onset and decay of the sound.

5.6 Understanding music

Music is a common auditory stimulus encountered in everyday life. The level to which an individual engages with music varies considerably, ranging from professional musicians to those who occasionally listen to music on the radio. This section further explores how pitch and timbre are perceived, before looking at which brain regions may be involved in processing different features of music. Finally, it briefly examines the wider impact of musical training on neural processing.

5.6.1 Features of music

The pitch of music is used to create melodies (patterns of pitch over time), chords (simultaneous presentation of multiple pitches) and harmonies (simultaneous melodies), and is therefore critical to our perception of music (Warren, 2008). Musical sounds have a definite pitch to them and are produced by a steadily vibrating sound source such as a string, reed or lips for instrumental music: the faster the vibration, the higher the pitch.

The upper panel of Figure 5.6 shows the first 500 ms of the periodic waveform of an oboe note in terms of the change in pressure over time. The instrument is starting to play the note F#, which has a fundamental frequency of 740 Hz that corresponds to the rate at which the reed in the oboe is vibrating. The lower panel shows a spectrogram of the waveform. Recall from Activity 2.1 that a spectrogram is a way of displaying how much energy is present, corresponding to the different frequencies comprising a sound (shown on the *y*-axis) at different time points (shown on the *x*-axis). The amount of energy present is depicted by the depth of shading, such that the darker shading indicates more energy.

The spectrogram shows that there is energy at the harmonic frequencies. Note that, for this oboe, the second frequency component is stronger, with a darker bar than the other harmonics. This is in line with what you read in Section 2.3.1, in that the higher harmonics have lower amplitudes. The brain then recognises the pitch of this note mainly from the frequencies of these first few harmonics.

Recall that the timbre of the sound relates to the relative amplitudes of the different harmonics as well as temporal features. For musical instruments, the onset of a note is particularly important in giving the listener clues to what

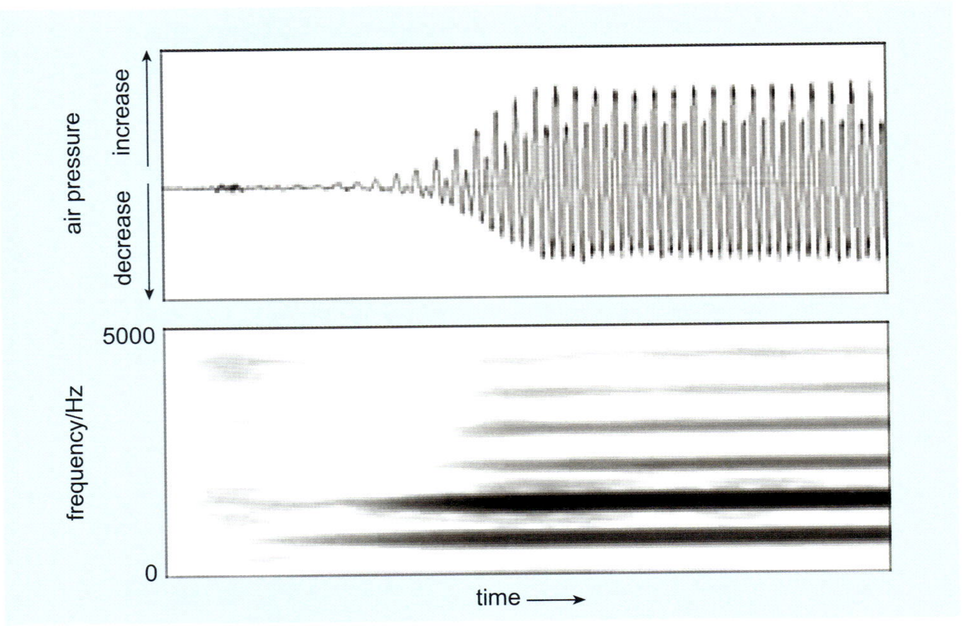

Figure 5.6 Waveform (upper panel) and spectrogram (lower panel) of the start of the note F sharp (F#) on an oboe.

instrument it is, particularly the 'onset transient' time period, which lasts about 50 ms. However, we know very little about how rapidly changing, complex sounds such as these are coded by the brain. Note in the spectrogram of Figure 5.6 that the oboe's note starts in a complicated way with a burst of noise at a number of frequencies, followed by the various harmonics appearing at different times. This shows that the harmonics of a note start at different times, and each one can have complex changes in amplitude before the note settles down.

Although pitch and timbre are clearly important for perceiving music, there are many other qualities that are also vital, such as the emotional content or rhythm. A full discussion of these is beyond the scope of this module, however, a brief look at the brain regions involved in processing music illustrates the complexity.

The processing of music requires a considerable network of brain regions and is thought to be as complex a system as that required for language processing (Warren, 2008). Also, brain imaging studies show that no single structure is exclusively dedicated to the perception of music. Figure 5.7 shows the brain regions involved, their possible roles, and the predominant flow of information between cortical areas (Figure 5.7b). Many of the qualities of music are processed within the auditory system while others, such as those relating to emotion and memory, require interaction with other brain regions. This creates a hierarchical structure to the processing of music with more complex and abstract properties represented by areas beyond the primary auditory cortex (A1).

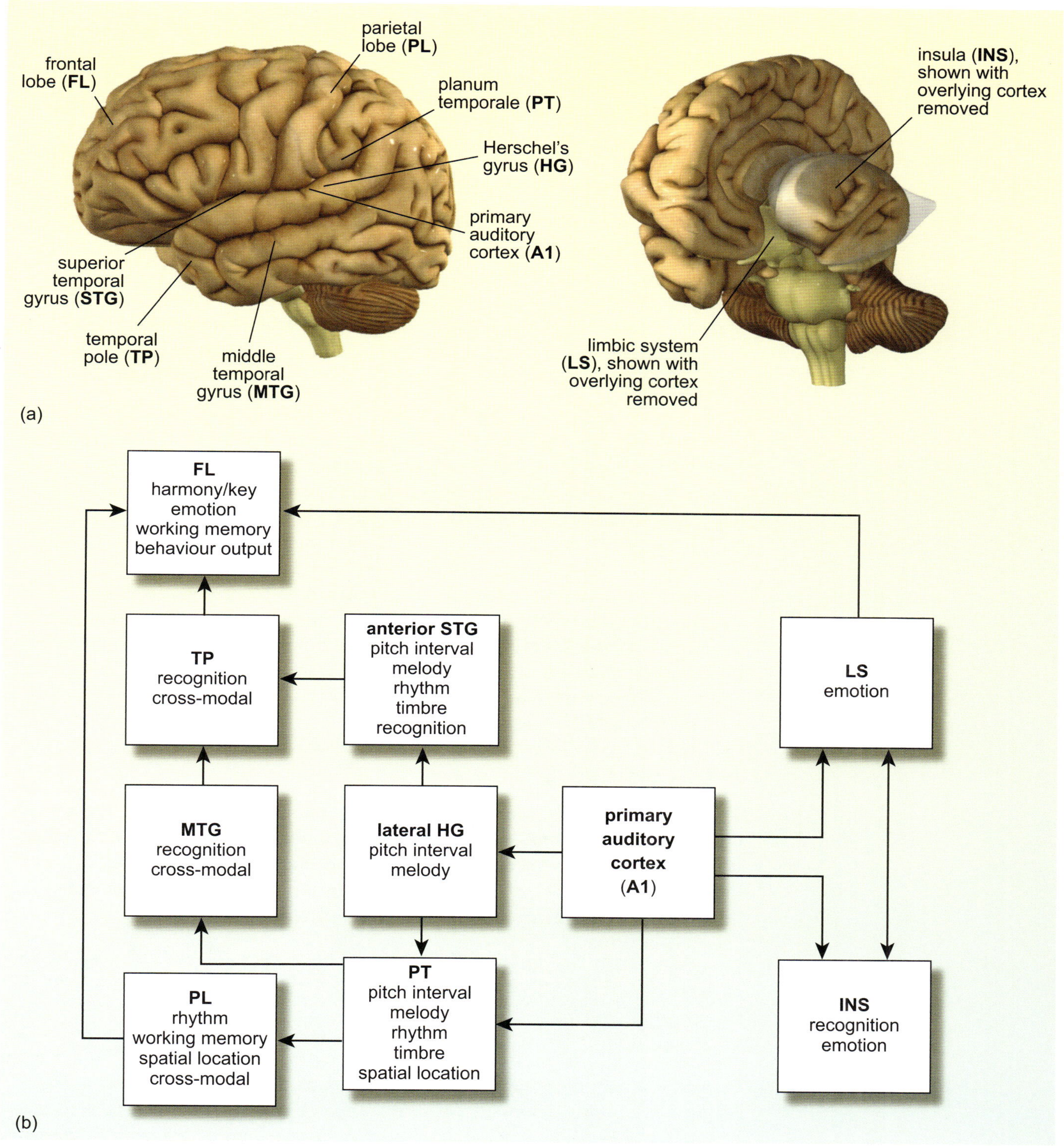

Figure 5.7 (a) Key brain regions involved in processing music; (b) their proposed roles and the connections between them (based on Warren, 2008).

5.6.2 Musical training and brain development

In the previous section you read that the processing of music requires a number of brain structures, and is not limited to those involved in hearing. In addition, further brain areas are involved if people learn to produce music rather than simply listen to it, such as those for fine motor control and visual–motor integration as the visual symbols for musical notes are translated into fine movements on an instrument, for example.

Researchers are beginning to reach a consensus that musical training can have important effects beyond those associated with performing music. Indeed, findings have consistently shown that music involves the activation of areas linked to language and it is thought that language ability correlates with musical ability. The exact reasons for this relationship are not clear, but it is probable that musical training could help the development of parts of the brain involved in hearing and therefore aid the development of language.

Recent studies have shown that music can have an impact on a number of more general measures: for example, work by a Canadian research group led by Sylvain Moreno found that short-term musical training improved measures of intelligence and decision making (Moreno et al., 2011). Previously, music had been linked to measures like this, but what made this study particularly interesting is the fact that it was able to show musical training could actually lead to these improvements. This was possible because the research group designed their investigation carefully to include a control group, and worked with children who were not musicians. In contrast, many previous studies in the field involved existing musicians and therefore it was impossible to tell if their IQ, for example, was higher because of their music abilities or whether children with a higher IQ elect to study music.

5.7 Speech perception

This section considers how the complex acoustical patterns of speech are perceived by the brain. Before you begin reading it, however, it is important to note that, despite many years of investigating speech and language, the picture is still somewhat incomplete, therefore this section is not intended to be an exhaustive review of what we know. Rather, in this block we have selected information that helps you to build directly on your existing knowledge of the auditory system, and to give you a broad sense of the topic should you wish to engage in the further reading listed on the module website. We return to the topic of language more broadly in Block 5 in the context of how written language is understood.

Speech is really important in our daily lives, and is often treated separately from other stimuli. This is because researchers investigating speech perception have often argued that speech has its own special kind of perception because of, among other things, the apparently distinct pattern of brain activity that it evokes and the variable nature of speech. The latter can be illustrated by spending a moment or two thinking about how speech can vary. For example, the pitch, loudness and timbre of speech, and the speed of speaking, can all differ with context. This means that the actual acoustic stimulus cannot be mapped to any particular feature or unit of speech, making research very challenging. However, this issue has not prevented researchers considering the different units of speech and theories of perception, as you will see next.

5.7.1 Units of speech

When you read the heading of this section, one of the first things that might have come to mind was probably words as the units of speech. However, speech can be broken down into smaller units called **phonemes**.

If you have ever completed the puzzle in a newspaper where you had to get from a starting word to an end word, via three new words that you must create by changing just a letter at a time, you are probably already familiar with phonemes. These can be defined as the smallest unit of sound that can differentiate one word from another. Individual phonemes themselves have no meaning and vary across languages. It is noteworthy that not all researchers in speech perception consider the phoneme a useful unit but, because much research has been conducted at this level, we have introduced it. For the sake of completeness, you should also be aware of the other levels of analysis for speech and language research, as shown in Table 5.2.

Table 5.2 Levels of speech perception studies.

Level of study	Focus of study
Phonology	rules about how phonemes can and cannot be put together in a language which vary from language to language
Morphology	rules that define the structure of words, such as adding an 's' to make a word plural
Syntax	rules that govern the way individual words are put together into sentences
Semantics	the meaning of words and sentences

Now that you are aware of the units of speech that may be used when investigating speech perception, we next consider some different theories of this perception.

5.7.2 Theories of speech perception

There are a number of theories of speech perception and, as outlined at the start of this section, there is – at the time of writing – no real consensus over which (if any) is correct. Given this, and the fact that it is possible to write an entire module on the topic, we will provide a brief overview of three such theories, which are suitably distinct, to give you a sense of the breadth of current theories.

The motor model

This model was put forward by Liberman and colleagues in the 1960s and suggests that we perceive speech by detecting phonetic gestures performed by the speaker (Liberman et al., 1967). A phonetic gesture is an organised movement of one or more vocal-tract structures that result in a specific phonetic utterance. For example, the sound 'bah' begins with a gesture that involves both lips coming together. (Try saying 'bah' aloud and then saying 'ah' to help you recognise this gesture.) This model then proposes that the necessary item for perception is gestural rather than acoustic, namely it is the movement and not the sound that is important. Liberman et al. (1967) proposed that these gestures are invariant representations of vocal-tract activity that underlie the most salient part of the phoneme.

One piece of evidence that supports the critical gesture not being acoustic comes from the McGurk effect. This is a phenomenon that occurs when individuals are presented with a voice repeatedly uttering a particular syllable (e.g. 'bah'), while they are simultaneously shown synchronised lip movements associated with another syllable (e.g. 'gah'). Surprisingly, the majority of participants report hearing a different syllable in this situation (e.g. 'dah'), demonstrating that the phoneme that people *hear* can be modulated by *seen* lip movements, which is information that is not carried in the acoustic signal. This outcome occurs even when people know that what they are hearing and seeing are incongruent, suggesting that the audiovisual integration leading to speech perception may occur automatically.

However, although there is evidence that the key information may not be acoustic, these phonetic gestures are actually quite variable, which led to the model being revised to focus on intended gestures which were proposed to be invariable, unlike actual gestures.

The model also suggests that speech production and perception are linked through these gestures and the perception is mediated by an innate, specialised speech processor that we have no conscious awareness of. The original proponents of the model provided no evidence for an actual mechanism for turning the acoustic signal into a perceived intended gesture, limiting how this model may be used. However, more recently, Wilson et al. (2004) used fMRI to examine brain activation while participants listened passively to monosyllables and produced the same speech sounds. The study showed that listening to speech activated bilaterally the areas of the motor cortex involved in speech production. While this does not, of course, prove the motor model, it does support the view that speech perception is mediated by speech production mapping in the motor system.

Invariant feature or cue-based theories

These theories began to emerge in the 1980s (e.g. Stevens, 1980) and have continued to be developed. They take a different approach from the motor model because they do not rely on phonetic gestures, but rather look for phonetic features that do not vary. These theories purport that each word can be described by a set of binary features and that processing can occur in a number of stages (Moore, 2012):

1. Detection of peaks, troughs and discontinuities in frequency range to provide an acoustic landmark.
2. Extraction of cues from the signal close to landmarks to determine the actions of lips and tongue (articulators).

3 Combination of information from landmarks and articulators to derive a sequence of specific segments.
4 Information on segments is compared with a bank of segment information for words to generate candidate words.
5 Synthesising of sound pattern for candidate words to see which one best matches the auditory input.

While these kinds of model can accommodate top-down influences on speech perception, there can be difficulties defining the acoustic features necessary.

The TRACE model

This model was developed by McClelland and Elman (1986) and uses a connectionist approach (see Box 5.2). The concept aimed to identify single words by making use of both top-down and bottom-up information. These types of information refer to using higher level knowledge and stimulus data, respectively. TRACE uses a neural network with a number of interconnected units called nodes that learn to classify input by examining patterns and comparing them with stored information. The lowest level nodes represent phonetic features, followed by phonetic segments and then, finally, words. You can think of each node as a bit like a bingo player with a specific set of numbers, or in this case a phonetic feature, segment or word. When a stimulus is presented, the node collects evidence for its own specific requirements. If the specific requirements are present, the node 'fires' (a connectionist version of calling 'Bingo!').

Box 5.2 Connectionism and neural networks

One way in which psychologists and neuroscientists investigate the functioning of the brain is to create computer models of it. These models can take on a number of forms and range from relatively simple constructs to highly complex ones.

Connectionist models of the brain draw their inspiration from the millions of interconnected neurons within the organ that enable information to be processed in parallel. A connectionist model typically consists of a number of units (modelling the neurons in the brain) organised into three layers. Each unit will have input from units in the layer beneath it and output to units in the layer above it. Additionally, the strength of the connections can be allocated different weightings such that some connections are more effective than others.

As with the other models, this one is not without difficulties. For example, it does not address how the incoming signal is processed to extract phonetic features, and it ignores certain factors that are known to affect word segmentation such as rhythmic structure. Also, in some cases, the top-down processes appear a little too powerful, causing the model to ignore the mispronunciation of words.

5.7.3 Neural processing of speech

In the previous chapter you read that auditory information travels from the cochlea to the primary auditory cortex (A1) and then to various other cortical regions via the dorsal ('where') and ventral ('what') streams. But which of these regions are critical for speech perception?

Non-invasive brain imaging techniques have allowed this question to be addressed and research indicates that this speech specificity occurs beyond A1. For example, Binder et al. (2000) measured auditory responses to various sound stimuli, including white noise, reversed speech and pseudowords (e.g. nonsensical terms like 'sked'). They found that A1 responded equally well to all of the stimuli, suggesting that it may be activated by the basic acoustic elements present in all of the stimuli, rather than specifically to speech. This indicates that speech-specific processing must rely on cortical areas beyond A1.

Indeed, it is now generally accepted that both cortical streams extending from A1 within the superior temporal gyrus (STG) have distinct roles in speech, and that these roles are explained by the **dual-stream model** (Figure 5.8) of speech processing proposed by Hickok and Poeppel (2007). From A1, information is sent to the posterior superior temporal sulcus (STS), which is associated with phonological-level processes. From here, information can enter the ventral stream (shown in pink in the figure) corresponding to the lexical interface, which links phonological and semantic information. These three areas (STG, STS and the ventral stream) show bilateral activation. By contrast, the dorsal stream (shown in blue in the figure), which is thought to be a sensorimotor interface, is strongly left-hemisphere dominant.

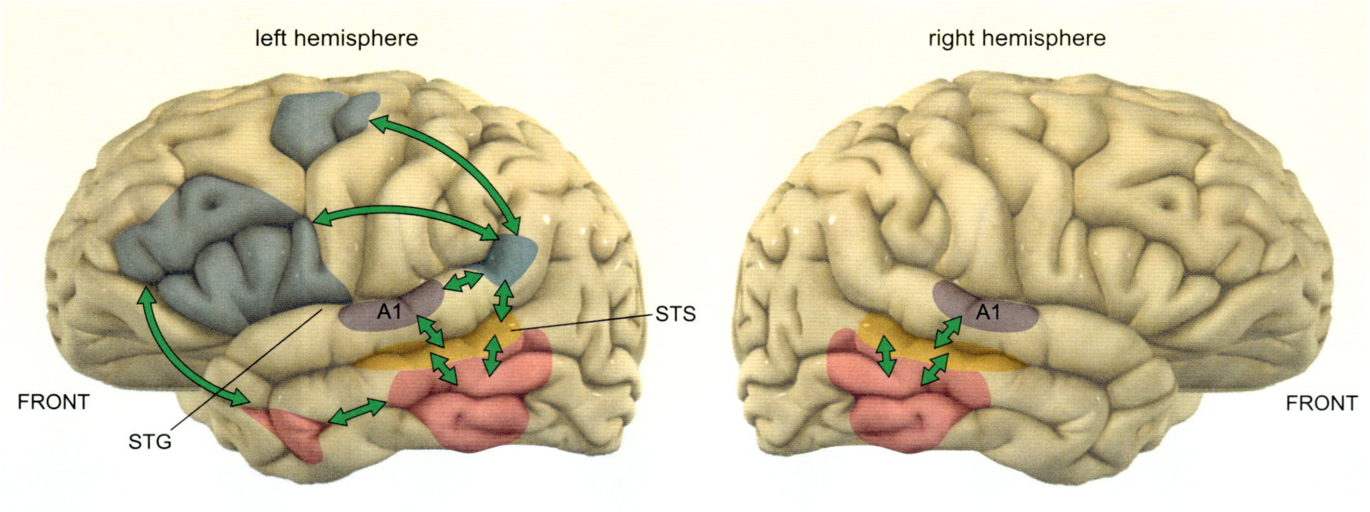

Figure 5.8 Locations of the dual-stream model components of both brain hemispheres; pink = ventral stream; blue = dorsal stream; STS, superior temporal brain sulcus; STG, superior temporal gyrus; A1, primary auditory cortex.

Role of the ventral stream

The ventral stream is thought to be critical for speech comprehension. A number of levels of processing are needed in order to understand speech, from analysis of phonemes to semantic information. Functional imaging suggests that speech comprehension is located bilaterally. That is not to say there are no differences between processing in the two brain hemispheres (they differ, for example, in the timescales over which they integrate information) but rather that they both show activation related to speech comprehension. It has been found consistently that listening to speech activates the STS and dorsal STG in both hemispheres, and that this is maintained when speech is compared with non-speech sound.

■ Why is it important to know that the activation persists when speech is compared with non-speech sounds as opposed to silence?

□ The studies comparing speech with silence would not tell you whether it is speech specifically that activates the brain regions or just the presence of any auditory stimulus.

In fact, devising a suitable control for speech experiments can be difficult because it is necessary to have an equally complex stimulus. A variety of different control stimuli have been used for this task, including time-reversed speech and spectrally rotated speech.

Speech comprehension requires some phonological processing in terms of consideration of how the phonemes are combined. The STS appears particularly important for this level of processing, with research demonstrating that modulating the phonological characteristics can modulate activity in this region (Buchsbaum et al., 2001; Hickok et al., 2003).

The next level of processing in comprehension that has received considerable research focus is the neural processes allowing access to existing lexical and semantic information, which is critical for understanding. Researchers now agree that this activity involves the posterior middle temporal regions (Hickok and Poeppel, 2007). However, it may also involve the anterior temporal lobe (ATL). Imaging studies such as Friederici et al. (2000) have revealed increased activation in the ATL when participants read or hear sentences as opposed to unstructured word sequences. Furthermore, patients with a specific kind of dementia called semantic dementia, which is associated with bilateral degeneration of the ATL, struggle with lexical tasks.

Role of the dorsal stream

The dorsal stream was originally labelled the 'where' pathway, indicating a role in the spatial element of hearing. However, more recent evidence suggests that it also offers a way in which the auditory system can communicate with the motor system. Auditory–motor integration is critical for speech; indeed, learning to speak requires motor learning. There must therefore be a way of using speech sounds to guide speech gestures so that sounds are accurately produced. According to the dual-stream model, it is the dorsal pathway that is important for speech perception and production. This idea is supported by a number of observations.

- Damage to the left dorsal STG and temporoparietal junction is associated with conduction aphasia, a condition in which there is good comprehension of speech but error-laden production of it (Damasio and Damasio, 1980). It is thought that the comprehension aspect is unaffected because the ventral stream is intact, and because the right hemisphere may compensate for the deficit in perception created by left-hemisphere damage.
- Brain imaging studies have identified the boundary between the frontal and parietal lobes as important in auditory–motor integration.

This dual-stream model has a considerable level of research supporting it, but you may be wondering about how this model fits with the idea of lateralisation of speech and language. Indeed, one of the best-known generalisations about language is that it is represented in the left hemisphere. However, the ventral and dorsal streams are found bilaterally; so can these two features be reconciled? Fortunately, it seems that they can be, because, although both streams are present in both hemispheres, the dorsal stream is left-dominant. This could account for speech-production deficits being more commonly found after dorsal and frontal damage and why left-hemisphere injury substantially impairs speech perception.

5.8 Separating mixtures of sounds

The two preceding sections examined the features used in the perception of music and speech: both everyday sounds. However, in each case the discussion was restricted to processes that occur when only one sound is occurring at a time – something that is distinctly rare in everyday circumstances. Indeed, in most cases there is more than one sound stimulus present and this gives rise to two interesting problems:

- simultaneous grouping
- sequential grouping.

Consider a snapshot of the sound coming into the ear at any particular time. Now, decide how many different sounds are present, and which parts of the total sound come from each sound source. This illustrates the problem of simultaneous grouping.

The sequential problem can be illustrated as follows: imagine that you have successfully split up the total sound at time t_1 into a number of different sources, and also at time t_2. Now which (if any) of the sources at t_1 are the same as those at t_2?

Bregman (1990) suggested that there are two ways in which the brain might solve these problems. One is through learned, top-down schema-based mechanisms, where the listener uses detailed knowledge about what specific sounds are like to select a relevant subset of the total sound. The other is through unlearned, bottom-up primitive grouping mechanisms, which use generally useful cues to separate sound into different sources. An example of a primitive cue that can be used to help solve the simultaneous grouping problem is onset-time – components of the same sound source tend to start at the same time.

Another clue which applies to periodic sounds, such as music and speech sounds with a definite pitch, is that the frequency components all form a harmonic series. If two instruments play the same note at exactly the same time, it is difficult to recognise the individual sound of either instrument. An example of this is at the beginning of Schubert's *Unfinished Symphony*, where the theme is played by two different wind instruments. If the performance is by an orchestra with players who are in tune and perfectly in time, it is very difficult to tell which two wind instruments are playing; but if the players are less accomplished, the task is easier. The fusion of the two well-played instruments' timbres creates a new timbre that is a composite of the original two.

An example of schema-based grouping involves the remarkable ability of listeners to understand **sine-wave speech**. This is a transformation of natural speech, which strips the speech of its acoustic constituents, leaving just three sine waves. These three sine waves follow the first three formant frequencies. These are the frequencies that are amplified, for example through movement of the lips, and therefore appear as peaks on the frequency spectrum. Although there are few primitive grouping cues to tell listeners that they form a single sound source (the sounds are not harmonically related), none the less, listeners have little difficulty in interpreting what is being said. Here, knowledge of how frequencies change to produce different speech sounds is probably helping the brain to treat the sound as a single (speech) sound source rather than just as three independent whistles.

An important practical problem linked to sound-source separation is distinguishing the voice of a single talker from background sounds, which are often the sounds of other talkers. The problem is important for two reasons. First, individuals with a certain type of hearing loss have particular difficulty understanding speech against a background of other sounds (such as from a television in the same room). If hearing aids could remove the background noise, they would be much more useful. Second, although computers can recognise speech moderately well when the speech is spoken in quiet conditions (or with a close, directionally sensitive microphone), they are very much worse at recognising speech when there are background sounds present. It is likely that a solution to this problem will use a combination of both types of mechanism proposed by Bregman (1990).

5.9 Abnormal auditory processing

The next chapter discusses hearing impairments that can be found to have causes within the auditory system. However, the abnormal perception of auditory information can occur in a number of other conditions that are not defined primarily as hearing, or even sensory, conditions. In this section we briefly consider three such conditions – schizophrenia, autism and diabetes.

5.9.1 Schizophrenia

Schizophrenia is one of the most common mental health conditions, affecting around 1% of people worldwide (WHO, 2013). It is characterised by a number of core symptoms, including hallucinations. These hallucinations may take on a number of forms, including auditory–verbal hallucinations, where the individual experiences hearing voices.

Imaging technologies have allowed neuroscientists to observe which areas of the brain are activated during auditory–verbal hallucinations. Such studies have consistently demonstrated that the primary and some non-primary auditory cortices are activated during these episodes, as shown in the fMRI scans in Figure 5.9. However, activation is not limited to the sensory regions, and those involved in emotion processing are also found to be activated. Extensive research now supports the view that auditory–verbal hallucinations are linked to an impaired ability of internal speech plans to modulate neural activation in sensory language areas (Brown and Thompson, 2010).

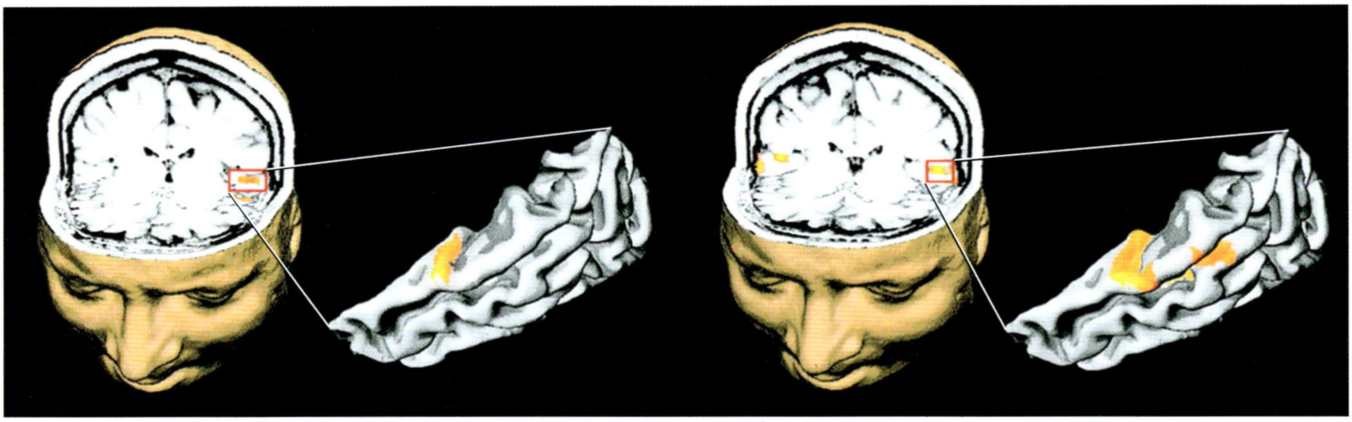

(a) (b)

Figure 5.9 Scans of the primary auditory cortex in a person with schizophrenia showing transversal and coronal sections (left) and a reconstruction of the grey–white matter boundary of the left temporal lobe (right, inset) during (a) hallucinations and (b) acoustical stimulation (Dierks et al., 1999).

5.9.2 Autism

Autism is typically characterised by three groups of symptoms:

- impaired social interaction
- language and communication difficulties
- restricted, repetitive and stereotyped behavioural patterns.

However, there is also considerable evidence for atypical processing of auditory information in some individuals with autistic conditions (O'Connor, 2012). The range of abnormalities of processing is extensive, including high prevalence of absolute pitch and reduced orientation to auditory stimuli, especially speech. Furthermore, Rosenhall et al. (1999) reported that 18% of individuals with autism display hyperacusis: abnormally acute hearing, resulting in intolerance to normal levels of sound. Interestingly, the sensory abnormalities noted have been both deficits (as in speech perception) and enhancements (in pitch and music perception) of normal functioning (Kellerman et al., 2005).

5.9.3 Diabetes

You read in Blocks 1 and 3 that diabetes can result in sensory impairment, specifically the damaging loss of pain perception. The condition also affects the auditory system. Bainbridge et al. (2008) discovered, while analysing national-health-survey data in the USA, that 21% of the people with diabetes surveyed had hearing loss, compared with only 9% of people without the condition. A number of possible reasons for the hearing loss that may result from diabetes have been identified, including damage to cochlear blood vessels and abnormal metabolic activity (Frisina et al., 2006).

5.10 Chapter 5 summary and questions

- Complex sounds such as speech and music can be considered in terms of their pitch and timbre.
- Music perception involves a number of auditory and non-auditory areas within the brain.
- Speech processing requires both the dorsal and ventral cortical streams, each of which fulfils slightly different roles in the process. This is known as the dual-stream model of processing.
- The separation of mixtures of sound can use both bottom-up and top-down processing.
- Abnormalities of sound processing can occur in conditions not primarily defined by changes to sensory processing, such as schizophrenia, autism and diabetes.

Self-assessment questions

Question 5.1

(a) What would be the difference in loudness between a 100 Hz tone and a 1000 Hz tone if each was broadcast at an intensity of 100 dB SPL through headphones? Explain your answer.
(b) How loud must a 100 Hz tone and a 1000 Hz tone be (in dB SPL) in order to have a loudness level of 50 phons?

Question 5.2

What properties of a sound determine its pitch and its timbre?

Question 5.3

What evidence is there to suggest that absolute pitch is not an auditory perception phenomenon?

Question 5.4

Which brain regions are likely to be involved in processing the emotional content of music?

Hearing impairment

6

> There are two kinds of deafness. One is due to wax and is curable: the other is not due to wax and is not curable.
>
> *(Sir William Wilde, attributed)*

It is almost 150 years since Sir William Wilde, one of the first British surgeons to call himself an 'otologist' (someone who specialises in the ear and its diseases), considered the causes of deafness in this pessimistic way. Our present understanding is fortunately very different.

Hearing impairments are normally divided into groups based on the anatomical site of their cause. One category of impairment is **conductive hearing loss**, which refers to loss originating in the outer ear or middle ear. By contrast, cochlear hearing loss stems from the inner ear, retrocochlear hearing loss from the cochlear nerve, and central hearing loss from the brain. The standard tests of hearing easily distinguish conductive losses from the other types but are less good at distinguishing cochlear, retrocochlear and central auditory problems from each other. The latter three causes are therefore, in practice, often amalgamated into **sensorineural hearing loss**.

In this chapter we consider the different causes of the types of hearing loss mentioned above, and the many treatments and strategies that can be utilised to rehabilitate people with such conditions. However, before doing so, we first briefly discusses how hearing impairment is assessed in a clinical setting.

6.1 Measuring hearing impairment in a clinic

When a hearing impairment is suspected, some attempt must be made to measure the extent of potential loss of perception. This can be done using a specific instrument called an audiometer, which produces different frequencies of sound that can be played to an individual through headphones. The threshold for hearing each of these frequencies is calculated relative to a known standard that is based on the threshold found in young, healthy listeners (set at 0 dB).

Because the thresholds recorded by the audiometer are not compared with the standard reference pressure of 20 μPa, they are not measured in dB SPL, but rather in dB HL ('hearing level'). The intensity in dB HL required for each of the frequencies tested to be audible is then plotted onto an audiogram, which displays the sound level in dB HL on the *y*-axis (where a value of zero would indicate unimpaired hearing), and frequency on the *x*-axis. Frequency is normally plotted as a logarithmic scale.

Figure 6.1 shows an example of an audiogram, the red line indicating unimpaired hearing function and the blue line showing the level of hearing loss found. You should note when looking at this figure that audiograms use positive values to indicate a hearing threshold that is higher than that found in a healthy, unimpaired individual, and therefore hearing loss, but that conventionally this scale extends downwards rather than upwards.

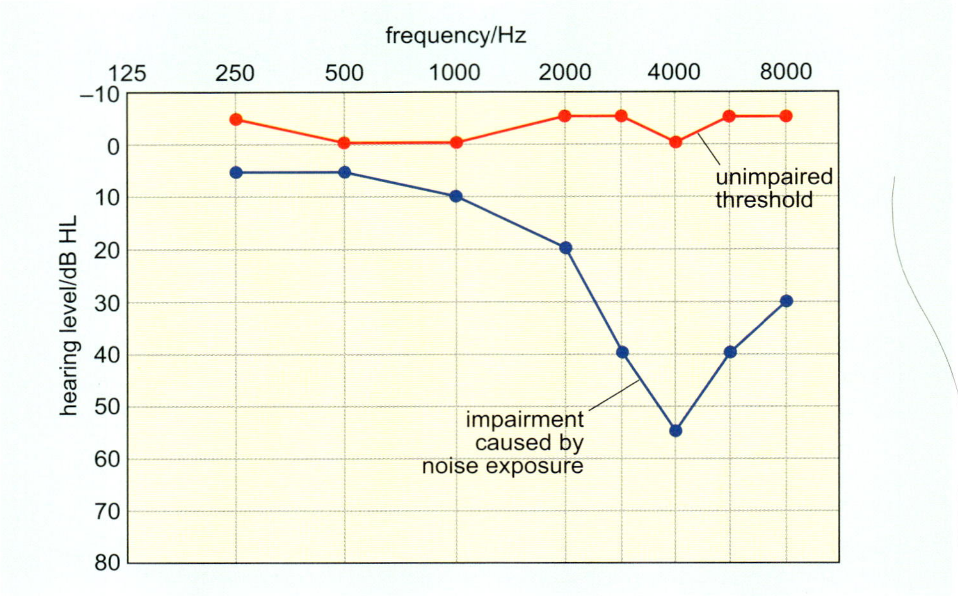

Figure 6.1 Example of a clinical audiogram showing hearing loss at the higher frequencies following noise exposure.

It is useful clinically to categorise the severity of hearing loss, and this can be done using the audiogram. Table 6.1 shows how the altered hearing level can be related to specific classifications of hearing loss. Additionally, the table shows how this kind of hearing impairment may be experienced by the people who have it.

Table 6.1 Categorisation of levels of hearing loss.

Hearing loss classification	Hearing level (dB HL)	Impairment experience
Mild	20–39	following speech may be difficult, especially in a noisy environment
Moderate	40–69	difficulty following speech without hearing aid
Severe	70–89	usually need to lip-read or use sign language even with hearing aid
Profound	90–120	usually need to lip-read or use sign language; hearing aid ineffectual

6.2 Conductive hearing loss

Disease or damage to any part of the middle or outer ear can result in conductive hearing loss. However, even if you have no meatus, tympanic membrane or ossicles, sound signals can still reach your inner ear via transmission through the temporal bone of the skull directly to your cochlea.

■ What is the term given to this kind of conduction of the sound signal?

□ Bone conduction (see introduction to Chapter 3).

The maximum effect of a conductive hearing loss is to remove the contribution of the outer and middle ear to hearing, and this equates to a hearing loss on an audiogram with an extent of 40–50 dB. In other words, the hearing loss would be classed as moderate.

Normally in cases of conductive hearing loss the individual's **auditory discrimination**, that is their ability to hear and concentrate on a sound in a noisy environment, is intact. Rather, there is an increase in **hearing threshold** (the quietest sound they can hear in a sound-proofed environment), which is unsurprising given the loss of contribution of the conductive hearing pathway. An individual with an increased hearing threshold but normal auditory discrimination will be helped simply by making the sound louder, and this is the basis of some treatments for conductive hearing loss.

6.2.1 Causes of impairment

The extent of hearing impairment and the type of treatment required depends in part on the exact location of damage within the outer and middle ear. Therefore, this section follows this pathway, considering how impairment can arise from each region.

Pinna

The pinna can be congenitally deficient or damaged by trauma or tumour. Although this particular anatomical feature has a small effect in funnelling sound and contributing to sound localisation, it is not of major importance in humans. Some other mammals, such as horses and cats, have more highly developed external ears and have a much enhanced ability to localise sound accurately. Disease of the human pinna can cause marked cosmetic deformity, but generally does not cause significant deafness.

Meatus

The meatus can become blocked due to wax or a foreign body, or it can become swollen due to infection or inflammation. This impedes the passage of sound to the tympanic membrane. It is easy to mimic this hearing impairment by simply putting your fingers in your ears! The extent of the resultant hearing loss depends on the extent of blockage.

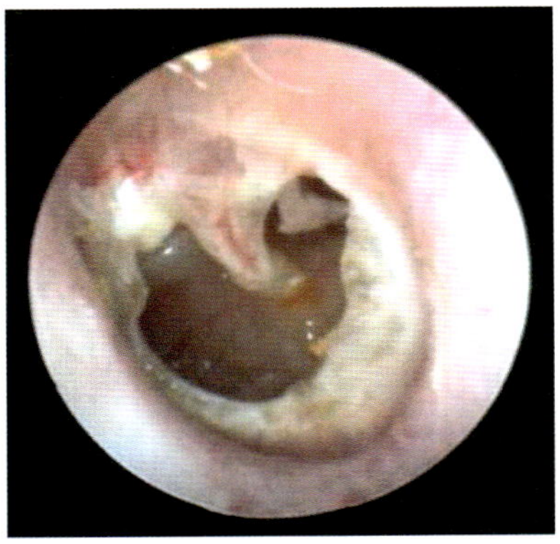

left ear

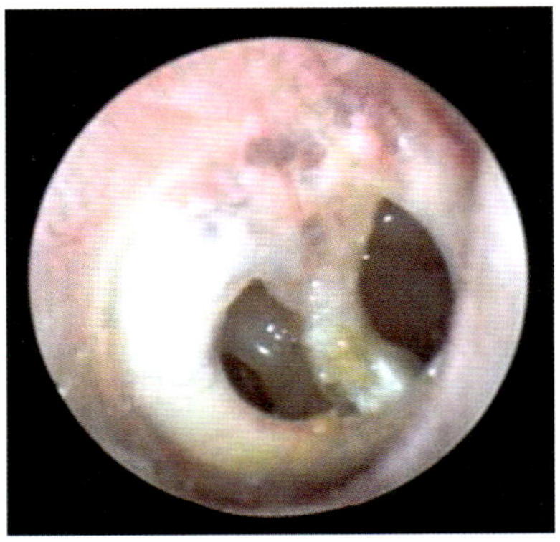

right ear

Figure 6.2 Perforation of the tympanic membrane in the left and right ear.

Tympanic membrane

The tympanic membrane can be damaged by trauma, such as a blow to the side of the head, or by fluid resulting from infection in the middle ear bursting its way out through the membrane. These factors can cause holes or perforations of the membrane that reduce the amount of sound energy captured by the ear, thereby causing hearing loss (Figure 6.2). The membrane can also become scarred as a result of repeated infection. This scarring, referred to as **tympanosclerosis**, increases the stiffness of the membrane, which reduces its efficiency as a sound transmitter.

Middle ear cavity

The middle ear cavity normally contains moist air, which is supplied via the Eustachian tube that passes from the back of the nose up to the ear. If this tube becomes blocked, air cannot reach the middle ear cavity and the ears feel blocked: you have probably experienced this feeling temporarily during a bad head cold, or after swimming underwater. If the tube malfunctions for a longer period, the middle ear cavity gradually fills up with fluid that is produced by the lining of the cavity itself. This fluid may be thin and watery or it may be the thick, viscous sticky fluid that gives the condition the colloquial name 'glue ear'.

■ How would the presence of fluid in the middle ear affect the acoustic impedance at the outer and middle ear boundary?

□ As a healthy middle ear is air-filled, there is normally no change in acoustic impedance from the outer to the middle ear. However, if the middle ear fills with fluid, there will be at greater acoustic impendence at this boundary and more of the signal will be reflected back.

The more correct medical terms for glue ear are **otitis media with effusion**, or secretory otitis media. Although the condition can occur at any age, it is most prevalent in children, partly due to immaturity of the Eustachian tube and the physiological enlargement of adenoid tissue in this age group. The adenoids are swellings of lymphoid tissue at the back of the nose that help the body to respond to infections. Unfortunately, they are very close to the openings of the Eustachian tubes and adenoidal swelling can result in tubal blockage.

Otitis media with effusion is by far the most common cause of conductive hearing loss in the UK, and its causes and effects have been closely examined. A number of risk factors have been identified, and these are detailed in Box 6.1. Additionally, it is now known that as well as the loss of hearing itself, acute and chronic otitis media can result in sleeping difficulties, poor eating, balance problems and irritability. Behavioural problems as well as difficulties with speech and social development have also been identified (Brouwer et al., 2005). It seems likely that other hearing problems that affect an individual for a similar period of time could also have such effects.

Box 6.1 Risk factors for glue ear

Several risk factors have been identified for otitis media that can be related to either the individual or their environment.

First, it is thought that there is a genetic predisposition to developing the condition; for example, a Norwegian study of 2750 twin pairs concluded that heritability of otitis media was 74% among girls and 45% among boys (Kvaerner et al., 1997). In addition, individuals with suppressed action of the immune system are also more at risk. The influence of allergy as a risk factor for otitis media is contentious with only some studies noting an association (Skoner et al., 2009).

In terms of environmental risk factors, the largest factor is day-care attendance by children, with 20% of children in full-time day-care receiving treatment for glue ear. This trend is directly related to the number of children in each day-care centre (Wald et al., 1988) and may reflect the increased risk of upper respiratory tract infection in day-care. The same factors hold for overcrowding in homes and families with a number of older siblings (Pukander, 1985). Passive cigarette smoking also increases the risk of otitis media (Uhari et al., 1996), possibly through increasing the production of specific proteins (Cho et al., 2009).

Meta-analyses by Uhari et al. (1996) have also found the use of a dummy beyond 11 months of age to be associated with otitis media, and that breast feeding can have a protective effect on the development of middle ear problems; an effect thought to be mediated by the immunological properties of breast milk.

Ossicles

The ossicles can be damaged by infections that cause scar tissue to develop around them. Some conditions cause persistent negative pressure in the middle ear, which can suck part of the tympanic membrane inwards. The inside-out portion of the membrane traps layers of dead skin that can then become infected. This small growth is called a **cholesteatoma**, and the infectious material slowly, inexorably, eats away the normal structures in the middle ear. The middle of the three ossicles, the incus, is especially prone to damage in this process. This uncommon disease tends to occur in later childhood or adulthood.

Trauma can also damage the ossicles; a severe head injury can dislocate the delicate joints between the tiny bones. Equally, in the condition of **otosclerosis**, new bone forms around the footplate of the stapes, fusing the bone rigidly with the bone of the inner ear. This reduces the ear's ability to conduct sound from the ossicular chain to the transduction mechanism of the cochlea.

6.2.2 Treatment

As individuals with conductive hearing loss often have unimpaired auditory discrimination, they generally find that hearing aids improve their sound perception, but this is rather ironic, since this is the same group of people who are most likely to benefit from surgery. A foreign body or earwax can be removed, a perforated tympanic membrane can be repaired with a graft taken from one of the patient's own muscle tendons, and a dislocated ossicular chain can be reset using microsurgical techniques. Cholesteatomas can be excised and the damage they have caused can in many cases be repaired. In cases of otosclerosis, the diseased stapes can be replaced with a minute prosthetic ossicle. Such stapedectomy surgery often returns hearing sensitivity back to unimpaired, or near-unimpaired, levels.

Otitis media with effusion can also be treated with surgery developed to alleviate the potential impairment. The surgery involves making a tiny incision in the tympanic membrane, removing any fluid in the middle ear, and inserting a tiny plastic or metal tube. This ventilation tube or **grommet** allows air to get from the atmosphere, through a hole in the grommet into the middle ear cavity. This equalises the pressure on either side of the tympanic membrane, preventing the build-up of fluid in the middle ear. Two different types of grommet are shown in Figure 6.3. The tympanic membrane grows throughout life and this normal growth eventually results in the grommet being extruded. This process takes approximately one year and, in the majority of cases, by the time extrusion is complete, the patient's Eustachian tube function has returned to normal and the otitis media with effusion does not recur.

Figure 6.3 A T-tube and a Shah grommet.

Initial results from this procedure were good, and the operation became very popular. However, more detailed surveys showed that the otitis media with effusion was short-lived in many cases and the insertion of grommets was not without its own problems. Scarring of the tympanic membrane often followed grommet insertion and, in some cases, the degree of hearing improvement was disappointing. A sensible middle-ground approach has now been adopted whereby most individuals with otitis media with effusion undergo a period of 'watchful waiting' (careful monitoring of hearing over time) prior to considering surgery. In some otology units, hearing aids are provided for mild cases of impairment, surgery being reserved for the more seriously affected.

6.3 Cochlear hearing loss

The delicate structures of the cochlea were described earlier in this block, and it should come as no surprise that they are vulnerable to trauma, infection and degenerative processes, leading to a reduction in hearing sensitivity. The extent of cochlear hearing loss can be mild, moderate, severe or profound, and can have almost any conceivable frequency configuration, although most often the extent of loss is greater in the high frequencies. Auditory discrimination tends to be more affected in this type of loss than in conductive hearing loss, meaning that clinical interventions that merely amplify the sound are of limited use.

6.3.1 Causes of impairment

This section considers a number of causes of cochlear hearing loss, beginning with those that are present from birth, before considering some of the causes of hearing loss that can start later in life.

Congenital impairment

In more wealthy countries, approximately one in every thousand live births is a child with severe to profound bilateral cochlear hearing loss, and in approximately two-thirds of these cases the cause of the impairment is genetic (Terrinoni et al., 2009). In the other third, factors such as intrauterine infection, hypoxia or neonatal jaundice are responsible.

Without early identification and treatment, children with such hearing loss have almost insurmountable difficulties in the development of speech, and sign language may become vital for communication. Early identification is possible with tests during the neonatal period, although care has to be taken to allay parental anxiety.

Noise-induced hearing loss (NIHL)

It is thought that as much as 5% of the world's population experiences noise-induced hearing loss (NIHL), causing great economic cost and detriment to the quality of life of the affected individuals (Oishi and Schacht, 2011). This loss may be caused by noise from industrial or military sources, or from recreational activities, including listening to loud music. The loss is usually bilateral and reasonably symmetrical, and is the second most self-reported occupational injury despite many years of research into regulation and interventions intended to prevent such damage (Nelson and Hinojosa, 2006).

Verbeek et al. (2009) state that the probability of hearing impairment occurring in individuals not exposed to loud noise at the ages of 35 and 65 is estimated to be 10% and 55%, respectively, because hearing impairment increases with age. By contrast, if an individual experiences ten years of exposure to loud noise, the probability rises to 94.5% and 99.5%, respectively. In addition, individuals who are subjected to industrial noise may also experience concurrent exposure to ototoxic substances (substances which can damage hearing) such as solvents and heavy metals, which can increase the damaging potential of the noise (Morata et al., 1993).

The actual mechanism of damage underlying NIHL is unclear; however, a number of potential explanations have been identified. For example, heavy noise exposure is known to induce the production of free radicals in the cochlea (reviewed by Henderson et al., 2006). These are highly reactive clusters of atoms and, in excess, can damage cellular membranes, proteins and DNA, and therefore have the potential to damage the delicate structure of the cochlea (Le Prell et al., 2007). Damage can be quite visible in both inner and outer hair cells (Figure 6.4) but it is also found in supporting cells such as pillar cells (Henderson et al., 2006).

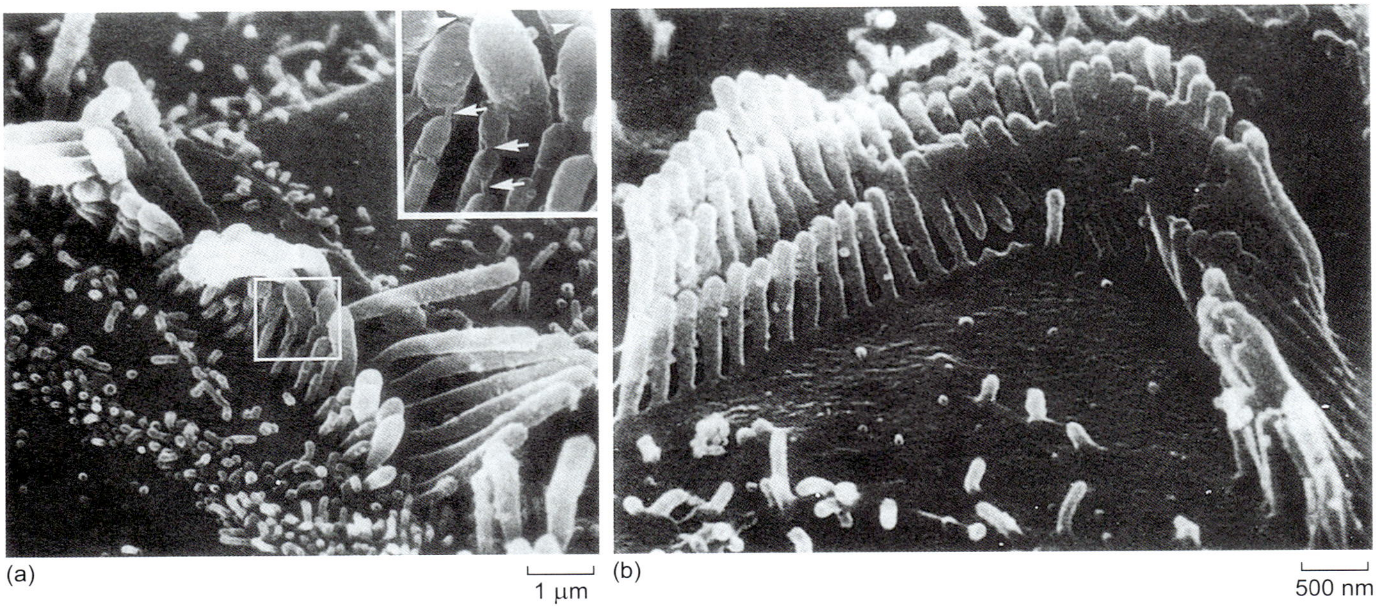

Figure 6.4 Scanning electron micrographs of hair cells damaged by excessive noise: (a) inner hair cells, inset showing some links between stereocilia are broken (indicated by arrows); (b) outer hair cells, showing fused or detached stereocilia. (Adapted from Pickles et al., 1987)

Presbycusis

Presbycusis refers to a decrease in cochlear sensitivity with age. As the population ages, this condition represents a significant concern and health care cost, especially as it is known to contribute to social isolation and loss of autonomy associated with anxiety, depression and cognitive decline.

Much like NIHL, presbycusis is thought to involve cell damage caused by free radicals, and Nelson and Hinojosa (2006) report the loss of both inner and outer hair cells, as well as spiral ganglion cells. Seidman et al. (1997) proposed that ageing is associated with the accumulation of reactive species in the cochlea and DNA damage, such that when a critical level is reached, cell death (lysis) is triggered. However, it seems that the mechanism could be twofold, with not only this increase in DNA damage with age, but also a decrease in natural cell protection mechanisms (Sha et al., 2010).

As with NIHL, presbycusis normally results in bilateral and reasonably symmetrical hearing loss, which is typically greater for higher frequencies (>2000 Hz).

- ■ Recall from Chapter 5 why hearing loss is often greater at the higher frequencies.
- □ The region of the basilar membrane, and therefore the hair cells, stimulated by high-frequency sounds are also affected by low-frequency sounds. This means there is more opportunity for them to become 'worn out' or damaged (see Section 5.2.1).

Ototoxic medications

In discussing NIHL, we briefly mentioned ototoxic substances that may be found in industry. However, many ototoxic substances are medications and they can result in bilateral hearing loss and a form of impairment called tinnitus (see Section 6.6). One of the most common classes of medication known to be ototoxic is aminoglycoside antibiotics, such as streptomycin. Despite the potential adverse effects on the hearing system, these antibiotics remain important drugs in the treatment of bacterial infections, cystic fibrosis and tuberculosis.

Although the exact mechanism of ototoxicity depends on the specific drug used, and is not well understood, a recent breakthrough has revealed how these chemicals reach the inner ear. Li and Steyger (2011) have provided evidence that these antibiotics can cross a special barrier that normally protects hair cells from damaging substances in the blood. Assuming this is the case, it remains to be seen whether it will be possible to block this trafficking to the inner ear.

Menière's disease

Menière's disease is a disorder of the inner ear that is characterised by episodes of hearing loss, tinnitus and vertigo. The hearing loss is normally unilateral, and the ear often feels blocked prior to these attacks. Between acute episodes, the person affected may return to their normal level of hearing, although as the disease progresses hearing loss may become permanent.

This distressing condition is thought to be due to a build-up of endolymph within the inner ear that distorts the delicate membranes of the cochlea and vestibular apparatus, thereby affecting both hearing and balance. In some rare cases the body's immune system may malfunction, attacking normal tissues such as the components of the inner ear and causing a sudden or progressive hearing loss. The cochlea is also vulnerable to a number of specific viruses. The hearing impairment associated with the disease means that its impact on quality of life may be substantial, as described in Box 6.2.

Box 6.2 Living with Menière's disease

Ryan Dempsey lives with his wife and children and works as a web designer. He also plays and records music and races cars. Here he describes what it is like to have Menière's disease.

> Being a positive thinker, it's taken me a long time to admit this to myself, but I've got Menière's disease. It's not life threatening or contagious or anything but it has changed my life considerably.
>
> I started noticing some hearing loss in my early twenties and continued to lose hearing in my right ear to the point it's almost gone. I often get pretty bad tinnitus too, an annoying white noise and ringing in my ear. I used to love singing and playing in bands. My hearing got so bad that I started to have

> difficulty singing in tune most of the time. I remember being on stage where I was supposed to be singing a duet with a girl. I couldn't find the tune and just stood there silently feeling like an idiot. The last time I sang in public was at a coffee shop. Again, I just couldn't hear the tune correctly in my head and just played instrumentals on my guitar instead.
>
> *(Dempsey, 2010)*

6.3.2 Treatment

The exact treatment for cochlear hearing loss very much depends on the cause of impairment in the individual being treated and the availability of treatment. The latter is likely to be significantly poorer in less developed countries, where some forms of hearing loss will be greater. This increase in occurrence is due to lack of education about the impact of noise and the higher prevalence of conditions that require treatment with ototoxic medications. In addition, the majority of treatments currently available focus on the hearing loss rather than the impact it can have on quality of life, such as the increased isolation experienced in individuals with presbycusis.

Preventive treatments

Interestingly, some of the forms of cochlear hearing loss outlined can be avoided or treated using a prevention-rather-than-cure approach. For example, with NIHL, hearing protection equipment within occupational settings and appropriate education on how to use it may be effective (Verbeek et al., 2009). In addition, understanding the mechanisms involved in lysis within the cochlea in NIHL, presbycusis and following ototoxic exposure can provide potential new treatments. For example, for some people, hearing loss could be avoided by blocking the actions of free radicals or preventing the transport of ototoxic substances to the inner ear.

Although no treatments are available to prevent the initial onset of Menière's disease, there are some specific, but controversial, treatments available to prevent or ameliorate attacks.

- Drugs are used to try to improve cochlear blood flow and to control the vertigo.
- Surgery is undertaken in some patients to try to reduce the build-up of endolymph.
- Other patients have operations to sever the balance nerves and prevent the disabling vertigo.

In addition, a number of people with Meniere's disease rely on complementary and alternative medicines (CAM), although there is little published information about how such treatments may help (Long and Bennett, 2009).

Hearing aids

It appears that about one in ten adults with cochlear hearing loss would benefit from using hearing aids. However, unlike conductive hearing impairment, the effect of cochlear damage is not only to reduce hearing sensitivity, but also to reduce the person's ability to make fine auditory discrimination in frequency and temporal domains. In addition, tolerance to loud sound may be reduced. The consequence for someone with a cochlear impairment is that sound may be distorted, even when amplified.

Hearing aids may also provide a suitable initial treatment in children with congenital deafness, along with intensive support for both the child and the parents and correction of any coexisting conductive hearing loss such as otitis media with effusion. In some cases, however, the hearing loss is beyond the reach of even the most powerful and sophisticated hearing aids. Thus, the benefits of hearing aids in cochlear hearing loss may be limited.

Cochlear implantation

The idea that it is possible to induce sound perception by electrical stimulation dates as far back as Volta, who in 1800 electrically stimulated of his own ear after filling the ear canal with saline solution. The electrical charge gave rise to an extremely loud bang, and Volta appears not to have repeated the experiment!

In the 1970s, the possibilities of using electrical stimulation to give profoundly deaf people some experience of sound formed the basis of **cochlear implantation**. A cochlear implant is a small electrical device consisting of a number of electrodes, which can be placed in the cochlea. The electrodes produce an electrical current, allowing them to stimulate the cochlear nerve directly. You will find out more about cochlear implantation by now completing Activities 6.1 and 6.2.

Activity 6.1 Core reading

Allow 3 hours

(*Relevant module learning outcomes: KU5 and KU6*)

Access the core reading associated with this activity, which is available from the *Block 4 Activities* resource on the module website. The reading is an essential part of the module, so you should treat it as you would the module text and devote an adequate amount of time to studying it. You will find questions and guidance on how to approach your reading of this text in the activity.

Now that you have an understanding of the science behind cochlear implants and the factors affecting the outcome of implantation, complete Activity 6.2.

Activity 6.2 Cochlear implants: a wider context

Allow 1 hour

(*Relevant module learning outcome: KU6*)

Access and watch the programme entitled 'Rita Simons: My Daughter, Deafness and Me', which is available from the *Block 4 Activities* resource. In this programme, Rita explores the issues around cochlear implantation for her daughter Maiya, who was diagnosed with deafness at 6 months of age. As you watch the programme, make brief notes on the different opinions and issues surrounding cochlear implants.

6.4 Retrocochlear hearing loss

Retrocochlear hearing loss results from damage to the cochlear nerve projecting from the cochlea to the brainstem. People with this condition normally experience a loss of sound intensity and sound discrimination. It is considered to be an irreversible condition.

6.4.1 Causes of impairment

Tumours

The cochlear and vestibular nerves run side by side within the internal auditory meatus, a bony canal that passes through the temporal bone from the inner ear structures towards the brainstem. A region of cellular instability on the vestibular nerve can give rise to a benign tumour, derived from the Schwann cells that surround and insulate axons. These tumours are correctly known as **vestibular schwannoma** but they are more often called acoustic neuromas.

Vestibular schwannoma usually cause unilateral hearing loss (typically resulting in poor auditory discrimination) and tinnitus. Although these tumours are often benign, if left untreated they can grow to fill the internal auditory meatus and then encroach towards the brainstem where, after some years, the compressive effects of the tumour may compromise functions vital for life. Vestibular schwannomas are diagnosed in 1 in 50 000 adults per year in the UK, and such diagnosis has been greatly facilitated by magnetic resonance imaging (MRI), as highlighted in Figure 6.5.

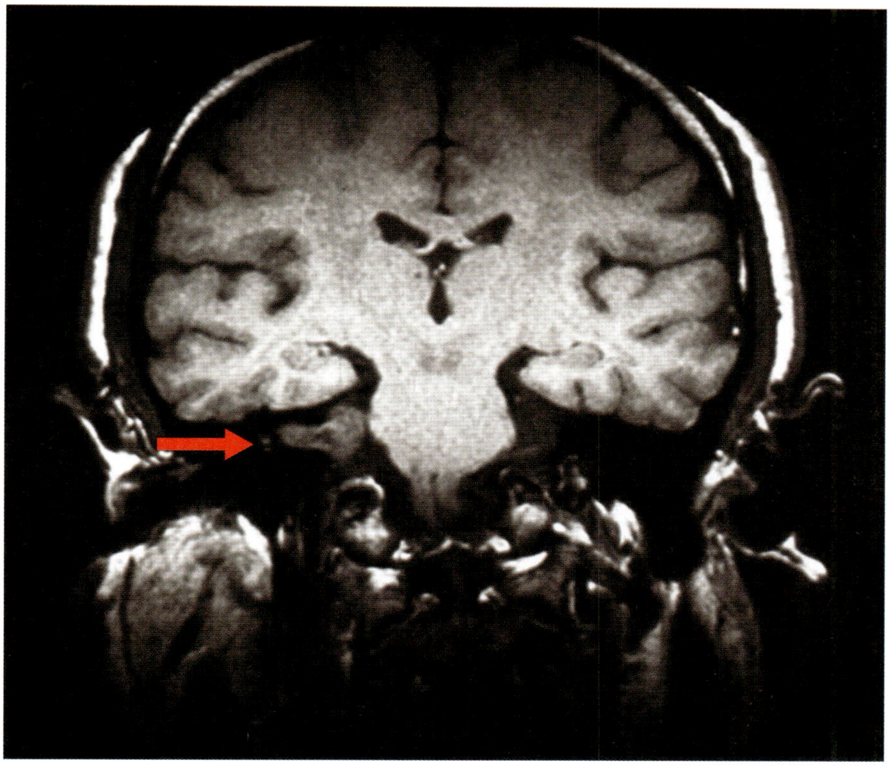

Figure 6.5 MRI scan of brain; arrow indicates right vestibular schwannoma.

Auditory neuropathy

The move towards the diagnosis of hearing impairment in newborn babies has uncovered another situation of interest. In the 1970s, biophysicist David Kemp discovered that our ears emit a small amount of sound in response to sound input (Kemp, 1978). It has been since been discovered that these **otoacoustic emissions** originate from the movement of the outer hair cells, and they are used as the basis of a hearing test in infants.

A small number of babies have regular otoacoustic emissions (suggesting healthy cochlear function) but, when tested using auditory brainstem responses, show results indicative of significant dysfunction in the activity of the retrocochlear neural pathway that is beyond the cochlea. This condition was named auditory neuropathy or auditory desynchrony (Sininger, 1995) and its cause was proposed to be abnormalities in the cochlear nerve (Starr et al., 1996).

However, later research indicated that, at least in some cases, the problem was in the cochlea. Gibson and Sanli (2007) demonstrated that in 75% of cases the abnormality was caused by a loss of inner hair cells but survival of outer cells, which resulted in the cochlea being tuned atypically and effectively giving a chaotic signal. Treatment with hearing aids was ineffective in these individuals because the aberrant signal remained, but surgical treatment with cochlear implants was found to be largely beneficial, as may be expected for treating a condition based in the cochlea.

It has since been suggested that the umbrella term of 'auditory neuropathy' is somewhat unhelpful and that, for true auditory neuropathy, abnormalities must be associated with the cochlear nerve, brainstem pathways or higher structures. Here, auditory neuropathy is included under the heading of retrocochlear hearing loss because the cochlear nerve is the first point at which abnormalities may result in true auditory neuropathy.

6.4.2 Treatment

If a tumour is present, the treatment used will depend on the size of the tumour, the symptoms present and the rate of tumour growth. Where the tumour is large – causing significant symptoms and growing quickly – it is likely to be removed surgically. If the tumour is located in such a position that removal would be too difficult, stereotactic radiosurgery may be used.

The equipment for this latter approach is shown in Figure 6.6. The gantry of the machinery contains 192 highly radioactive sources of the isotope cobalt-60 (^{60}Co), which produce high-energy gamma rays. These rays are directed at the tumour from different directions around the head so that a very large radioactive dose is given to the tumour, while the dose to surrounding, sensitive tissue remains as low as possible.

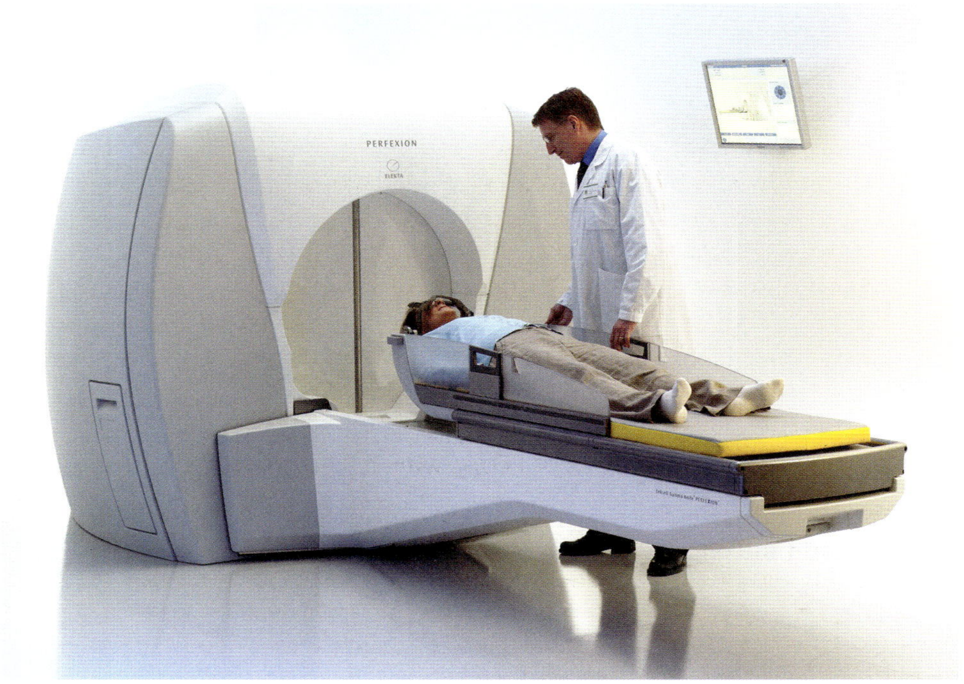

Figure 6.6 Equipment used for stereotactic radiosurgery. (Courtesy of Elekta)

Despite its name, stereotactic radiosurgery is not actually considered a surgical technique but rather a form of radiation therapy whereby the electromagnetic waves can reduce or stop tumour growth. However, like surgical excision, this treatment may result in unilateral, total and permanent hearing loss depending on the level of damage to the cochlear nerve prior to the removal or irradiation of the tumour.

- Why would a cochlear implant not be a suitable treatment for an individual whose hearing has been lost following the removal of vestibular schwannoma?

- The problem is caused by damage to the nerve, which is beyond the cochlea. Therefore, the cochlea may be functioning appropriately and, even if it were not, improving cochlea function will not help if the nerve transmitting the information to the brain is damaged. Additionally, damage is only unilateral and cochlear implants are provided where there is bilateral hearing loss.

In fact, implantation methods can be used following removal of the tumour if this leaves the individual with bilateral hearing loss. This may be the case if they were already deaf in one ear before the removal of the tumour in the other ear or if they had bilateral tumours, as can be found with the condition neurofibromatosis type 2. However, rather than targeting the cochlea, the implants must be beyond the damaged nerve, and you will now discover more about this idea by completing the next activity.

Activity 6.3 Core reading

Allow 45 minutes

(*Relevant module learning outcomes: KU5 and KU6*)

Access the core reading associated with this activity, which is available from the *Block 4 Activities* resource on the module website. The reading is an essential part of the module, so you should treat it as you would the module text and devote an adequate amount of time to studying it. You will find questions and guidance on how to approach your reading of this text in the activity.

- Based on what you have read in Activity 6.3, would you expect a brainstem implant to benefit someone with auditory neuropathy?

- It would depend on the location of the damage and the implant. If the issue is in the cochlear nerve, this form of implant may be beneficial. However, if the damage is beyond the brainstem, the impact may be lost.

Away from these techniques, current research is working towards identifying the key molecules involved in the proliferation and survival of the tumours. This raises the possibility of drug treatments being developed to block tumour growth or survival (Miller et al., 2012).

6.5 Central auditory processing disorders

One interesting group of patients who are referred to audiologists and otologists believe themselves to have a hearing problem, although they perform normally in standard hearing tests. More detailed psychoacoustic tests show that their auditory discrimination is markedly worse than their peers.

In the UK, these symptoms were carefully considered in the 1980s and the condition was named obscure auditory dysfunction (OAD). In the USA, the name **central auditory processing disorder (CAPD)** has been used for the same set of symptoms. This was coined after the specific investigation of children who had regular hearing acuity on pure tone and otoacoustic emission testing but who had quantifiable and significant difficulties in noisy environments, such as a classroom. CAPD is gradually becoming the more accepted terminology.

6.5.1 Causes of impairment

At present the specific mechanisms involved in CAPD have not been identified. Furthermore, there are likely to be various pathophysiologies involved rather than one alone, meaning that CAPD is an umbrella term. So, for now, Box 6.3 provides a personal insight into the impact that this condition can have.

Box 6.3 Living with CAPD

The following account is by Andrea, a blogger and science author who has CAPD.

> I am walking across campus when someone stops me. While I am standing there desperately trying to figure out who this out-of-place person is, they ask me, 'Are you going to the four-meter spa?'
>
> I blink with confusion, and then realise that I am scrambling these sounds, so ask for a repeat, but it makes no more sense. Apparently this is an important question, so I ask for a rephrase, and finally it all clicks: this is Elverta and she is asking me, 'Are you going to tutor for me this fall?' This kind of auditory miscomprehension is a real problem; I end up answering the wrong questions, and sometimes the person and I do not realise that we are engaged in a dialog about entirely different subjects.
>
> [...]
>
> Over the years, my family, teachers, graduate school advisor, and employers have complained at me for not understanding what was going on, for forgetting what they told me, for taking things too literally, or for ignoring them. I do what I can in class and meeting situations: I sit up front, do the readings beforehand, and watch what the speaker is saying. But many times I am caught between an air conditioner fan or steam-heat

radiators, flickering or buzzing lights, and a whining projector, and thus can barely understand the speaker despite the fact that I am just a few feet away. Sometimes I ask them to speak up, but it really isn't their volume – it is me having difficulty discriminating between the voice and the background noises, plus my mental decoding of his discussion into these new words, plus my double-time processing of trying to figure out what is being said in words and what it means in content. Often I cannot understand people when more than one person is speaking. I've tried recording lectures, but generally it's not any clearer the second time around.

(Andrea's Buzzing About, 2006)

6.5.2 Treatment

The management of CAPD involves a variety of measures that depend on the exact nature of the deficit and the age of the individual affected. In general, there are two treatment approaches:

- improving the quality of the auditory signal
- enhancing the individual's auditory perception skills.

The first of these approaches can be achieved with various changes aimed at increasing the strength of the signal that the individual is striving to hear relative to the competing background noise. In a classroom setting, this can be accomplished by simple measures such as moving the individual closer to the teacher or lecturer, speaking clearly, rephrasing information, and using visual aids to supplement auditory information. Some of these are mentioned in Box 6.3. The careful use of hearing aids can also help.

Additionally, FM radio aids may be useful. These devices allow the sound signal of a human voice to be sent via radio waves from a transmitter worn by the speaker to a receiver worn by the listener. This has the effect of reducing background noise, which can otherwise be a problem for people with hearing aids if the speaker is more than an arm's length away.

Outside an educational setting, it is often more difficult to manipulate the acoustic environment and, in these cases, counselling and the teaching of specific hearing tactics are the most common treatment options. In order to enhance perception skills, individuals may undergo specific forms of listening training, which have been shown to improve perception by, for example, increasing speech recognition amid background noise (Putter-Katz et al., 2008).

6.6 Tinnitus

The word tinnitus comes from the Latin for 'ringing', and it was defined in a publication by the Committee on Hearing, Bioacoustics, and Biomechanics (McFadden, 1982). The term refers to the phenomenon of hearing sound in the absence of any external stimulation (or sound wave).

Experiencing some short-lived (<5 minutes) spontaneous tinnitus is quite common but around 10% of the UK adult population experience persistent, albeit mild forms of tinnitus. Furthermore, in 1% of the UK population tinnitus has a severe effect on quality of life, making this an auditory dysfunction worthy of scientific consideration and of effective therapy (Action on Hearing Loss, 2013).

6.6.1 Causes of impairment

It is important to recognise that tinnitus involves symptoms beyond those that relate to sound. A useful model of the condition was proposed by neuroscientist Pawel Jastreboff (1990) to show that it involves areas beyond the auditory systems, such as the sympathetic and the limbic system (specifically the amygdalae – structures in the brain that play a critical role in the formation and modulation of emotionally influenced memory). Jastreboff postulated that the perception of tinnitus becomes associated with negative emotions, thereby involving the limbic system, which in turn activates the autonomic nervous system, resulting in annoyance. This concept is depicted in Figure 6.7.

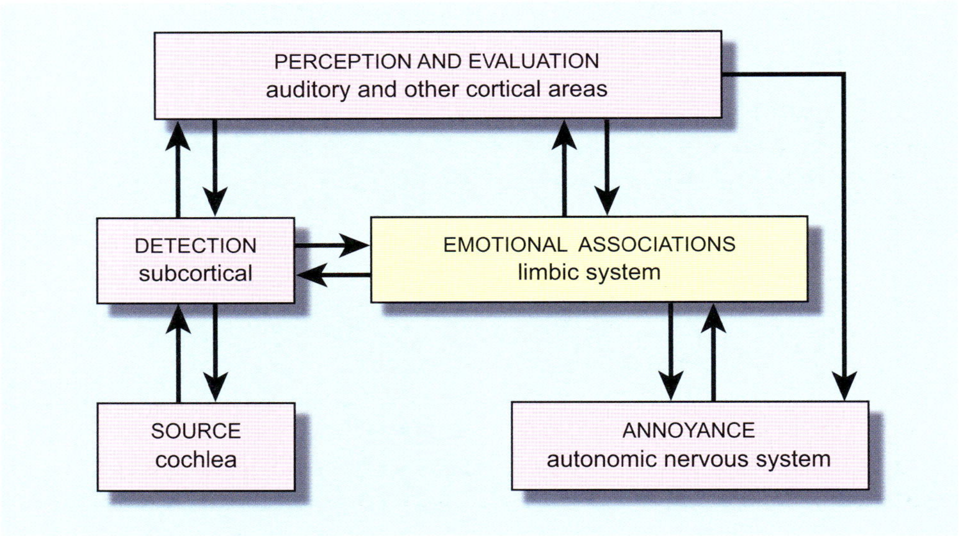

Figure 6.7 The neurophysiological model of tinnitus (Jastreboff, 1990).

This notion of causation beyond the auditory system is also supported by work in animal models of tinnitus, which have revealed hyperactivity in auditory and non-auditory brain regions and provided insights into how tinnitus may develop.

Currently, it is thought that tinnitus can be triggered by injury to the ear, which results in a decrease in activity in the cochlear nerve. In response to this decrease in activity, spontaneous activity increases in the central auditory system. This increased activity is believed to result from both reductions in the activity of neurotransmitters exerting an inhibitory effect, such as GABA, and rises in the activity of neurotransmitters exerting an excitatory effect, such as glutamate (Kaltenbach, 2011).

At a clinical level, non-auditory symptoms are also evident, with individuals experiencing a wide range of symptoms including emotional components such as sleep disturbance, anxiety, depression, irritation, and difficulties with concentration (Langguth, 2011). It is unclear whether all of these components are a consequence of living with the hearing problems of tinnitus or a distinct factor in the condition. However, recent research has suggested that depression in tinnitus may result from the overlap in pathology between tinnitus and depression rather than purely as a reaction to the tinnitus (Langguth, 2011).

6.6.2 Treatment

Treatment for tinnitus is varied. Drug therapy has not been effective, although antidepressant medication can help to alleviate the depression associated with tinnitus. Surgery is not usually recommended, although some conditions that may require this approach (such as vestibular schwannoma and Menière's disease) include tinnitus in their symptom profiles.

A number of psychological treatments exist, and rely on counselling and relaxation therapies to reduce agitation and emotional responses to tinnitus. The effectiveness of such treatments is not always easy to evaluate because there may be considerable variation in how the treatments are used. However, Hesser et al. (2010) conducted a meta-analysis into the effectiveness of cognitive-behavioural therapy (CBT) for tinnitus. Such approaches may include a number of elements, for example relaxation, restructuring of negative beliefs about tinnitus, attention exercises and positive imagery. Hesser and colleagues (2010) found that CBT did offer an effective treatment, reducing the tinnitus symptoms and associated anxiety and depression.

Finally, treatment may take the form of auditory training. This process commonly involves frequency discrimination tasks but it can also include activities relating to loudness and localisation. One specific strategy, named 'tinnitus retraining therapy', is based on the model put forward by Jastreboff (1990) and shown in Figure 6.7. It approaches the treatment of tinnitus from several different angles: the condition is thoroughly explained; the patient is counselled; relaxation techniques may be taught; and sound therapy is used in some cases. However, as yet there is a lack of high-quality studies evaluating training interventions, making it impossible to judge their efficacy (Hoare et al., 2010; Phillips and McFerran, 2010).

There may be some controversy over the methods of tinnitus therapy, but there is a consensus about the objective: that patients should habituate to the signal within their auditory system; that is, they should learn to ignore it. A person is unlikely to do so if they are anxious or upset by tinnitus or concerned about the potential seriousness of the sound, and so careful, authoritative reassurance might well be helpful, and indeed has long been practised by health care professionals working in this field.

6.7 Concluding remarks on hearing

Chapters 2–6 examined in some detail the sense of hearing, looking at the physical characteristics of pure sound waves and how these relate to the perception of specific features such as pitch. We also explained how complex sounds, including those comprising speech and music, differ from simple waves and how the auditory system can transduce these signals to provide an informative and reliable neural representation of sound. We described the pathway such information takes to the brain and the different processing that occurs.

We also discussed how the perception of these complex sounds occurs, specifically focusing on different theories of speech perception and you should now recognise that, despite significant advances, there is no clear consensus on how this perception occurs. Moreover, speech perception is also influenced by visual information (e.g. the McGurk effect; see Chapter 5), therefore examining the auditory system in isolation may not reveal the full extent of processing for such stimuli.

Finally, you saw how auditory impairments can impact on individuals and what treatment options are currently available for those with hearing loss. As you worked through Chapter 6, you should have become aware that impairment of the auditory system also affects functions such as balance, which is why we chose to consider the vestibular system in the final chapter in this block on hearing and balance.

6.8 Chapter 6 summary and questions

- Hearing loss can be categorised according to where the impairment originates.
- Conductive hearing loss is the result of impairment of transmission of the sound signal to the cochlea. This type of impairment can often be treated effectively by removing any blockages or amplifying the signal.
- Cochlear hearing loss results from damage to the cochlea itself. There are a number of causes of this, ranging from congenital conditions and excessive noise exposure to age-related hearing loss. Treatment may be preventive or involve amplification. Where there is severe to profound bilateral hearing loss, cochlear implants may be considered. The outcome of implantation ranges widely and may be affected by many factors.
- Retrocochlear hearing loss results from damage beyond the cochlea itself and is commonly a result of vestibular schwannomas (tumours). The exact treatment applied varies with cause, but it may involve the use of implants.
- 'Central auditory processing disorders' (CAPD) is an umbrella term for a number of hearing problems originating from within the central auditory system. Treatments focus on improving signal quality and perceptual skills.
- Tinnitus is a complex disorder for which treatments are limited, although some benefit may be gained from psychological interventions.

Self-assessment questions

Question 6.1

Which part of the auditory system is associated with otosclerosis, and how can this condition be treated?

Question 6.2

Referring to Figure 6.7, suggest why might antidepressants be effective in treating tinnitus.

Balance: the vestibular system

7

Although a primary function of the inner ear is to perceive sound, it also houses the vestibular system. Recall from Block 1 that the information from the vestibular system is proprioceptive in character. Thus, it deals with events within the body rather than exteroceptive events outside the body (as in the case of the response of the cochlea to sound). However, the system is concerned only with the head and therefore is generally considered separately from the concepts you learned about in Block 3.

During movement, signals from the vestibular system about the position and motion of the head are combined with visual and proprioceptive input from elsewhere in the body. This amalgamation of information provides the basis for postural control, motion perception and stabilising reflexes by reducing movement of the head and ensuring images remain stable on the retina. As with other proprioceptive information, such as that received by joint receptors and Golgi tendon organs, the importance of a functional vestibular system is considerable in everyday life and yet we are often only actively conscious of the vestibular system when it is damaged through illness. Such illnesses can be extremely debilitating, producing effects like vertigo (dizziness and loss of balance), which can considerably reduce the person's quality of life.

As with hearing and the other sensory systems explored in this module, the focus of this chapter progresses from the initial signal to the perception of vestibular information, before considering the impact of the different types of vestibular disorders that can affect people. However, because the signal results from within the body, we begin by describing the apparatus that results in the signal, followed by how it is detected. You should note that there are a number of similarities between hearing and vestibular apparatus and functioning, so you will need to draw on your knowledge of hearing to answer some of the questions in this chapter.

7.1 Structure of the vestibular apparatus

As you know from your understanding of hearing, the inner ear consists of a system of tunnels: the bony labyrinth in the hardest part of the temporal bone (Figure 7.1). The two structures of the vestibular system – the **vestibule** and the **semicircular canals** – are found within this labyrinth. The vestibule houses two membranous sacs – the **utricle** and the **saccule** – which are known as **otolithic organs**. Likewise, there are three semicircular canals, each oriented at right angles to one another, and these are termed the superior, posterior and lateral canals. At one end of each canal there is a swelling of the tube called an **ampulla**. Both ends of each canal open into the utricle.

To give some impression of their size, the vestibule in humans is about 3–5 mm across, while the semicircular canals range from 12 mm up to 22 mm in length. The bony labyrinth is lined by an outer membrane sheath that encloses an inner membranous labyrinth. This arrangement means that the system contains two almost concentric compartments both filled with fluid.

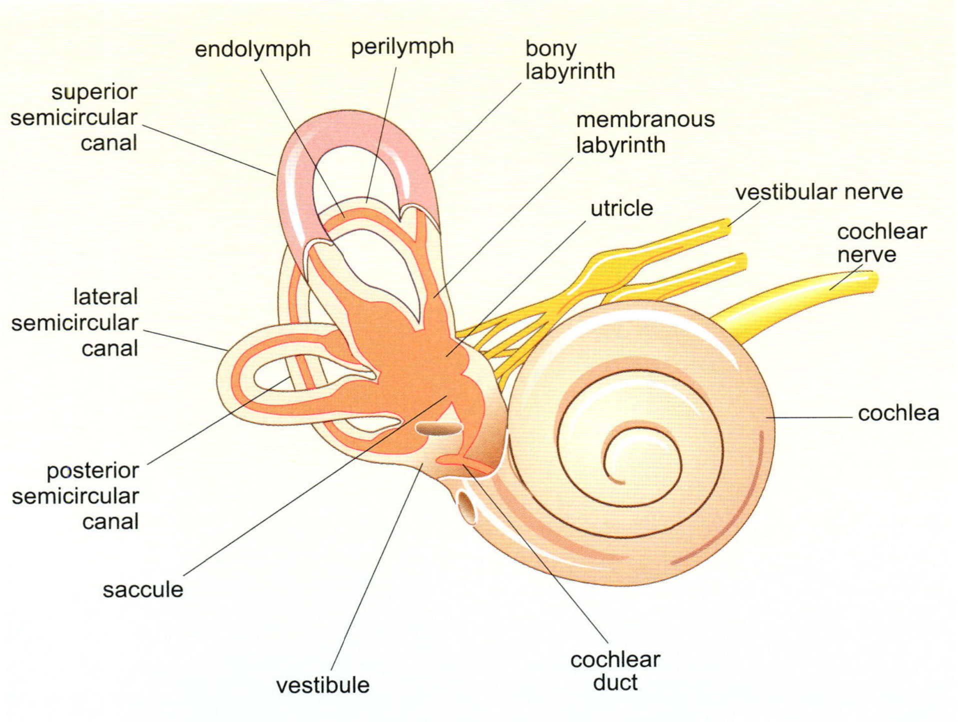

Figure 7.1 Structure of the vestibular system.

The outer compartment contains perilymph and the inner compartment contains endolymph.

- Which ions are present in the highest concentration in the perilymph and endolymph fluids?

- Perilymph is similar in composition to extracellular fluid and rich in sodium ions, while endolymph is rich in potassium ions, similar to intracellular fluid.

As with the cochlea, the otolithic organs and the semicircular canals contain hair cells. These cells are positioned within an epithelium that also contains the nerve processes connecting to the hair cells, and supporting cells. In the saccule and utricle, the sensory epithelium is a flat plaque called a **macula** (Figure 7.2a), while in the ampullae of the semicircular canals there is a ridge called a **crista** (Figure 7.2b). The hair bundles of both structures project into specific overlying structures. For the otolithic organs, this is the **otolithic membrane**, the surface of which is covered by a blanket of calcium carbonate crystals called **otoliths**. For the semicircular canals, the hair cells project into a gelatinous mass called the **cupula**.

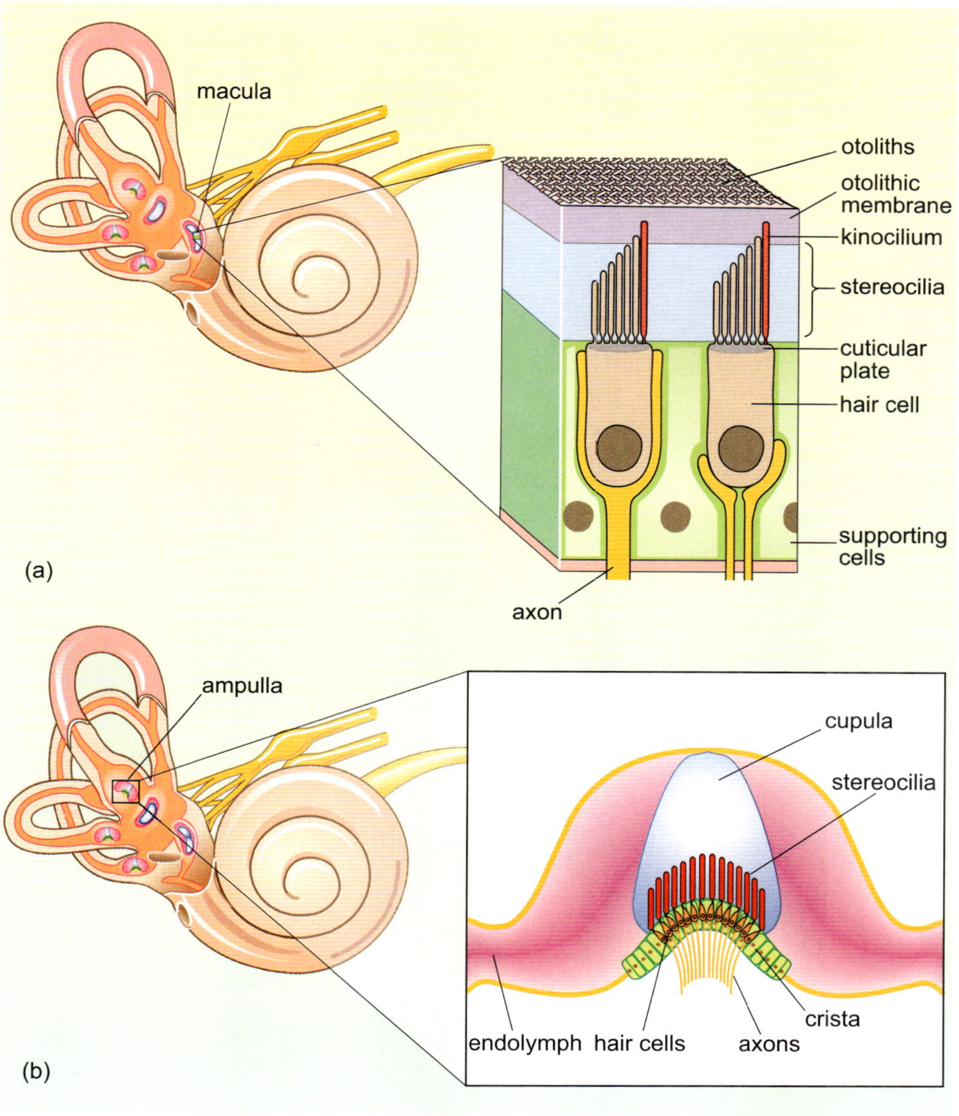

Figure 7.2 Structure of the macula and the ampulla. (a) Hair cells in the otolithic organs project upwards into the otolithic membrane which is coated with calcium carbonate crystals. (b) Cross-section through the ampulla of a semicircular canal, showing the crista. The stereocilia of the hair cells penetrate into the gelatinous cupula. The cupula is bathed in endolymph, which fills the canals.

There are two types of hair cell, as highlighted in the cross-section of the utricular macula shown in Figure 7.3. Type I hair cells are flask-shaped and are innervated by an afferent neuron that forms a cup, or calyx, around the cell body. The calyx is sometimes shared with other hair cells. In contrast, Type II hair cells are more cylindrical and have small round afferent endings onto the cell body. Efferent nerves for Type II hair cells end directly on the cell bodies, rather than the calyx.

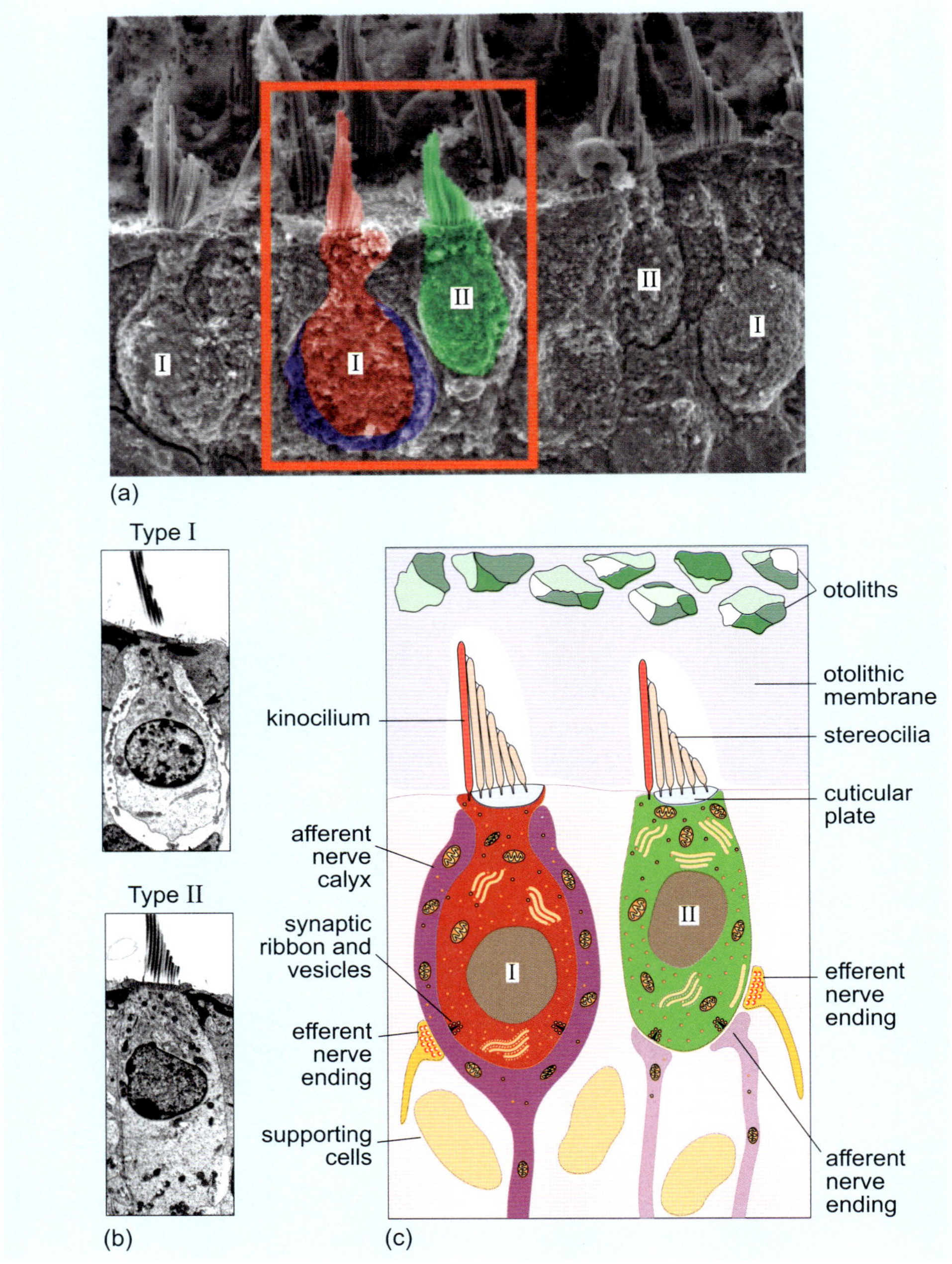

Figure 7.3 The structure of vestibular sensory epithelia: (a) scanning electron micrograph with Type I and Type II hair cells highlighted; (b) transmission electron micrographs of the two types of hair cell; (c) schematic representation.

7.2 Vestibular mechanoelectrical transduction

The mechanism of transduction in the vestibular system is very similar to that found in the cochlea. Moreover, the same process is employed in both the vestibule and the semicircular canals. This section therefore provides a general overview of the mechanism, using the cochlea as a point of reference, before considering in more detail how the two parts of the vestibular system are able to detect different types of movement of the head.

7.2.1 General mechanisms of transduction

As with the cochlea, the hair bundles of the vestibular system consist of a single kinocilium and multiple stereocilia contacting the cuticular plate (see Figure 7.2a). The stereocilia and cuticular plate contain complex cytoskeletal networks of actin-associated proteins such as myosin that influence how the hair bundle moves.

■ What is the function of myosin in hair cells?

□ Myosin controls the tension in the tip links, and therefore the force applied to the mechanically-gated ion channel.

The stereocilia form rows increasing in height across the bundle, forming a 'staircase' (Figure 7.4) that may vary in size from as little as 0.5 μm to over 9 μm high. Bundle shapes vary quite considerably compared with the hair bundles of cochlear hair cells, but the functional orientation of the hair cell is always determined by the direction of the staircase.

As with cochlear hair cells, the stereocilia in the vestibular system are interconnected by tip links, attaching each stereocilium to the one immediately adjacent (Figure 7.4c). The kinocilium occurs on the side of the hair bundle immediately adjacent to the tallest row. Its position is shown in Figure 7.4d, which represents a view looking down onto a hair bundle.

■ What causes the hair cell bundle to move in the cochlea?

□ As the basilar membrane vibrates with the incoming sound stimuli, the hair cell bundles shear against the overlying tectorial membrane or are deflected by fluid forces.

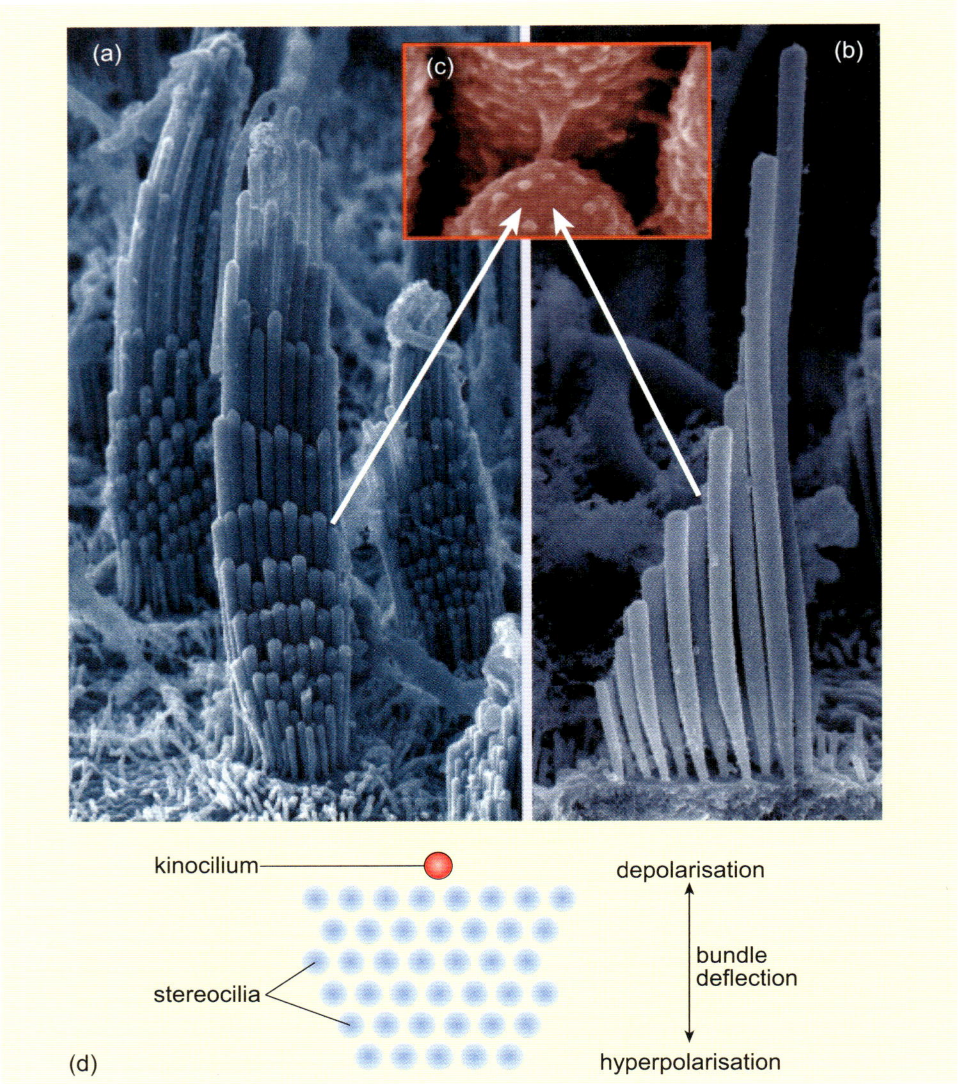

Figure 7.4 Scanning electron micrographs of (a) a front view and (b) a side view of vestibular hair bundles. (c) The tip link between adjacent stereocilia. (d) Schematic representation of how bundle orientation and deflection produce changes in membrane polarisation.

In the vestibular system there is no external signal such as a sound wave causing deflection. Rather, the hair cell bundles are deflected because when the head moves, the otoliths in the utricle and saccule (Figure 7.5a) lag behind due to inertia, and this effect is mirrored in the endolymph in the semicircular canals when the head rotates (Figure 7.5b). This lag is communicated to the otolithic membrane and cupula respectively, causing deflection of the hair cell bundles.

Deflection of the hair bundle towards the kinocilium is excitatory and results in depolarisation of the hair cell and an increase from spontaneous firing in the afferent neuron; deflections in the opposite direction cause the cell to hyperpolarise, which results in a decrease in spontaneous firing.

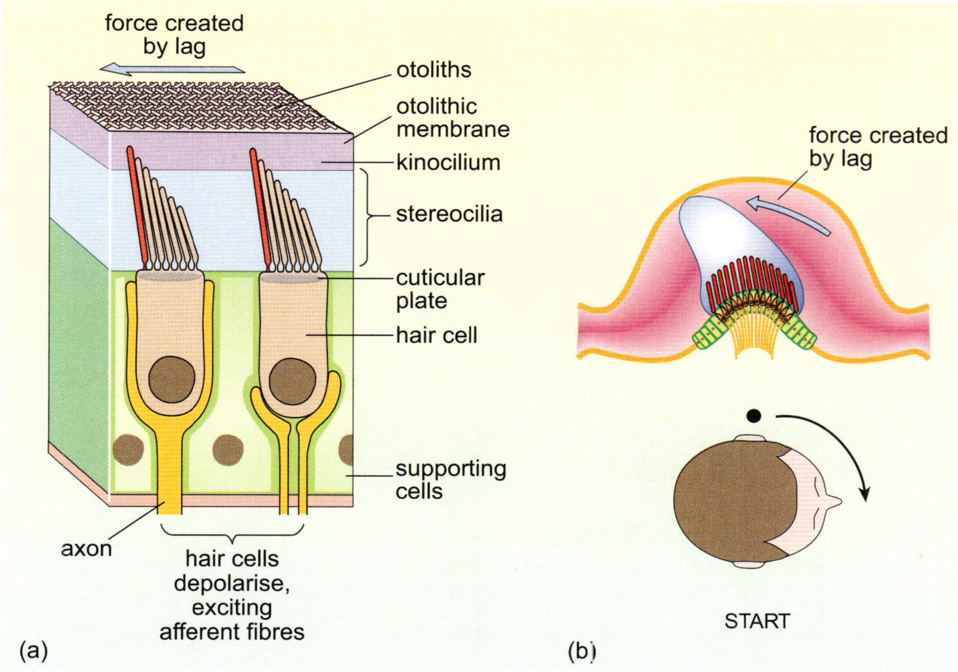

Figure 7.5 Movement of the head causes (a) lag of the otoliths, which is transmitted through the otolithic membrane to cause deflection of the hair cells. Similarly, lag of the endolymph (b) is transmitted through the cupula to the hair cells, resulting in deflection.

- ■ What causes spontaneous firing in the afferent neuron? (*Hint*: this is the same as for the cochlea.)
- □ At rest, in the absence of deflection of the hair cell bundle, a small number of ion channels are open and this allows an influx of potassium ions.

At rest, around 10% of ion channels are open in the vestibular hair cells bundles, resulting in the release of what is thought to be the same neurotransmitter as is found in cochlear hair cells.

- ■ Which neurotransmitter is this, and what effect does it have on the postsynaptic neuron?
- □ The neurotransmitter is glutamate, which tends to have an excitatory effect.

At these afferent synaptic contacts, the hair cells contain synaptic ribbons with neurotransmitter vesicles around them.

- ■ Thinking back to the information on hearing, what is the main advantage of synaptic ribbons?
- □ They allow a larger pool of readily releasable neurotransmitter to be available.

The supporting cells may also be directly involved in the transmission process. They contain glutamate transporter molecules that rapidly take up extracellular neurotransmitter. These proteins help to terminate glutamate action at the synapses, making them ready for further activation. They also provide a vital protective function because glutamate is excitotoxic, so causes cell damage if allowed to remain around the neuron.

Finally, as with the hair cells in the cochlea, those in the vestibular apparatus can show adaptation through calcium-dependent mechanisms that effectively reset the hair cells so that they can continue to detect further movements.

7.2.2 Transduction in the otolithic organs

The otolithic organs are able to respond to changes in the position of the head with respect to gravity. Such movement is referred to as linear acceleration (see Box 7.1), which can be in any direction. For example, if you imagine the experience of sitting on a train pulling out of the station then that is acceleration in a horizontal plane; or if you jump or a rollercoaster lifts you upwards, that is in a vertical plane (Figure 7.6). The semicircular canals are able to detect another form of acceleration, which is explained in the next section.

Figure 7.6 Examples of linear acceleration in (a) horizontal and (b) vertical planes which can be detected by the utricle and the saccule, respectively.

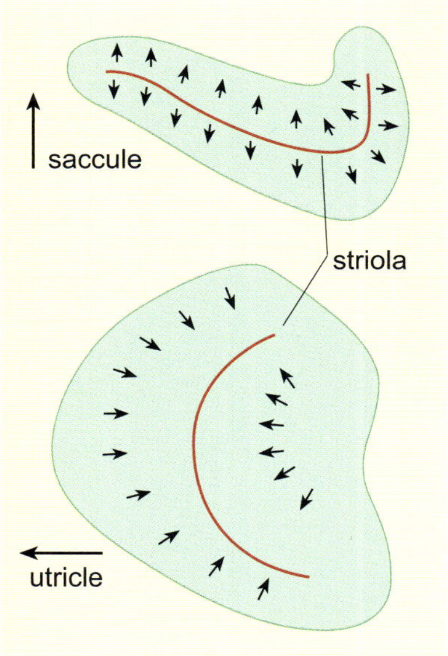

Figure 7.7 Shape and orientation (large arrows) of the maculae of the saccule and utricle. The orientation of the hair bundles is indicated by the small arrows showing the excitatory direction, with opposing directions on each side of the striola.

It is possible for us to detect these two different planes because the maculae in the utricle and saccule differ in orientation. In the utricle, the macula projects from the anterior wall and lies primarily in the horizontal plane (Figure 7.7a), therefore detecting acceleration in a horizontal plane. In the saccule, the macula is in a vertical plane and has an elongated shape resembling the shape of the letter 'j'. It detects movement in the sagittal plane (up and down, forward and back; see Figure 7.7b).

In both otolithic organs, the macula is divided by the striola, a zone that separates two populations of hair cells with opposite orientations. This means that when the head moves and deflection of the hair bundles occurs, some hair cells are excited and some are inhibited. In the utricle, the orientation of the hair bundles reverses along the striola so that the excitatory direction always points towards this zone. A similar distribution of hair bundle orientations occurs in the saccular macula, but here the excitatory directions in the two populations of cells point away from the striola. In both cases, the orientation of each bundle changes gradually with the curvature of the striola. This results in the central nervous system (CNS) receiving a unique pattern of signals for any linear acceleration of a given magnitude and orientation.

Box 7.1 Principles of linear acceleration

A body (i.e. an object) that is travelling in a straight line at constant speed is said to be moving at constant velocity. Velocity is a vector quantity – that is, it has both magnitude (a speed, in SI units of m s^{-1}, for example) and direction.

Isaac Newton's first law of motion states that a body that is not subjected to the action of a force will continue to move at constant velocity. If a force is applied to the body then there is a change in the speed or the direction, or both, and the object then has an acceleration (strictly speaking, a linear acceleration). The acceleration is the rate of change of the velocity and the SI unit of this quality is m s^{-2}.

Newton's second law of motion states that the linear acceleration experienced by the body is proportional to, and in the same direction as, the applied force. Note that although we normally think of acceleration as being an increase in speed, such as when we accelerate while driving, it can actually be either an increase in velocity or a decrease in velocity (often referred to as deceleration), depending on the direction in which the force is acting.

If you have ever experienced travelling at constant velocity without being able to see the exterior (for example, in an aeroplane or a train) you will know that it is hard to tell in which direction you are travelling. In fact, it was Galileo Galilei who first pointed this out in 1632, using the example of someone in the lower decks of a ship on a calm sea, and the concept is known as the Galilean principle of relativity (named long before Einstein's one!). So, neither the ears nor any other physical instrument can detect motion at constant velocity. However, once there is acceleration, whether it is due to a change in speed or a change in direction, it is possible for us to detect this variation and this is facilitated by the otolithic organs, as described in the text.

7.2.3 Transduction in the semicircular canals

The semicircular canals detect a different kind of movement to the otolithic organs: the acceleration that occurs whenever an object alters its rate of rotation about an axis. This is called angular acceleration (see Box 7.2). Our head undergoes angular acceleration when it turns or tilts on the shoulders, during rotatory body movements, and in turning movements during passive or active locomotion. The three semicircular canals in each ear detect these angular accelerations and report their magnitude and orientation to the brain.

Box 7.2 Principles of angular acceleration

When a solid body rotates about an axis, different parts of it are going in different directions at different times, so the concept of velocity as used for describing linear motion is not helpful. Instead, we can define an angular velocity – usually given the symbol ω (omega), which, like linear velocity, is a vector quantity. The magnitude of the velocity is simply the rotational speed measured in radians s^{-1}, because that has the same value over the entire body. The direction is defined as being along the axis of rotation.

If the angular velocity changes, again in either direction or magnitude, then there is said to be an angular acceleration, defined as the rate of change of the angular velocity and the units are usually radians s^{-2}.

You may be aware that rotational motion at constant speed always requires acceleration towards the centre of rotation, as exemplified in the motion of the Moon around the Earth. In this case, the acceleration towards the Earth is provided by a gravitational force between the two bodies. If there was no force, the Moon would fly off into space! So, unlike the case of uniform linear motion, in uniform rotational motion there is always acceleration involved because the direction of the velocity is constantly changing. However, at constant angular velocity, that acceleration is towards the centre of the circle and it is *not* an angular acceleration as defined above. It is the angular acceleration defined above that is detected by the semicircular canals, as explained in the text.

This kind of acceleration can be a little more confusing than linear acceleration, so we briefly return to the process of how the hair cells are deflected. When the head starts turning, the endolymph fluid in the semicircular canals lags behind the movement of the rest of the structure and bends the cupula, and therefore the hair bundles of the crista, in the direction opposite to the head movement (Figure 7.8a). Bending of the stereocilia stimulates the associated hair cells and may produce an action potential in the afferent nerve.

As the movement of the head continues, typically after 15–20 seconds of continuous uniform rotation, the endolymph and the cupula move at the same rate as the rotatory movement of the head and the stereocilia become erect. As long as the head is moving in a constant direction at a constant speed, or is rotating with a constant angular speed, the cupula and stereocilia remain erect, as is the case if there is no head rotation at all (Figure 7.8b).

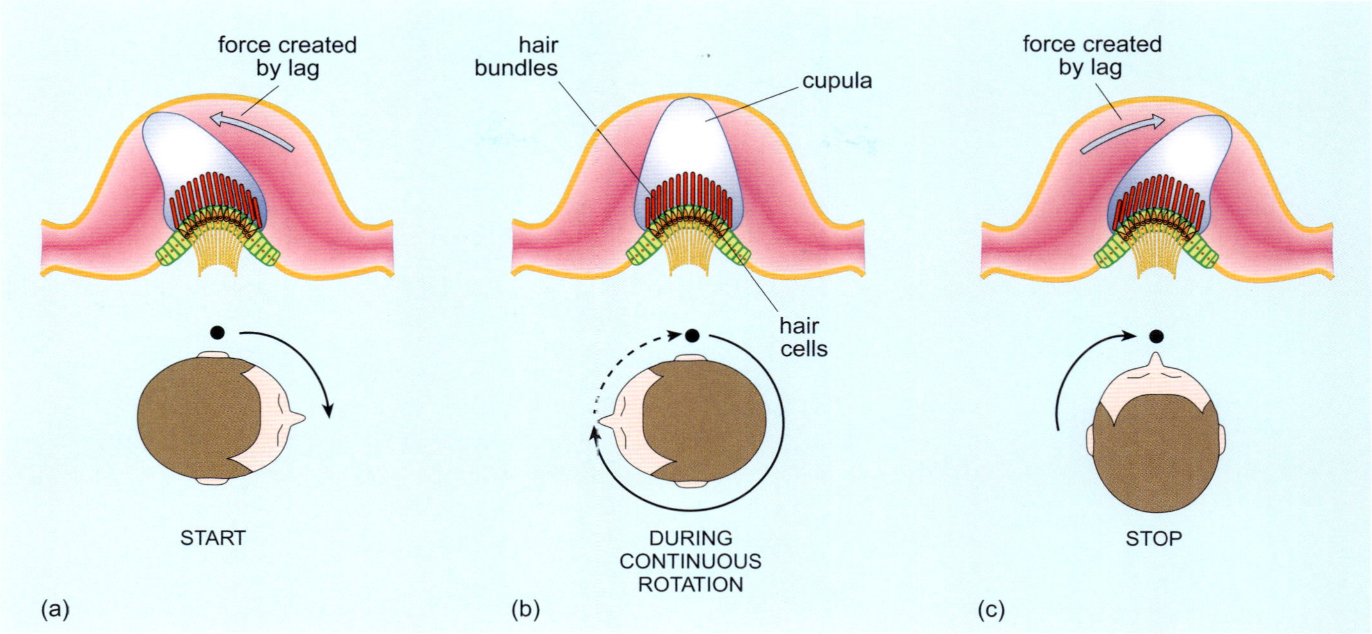

Figure 7.8 Schematic diagram of the movement of the cupula in response to rotatory movement of the head.

When head movement stops, the inertial force of the endolymph carries the cupula forward in the direction that the head had been rotating in, and the stereocilia are bent in that direction (Figure 7.8c). Therefore, starts and stops in rotation bend the stereocilia in the semicircular canals, whereas constant motion produces no deflection. As all the hair bundles in the canals share a common orientation, acceleration in one direction depolarises the hair cells and excites afferent neurons, while acceleration in the opposite direction hyperpolarises the hair cells and diminishes spontaneous neural activity.

Naturally, the arrangement of semicircular canals is mirrored on both sides of the head. This means that generally, when the cells on one side of the head are excited, the cells on the other side of the head will be inhibited. This idea is illustrated in Figure 7.9, which depicts a bird's-eye view of the lateral semicircular canals. When the head rotates anticlockwise, the endolymph moves in a clockwise direction with respect to the canals. This causes the stereocilia in the left canal to be excited, while those in the right canal are inhibited. The reverse is true when the head rotates in a clockwise direction. The balance of excitation and inhibition of all three pairs of canals can thus represent the direction and speed of any angular rotation of the head.

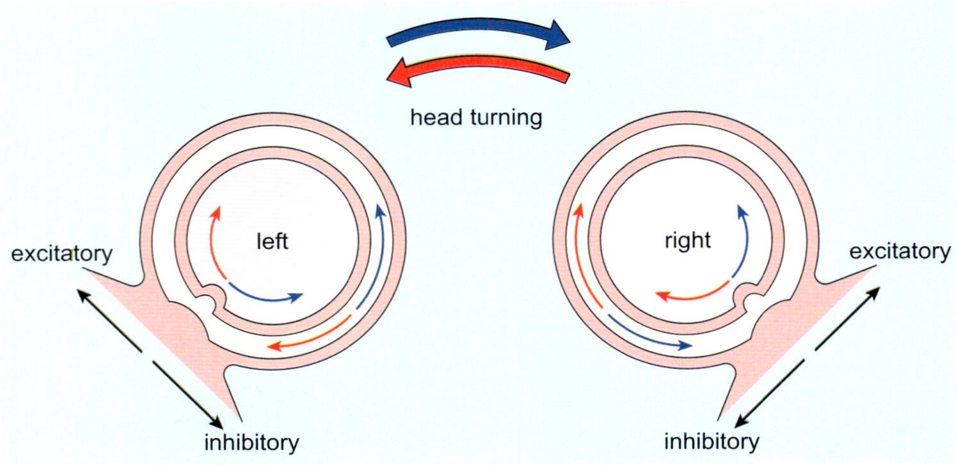

Figure 7.9 Rotation of the head causes a balance of excitation and inhibition of the supercilia in the ears' semicircular canals.

7.3 Central processing of vestibular information

You have now read about how linear and angular acceleration are detected in the inner ear and that this information can be combined to give a unique signal detailing the orientation and speed of the movement of the head or body. In this section, we describe where this information travels to in the CNS and the functional significance of the different brain regions involved. However, unlike the auditory pathway you examined in Chapter 4, once vestibular information reaches the brainstem, it both ascends through the brain and descends down the spinal cord. Therefore, this section is structured slightly differently from our coverage of auditory pathways and begins with a description of the vestibular nuclear complex in the brainstem, from which both ascending and descending pathways originate.

7.3.1 Vestibular nuclei complex

The hair cells of the vestibular apparatus send information to the brain via the vestibular nerve, which is the vestibular component of the vestibulocochlear, or VIIIth (eighth), cranial nerve. These afferent fibres are peripheral processes arising from bipolar neurons: that is, neurons with two processes, one entering each side of the cell body.

The cell bodies are located in two subdivisions of Scarpa's ganglion (the superior and inferior; Figure 7.10). The peripheral process is like a dendrite, in that it carries signals to the cell body of the neuron rather than away from it, but is also like an axon because, except where it enters the epithelium, it is myelinated and carries action potentials. The process leaving the opposite pole of the cell body is the true axon of the neuron, and this enters the brainstem at the junction of the medulla and pons. Although some axons enter the cerebellum via the inferior cerebellar peduncle, the majority fork into two and branch further to form excitatory connections in the different parts of the **vestibular nuclear complex**.

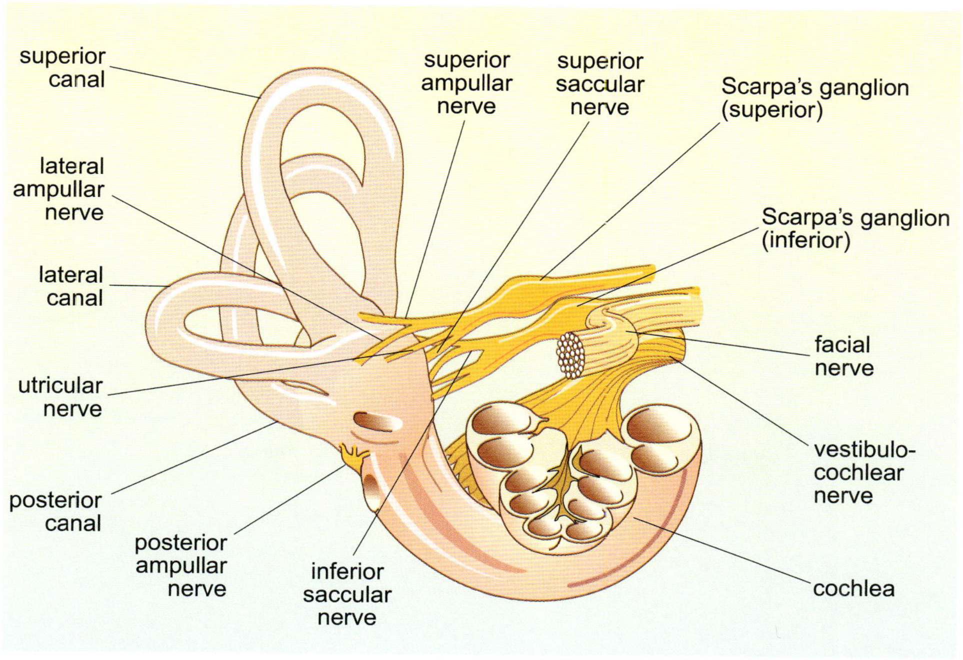

Figure 7.10 Innervation of the vestibular system. Afferent neurons leave each of the sensory epithelia via distinct nerves and enter the two subdivisions of Scarpa's ganglion before joining the vestibulocochlear nerve.

The complex contains four vestibular nuclei (inset in Figure 7.11) which differ in the pattern of their afferent and efferent connections and in the different populations of neurons they possess. The superior nucleus, in the caudal pons, and the medial and inferior nuclei, in the rostral medulla, contain small to medium-sized neurons. The lateral nucleus (also known as Deiters' nucleus) is in the medulla and contains mainly large multipolar neurons.

Studies of the physiology of neurons in these nuclei show that some receive inputs from both the utricle and the saccule and others from both canals and otolithic organs. Also, many neurons receive inputs from the vestibular system on both sides of the head, as indicated by pathways crossing the midline in Figure 7.11. These convergent inputs of various kinds mean that information from the different vestibular sensory organs and from both sides of the head is rapidly integrated, increasing the accuracy of the directional information obtained, for example, by reducing the possibility of error from spontaneous or random activity in one organ.

As with the cochlea, there is a pathway extending from the brainstem to the hair cells of the vestibular system. Efferent stimulation has varied effects on hair cells and, at present, the role of this efferent pathway is not properly understood.

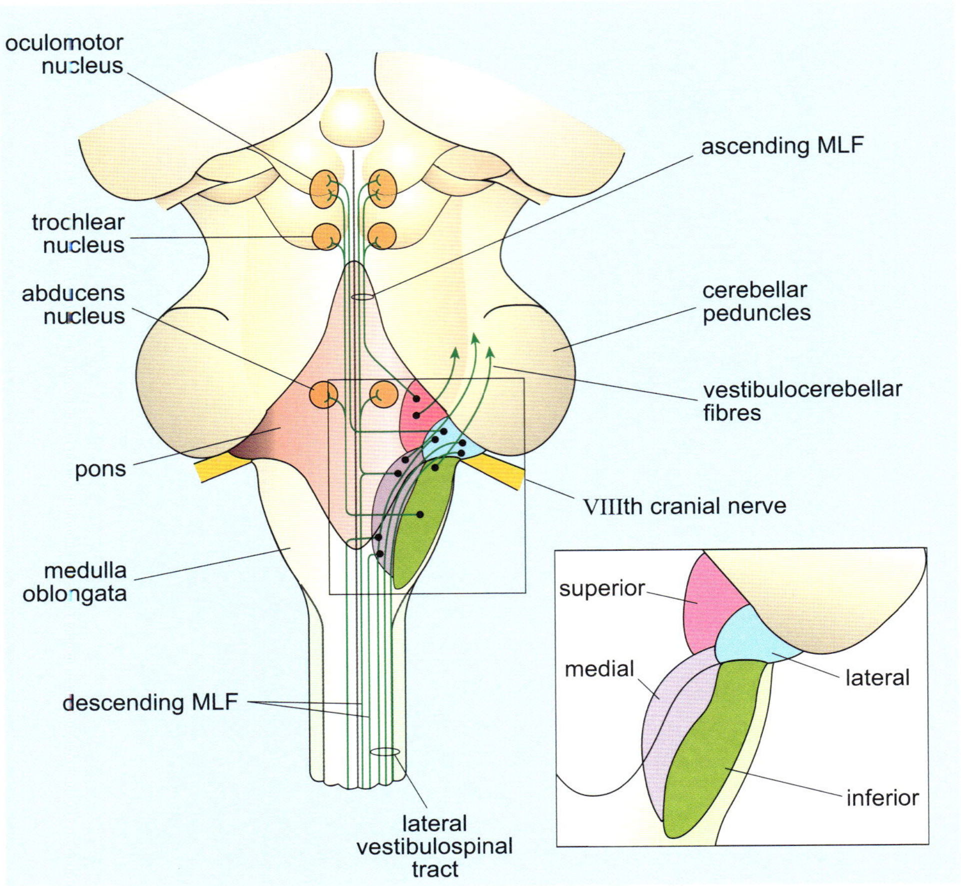

Figure 7.11 Vestibular brainstem nuclei and their connections to other nuclei. The vestibular nuclear complex is shown in the inset.

7.3.2 Ascending pathways

Oculomotor system

There are ascending tracts arising from the superior and medial nuclei in the vestibular nuclear complex, which travel in the ascending branch of the medial longitudinal fasciculus (MLF) to three **oculomotor nuclei**: the oculomotor nucleus, trochlear nucleus and abducens nucleus (Figure 7.11). These tracts are critical for coordinating eye movements in response to head movements in order to maintain a stable image on the retina.

This result is achieved by the **vestibulo-ocular reflex (VOR)**. The effectiveness of the VOR can be demonstrated by shaking your head while reading this paragraph. You will find that you have no trouble staying focused on it. This is because when you move your head while keeping the text still, the vestibular system signals to the brain how fast the head is moving and the oculomotor system then uses this information to stabilise the eyes in order to keep the visual image motionless on the retina.

The VOR can be divided into the static VOR, which is dependent on information from the otolithic organs, and the dynamic or rotational VOR, based on semicircular canal activation. The static VOR can be further subdivided into the translational VOR, which compensates for linear head movements, and the ocular counter-rolling response, which counteracts head tilt in the vertical plane. However, in all cases the nerve pathways lead to and directly control contraction in the eye muscles. This involves two routes, one staying on the same side of the brainstem and one crossing over the midline, both to the abducens and oculomotor nuclei. The crossing over is necessary to enable both eyes to receive appropriate signals from both inner ears. These pathways work together to provide signals directly from the vestibular system to the eye muscles.

Each eye has three pairs of **extraocular muscles** that pull on the eye to rotate it in three orthogonal planes that match, approximately, the three planes of the semicircular canals. Stimulation signalling, for example a leftward head movement, causes excitation in the left lateral canal and inhibition in the right. These signals go via the vestibular nuclei into the two routes to produce complementary contraction and relaxation of the appropriate muscle pairs on both sides. This produces movement of both eyeballs in synchrony (termed conjugate eye movements) which compensates for the rotation of the head and keeps the centre of gaze fixed on the object of interest.

As well as vestibular input, the VOR is strongly influenced by the visual system, especially information regarding the distance to an object. This is not surprising because an object that is closer would appear to move more than an object that is further away for the same amount of head rotation, which would affect the amount of compensatory movement required to keep the gaze fixed on it.

The VOR is not the only reflex that operates to ensure the stability of the image on the retina during head movement. You are probably not surprised to learn that the other main reflex, termed the **visual pursuit reflex**, is controlled by the visual system. This reflex generates an eye movement to match the speed at which an image is moving across the retina. However, it involves relatively slow cortical processing and in consequence fails to operate effectively at the higher frequencies of target movement. At these higher frequencies, head movement to follow the stimulus can maintain a stable retinal image using the VOR.

Information from the vestibular system can also be used to determine whether perceived motion is due to self-motion. Where visual image movement is of the whole visual scene rather than of objects within it, the resulting perception is of self-motion with respect to a stable outside world. Whether the motion is self-motion may also determine the emotional and cognitive response to the situation.

The brain possesses mechanisms for detecting differences between perceived motion from the visual and vestibular systems. Furthermore, the detection of persistent inconsistencies provokes a pattern of symptoms which include lethargy, light-headedness, sweating, nausea and ultimately vomiting: a phenomenon we know as motion sickness (see Box 7.3).

Box 7.3 Motion sickness

What is the nature of the stimulus that provokes the unpleasant sensation of motion sickness, and what is the condition's purpose? The theory that best explains motion sickness is that it is caused by sensory conflict, either within the vestibular system itself or between visual and vestibular evidence of motion. All pedestrian motion takes place against a background of a fixed visual environment and a gravitational force that is constant in direction and magnitude. From this scenario it is possible to formulate three rules that determine the interaction between visual and vestibular motion sensors:

- When rotational motion is sensed by the semicircular canals, there should be an equivalent rotation of the visual scene in the opposite direction.
- If the head is rotated either forwards or backwards, or to the left or right, there is an expectation that the degree of rotation sensed by the semicircular canals is matched by an equivalent change in the direction of gravity as sensed by the otolithic organs.
- Normal locomotor activities such as walking or running generate alternating vertical forces corresponding to the up-and-down movement involved. These forces are sensed by the otolithic receptors as transient oscillations in the intensity of gravity.

The brain seems to recognise frequencies of oscillation that are significantly below those found in everyday activities, and exposure to vertical oscillation at frequencies below 0.5 Hz gives rise to nausea and vomiting. This type of motion stimulus predominates in rough conditions at sea and its measured intensity aboard ships correlates well with the incidence of seasickness.

While the notion of sensory conflict offers an explanation of the characteristics of motion that result in sickness, this does not explain why such stimuli would evoke the symptoms of nausea and vomiting. It is perhaps even more puzzling to find that many animals exposed to similar types of motion also vomit. Neither these creatures, nor indeed humans, can have evolved this emetic mechanism as a purposeful response to types of motion that they could never have encountered in their past. On the other hand, vomiting has a more obvious evolutionary benefit if it results in the removal of potentially toxic substances.

The most convincing explanation for the symptoms of motion sickness is that the brain uses the constancy of the gravitational and visual environment as a form of self-calibration. If the expected integration between vestibular and visual sensory information is not found, this is interpreted as a malfunction of the brain itself. If such a malfunction were the result of some ingested neurotoxin then vomiting might be an appropriate response to eliminate any that still remained in the gut.

Cerebellum

While some vestibular afferents travel directly to the cerebellum, the majority do so via the medial and inferior vestibular nuclei, travelling from these nuclei to the cerebellum in the inferior cerebellar peduncle (a stalk-like bundle of nerve fibres). Most of the vestibular information enters the flocculonodular lobe of the cerebellum (Figure 7.12). These connections are critical for postural adjustments.

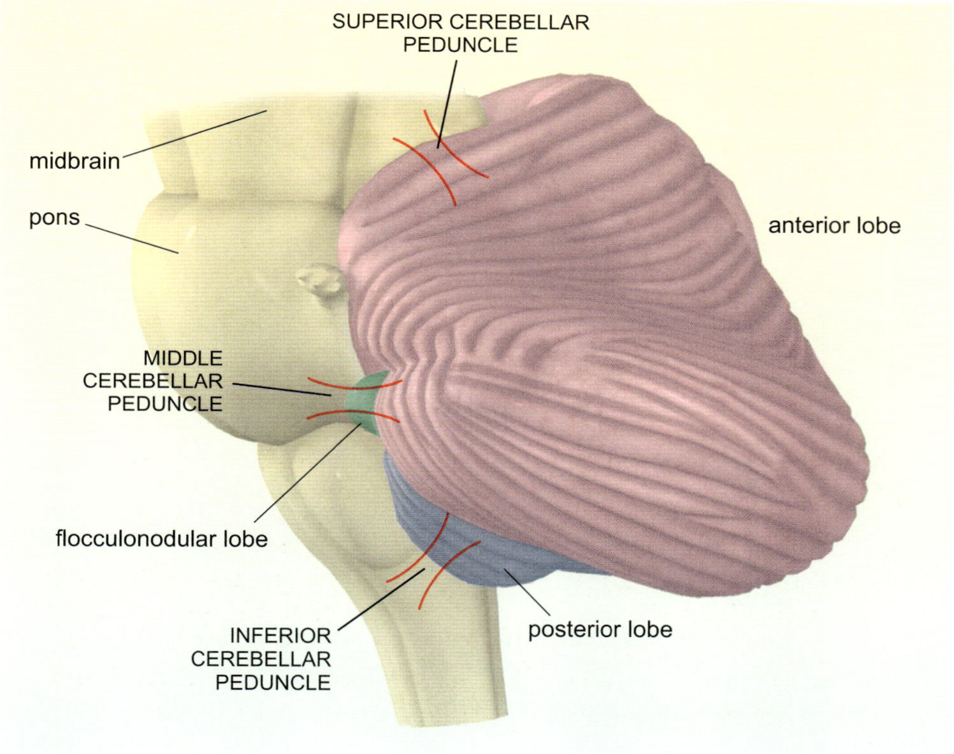

Figure 7.12 The majority of vestibular information travelling from the vestibular nuclear complex innervates the flocculonodular lobe of the cerebellum.

Vestibular cortex

It has also been suggested that there is an ascending pathway that gives rise to conscious perception of vestibular information. This pathway is thought to originate in the superior vestibular nucleus and travels within either the lateral lemniscus or the reticular formation to the ventral posterior intermediate nucleus of the thalamus. From here, it is thought to enter the vestibular cortex.

There is still some debate over where the vestibular cortex is located with some believing it is positioned just behind the area of the somatosensory cortex relating to the head and others believing that it is closer to the primary auditory cortex. This pathway is bilateral.

Other areas

The vestibular nuclei also send projections to respiratory centres, which alter breathing rate in relation to position. A connection to the visceral centres that influences the digestive system may be the origin of nausea and vomiting in motion sickness (see Box 7.3), caused by conflicting visual and vestibular signals.

7.3.3 Descending pathways

The **lateral vestibulospinal tract** arises from the lateral nuclei and descends ipsilaterally to the sacral regions of the spinal cord (see Figure 7.11). Signals from the lateral vestibular nucleus derived originally from the vestibular organs affect the tone of the body's muscles. This is illustrated by the fact that stimulation of this nucleus results in excitation of extensor muscles and inhibition of flexor muscles in the lower limb, causing the foot to be pressed firmly down to maintain balance. Around 40% of body musculature is involved in maintaining posture and balance against gravity, so signals from the otolithic organs are particularly important.

The **medial vestibulospinal tract** arises from the medial nucleus and travels bilaterally within the descending part of the MLF. However, it only extends as far as the mid-thoracic region of the spinal cord, and functions to control muscles in the neck and shoulder. This descending pathway underlies the **vestibulocollic reflex (VCR)**, which maintains the correct positioning of the head. The VCR, in conjunction with the VOR, acts to stabilise the gaze.

7.4 Integration with vision and proprioception

We have previously described the information collected by the vestibular system as proprioceptive in nature, and said that these inputs are combined with those collected by proprioceptors throughout the body to allow us to balance. Also, in this chapter we have discussed how vestibular signals can be important in visual processes such as maintaining appropriate eye position. In addition, we briefly touched on the consequences of a mismatch between visual and vestibular information with the example of seasickness.

From the limited examples given here, we hope that it is apparent to you that effective, everyday functioning very often relies on integration of the information from different sensory systems. Moreover, any conflict arising as a result of combining transduced signals from different systems can lead to abnormal perception. A consequence of this integration is that disorders in one sensory system may have consequences for the processing of information in a different sensory modality, for example visual processing may be disrupted by vestibular disorders. We continue this theme in the next section by looking specifically as vestibular disorders, and you should keep in mind the impact on other sensory systems as you work through the associated activities.

7.5 Vestibular disorders

You have now examined the structure of the vestibular system and its role in a number of critical reflexes and functions. By discussing motion sickness we have touched on the very unpleasant symptoms that can arise when the vestibular system functions abnormally, or is perceived to do so.

Activity 7.1 Core reading

Allow 3¼ hours

(*Relevant module learning outcomes: KU5 and KU6*)

Access the core reading associated with this activity, which is available from the *Block 4 Activities* resource on the module website. This reading is an essential part of the module, so you should treat it as you would treat the module text and devote an adequate amount of time to studying it. You will find questions and guidance on how to approach your reading of this text in the activity.

Activity 7.2 Living with benign paroxysmal positional vertigo (BPPV)

Allow 15 minutes

(*Relevant module learning outcome: KU5*)

Finish your study of this chapter by completing this activity, which is available from the *Block 4 Activities* resource. You will hear an audio interview with someone with BPPV and be required to answer questions about her experience. As you listen to the interview, as well as answering the specific questions detailed online, consider the overall effect this condition has on the individual's everyday life.

7.6 Concluding remarks on the vestibular system

This chapter has described the vestibular system, drawing on much of your previous knowledge of the auditory system and proprioception from Block 3. It has also discussed how the vestibular system uses signals derived from the movement of fluid within the inner ear to code for linear and angular acceleration, and drawn parallels between transduction within the auditory system and the vestibular system.

You have also considered the pathways to the brain and how this information is combined with other proprioceptive input to allow us to balance, for example. Finally, you have read about the causes, impacts of and treatments available for vestibular disorders.

Reading this chapter should have reiterated the main message from Block 3 on proprioception, which is that effective proprioception functioning requires input from multiple sensory systems.

7.7 Chapter 7 summary and questions

- The vestibular system consists of the vestibule and the semicircular canals, both of which are housed in the inner ear with the cochlea.
- The vestibule comprises two membranous sacs called the utricle and the saccule, and together these are referred to as the otolithic organs.
- Transduction occurs at hair cells in the vestibular system in much the same way as it does in those within the cochlea.
- Orientation of the hair cells allows those in the utricle to detect horizontal linear acceleration, while the saccule detects vertical linear acceleration. The semicircular canals provide information about head rotation.
- Information leaves the inner ear in the vestibular portion of the vestibulocochlear nerve and travels to the vestibular nuclear complex in the brainstem. Both ascending and descending pathways project from here.
- These pathways are involved in a number of distinct reflexes such as the vestibulo-ocular reflex (VOR), the vestibulocollic reflex (VCR) and spinal postural reflexes.
- Information from the vestibular system is integrated with that from the visual and proprioceptive systems.
- Impairment of the vestibular system can significantly impact on quality of life and may cause recurrent conditions. Disorders may originate from the peripheral or central vestibular system, and many include symptoms that relate to other sensory systems, including the auditory and visual systems.

Self-assessment question

Question 7.1

Which part of the vestibular system would be activated by linear acceleration of the head, and how would his information be encoded?

Block 4 conclusion

You have now reached the end of this block on hearing and balance and are over half-way through this module. Before you progress to the next block, it is useful to reflect on the similarities and differences that you have found so far in your study of the senses.

One difference that may have stood out for you is in the level of our current knowledge of the various sensory systems. For example, when you were studying somatosensation we commented that the knowledge of this sense is far from complete, yet we seem to have more information on the workings of the auditory system. The same can be said of the vestibular system, although this is perhaps because of the similarities with hearing.

Despite the different depths of knowledge of the senses, there are a number of similarities. For example, in all the senses you have studied so far mechanoreceptors play a vital role. Additionally, one overriding similarity remains: that to study any sensory system and its impairment requires the consideration of other systems. This has been illustrated in this block with the discussion of the McGurk effect and the necessary integration of visual and proprioceptive information with vestibular inputs.

This leads us on nicely to the next block, in which you will study vision. For many people the visual system appears to be the dominant sense. Therefore, much research has gone into investigating it and the depth of current knowledge is significant. However, as you will see, we will focus on very specific elements.

Answers to questions

Block 3

Question 2.1

The term 'Merkel cell neurite complex' simply refers to the Merkel's disc afferent in close apposition to its accessory structure. This differs from the Pacinian corpuscle because in the Pacinian corpuscle the accessory structure is wrapped around the afferent nerve.

Question 2.2

Both Meissner's corpuscles and Pacinian corpuscles are rapidly adapting receptors, but Meissner's corpuscles have small receptive fields and they are much more numerous. Therefore, they can function to detect fine detail, for example when reading Braille, and can also more accurately locate a stimulus on the body surface. The Pacinian corpuscle provides information from a much larger area so does not signal location. While the Pacinian corpuscle is not sensitive to a single stimulus, it is very responsive to oscillating (vibratory) stimuli.

Question 2.3

Your diagram should resemble Figure 2.17, and show the sensory afferent axon branching in the dorsal horn of the spinal cord. One branch forms part of the dorsal column fibre tract. A second branch synapses once in the dorsal horn and a second-order neuron projects via the spino-cervical tract to the brain. The third branch gives rise to a local motor reflex loop.

Question 2.4

The evidence for this comes from the work of Blankenburg et al. (2006), as described in Box 2.3. They used a touch illusion to show that the pattern of activation of the somatosensory cortex reflects the perceived illusion rather than the actual sensory stimulation.

Activity 2.2 feedback

A completed version of Table 2.6 is shown below.

Table 2.7 Summary of axon types, based on information from the whole of Block 3.

Axon type	Specialised name	Diameter/μm	Function(s)
Aβ	mechanoreceptor	6–10	innocuous touch
Aδ	thermoreceptor thermo-nociceptor mechano-nociceptor	1–6	innocuous temperature noxious temperature noxious touch
Aα	proprioceptor	10+	proprioception
C	polymodal nociceptor	<1	nociception

Question 3.1

Active touch refers to voluntary touch exploration and is important for body schema. In order to perform a movement for touch exploration – namely to reach out and pick up an object and undertake the movements defined in Lederman and Klatzky's taxonomy (1987) – it is necessary for the brain to know where the limbs involved are in relation to each other at a given point in time.

Question 3.2

The cutting sensation is felt at the blade surfaces because scissors are a tool that has become incorporated into an extended body schema in the somatosensory cortex.

Question 3.3

Evidence for cross-modal processing at the cortical level comes from studies of sighted people who find that their tactile discrimination of an object's orientation is disrupted by the application of transcranial magnetic stimulation to the occipital cortex. This evidence shows that the visual cortex may process more than just visual inputs.

Activity 3.1 feedback

The temperature-sensing capabilities of the skin detect relative temperature in terms of variation from a fixed point because the neurons signalling temperature adapt rapidly. Thus, by placing one of your hands in a bowl of cool water for a short while you cause sensory adaptation to occur to the thermoreceptors in that hand. When you move this cold-adapted hand to the warmer room-temperature water bath, you feel the latter to be warm because it *is* warmer *relative* to the cool bowl. On the other hand (literally), if you adapt your thermoreceptors at a hot temperature (using the bowl containing hot water) and then place your hand in the room-temperature water bath, the water feels cool because your thermoreceptors are reporting cold environmental stimuli relative to the level at which they were adapted.

Question 4.1

Information ascends from the spinal cord to the brain in either the dorsal column medial lemniscal tract, the spino-cervical-thalamic tract, or the spino-cerebellar tract.

Question 4.2

When a muscle contracts, the resulting shortening would cause the muscle spindles to become slack and unresponsive if it were not for the firing of the gamma (γ) neurons. This action stretches the spindles at the end portions of the fibres, effectively contracting the middle portion and taking up the slack.

Question 4.3

Type Ib afferents innervate the Golgi tendon organ, while Type Ia and Type II afferents innervate the muscle spindle.

Activity 4.1 feedback

You may have found that your arms were not exactly parallel to each other once you attempted to align them and opened your eyes. Specifically, the arm that was at the angle bringing it closer to your face during the conditioning part of the task may have remained slightly higher than the other arm when you tried to bring both to the test position. The conditioning procedure can result in substantial changes to spindle firing rates, which causes these errors in limb positioning.

Activity 4.2 feedback

Even when standing on both legs, we are not very stable because our centre of mass is very high, being somewhere around the hips. So, a slight movement can cause your centre of mass to move beyond the base provided by your feet, and you start to topple. However, a range of receptors communicate this unsatisfactory state of affairs to your brain. For example, somatosensory receptors in your two feet will be reporting a difference in pressure as you start to topple.

Question 5.1

The main route that pain information takes to the cortex occurs is the spinothalamic tract (STT). The origin is a dorsal root ganglion neuron that projects to the dorsal horn of the spinal cord. Projections then cross to the other side of the spinal cord and ascend to the thalamus before reaching the somatosensory cortex.

Question 5.2

'Wind-up' refers to the sensitisation of nociceptors leading to increased pain perception. This occurs via a lowering of the nociceptor firing threshold.

Question 5.3

The arachidonic acid cascade is a string of molecular events that leads to the creation of prostaglandins from arachidonic acid. Some prostaglandins are capable of sensitising nociceptors, leading to enhanced pain perception.

Question 6.1

Pain may have adaptive value because it teaches the avoidance of negative, painful stimuli via learning mechanisms such as instrumental conditioning.

Question 6.2

The physiological mechanism that underlies phantom limb pain is a background level of cortical activity in the somatosensory cortex in the absence of sensory input.

Question 6.3

People die from using NSAIDs because they have a general action on blocking the enzyme COX. There are two forms of COX: COX-1 produces beneficial prostaglandins that are important in gastrointenstinal and renal functioning, and taking drugs which block this form of COX as well as the inflammatory form – COX-2 – leads to severe gastrointestinal and renal complications.

Question 6.4

Pain is a complex phenomenon that has psychological components, thus it follows that therapies which target these psychological components may be able to produce pain relief. A classic example is the placebo effect, where the simple expectation of pain relief is capable of producing that result.

Block 4

Question 2.1

The speed of sound in air at 293 K is 343 m s^{-1} and in water it is 1480 m s^{-1} (see Table 2.2). The wavelength of middle C can be found from the equation

$$\lambda = \frac{c}{f}$$

where c = the speed of sound, f = frequency and λ = wavelength.

Substituting these symbols for our known values gives:

(a) in air: $\lambda = 343\ \text{m s}^{-1}/262\ \text{Hz} = 1.3\ \text{m}$

(b) in water: $\lambda = 1480\ \text{m s}^{-1}/262\ \text{Hz} = 5.6\ \text{m}$

Question 2.2

Relative intensity = $10 \log_{10} (I_1/I_2)$ dB

If $I_1/I_2 = 2$, the relative intensity in dB is $10 \log_{10} 2 = 3.01$ dB. This is a useful figure to remember – a drop of 3 dB corresponds to a halving of the intensity of the sound.

Question 2.3

Your sketches should look something like those in Figure 2.17.

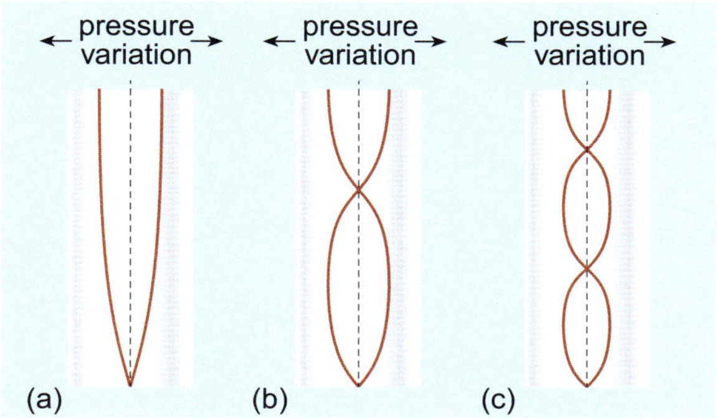

Figure 2.17 Sketches of standing waves in a tube: (a) the fundamental frequency; (b) and (c) the first and second harmonics of that wave, respectively.

Question 3.1

The middle ear compensates for differences in acoustic impedance as sound travels to the inner ear via two physical systems.

(a) Measurements have shown that the area of the tympanic membrane that vibrates in response to high-intensity sound is much greater than the area of the footplate which makes contact with the oval window. Assuming that all of the force exerted on the tympanic membrane is transferred to the footplate, the ratio of the two areas creates a greater pressure on the oval window than was experienced at the first of these two structures.

(b) The lever action of the ossicles increases the force at the tympanic membrane by a factor of 1.2 at the footplate.

Question 3.2

The motion set up on the basilar membrane in response to movement of the cochlear fluids is analogous to a travelling wave. The wave propagates from the base of the membrane towards the apex. How far the wave travels is determined by the frequency of the incoming sound.

Question 3.3

To determine the characteristic frequency of a cochlear nerve axon, you would construct a tuning curve. Tuning curves indicate the sound pressure level at the tympanic membrane that is sufficient to elicit a predefined firing rate of a cochlear nerve neuron, as a function of the frequency of a pure tone stimulus. For each neuron, the lowest intensity of a pure tone that will produce this level of response is determined for a range of pure tones. The frequency of the tone for which the threshold of a given axon is lowest is called the characteristic frequency (CF).

Question 3.4

There are two features of the hair cell that allow it to respond with high temporal precision.

(a) The synaptic ribbon allows synchronised release of large amounts of neurotransmitter in response to a stimulus.

(b) The close proximity of the Ca^{2+} channels and the sensors for exocytosis ensures changes in calcium influx can be responded to very quickly.

Question 4.1

(a) The travelling wave on the basilar membrane peaks at a specific location determined by the frequency of the incoming sound wave. For low-frequency sounds, the peak is located at the apical end while for high-frequency sounds, the peak is located at the basal end.

Hair cells are located along the basilar membrane. Cells that are located at the position at which the wave peaks are stimulated, resulting in the generation of action potentials in the cochlear nerve axons contacting those hair cells. Axons on the outside of the cochlear nerve innervate the basal hair cells and therefore fire in response to high-frequency sounds whereas axons on the inside of the cochlear nerve innervate apical hair cells and therefore fire in response to low-frequency sounds. This is the basis of the place coding of frequency.

The second way in which the basilar membrane provides information about frequency is through its rate of vibration, which can be preserved in the hair cell receptor potential and axon firing in the cochlear nerve. This is the basis of the temporal coding of frequency.

(b) The higher the intensity of the sound impinging on the ear, the greater the amplitude of the wave produced on the basilar membrane. The higher amplitude wave causes neurons to fire at a greater rate or causes more neurons to fire (auditory neurons have different thresholds and the greater the displacement of the membrane, the greater the number of neurons that reach threshold).

Question 4.2

The binaural processing of information begins in the superior olivary complex, using interaural time delays and intensity differences.

- In the medial superior olivary (MSO), neurons increase their firing rate in response to sounds from both ears, and will increase their discharge rate even further when sounds reach both ears with a certain delay (interaural time delays, excitation–excitation, or EE, responses).
- In the lateral superior olivary (LSO), neurons increase their firing rate in response to sounds in the ipsilateral ear and are inhibited from firing by sounds in the contralateral ear. So stimulation from both ears may decrease the firing rate of neurons compared with stimulation by one ear (excitation–inhibition, or EI, responses).

Question 5.1

(a) They will actually sound equally loud; they both fall on approximately the same equal-loudness contour, as shown in Figure 5.4.

(b) The 100 Hz tone must be about 59 dB SPL and the 1000 Hz tone about 50 dB SPL (see Figure 5.4).

Question 5.2

Pitch is mainly determined by the frequencies of the low-numbered harmonics in a sound, whereas timbre is determined by which frequency regions have more energy: the relative intensities of different harmonics. Timbre may also be influenced by other features such as onset characteristics.

Question 5.3

Studies of the neural basis of absolute pitch have revealed that, in fact, it does not appear to relate to differences in perception, and activation of auditory structures in people with absolute pitch is not different from that found in people with relative pitch. Instead, there are differences in activation of the posterior dorsolateral frontal cortex, an area involved in learning, and researchers now believe that absolute pitch is a labelling ability, rather than a perceptual ability.

Question 5.4

The limbic system, frontal lobe and insula (see Figure 5.7).

Question 6.1

In otosclerosis, new bone forms around the footplate of the stapes, fusing those components rigidly with the bone of the inner ear and reducing the ear's ability to conduct sound from the ossicular chain to the transduction mechanism of the cochlea. Treatment for this condition involves surgically removing the diseased stapes and replacing them with a prosthetic ossicle.

Question 6.2

Emotional associations feed into the processes of detection, perception and evaluation of the auditory signal. Therefore, any emotional difficulty that may be alleviated with antidepressants could reduce the impact of tinnitus.

Question 7.1

The otolithic organs in the utricle and the saccule relay information about linear acceleration of the head. During acceleration, the otoliths lag behind the movement of the head, thereby bending the stereocilia.

- If these bend towards the kinocilium, the hair cell is excited and an increase in afferent neuron firing rate occurs.
- If they bend away from the kinocilium, the hair cell is inhibited and there is a decrease in afferent neuron firing rate.

When a constant speed is reached, the otoliths ‘catch up’ to the speed of the head, allowing the stereocilia to straighten, and the firing rate of neurons returns to resting rate. Upon deceleration, the head slows down and the otoliths continue in the original direction of travel, once again lagging due to inertia and bending the stereocilia in the opposite direction. This causes the opposite excitation pattern to that found during acceleration.

Each head movement results in a unique pattern of excitation and inhibition results, which is recognised by the brain and interpreted in terms of the position of the head with respect to gravity.

References

Block 3

Andersson, A., Bucher, B., Galzi, J.-L., Sterner, O., Bevan, S., Hogestatt, E. D. and Zygmut, P. M. (2011) 'TRPA1 mediates spinal antinociception induced by acetaminophen and the cannabinoid delta nine tetrahydrocannabinol', *Nature Communications*, vol. 2, p. 551.

Bach-y-Rita, P. and Kercel, S. W. (2003) 'Sensory substitution and the human-machine interface', *Trends in Cognitive Sciences*, vol. 7, no. 12, pp. 541–46.

Bach-y-Rita, P., Kaczmareck, K. A., Tyler, M. E., Garcia-Lara, J. A. (1998) 'Form perception with a 49 point electrotactile stimulus array on the tongue', *Journal of Rehabilitation Research and Development*, vol. 35, pp. 427–30.

Berman J. S., Birch, R. and Anand, P. (1998) 'Pain following human brachial plexus injury with spinal cord root avulsion and the effect of surgery', *Pain*, vol. 75, pp. 199–207.

Biguer, B., Donaldson, I. M. L., Hein, A. and Jeannerod, M. (1988) 'Neck muscle vibration modifies the representation of visual motion and direction in man', *Brain*, vol. 111, no. 6, pp. 1405–24.

Blankenburg, F., Ruff, C. C., Deichmann, R., Rees, G. and Driver, J. (2006) 'The cutaneous rabbit illusion affects human primary sensory cortex somatotopically', *PLoS Biology*, vol. 4, no. 3, p. e69.

Cardinali, L., Jacobs, S., Brozzoli, C., Frassineti, F., Roy, A. C. and Farne, A. (2012) 'Grab an object with a tool and change your body: tool use dependent changes of body representation for action', *Experimental Brain Research*, vol. 218, no. 2, pp. 259–71.

Chan, B. L., Witt, R., Charrow, A. P., Magee, A., Howard, R., Pasquina, P. F., Heilman, K. M and Tsao, J. W. (2007) 'Mirror therapy for phantom limb pain', *New England Journal of Medicine*, vol. 357, no. 21, pp. 2206–7.

Cohen, L. G., Celnik, P., Pascual-Leone, E., Corwell, B., Faiz, L., Dambrosia, J., Honda, M., Sadato, N., Gerloff, C., Catala, M. D. and Hallett, M. (1997) 'Functional relevance of cross modal plasticity in blind humans', *Nature*, vol. 389, pp. 180–3.

Cole, J. and Paillard, J. (1995) 'Living without touch and peripheral information about body position and movement: studies with deafferented subjects', in Bermudez, J. L., Marcel, A. and Eilan, N. (eds) *The Body and the Self*, London, MIT Press, pp. 245–67.

Cotzin, M. (1950) 'Facial vision: the role of pitch and loudness in the perception of obstacles by the blind', *American Journal of Psychology*, vol. 63, no. 4, pp. 485–515.

DeWall, C. N., MacDonald, G., Webster, G. D., Masten, C. L., Baumeister, R. F., Powell, C., et al. (2010) 'Acetaminophen reduces social pain: behavioral and neural evidence', *Psychological Science*, vol. 21, no. 7, pp. 931–7.

DiCarlo, J. J. and Johnson, K. O. (2002) 'Receptive field structure in cortical area 3b of the alert monkey', *Behavioural Brain Research*, vol. 135, pp. 167–78.

Dolin, S. J., Padfield, N. L. and Pateman, J. A. (eds) (1996) *Pain Clinic Manual*, Oxford, Butterworth–Heinemann.

Dr Strangelove or: How I Learned to Stop Worrying and Love the Bomb (1963) Directed by Stanley Kubrick [Film], Columbia Pictures Corporation.

Eisenberger, N. I., Lieberman, M. D. and Williams, K. D. (2003) 'Does rejection hurt? An fMRI study of social exclusion', *Science*, vol. 302, no. 5643, pp. 290–2.

Fillingim, R. B. (2000) 'Sex, gender and pain: women and men really are different', *Current Pain and Headache Reports*, vol. 4, no. 1, pp. 24–30.

Fisher, J. D., Rytting, M. and Heslin, R. (1976) 'Hands touching hands: effective and evaluative effects of an interpersonal touch', *Sociometry*, vol. 39, pp. 416–21.

Gescheider, G. A., Hoffman, K. E., Harrison, M. A., Travis, M. L. and Bolanowski, S. J. (1994) 'The effects of masking on vibrotactile temporal summation in the detection of sinusoidal and noise signals', *Journal of the Acoustical Society of America*, vol. 95, no. 2, pp. 1006–16.

Gibson, J. J. (1983) *Senses Considered as Perceptual Systems*, Connecticut, Greenwood.

Gold, M. S. and Gebhart, G. F. (2010) 'Nociceptor sensitisation in pain pathogenesis', *Nature Medicine*, vol. 16, no. 11, pp. 1248–57.

Goldstein, K. (1908) 'Zur lehre von der motorisschen apraxie', *Journal für Psychologie und Neurologie*, vol. XI, pp. 169–87.

Head, H. and Holmes, G. (1911) 'Sensory disturbances from cerebral lesions', *Brain*, vol. 34, pp. 102–254.

Horizon (1997) 'The Man Who Lost His Body', BBC Two, 16 October.

Ikoma, A., Steinhoff, M., Stander, S., Yosipovitch, G. and Schmelz, M. (2006) 'The neurobiology of itch', *Nature Reviews Neuroscience*, vol. 7, no. 7, pp. 535–47.

Ingber, D. E. (2006) 'Cellular mechanotransduction: putting all the pieces together again', *The FASEB Journal*, vol. 20, no. 7, pp. 811–27.

Iwamura, Y. and Tanaka, M. (1993) 'Information processing in the monkey somatosensory cortex for the recognition of objects', in Taketoshi, O., Fukuda, M., Squire, L. R., Raichle, M. E. and Perrett, D. I. (eds) *Brain Mechanisms of Perception and Memory: From Neuron to Behaviour*, New York and Oxford, Oxford University Press, pp. 71–82.

Lawson, H. C., Ohara, S., Greenspan, J. D., Coghill, R. C. and Lenz, F. A. (2009) 'Neurophysiology of cingulate pain responses and neurosurgical pain interventions', in Vogt, B. A. (ed.) (2009) *Cingulate Neurobiology and Disease*, London, Oxford University Press.

Lederman, S. J. and Klatzky, R. (1987) 'Hand movements: a window into haptic object recognition', *Cognitive Psychology*, vol. 19, pp. 342–68.

Lederman, S. J. and Klatzky, R. (1998) 'The hand as a perceptual system', in Connolly, K. J. (ed.) *The Psychobiology of the Hand*, London, McKeith Press.

Linde, K., Ramirez, G., Mulrow, C. D., Pauls, A., Weidenhammer, W. and Melchart, D. (1996) 'St John's wort for depression: an overview and meta-analysis of randomised clinical trials', *British Medical Journal*, vol. 313, pp. 253–8.

Liu, X. Y., Sun, Y. G., Ross, M., Kim, S., Tsai, F. F., Li, Q. F., Jeffry, J., Kim, J. Y., Loh, H. H. and Chen, Z. F. (2011) 'Unidirectional cross activation of GRPR by MOR1D uncouples itch and analgesia induced by opioids', *Cell*, vol. 147, no. 2, pp. 447–58.

Melzack, R. and Wall, P. D. (1965) 'Pain mechanisms: a new theory', *Science*, vol. 150, no. 3699, pp. 971–9.

Melzack, R. and Wall, P. D. (1996) *The Challenge of Pain*, 2nd edn, London, Penguin Books.

Pailler-Mattei, C., Bec, S. and Zachouani, H. (2008) '*In vivo* measurements of the elastic mechanical properties of human skin by indentation', *Medical Engineering and Physics*, vol. 30, no. 5, pp. 599–606.

Pavlov, I. (1960 [1927]) *Conditioned Reflexes: An Investigation of the Physiological Activity of the Cerebral Cortex* (trans. and ed. G. V. Anrep), London, Oxford University Press.

Penfield, W. and Boldrey, E. (1937) 'Somatic motor and sensory representation in the cerebral cortex of man as studied by electrical stimulation', *Brain*, vol. 60, pp. 389–443.

Prochazka, A., Hulliger, M. and Zangger, P. (1985) 'Fusimotor set: new evidence for alpha-independent control of gamma-motoneurones during movement in the awake cat', *Brain Research*, vol. 339, no. 1, pp. 136–40.

Proske, U. and Morgan, D. L. (1999) 'Do cross-bridges contribute to the tension during stretch of passive muscle?', *Journal of Muscle Research and Cell Motility*, vol. 20, pp. 433–42.

Ramer, M. S. (2012) 'Endogenous neurotrophins and plasticity following spinal deafferentiation', *Experimental Neurology*, vol. 235, no. 1, pp. 70–7.

Ribot-Ciscar, E., Hospod, V., Roll, J.P. and Aimonettie, A. M. (2008) 'Fusimotor drive may adjust muscle spindle feedback to task requirements in humans', *Journal of Neurophysiology*, vol. 101, no. 2, pp. 633–40.

Sacks, O. W. (1984) *A Leg To Stand On*, London, Duckworth.

Sacks, O. W. (1985) *The Man Who Mistook His Wife for a Hat*, London, Duckworth.

Schaefer, M. (2010) *Body in Mind: A New Look at the Somatosensory Cortices*, New York, Nova Science.

Schott, G. D. (2001) 'Delayed onset and resolution of pain: some observations and implications', *Brain*, vol. 124, no. 6, pp. 1067–76.

Sherrington, C. (1902) *The Integrative Action of the Nervous System*, New Haven, Conn., Yale Press.

Sherrington, C. S. (1906) *The Integrative Action of the Nervous System*, New York, Scribners.

Sun, Y. G. and Chen, Z. F. (2007) 'A gastrin-releasing peptide receptor mediates the itch sensation in the spinal cord', *Nature*, vol. 448, no. 7154, pp. 700–3.

Supa, M., Cotzin, M. and Dallenbach, K. M. (1944) 'Facial vision: the perception of obstacles by the blind', *American Journal of Psychology*, vol. 57, no. 2, pp. 133–83.

Valbo, A. B. and Johansson, R. S. (1978) 'The tactile sensory innervation of the glabrous skin of the human hand', in Gordon, G. (ed.) *Active Touch: the Mechanisms of Recognition of Objects by Manipulation: a Multi-Disciplinary Approach*, Oxford, Pergamon Press, pp. 29–54.

Voudouris, N. J., Peck, C. L. and Coleman, G. (1989) 'Conditioned response models of placebo phenomena: further support', *Pain*, vol. 38, pp. 109–16.

Weber, E. H. (1978) *The Sense of Touch* (trans. H. Ross), London, Academic Press.

Weiskrantz, L. (1996) 'Blindsight revisited', *Current Opinion in Neurobiology*, vol. 6, pp. 215–20.

Weiskrantz, L. and Zhang, D. (1987) 'Residual tactile sensitivity with self-directed stimulation in hemianaesthesia', *Journal of Neurology, Neurosurgery and Psychiatry*, vol. 50, no. 5, pp. 632–4.

Wells, M. J. (1960) 'Proprioception and visual discrimination of orientation in the octopus', *Journal of Experimental Biology*, vol. 37, pp. 489–99.

Williams, K. D., Cheung, C. K. T. and Choi, W. (2000) 'Cyberostracism: effects of being ignored over the internet', *Journal of Personality and Social Psychology*, vol. 79, no. 5, pp. 748–62.

Xing, G. G., Liu, F. Y., Qu, X. X., Han, J. S. and Wan, Y. (2007) 'Long term synaptic plasticity in the spinal dorsal horn and its modulation by electroacupuncture in rats with neuropathic pain', *Experimental Neurology*, vol. 208, no. 2, pp. 323–32.

Zhou, B., Xu, F., Chen, C. Q. and Lu, T. J. (2010) 'Strain rate sensitivity of skin tissue under thermomechanical loading', *Philosophical Transactions of the Royal Society A*, vol. 368, no. 1912, pp. 679–90.

Block 4

Action on Hearing Loss (2013) 'What is tinnitus?' [Online]. Available at www.actiononhearingloss.org.uk/your-hearing/tinnitus/what-is-tinnitus.aspx (Accessed 12 March 2013).

Andrea's Buzzing About (2006) 'Living with (central) auditory processing disorder', *Andrea's Buzzing About*, 19 July [Online]. Available at http://qw88nb88.wordpress.com/living-with-auditory-processing-disorder (Accessed 12 March 2013).

Bainbridge, K. E., Hoffman, H. J. and Cowie, C. C. (2008) 'Diabetes and hearing impairment in the United States: audiometric evidence from the National Health and Nutrition Examination Survey, 1999 to 2004', *Annals of Internal Medicine*, vol. 149, pp. 1–10.

Binder, J. R., Frost, J. A., Hammeke, T. A., Bellgowan, P. S., Springer, J. A., Kaufman, J. N. and Possing, E. T. (2000) 'Human temporal lobe activation by speech and nonspeech sounds', *Cerebral Cortex*, vol. 10, pp. 512–28.

Birks, R., and MacIntosh, F. C. (1961) 'Acetylcholine metabolism of a sympathetic ganglion', *Canadian Journal of Biochemistry and Physiology*, vol. 39, pp. 787–827.

Bracewell, R. N. (1986) *The Fourier Transform and Its Application*, New York and London, McGraw-Hill.

Bregman, A. S. (1990) *Auditory Scene Analysis: The Perceptual Organisation of Sound*, Cambridge, Massachusetts and London, MIT Press.

Brouwer, C. N., Maille, A. R., Rovers, M. M., Grobbee, D. E., Sanders, E. A. and Schilder, A. G. (2005) 'Health-related quality of life in children with otitis media', *International Journal of Pediatric Otorhinolaryngology*, vol. 69, no. 8, pp. 1031–41.

Brown, G. G. and Thompson, W.K. (2010) 'Functional brain imaging in schizophrenia: selected results and methods', *Current Topics in Behavioural Neuroscience*, vol. 4, pp. 181–214.

Buchsbaum, B., Hickok, G. and Humphries, C. (2001) 'Role of left posterior superior temporal gyrus in phonological processing for speech perception and production', *Cognitive Science*, vol. 25, pp. 663–78.

Cho, J. G., Woo, J. S., Lee, H. M., Jung, H. H., Hwang, S. J. and Chae, S. (2009) 'Effects of cigarette smoking on mucin production in human middle ear epithelial cells', *International Journal of Pediatric Otorhinolaryngology*, vol. 73, pp. 1447–51.

Coleman, N. (2012) 'Tinnitus: when the music stops', *Independent*, 31 January [Online]. Available at www.independent.co.uk/life-style/health-and-families/features/tinnitus-when-the-music-stops-6297145.html (Accessed 12 March 2013).

Dallos, P. (2008) 'Cochlear amplification, outer hair cells and prestin', *Current Opinion in Neurobiology*, vol. 18, pp. 370–6.

Damasio, H. and Damasio, A. R. (1980) 'The anatomical basis of conduction aphasia', *Brain*, vol. 103, pp. 337–50.

Dempsey, R. (2010) 'Meniere's disease really sucks', *Ryan Dempsey's Blog*, 6 March [Online]. Available at www.rjdempsey.com/blog/menieres-disease-really-sucks (Accessed 11 March 2013).

Dierks, T., Linden, D. E., Jandl, M., Formisano, E., Goebel, R., Lanfermann, H. and Singer, W. (1999) 'Activation of Heschl's gyrus during auditory hallucinations', *Neuron*, vol. 22, pp. 615–21.

Fettiplace, R. and Hackney, C. M. (2006) 'The sensory and motor roles of auditory hair cells', *Nature Reviews: Neuroscience*, vol. 7, pp. 19–29.

Friederici, A.D., Wang, Y., Herrmann, C. S., Maess, B. and Oertel, U. (2000) 'Localization of early syntactic processes in frontal and temporal cortical areas: a magnetoencephalographic study', *Human Brain Mapping*, vol. 11, pp. 1–11.

Frisina, S. T., Mapes, F., Kim, S., Frisina, D. R. and Frisina, R. D. (2006) 'Characterization of hearing loss in aged type II diabetics', *Hearing Research*, vol. 211, pp. 103–13.

Gibson, W. P. and Sanli, H. (2007) 'Auditory neuropathy: an update', *Ear Hear*, vol. 28, pp. 102S–106S.

Glowatzki, E., Grant, L. and Fuchs, P. (2008) 'Hair cell afferent synapses', *Current Opinion in Neurobiology*, vol. 18, pp. 389–95.

Goldstein, E. B. (1999) *Sensation and Perception*, 5th edn, London, Brooks/Cole Publishing Company.

Goldstein, J. L. (1973) 'An optimum processor theory for the central formation of the pitch of complex tones', *Journal of the Acoustical Society of America*, vol. 54, pp. 1496–516.

Henderson, D., Bielefeld, E. C., Harris, K. C. and Hu, B. H. (2006) 'The role of oxidative stress in noise-induced hearing loss', *Ear Hear*, vol. 27, pp. 1–19.

Hesser, H., Weise, C., Westin, V. Z. and Andersson, G. (2010) 'A systematic review and meta-analysis of randomized controlled trials of cognitive-behavioral therapy for tinnitus distress', *Clinical Psychology Review*, vol. 31, pp. 545–53.

Hickok, G. and Poeppel, D. (2007) 'The cortical organization of speech processing', *Nature Reviews Neuroscience*, vol. 8, pp. 393–402.

Hickok, G., Buchsbaum, B., Humphries, C. and Muftuler, T. (2003) 'Auditory-motor interaction revealed by fMRI: speech, music, and working memory in area Spt', *Journal of Cognitive Neuroscience*, vol. 15, pp. 673–82.

Hoare, D. J., Stacey, P. C. and Hall, D. A. (2010) 'The efficacy of auditory perceptual training for tinnitus: a systematic review', *Annals of Behavioural Medicine*, vol. 40, pp. 313–24.

Hofman, P. M., Van Riswick, J. G. A. and Van Opstal, A. J. (1998) 'Relearning sound localization with new ears', *Nature Neuroscience*, vol. 1, pp. 417–21.

Hood, J. D. (1950) 'Studies of auditory fatigue and adaptation'. *Acta Oto-laryngologica Supplementum*, vol. 92, pp. 1–57.

Hood, J. D. (1972) 'Fundamentals of identification of sensorineuronal hearing loss', *Sound*, vol. 6, pp. 21–6.

Jastreboff, P. J. (1990) 'Phantom auditory perception (tinnitus): mechanisms of generation and perception', *Neuroscience Research*, vol 8, pp. 221–54.

Jeffress, L. A. (1948) 'A place theory of sound localization', *Journal of Comparative and Physiological Psychology*, vol. 41, pp. 35–9.

Kaltenbach, J. A. (2011) 'Tinnitus: models and mechanisms', *Hearing Research*, vol. 276, pp. 52–60.

Kellerman, G. R., Fan, J. and Gorman, J. M. (2005) 'Auditory abnormalities in autism: toward functional distinctions among findings', *CNS Spectrums*, vol. 10, pp. 748–56.

Kemp, D. T. (1978) 'Stimulated acoustic emissions from within the human auditory system', *Journal of the Acoustical Society of America*, vol. 64, pp. 1386–91.

King, A. J. and Nelken, I. (2009) 'Unraveling the principles of auditory cortical processing: can we learn from the visual system?', *Nature Neuroscience*, vol. 12, pp. 698–701.

Kvaerner, K. J., Tambs, K., Harris, J. R. and Magnus, P. (1997) 'Distribution and heritability of recurrent ear infections', *Annals of Otology, Rhinology and Laryngology*, vol. 106, pp. 624–32.

Langguth, B. (2011) 'A review of tinnitus symptoms beyond "ringing in the ears": a call to action', *Current Medical Research and Opinion*, vol. 27, pp. 1635–43.

Le Prell, C. G., Yamashita, D., Minami, S. B., Yamasoba, T. and Miller, J. M. (2007) 'Mechanisms of noise-induced hearing loss indicate multiple methods of prevention', *Hearing Research*, vol. 226, pp. 22–43.

Levitin, D. J. and Rogers, S. E. (2005) 'Absolute pitch: perception, coding, and controversies', *Trends in Cognitive Sciences*, vol. 9, pp. 26–33.

Li, H. and Steyger, P. S. (2011) 'Systemic aminoglycosides are trafficked via endolymph into cochlear hair cells', *Scientific Reports*, vol. 1, p. 159.

Liberman, A. M., Cooper, F. S., Shankweiler, D. P. and Studdert-Kennedy, M. (1967) 'Perception of the speech code', *Psychological Review*, vol. 74, pp. 431–61.

Long, A. F. and Bennett, T. (2009) 'Coping with Menière's disease: experience and benefits from the use of complementary and alternative medicine', *Chronic Illness*, vol. 5, pp. 219–32.

McClelland, J. L. and Elman, J. L. (1986) 'The TRACE model of speech perception', *Cognitive Psychology*, vol. 18, pp. 1–86.

McFadden, D. (1982) *Tinnitus: Facts, Theories, and Treatments*, Working Group 89, Committee on Hearing, Bioacoustics, and Biomechanics, National Research Council, Washington, DC, National Academies Press.

Miller, C., Igarashi, S. and Jacob, A. (2012) 'Molecular pathogenesis of vestibular schwannomas: insights for the development of novel medical therapies', *Otolaryngologi Polska*, vol. 66, pp. 84–95.

Moore, B. C. J. (2012) *An Introduction to the Psychology of Hearing*, 5th edn, Bingley, Emerald.

Morata, T. C., Dunn, D. E., Kretschmer, L. W., Lemasters, G. K. and Keith, R. W. (1993) 'Effects of occupational exposure to organic solvents and noise on hearing', *Scandinavian Journal of Work, Environment and Health*, vol. 19, pp. 245–54.

Moreno, S., Bialystok, E., Barac, R., Schellenberg, E. G., Cepeda, N. J. and Chau, T. (2011) 'Short-term music training enhances verbal intelligence and executive function', *Psychological Science*, vol. 22, pp. 1425–33.

Moser, T., Neef, A. and Khimich, D. (2006) 'Mechanisms underlying the temporal precision of sound coding at the inner hair cell ribbon synapse', *Journal of Physiology*, vol. 576, pp. 55–62.

Mountain, D. C. (1980) 'Changes in endolymphatic potential and crossed olivocochlear bundle stimulation alter cochlear mechanics', *Science*, vol. 210, pp. 71–2.

Nedzelnitsky, V. (1980) 'Sound pressures in the basal turn of the cat cochlea', *Journal of the Acoustical Society of America*, vol. 68, pp. 1676–89.

Nelken, I., Fishbach, A., Las, L., Ulanovsky, N. and Farkas, D. (2003) 'Primary auditory cortex of cats: feature detection or something else?', *Biological Cybernetics*, vol. 89, pp. 397–406.

Nelkon, I. (2004) 'Processing of complex stimuli and natural scenes in the auditory cortex', *Current Opinion in Neurobiology*, vol. 14, pp. 474–80.

Nelson, E. G. and Hinojosa, R. (2006) 'Presbycusis: a human temporal bone study of individuals with downward sloping audiometric patterns of hearing loss and review of the literature', *Laryngoscope*, vol. 116, pp. 1–12.

Nouvian, R., Beutner, D., Parsons, T. D. and Moser, T. (2006) 'Structure and function of the hair cell ribbon synapse', *Journal of Membrane Biology*, vol. 209, pp. 153–65.

Oishi, N. and Schacht, J. (2011) 'Emerging treatments for noise-induced hearing loss', *Expert Opinion on Emerging Drugs*, vol. 16, pp. 235–45.

O'Connor, K. (2012) 'Auditory processing in autism spectrum disorder: a review', *Neuroscience and Biobehavioral Reviews*, vol. 36, pp. 836–54.

Phillips, J. S. and McFerran, D. (2010) 'Tinnitus retraining therapy (TRT) for tinnitus', *Cochrane Database of Systematic Reviews*, vol. 3, CD007330.

Pickles, J. O., Osborne, M. P. and Comis, S. D. (1987) 'Vulnerability of tip links between stereocilia to acoustic trauma in the guinea pig', *Hearing Research*, vol. 25, pp. 173–83.

Plomp, R. (1970) 'Timbre as a multidimensional attribute of complex tones', in Plomp, R. and Smoorenburg, G. F. (eds) *Frequency Analysis and Periodicity Detection in Hearing*, Leiden, Sijhoff pp. 397–414.

Plomp, R. (1976) *Aspects of Tone Sensation*, London, Academic Press.

Plomp, R. and Steeneken, H. J. M. (1969) 'Effect of phase on timbre of complex tones', *Journal of the Acoustical Society of America*, vol. 46, pp. 409–21.

Plomp, R., Pols, L. C. W. and van de Geer, J. P. (1967) 'Dimensional analysis of vowel tones', *Journal of the Acoustical Society of America*, vol. 41, pp. 701–12.

Pukander, J. (1985) 'Akillisen välikorvantulehduksen esiintyvyys ja taustatekijät' ['Occurrence of acute otitis media and its risk factors'], *Duodecim*, vol. 101, no. 7, pp. 623–9.

Putter-Katz, H., Adi-Bensaid, L., Feldman, I. and Hildesheimer, M. (2008) 'Effects of speech in noise and dichotic listening intervention programs on central auditory processing disorders', *Journal of Basic and Clinical Physiology and Pharmacology*, vol. 19, pp. 301–16.

Rizzoli, S. O. and Betz, W. J. (2005) 'Synaptic vesicle pools', *Nature Reviews: Neuroscience*, vol. 6, pp. 57–69.

Robles, L., Ruggero, M. A. and Rich, N. C. (1986) 'Basilar membrane mechanics at the base of the chinchilla cochlea; I; input–output functions, tuning curves, and response phases', *Journal of the Acoustical Society of America*, vol. 80, pp. 1364–74.

Rose, J. E., Hind, J. E., Anderson, D. J. and Brugge, J. F. (1971) 'Some effects of stimulus intensity on response of cochlear nerve fibers in the Squirrel Monkey', *Journal of Neurophysiology*, vol. 34, pp. 685–99.

Rosenhall, U., Nordin, V., Sandstrom, M., Ahlsen, G. and Gillberg, C. (1999) 'Autism and hearing loss', *Journal of Autism and Developmental Disorders*, vol. 29, pp. 349–57.

Ryan, A. and Dallos, P. (1975) 'Effect of absence of cochlear outer hair cells on behavioural auditory threshold', *Nature*, vol. 253, pp. 44–6.

Schouten, J. F. (1940) 'The residue and the mechanism of hearing', *Proceedings of the Koninklijke Nederlandse Academie van Wetenschappen*, vol. 43, pp. 991–9.

Schouten, J. F. (1968) 'The perception of timbre', *Reports of the Sixth International Congress on Acoustics*, Tokyo, GP-6-2, 21–28 August 1968, Tokyo, Maruzen; Amsterdam, Elsevier.

Seebeck, A. (1841) 'Beobachtungen über einige Bedingungen der Entschung von Tönen' ['Observations on some conditions for the creation of sound'], *Annalen der Physik*, vol. 53, pp. 417–36.

Seidman, M. D., Bai, U., Khan, M. J. and, Quirk, W. S. (1997) 'Mitochondrial DNA deletions associated with aging and presbycusis', *Archives of Otolaryngology: Head and Neck Surgery*, vol. 123, pp. 1039–45.

Sha, S. H., Chen, F. Q. and Schacht, J. (2010) 'PTEN attenuates PIP3/Akt signaling in the cochlea of the aging CBA/J mouse', *Hearing Research*, vol. 264, pp. 86–92.

Sininger, Y. S. (1995) 'Filtering and spectral characteristics of averaged auditory brain-stem response and background noise in infants', *Journal of the Acoustical Society of America*, vol. 98, pp. 2048–55.

Skoner, A. R., Skoner, K. R. and Skoner, D. P. (2009) 'Allergic rhinitis, histamine, and otitis media', *Allergy and Asthma Proceedings*, vol. 30, no. 5, pp. 470–81.

Starr, A., Picton, T. W., Sininger, Y., Hood, L. J. and Berlin, C. I. (1996) 'Auditory neuropathy', *Brain*, vol. 119, no. 3, pp. 741–53.

Stevens, K. N. (1980) 'Acoustic correlates of some phonetic categories', *Journal of the Acoustical Society of America*, vol. 68, pp. 836–42.

Tanaka, K. (1996) 'Inferotemporal cortex and object vision', *Annual Review of Neuroscience*, vol. 19, pp. 109–39.

Terrinoni, A., Melino, G., Serra, V., Alessandrini, M., Napolitano, B. and Bruno, E. (2009) 'Deafness', *Encyclopedia of Life Sciences (ELS)* [Online]. Available at www.els.net/WileyCDA/ElsArticle/refId-a0001453.html (Accessed 11 March 2013).

Uhari, M., Mantysaari, K. and Niemela, M. (1996) 'A meta-analytic review of the risk factors for acute otitis media', *Clinical Infectious Diseases*, vol. 22, pp. 1079–83.

Verbeek, J. H., Kateman, E., Morata, T. C., Dreschler, W. and Sorgdrager, B. (2009) 'Interventions to prevent occupational noise induced hearing loss', *Cochrane Database of Systematic Reviews*, vol. 10, CD006396.

Wald, E. R., Dashefsky, B., Byers, C., Guerra, N. and Taylor, F. (1988) 'Frequency and severity of infections in day care', *Journal of Pediatrics*, vol. 112, pp. 540–6.

Warren, J. (2008) 'Medicine, music and the mind', *Clinical Medicine*, vol. 8, pp. 7–8.

Wen, B., Wang, G. I., Dean, I. and Delgutte, B. (2009) 'Dynamic range adaptation to sound level statistics in the cochlear nerve', *Journal of Neuroscience*, vol. 29, pp. 797–808.

Wever, E. G. and Bray, C. W. (1930) 'Auditory nerve impulses', *Science*, vol. 71, p. 215.

Wilson, S. M., Saygin, A. P., Sereno, M. I. and Iacoboni, M. (2004) 'Listening to speech activates motor areas involved in speech production', *Nature Neuroscience*, vol. 7, pp. 701–2.

World Health Organization (WHO) (2006) 'Face to face with hearing impairment', 3 May [Online]. Available at www.who.int/features/2006/hearing_impairment/en/ (Accessed 12 March 2013).

World Health Organization (WHO) (2013) 'Schizophrenia' [Online]. Available at www.who.int/mental_health/management/schizophrenia/en (Accessed 15 March 2013).

Zucker, R. S. and Regehr, W. G. (2002) 'Short-term synaptic plasticity', *Annual Review of Physiology*, vol. 64, pp. 355–405.

von Bekesy, G. (1947) 'The variations in phase along the basilar membrane with sinusoidal vibrations', *Journal of the Acoustical Society of America*, vol. 19, pp. 452–60.

Acknowledgements

Grateful acknowledgement is made to the following sources.

Block 3

Figure 2.7: Kandel, E. R. et al. (2000) *Principles of Neural Science*, The McGraw-Hill Companies Inc.; Figure 2.10: Knibestol, M. (1973) 'Stimulus-response functions of rapidly adapting mechanoreceptors in the human glabrous skin area', *Journal of Physiology*, vol. 232, Cambridge University Press; Figure 2.12: Schmidt, R. F. (ed.) (1978) *Fundamentals of Sensory Physiology*, Springer Verlag; Figure 2.13: Westling, G. K. (1986) 'Sensori-Motor Mechanism during Precision Grip in Man', UmeaUniversity Dissertation No. 171; Figure 3.4: Bsip, Astier/Science Photo Library; Figure 4.4b: Nicholl, J. G. et al. (2001) *From Neuron to Brain*, 4th edition, copyright 2011 Sinuaer Associates, Inc.; Figure 4.7: Proske, U. and Gandevia, S. C. (2009) 'The kinaesthetic senses', *The Journal of Physiology*, vol. 587, 2009, The Physiological Society; Figure 5.4: Anderson, D. J. (ed.) (1980) 'Touch and pain - facts and concepts, old and new', *Physiology: Past, Present and Future*, Pergamon Press Limited; Figure 5.5: Lynn, B. (1979) 'The heat sensitization of polymodal nociceptors in the rabbit and its independence of the local blood flow', *Journal of Physiology*, vol. 287, Cambridge University Press; Figure 5.10: adapted from Matthews, P. J. and Aziz, Q. (2005) 'Functional abdominal pain', *Postgraduate Medical Journal*, 2005; vol. 81, The Fellowship of Postgraduate Medicine; Figure 6.6: Solonen, K. A. (1962) 'The phantom phenomenon in amputated Finnish war veterans', *Acta Orthopaedica Scandinavica, Supplementum*, no. 54, Blackwell Publishers Limited.

Block 4

Figure 2.15: Schnupp, J., Nelken, I. and King, A. (2012) *Auditory-Neuroscience: Making sense of sound*, MIT Press; Figures 3.3 and 3.5: Rosowski, J. J. (1996) 'Models of External and Middle ear Function', Hawkins, H. L. et al. (eds), *Auditory Computation*, Springer-Verlag; Figure 3.7a: Picture by Mireille Lavigne-Rabillard, from 'Promenade around the cochlea' by Pujol, R. et al. (www.neuroreille.com/promenade/english/cochlea/fcochlea.htm); Figure 3.9b: Dr Goran Bredberg, Science Photo Library; Figure 3.11: Kandel, E. R., Schwartz, J. H. and Jessell, T. M. (2000) *Principles of Neural Science*, 4th edition, McGraw-Hill; Figure 3.15: Bekesy, G. V. (1953) 'Description of some mechanical properties of the organ of corti', *The Journal of the Acoustical Society of America*, vol. 25, no. 4, July 1953, American Institute of Physics; Figure 3.16b: Zemlin, W. R. (1981) *Speech and Hearing Science: Anatomy and Physiology*, 2nd edition, Prentice Hall Inc.; Figure 3.18: Yost, W. A. (2000) *Fundamentals of Hearing: An Introduction*, 4th edition, Academic Press; Figure 3.21: Palmer, A. R. and Russell, I. J.(1986) 'Phase-locking in the cochlear nerve of the guinea-pig and its relation to the receptor potential of inner hair-cells', *Hearing Research*, vol. 24, Elsevier Science; Figure 3.24: Marcotti, W. and Masetto, S. (Jan 2010) 'Hair Cells', *eLS*, John Wiley & Sons Ltd, Chichester, www.els.net [DOI: 10.1002/9780470015902.a0000181.pub2]; Figure 3.26: Kiang, N. Y. S. (1980) 'Processing of speech by the auditory nervous system', *The Journal of the Acoustical Society of America*, vol. 68, American Institute of Physics; Figure 3.27: Ulfendahl, M. and Flock, A. 'Outer Hair Cells Provide Active Tuning in the Organ of Corti', *Physiology*, June 1, 1998, vol. 13, no. 3, American Physiological Society; Figure 4.1a: Rose, J. E. et al. (1971) 'Some effects of stimulas intensity on response of auditory nerve fibers in the Squirrel monkey', *Journal of Neurophysiology*, vol. 34, The American Physiological Society; Figure 4.1b: Goldstien, E. B. (1999) *Sensation & Perception*, 5th edition, Brooks/Cole Publishing Company, A division of International Thomson Publishing Inc.; Figure 4.3: Zwicker, E. and Terhardt, E. (1974) *Facts and Models in Hearing*, Springer-Verlag; Figure 4.5: Egan, J. P. and Hake, H.W. (1950) 'On the masking pattern of a single auditory stimulus', *The Journal of the Acoustical Society of America*, vol. 22, no. 5, American Institute of Physics; Figure 4.6: Adapted from Wever, E. G. (1949) *Theory of Hearing*, John Wiley & Sons, Inc.; Figures 4.10, 4.13 and 4.19: Bear, M. F., Connors, B. W. and Paradiso, M. A. (1996) *Neuroscience: Exploring the Brain*, Williams & Wilkins; Figures 4.11 and 4.12b, c and d: Hackney, C. M., Osen, K. K. and Kolston, J. (1990) 'Anatomy of the nuclear complex of a guinea pig', *Anatomy and Embryology*, vol. 182, Springer-Verlag; Figure 4.12a: Ehret, G. and Romand, R. (1997) *The Central Auditory System*, Oxford University Press; Figure 4.16: The Digital Anatomist Project at the University of Washington, Seattle, Washington; Figure 4.17a: Webster, W. R. and Calford, M. B. (1984) *The journal of Comparative Neurology*, Wiley-Liss, Inc. a subsidiary of John Wiley & Sons, Inc.; Figure 4.17b: Stieber, I. (1986) *Neuroscience Letters*, vol. 65, Elsevier Science; Figure 4.20: adapted from Scott, S. and Rauschecker, J. (2009) 'Dual processing scheme for what and where, proposed for nonhuman primates on anatomic', *Nature Neuroscience*, vol. 12, no. 6, Nature American, Inc.; Figure 5.3: Sivian, L. J. and White, S. D. (1933) 'On minimum audible sound fields', *The Journal of the Acoustical Society of America*, vol. 4, American Institute of Physics; Figure 5.4: Fletcher, H. and Munson, W. A. (1993) 'Loudness, its definition, measurement and calculation', *The Journal of the Acoustical Society of America*, vol. 5, October 1933, The American Institute of Physics; Figure 5.7: adapted from Warren, J. D. (2008) 'How does the brain process music?', *Clinical medicine*, vol. 8, Royal College of Physicians; Figure 5.8: Hickok, G., Houde, J. and Rong, F. (2012) 'Sensorimotor Integration in Speech Processing: Computational Basis and Neural Organization', *Neuron*, vol. 69, no. 3, 10 February 2011, Elsevier Inc.; Figure 5.9: Dierks, D. et al. (1999) 'Activation of Heschl's Gyrus during Auditory Hallucinations', *Neuron*, vol. 22, no. 3, March 1999, Cell Press; Figure 6.1: Simon Fraser University, Canada; Figure 6.2: courtesy of Sullivan R. F., PhD, www.rcsullivan.com; Figure 6.4: Pickles, J. O. et al. (1987) *Hearing Research*, vol. 25, Elsevier Science; Figure 6.6: Scanner, courtesy of Elekta; Figure 6.7: Tyler, R. (2000) *Tinnitus Handbook*, Delmar, a division of Thompson Learning; Figure 7.3a: source unknown; Figure 7.3b: Quint, E., Furness, D. N. and Hackney, C. M. (1998) 'The effect of explantation and neomycin on hair cells and supporting cells in organotypic cultures of the adult guinea-pig utricle', *Hearing Research*, vol. 118, nos 1–2, April 1998, Elsevier Press; Figure 7.6a: Pako-Crestock Images; Figure 7.6b: Dallardyce.

Every effort has been made to contact copyright holders. If any have been inadvertently overlooked the publishers will be pleased to make the necessary arrangements at the first opportunity.

SD329 team

Module team

Eleanor Dommett (SD329 Chair, academic editor and author)
Terri Battrick (SD329 Manager)
Tracey Woodcraft (SD329 Assistant)
Paul Gabbott (Block 1 and 2 author and Block 6 Chair)
Claire Rostron (Block 3 author and Block 5 Chair)
David Robinson (Block 5 author and Block 4 Chair)
Claire Turner (Block 6 author and Block 3 Chair)
Katherine Leys (Block 6 author and Block 1 Chair)
Elizabeth Parvin (physics consultant author and Block 2 Chair)
Kate Bradshaw (Science Media Developer)

External module assessor

Peter Bailey

Critical readers

Iona Roth
Margaret Corbett

Production team

Robert Barnes (Media Project Manager)
Veda Beeharry (Media Assistant)
Greg Black (Interactive Media Developer)
Corinne Cole (Media Coordinator)
Roger Courthold (Graphics Media Developer)
Michael Francis (Media Developer)
Chris Hough (Graphics Media Developer)
Phillip Howe (Media Assistant)
Anna Hvass (Learning and Teaching Librarian)
Martin Keeling (Licensing and Acquisitions Coordinator)
Jonathan Martyn (Editorial Media Developer)
Matt Page (Media Assistant)
Federica Sacco (Editorial Media Developer)
Holly Tighe (Sound and Vision Assistant)
Will Rawes (Interactive Media Developer)

Other contributors

Matt Driver (editor and proofreader), Jane Henley (indexer), Amanda Smith (proofreader) and Fiona Williams (software developer).

We also gratefully acknowledge the contribution of the original SD329 team, on whose work this version of the module is based.

Index

Entries and page numbers in **bold** refer to glossary terms. Page numbers in *italics* refer to figures or tables.

A

B

I

J

K

L

M

N

O